31472400068676

THE AMA HANDBOOK OF BUSINESS WRITING

The AMA Handbook of Business Writing

The Ultimate Guide to Style, Grammar, Usage, Punctuation, Construction, and Formatting

KEVIN WILSON
and
JENNIFER WAUSON

AMACOM

AMERICAN MANAGEMENT ASSOCIATION

New York • Atlanta • Brussels • Chicago • Mexico City • San Francisco
Shanghai • Tokyo • Toronto • Washington, D. C.

This publication is designed to provide accurate and authoritative information in regard to the subject matter covered. It is sold with the understanding that the publisher is not engaged in rendering legal, accounting, or other professional service. If legal advice or other expert assistance is required, the services of a competent professional person should be sought.

Library of Congress Cataloging-in-Publication Data
AMA handbook of business writing : the ultimate guide to style, grammar, usage, punctuation, construction, and formatting / Kevin Wilson and Jennifer Wauson.
    p. cm.
  Includes bibliographical references and index.
  ISBN-13: 978-0-8144-1589-4
  Isbn-10: 0-8144-1589-x
  1. Commercial correspondence--Handbooks, manuals, etc. 2. Business writing—Handbooks, manuals, etc. 3. English language—Business English—Handbooks, manuals, etc. I. Wilson, K. (Kevin), 1958– II. Wauson, Jennifer. III. American Management Association.
  HF5726.A485 1996
  808'.06665—dc22   2009050050

About AMA
American Management Association (www.amanet.org) is a world leader in talent development, advancing the skills of individuals to drive business success. Our mission is to support the goals of individuals and organizations through a complete range of products and services, including classroom and virtual seminars, webcasts, webinars, podcasts, conferences, corporate and government solutions, business books and research. AMA's approach to improving performance combines experiential learning—learning through doing—with opportunities for ongoing professional growth at every step of one's career journey.

Printing number
10 9 8 7 6 5 4 3 2

CONTENTS

SECTION

The Writing Process

SECTION

2

The Business Writer's Alphabetical Reference

SECTION

3

Sample Business Documents

(See page xxiii for a list of sample documents figures.)

LIST OF BUSINESS DOCUMENTS FIGURES

INTRODUCTION

The AMA Handbook of Business Writing is a desktop job aid for all corporate communicators. The book is a collection of easy-to-find information on style, grammar, usage, punctuation, language construction, formatting, and business documents.

In writing three editions of the *Administrative Assistant's and Secretary's Handbook,* we have done extensive research on language usage. In addition, we are the founders of a corporate communications consulting business with over 25 years' experience working for many Fortune 500 companies like IBM, AT&T, Sony, Chevron, Hewlett Packard, and Cox Enterprises. In our work, we've developed hundreds of business documents including Web sites, brochures, reports, presentations, marketing plans, policy manuals, video programs, software tutorials, and training materials. In *The AMA Handbook of Business Writing,* we take the best of these corporate business writing guidelines and organize them in a way corporate writers will find useful.

We've written the book so you can easily find information on a particular topic and quickly get back to your writing project. We have alphabetized most of the book and included cross-references to assist you in finding alternatively worded entries.

The book is organized into three sections:

■ Section 1: The Writing Process

■ Section 2: The Business Writer's Alphabetical Reference

■ Section 3: Sample Business Documents

The book also includes a detailed table of contents and index that will assist you in quickly finding what you are seeking.

The Sample Business Documents section includes guidelines, tips, and a wide variety of business documents, including annual reports, brochures, business letters, business plans, grant proposals, mission statements, newsletters, policies, press releases, proposals, résumés, surveys, speeches, training manuals, user guides, and white papers.

We believe *The AMA Handbook of Business Writing* is an essential desk reference for the following business writers:

- Corporate communications writers and managers

- Marketing writers and managers

- Human resources administrators and managers

- Sales representatives and managers

- Training developers and managers

- Technical writers

- Grant writers

- Public relations writers

- Administrative assistants

ACKNOWLEDGMENTS

In writing this book, we referenced many sources to confirm guidelines we used throughout our professional careers while working with a variety of Fortune 500 companies. In addition, we used our own book, the *Administrative Assistant's and Secretary's Handbook,* as a source for content on language usage, grammar, and punctuation. We therefore thank James Stroman, who coauthored the *Administrative Assistant's and Secretary's Handbook.*

The following is a list of sources we referenced while writing this book to confirm the accuracy of our content:

James Stroman, Kevin Wilson, and Jennifer Wauson, *The Administrative Assistant's and Secretary's Handbook,* 3rd ed. (New York: AMACOM Books, 2007).

Microsoft Corporation Editorial Style Board, *Microsoft Manual of Style for Technical Publications,* 3rd ed. (Redmond, WA: Microsoft Press, 2004).

David A. McMurrey, Online Technical Writing, 2009. <http://www.io.com/~hcexres/textbook/acctoc.html#introduction> See also David A. McMurrey, *Power Tools for Technical Communication* (Heinle, 2001).

University of Illinois at Urbana-Champaign. *The Center for Writing Studies,* 2009. <http://www.cws.illinois.edu/workshop/writers/>

Purdue University. *The Purdue Online Writing Lab* (OWL), 2009. <http://owl.english.purdue.edu/>

UsingEnglish.com, *English Glossary of Grammar Terms,* 2009. <http://www.usingenglish.com/glossary.html>

The Writing Process

AUDIENCE ANALYSIS

When planning to write a business document, the most important consideration is to understand your audience. You must adapt your writing to the needs and interests of the audience.

For most business documents, the audience falls into one of the following categories:

- Subject matter experts—individuals who know the content completely and who focus on the details

- Technologists—people who manufacture, operate, and maintain products and services and who have a firm practical knowledge

- Management—people who make decisions about whether to produce and market products and services but who have little technical knowledge about the details

- General audience—people who may know about a product or service but who have little technical knowledge about the details

Another way to analyze your audience is to consider its characteristics:

- What are their background, education, and experience?

- Does your writing have to start with the basics, or can you work at a more advanced level?

    Example: If you are writing about a Windows-based software product, can you assume the audience already has a basic understanding of Windows, how to use a mouse, and so forth?

- What will the audience expect and need from your document?

- How will your document be used?

- Will users read it cover to cover or just skim the high points?

- Will they use your document as a reference to look up information when it is needed?

- What are the demographics of your audience?

- Consider the age, sex, location, and other characteristics of your audience.

Your writing may have more than one audience or an audience with a wide variety of backgrounds. With an audience of both experts and laypeople, it is best to organize your document into sections with easy-to-understand headings so that the individual users can find the areas that interest them. You may need to off-load the more technical information to an appendix.

Once you have analyzed your audience, you need to adapt your document to conform to its interests and needs.

- You may need to add information.

- You may need to omit information.

- You may need to add examples to help readers understand.

- You may need to write to a lower or higher level.

- You may need to include background information.

- You may need to strengthen transitions between sentences, paragraphs, and sections.

- You may need to write longer introductions and clearer topic sentences.

- You may need to change your sentence style.

- You may need change the type of graphics used.

- You may need to add cross-references.

- You may need to organize your content into headings with lists.

- You may need to use special fonts, font sizes, font styles, and line spacing for emphasis.

BRAINSTORMING

Brainstorming by jotting down notes is a great way to gather content ideas for a writing project.

- Don't worry about the order of the ideas.

- Let one idea lead you to other related ideas.

- Browse the Web to generate ideas.

- Review magazines, journals, and periodical indexes for ideas.

- Use free association to let your mind roam freely throughout the subject area.

- Use free association while commuting, while riding a bike, while walking, or even while taking a shower.

- Keep a pen and notepad or a digital recorder nearby.

As you think about the subject matter, consider the following angles:

- Are there any problems or needs?

- Is there a cause-and-effect relationship?

- What are the solutions to the problems?

- What is the history of the subject matter?

- What processes are involved?

- What needs to be described to readers?

- How can the subject matter be divided into smaller pieces?

- Are any comparisons involved?

- What needs to be illustrated with a graphic or photograph?

- How is the subject matter applied?

- Can you list any advantages and benefits?

- What are the disadvantages and limitations?

- Are there any warnings, cautions, tips, or guidelines?

- What are the financial implications of the subject matter?

- What is its importance?

- What does the future likely hold?

- What are the social, political, and legal implications of the subject matter?

- Can you draw any conclusions about the subject matter?

- Do you have any recommendations?

- What are the alternatives to the subject matter?

- What tests and methods are used?

- Can you use relevant statistics?

- Are there any legal issues?

- Should you consider applicable business situations?

After brainstorming, the next step is to narrow the list of ideas to the scope of the project.

- How does each brainstorm idea apply to your audience?

- Will your audience care about each brainstorming item?

- Does the idea help your audience understand the topic?

- Could you eliminate one or more ideas without sacrificing anything?

- Is the idea too general, too technical, or not technical enough?

After narrowing the list of topics, decide how to cover each and determine how to obtain the content details.

- Research online.

- Talk to subject matter experts.

- Use reference books.

- Test and evaluate the product or service yourself.

- Get testimonials from customers or users.

- Conduct tests.

- Record demonstrations using software or video.

For the narrowed list of topics, determine the audience level for each:

- Determine which topics apply to all audiences and should be more general.

- Determine which topics apply to individual audiences and should be more specific, include more details, or used to create separate audience-specific documents.

RESEARCH

The research phase of a business writing project consists of:

- Reviewing existing publications, periodicals, Web sites, and company documents

- Evaluating products and services

- Conducting tests of products and services

- Running tests

- Studying users

- Interviewing experts

- Conducting surveys using questionnaires or observations

Traditional print sources used in research include anything published in print form that is available in libraries and bookstores:

- Books

- Textbooks

- Newspapers

- Scholarly journals

- Trade publications

- Magazines

Materials available for research purposes on the Internet include:

- Web pages and blogs

- PDF documents

- eBooks

- Video and audio

- Online versions of print publications

- Press releases

- Message boards

- Discussion lists

- Chat rooms

- Web-based government reports

When searching for information at a library or on the Internet:

- Make a list of keywords related to your subject matter that will likely produce search results.

- Use the Library of Congress subject headings to search for keywords.

- Check *Books in Print* by subjects for any related keywords.

- Check the *Reader's Guide to Periodic Literature* for related articles.

- Use Google Scholar at www.scholar.google.com to search for articles across many disciplines and sources.

- Check the *New York Times Index* for relevant newspaper articles.

- Check a general encyclopedia for information about your topic.

Keep a list of the sources used in your research in order to document them in footnotes, endnotes, and a bibliography.

- Keep your notes organized on note cards or in a word processor.

- For research from *books,* include the title, authors, city of publication, publisher, date of publication, and the pages for specific quotes and other information.

- For research from *magazines,* include the title of the article, the magazine's name, the issue date, and beginning and ending page numbers of the article.

- For *encyclopedia articles,* include the title, edition number, date of publication, and the author's name.

- For *government documents,* include notes about the department, administration, or agency name, along with any cataloging number.

- For *private sources* of research from interviews, make notes about the date of the communication, the source's full name, title, and organization.

When making notes from your research sources, you can record any of the following:

- A few sentences or some statistics

- Direct quotes from a publication

- Paraphrased information in your own words

- Summaries that condense the main ideas in an article

INTERVIEWING

Interviews with subject matter experts, customers, end users, and members of your general audience provide you with insight and testimonials for use in your writing project.

Interviews can be conducted in a number of ways:

- Face-to-face

- In focus groups

- By telephone

- In a computer chat

- Via email

- On a message board

- By means of a discussion list

- By mail

Interviews that are conducted face-to-face or on the telephone can be recorded with the interviewee's permission and later transcribed.

- In informal conversational interviews, interview questions often flow from the context of the discussion.

- Structured interviews follow a checklist to make sure all relevant topics are covered, and the interviewer may ask impromptu questions based on the answers.

- In an open-ended interview, open-ended questions are asked, allowing the subject to share opinions and ideas.

When asking interview questions, consider the following:

- Ask clear questions whose language makes sense to the interviewees.

- Ask one question at a time, rather than multipart questions.

- Ask opened-ended questions with no predetermined answers.

- Ask questions about interviewees' experience with the subject matter before asking for their opinions on it.

- Order the questions from general to specific, from broad to narrow.

- Ask probing and follow-up questions when a different level of response or detail is needed.

- Be able to interpret the answers and clarify the responses to confirm that what you heard is what the interviewee meant.

- Avoid sensitive or deep questions that may irritate the interviewee.

- Allow free-form discussion, but keep the interview session under control by having a checklist of questions you want to ask.

- Establish and maintain a rapport with the interviewee through attentive listening, purposeful voice tone, and responsive expressions and gestures.

OUTLINING

Outlines are useful in the writing process as a strategy for brainstorming and the logical ordering of content. An outline lists the headings and subheadings for various topics and ideas. Several levels of subheadings may be used to group ideas.

To create an outline:

- Determine the purpose of the document.

- Determine the audience.

- Brainstorm ideas to include in the document.

- Organize the ideas by grouping similar ones together.

- Determine a logical order for the ideas.

- Label the groups of ideas for use as headings and subheadings in the outline.

In the most common outline format, numbers or letters are assigned to each level of heading or subheading. For example:

   I. Roman numerals

      A. Capitalized letters

         1. Arabic numerals

            a.   Lowercase letters

Keep the following ideas in mind when creating an outline:

- Use parallel structure for headings and subheadings.

- Heading content at the same level should be equally significant.

- A heading can contain just a few words or an entire sentence.

- Each heading should have at least two or more items of subordinated content or subheadings.

- Headings should be general, and subheadings should be more specific.

Example:

   I.   Introducing the transactional Web site

      A.   What is a transactional Web site?

      B.   Who uses this type of Web site?

   II.   Finding a transactional Web hosting service

      A.   Bandwidth pricing

      B.   Shopping cart service

      C.   Credit card merchant service

  III. Typical Web transactions

      A.   Services

      B.   Research

      C.   Downloadable software

      D.   Products

WRITING A DRAFT

After completing the prewriting stages of audience analysis, brainstorming, research, interviewing, and outlining, you can begin the writing process by creating a first draft. Start by copying your research notes into the related sections of your outline. Phrase your notes as complete sentences, and fill in the gaps with transitions and other commentary. As you work on your first draft, keep the following tips in mind:

- Add introductions and conclusions to the various sections of the outline.

- Don't worry about choosing the best wording when writing your draft; you'll have an opportunity to read and rewrite later.

- If you get stuck on a section, leave it and move on to the next one.

- If you don't like how a particular section sounds, keep writing and revise it later.

- Write notes to yourself with ideas for additional content or revisions using a different-colored font or highlighting tool.

After completing the first draft, look for ways to improve it by proofreading and revising.

BUSINESS WRITING STYLE

The overall tone of a business document, as seen through the choice of words and commentary, reflects the writer's attitude. Business writers must consider the overall tone of their messages, whether they are writing a letter or a formal report.

To decide on the appropriate tone for your documents, make sure you can answer the following questions:

- Why am I writing this document?

- For whom am I writing it?

■   What do I want the readers to understand?

The overall tone of a business document should be confident, courteous, and sincere. It should use nondiscriminatory language and be written at the appropriate level for the audience. In addition, your writing should focus on the benefits to the reader. To write with the appropriate tone:

■   Be knowledgeable and prepared so that readers will accept your ideas.

■   Be persuasive so that readers will follow your instructions.

■   Don't be arrogant or presumptuous.

■   Strive for politeness with sincerity to avoid sounding condescending.

■   Consider your word choices and think about how the reader will perceive them.

■   Use strategies to emphasize key points by using short sentences, placing key points at the beginning of paragraphs, and positioning subordinate information in the middle of paragraphs.

■   Use the active voice to describe what a reader should do, and use the passive voice to describe actions being performed.

■   Avoid language that is sexist or biased based on race, ethnicity, religion, age, sexual orientation, or disability.

■   Write from your readers' perspective and clearly explain the benefits for them.

■   Use language and details that are appropriate to the target audience's level of understanding.

USING VISUALS

Visuals in a business document should support the text and avoid confusing the reader. Visuals are a part of the overall message and should be used to communicate important ideas. When creating and placing visuals, keep the following in mind:

- Readers must be able to understand a figure without having to read any of the surrounding text.

- Introduce all figures by referring to them in the text.

- Place visuals in a logical place close to the reference text.

- Charts with content of interest only to specific audiences should be saved for an appendix.

- Visuals should not repeat the content of the text.

- Never use charts to distort research findings.

- Be aware of what multicolored images and graphs will look like in black and white.

Statistical information can be presented in tables or graphs. Graphs in particular help the reader conceptualize information that is not as easily seen in tabular form. Graphs can display the relationships between sets of data. When creating graphs:

- Don't overly complicate graphs with grid lines and data points.

- Use line graphs to show a relationship between two values.

- Employ pie charts to show a relationship between multiple values that make up a whole.

- Utilize bar charts to show comparisons, distributions, and trends.

- Use pictographs like bar charts but with symbols to make up each bar.

- Use organizational charts to show the hierarchy of an organization.

- Employ flowcharts to show the steps in a process.

A variety of other types of illustrations can be used effectively in business documents:

- Diagrams show the structures, mechanisms, or organisms that make up an object.

- Drawings depict an object or organism.

- Maps show geographic, demographic, agricultural, or weather data.

- Photographs present realistic views of a subject.

PAGE DESIGN

Page design involves the use of typographical elements and formatting techniques to lay out content in a pleasing way that helps communicate the message. Page design involves the use of the following:

■ Headings

■ Lists

■ Tables

■ Fonts and color

■ Font styles

■ Margins

■ Indention

■ Alignment

■ Footers

■ Graphical elements

■ Visuals

The first step in creating a page design for a document using a word processor is the document setup:

■ Setting the page size

■ Setting the margins

■ Creating paragraph styles

■ Customizing the color pallet

■ Selecting a document template

The text used in a document can take on many different forms. You can apply different fonts, font colors, styles (bold, italic, underlined), and paragraph styles (block, paragraph, hanging). Text can be organized visually on the page by using headings and lists. When formatting text on a page:

■ Make headings descriptive of the content that follows.

■ Use different font styles and margins for headings to make them stand out.

- Use parallel wording for all headings on the same level.

- Use numbered lists for things that must be done in a specified order.

- Use bulleted lists for items when no particular order is required.

- Introduce all lists with a lead-in sentence.

- Punctuate list items with a period only if they are complete sentences.

- Use font styles, such as bold or italic, for emphasis.

- Indent paragraph margins for emphasis.

- Use different font colors for headings for artistic design purposes.

- Use fonts for headings that are different from the text font.

- Use background shading and light-colored text for table column headings.

PUBLICATION DESIGN

Publication design involves creating and organizing the components of a business document. The components vary depending on whether the document is a letter, brochure, or report. No single publication uses all the possible publication components. Nor is there a single style guide for how these components should be used and organized, because style varies depending on the needs and requirements of the individual business.

The following publication design components are commonly used in business documents:

- Front and back covers—the organization's name, publication title, logo or artwork, and date

- Title page—information on the front cover that is often duplicated on the title page

- Edition notices—publication edition, publication date, and copyright notice, included on the backside of the title page

- Disclaimers—legal wording included as part of the edition notices on the backside of the title page, stating the document may not be free from errors

- Trademark lists—a list of trademarks used in the document, a separate element or part of the edition notices

- Warranties—additional legal wording regarding the company's products or services, sometimes on a separate page

- Safety notices—publications about products, possibly including a summary of all safety warnings found elsewhere in the publication

- Communication statements—statements required by government regulation

- Preface—a brief passage that describes the content and purpose of the publication as well as the target audience, included just before the table of contents

- Table of contents—a list of chapters and of at least a second level of heading detail, included so that readers can find information they need when using the publication as a reference

- List of figures—a list of all the figures used in the publication, along with their caption titles

- Content chapters—the actual text of the publication, possibly organized as chapters, topics, and sections

- Appendixes—details and content that is only suitable for subsections of your audience and that is included at the end of the publication

- Glossary—a list of specialized terms, along with their definitions, positioned at the end of the publication

- Index—references to specific topics and terms, along with page numbers

- Reader response form—a document that readers can fill out to provide feedback and to ask questions

EDITING

Editing consists of reading a draft document, checking for errors, rewriting sentences, adding missing content, and deleting unnecessary content. You can use word processing grammar and spelling checkers to point out potential problems, but don't rely on these tools in place of a thorough editing and proofreading. During the editing process, keep the following principles in mind:

■ *To be* verbs (*is, was, were*, etc.) should be replaced with strong active verbs.

Example: The form was filed by Allan.

Revision: Allan filed the report.

■ Rewrite the excessive use of prepositions.

Example: The company's annual report is overshadowed by the company's feeling of dread over the upcoming legislation pending in their state government.

Revision: A feeling of dread over the upcoming state government legislation pervaded the company's annual report.

■ Eliminate words that add no meaning or are redundant.

Example: He carelessly and nonchalantly tossed the confidential report into the nonsecure trash bin.

Revision: He carelessly tossed the confidential report into the nonsecure trash bin.

■ Vary sentence structure and sentence length.

■ Don't start every sentence with the main subject followed by a verb.

■ If there are too many sentences of the same length, rewrite them into compound sentences.

Example: I stopped checking my email when I went on vacation. There were over 300 messages waiting for me when I returned.

Revision: Because I did not check email while on vacation, over 300 messages were waiting when I returned.

- Add transitional words and phrases to connect sentences and show a relationship between sentences and paragraphs.

> **Example:** The copier on our floor broke. I went down to the copy center in the basement to copy the report.
>
> **Revision:** The copier on our floor broke. So I went down to the copy center in the basement to copy the report.

Use the following checklist when editing a document:

- Are the headings and subheadings consistently used?

- Is the spelling correct?

- Are all proper names accurate?

- Are all lists parallel in structure?

- Do all nouns and verbs agree?

- Are numbered lists correctly numbered?

- Are all dates correct?

- Are all alphabetical lists in alphabetical order?

- Is all punctuation correct and consistent?

- Is all capitalization correct and consistent?

- Are all bibliographical references accurate and consistent?

PROOFREADING

Proofreading is the checking of your documents for grammar, spelling, and punctuation, as well as for accuracy with respect to the edited version and adherence to style. If someone else proofreads your documents, the reader notes any needed corrections using proofreading marks and abbreviations. Figure 1.1 lists the standard proofreading symbols and abbreviations.

Figure 1.1 Proofreading Symbols

Notation	Meaning	Example	Becomes
wf	Wrong font	The last word is in wrong **font**.	The last word is in wrong font.
lc	Make lower case.	Decision-Making Mode	Decision-making mode
lc	Make all lower case.	CAPITAL LETTERS	Capital letters
c	Set in capitals.	capital letters	CAPITAL LETTERS
Caps/lc	Set in caps and lower case.	CAPS AND LOWER CASE	Caps and Lower Case
sc	Set small caps.	Set in small caps.	SET IN SMALL CAPS.
c & sc (c/sc)	Set in caps and small caps.	Set in caps and small caps.	SET IN CAPS AND SMALL CAPS.
roman	Set roman.	Set roman.	Set roman.
italic	Set italic.	Set italic.	Set *italic*.
lf	Set lightface.	Set **lightface**	Set lightface.
bf	Set boldface.	Set boldface.	Set **boldface**.
$\sqrt{}^2$	Set as superior ("super").	Set super 2.	Set super ^{2}.
$/_2$	Set as inferior ("sub").	Set sub 2.	Set sub $_2$.
⊐	Move to right.	Move to right⊐	Move to right.
⊏	Move to left.	⊏Move to left.	Move to left.
⊐ *ctr* ⊏	Center.	⊐Center.⊏	Center.
⊔	Lower.	Lower type.	Lower type.
⊓	Raise.	Raise type.	Raise type.
	Straighten (horizontally).	Straighten type.	Straighten type.
‖	Align (vertically).	‖⊏ Align type.	Align type.
tr	Transpose.	Transpose.	Transpose.
⌢	Close space (completely).	Close sp ace.	Close space.
#	Close space (partially).	Close # space.	Close space.
Eq #	Equal space.	Equal spaces between words.	Equal spaces between words.
#	Insert space.	Insert space.	Insert space.
Space out	More space.	More space between words.	More space between words.
∧	Insert ("caret").	Insert word "the."	Insert the word "the."
ℓ	Delete.	Take the word it out.	Take the word out.
ℓ	Delete and close space.	It is spelled "judgement."	It is spelled "judgment."
ℓ	Correct this letter.	Correct this latter. /e	Correct this letter.
Stet	Leave it the way it was ("stet").	Leave it the way it was.	Leave it the way it was.
⌐	Start new line.	Hopscotch in the Headlines	Hopscotch in the Headlines
¶	Start a new paragraph.	Start a new paragraph. It's ...	Start a new paragraph. It's ...
Run in	Run in to previous paragraph.	Start a new paragraph. It's ...	Start a new paragraph. It's ...
Flush	Make this flush.	Make this flush.	Make this flush.
⊙	Insert period.	Insert period	Insert period.
∧	Insert comma.	Insert comma now.	Insert comma, now.
;	Insert semicolon.	Insert semicolon here's how.	Insert semicolon; here's how.

Notation	Meaning	Example	Becomes
⊙	Insert colon.	Insert colon⌄cows, pigs, horses ...	Insert colon: cows, pigs, horses ...
⌄" ⌄"	Insert quotation marks.	He said,⌄What?⌄	He said, "What?"
⌄'	Insert apostrophe.	It⌄s about time.	It's about time.
Set ?	Insert question mark.	Insert a question mark⌃?	Insert a question mark?
Set !	Insert exclamation point.	Insert an exclamation point⌃!	Insert an exclamation point!
=	Insert hyphen.	Decision=making	Decision-making
⌿m	Insert an em dash.	Like⌿m wow!	Like—wow!
⌿n	Insert an en dash.	Pages 156⌿n175	Pages 156–175
⌿(⌿)	Insert parentheses.	⌿(These are parentheses⌿)	(These are parentheses.)
⌿[⌿]	Insert brackets.	⌿[These are brackets⌿]	[These are brackets.]
⊗	Broken type.	Brok⊗n type.	Broken type.
↻	Reverse upside down type.	Reverse upsi↻down type.	Reverse upside down type.
sp	Spell.	Spell the number ④	Spell the number four.
◯	Set as numeral.	Don't spell⟨twenty-six⟩	Don't spell 26.
Au?	Query to author.		
Ed?	Query to editor.		

Use the following checklist when proofreading a document:

- Are all headings and other text elements consistent in style and layout?

- For letters, are the dateline, reference line, initials, enclosure, and carbon-copy notation accurate?

- Are all cross-references accurate?

- Are all margins consistent and proper?

- Are all tables aligned consistently?

- Have any footnotes been omitted?

- Are all end-of-line word divisions accurate?

- Are any words accidentally repeated in the same sentence or paragraph?

- Are the page numbers correct?

- Are all headings and captions separate elements, that is, on lines by themselves?

Rather than make edits on paper, you can make edits electronically in a word processing document using the Track Changes feature (in Microsoft Word). The revisions show up in a different color. When you proofread the document, you can review each revision and either accept or reject it.

DOCUMENT REVIEW

Prior to its release or publication, a document should be reviewed by subject matter experts, management, or your peers. The purpose of this review is to evaluate the document, criticize it, and suggest improvements. Writers are often uneasy about having their documents reviewed out of fear their egos will be bruised. People who are asked to review a document are also often uneasy about offering criticism. Prior to the review, the writer should meet with the reviewers and discuss the following points:

- The writer's goals and concerns for the document including its topic, audience, and purpose

- Potential problems and concerns uncovered during the writing process

- Questions about accuracy that subject matter experts need to answer

When asked to review another writer's document, review the document several times and look for:

- Grammar, spelling, and punctuation issues

- Appropriate tone and level for the target audience

- Organization of the content

- Clarity of the writing

- Sentence style

- Use of graphics

When offering feedback, avoid making criticisms based on your own writing style. Instead, do the following:

- Base your comments on guidelines, concepts, and rules.

- Document your comments in the margins of the review copy or on a separate document.

- Provide specific details to explain your comments.

- Offer suggestions for correcting any problems you see.

- Avoid going overboard and rewriting the draft completely.

REVISIONS

In the revision process, you rewrite content to make improvements to the language, level of clarity, content organization, and tone that may be the result of a reviewer's comments or your own review. As you revise your document, consider the following questions:

- Have you adequately defined all the key terms used in the document?

- Do some things in the document, such as products, services, or people, need to be described in more detail?

- Do some processes in the document need more description?

- Do you need to add analogies or comparisons to make a particular concept easier to understand?

- Does the document have subcategories of information that need their own subheadings and introductory sentences?

- Is the content in the correct order?

- Have you provided sufficient examples?

- Do you need to provide more historical background to help readers better understand the content?

- Have you provided any necessary instructions in the correct step-by-step format?

- Do you need to insert overviews at key points to summarize topics?

- Do you need to add topic sentences that introduce new topics?

- Do the transitions between paragraphs and topics allow the ideas to logically flow from one to another?

- Do you need to break long paragraphs into shorter ones?

- Do you need to rewrite redundant or wordy phrases?

- Do you need to rewrite passive sentences in the active voice?

- Are there any subject-verb mismatches in your sentences?

- Are there series of sentences that are either all the same length, all too long, or all too short?

DOCUMENTING SOURCES

Always acknowledge the work of other writers to allow readers not only to judge the quality of the information based on its source but also to verify the information.

Some writers document sources in parenthetical references. Others use footnotes or endnotes.

You should document your sources when:

- The information is not already common knowledge.

- You use a direct quotation.

- The concepts are unique to the source.

Footnotes and Endnotes

Footnotes are short notes set at the bottom of the page. Endnotes are placed at the end of a document. Usually, both footnotes and endnotes are numbered. A small (so-called superior) number is inserted at the end of the text in question. Then, either a correspondingly numbered footnote is placed at the bottom of the page or a numbered endnote is listed at the end of the document.

Book information in footnotes and endnotes should include the authors' names, the book title, the city of publication, the publisher, the year of publication, and the page reference.

> **Example:** Kevin Wilson and Jennifer Wauson, *The AMA Handbook of Business Writing* (New York, AMACOM Books, 2010), page 24.

Parenthetical references are inserted within a document in parentheses.

> **Example:** ... (Wilson and Wauson, 2010)

Sometimes a footnote is used for the first usage of a reference source, and in subsequent references just the author names and page number are listed.

> **Example:** [1]Kevin Wilson and Jennifer Wauson, *The AMA Handbook of Business Writing* (New York, AMACOM Books, 2010), page 24.
>
> [2]Wilson and Wauson, page 43.

Magazine information should include the authors' names, followed by a period, the title of the article in quotes and ending with a period, followed by the name of the magazine in italics, followed by a period, then the date of the issue, followed by the beginning and ending page numbers.

Example: Jennifer Wauson. "Positively Pranic Cooking." *Yogic Cooking Journal* (March 1, 2011), 32–42.

Government report information does not need to include the author's name but should include the group or agency name with a comma, the title of the report in italics with a period, then the report number with a period, the city of publication with a colon, the name of the publisher with a comma, and the publication date ended with a period.

Example: Security and Exchange Commission, *SEC 2010 Annual Report.* NAA 6463:3. Washington, DC: U.S. Government Printing Office, 2012.

Personal interview information should include the name of the source, followed by a comma, the person's title with a period, the person's organization with a period, the interview location with a period, the type of information with a period, followed by the interview date ended with a period.

Example: James H. Stroman. Administrative Assistant to the Governor of Oklahoma. Governor Raymond Gary's Office. Oklahoma City, OK. Email interview. July 1, 2012.

Product brochure information should include the company name as author, followed by a period, the product name or model number with a period, the title of the brochure in italics with a period, the type of information with a period, and a date ended with a period.

Example: Greenway Manufacturing. Green Harvester. *Farm Products Catalog.* Acres in cultivation. 2012.

Online source information should include the author's name with a period, the title of the work in italic with a period, the date of the publication with a period, the date of access followed by a period, and the URL in angle brackets.

Example: Videologies, Inc. *Grammar Gotchas.* 2012. Retrieved March 20, 2012. <http://www.videologies.com/amahandbook>

Example: Wilwau, M. B. *Famous Banana Recipes for Fun and Profit.* April 21, 2012. Retrieved July 1, 2012. <http://www.bananafun.com/recipes.htm>

Email message source information should include the author's name with a period, the subject of the email in quotes with a period, the words "Email to the author" with a period, and then the date with a period.

Example: Wilson, Brian. "Editing Techniques on the Mac." Email to the author. August 22, 2012.

Bibliographies

Bibliographies list all the works citied in report footnotes or parenthetical references. Research sources that were not cited in a foot- or endnote but that were used to create the report may also be listed.

The bibliography listings are ordered alphabetically by author's last name. If there's no main author, then use the book title. The author's surname comes first. Additional authors are listed in the normal order: first name, last name.

Example: Wilson, Kevin, and Jennifer Wauson, *The AMA Handbook of Business Writing* (New York, AMACOM Books, 2010), page 26.

GLOBAL COMMUNICATIONS

When writing for an international audience, you can easily create problems with clarity and miscommunication. To overcome this problem, you need to avoid using slang or words with double meanings that can be misunderstood by non-native English speakers. To adjust your writing for an international audience:

■ Use both the active and passive voice (some cultures—for example, in Japan and China—consider the active voice to be condescending and prefer the passive voice).

■ Use a direct rather than indirect style; the indirect style can be confusing.

■ Avoid using abbreviations (e.g., "to be done asap") and brand names (e.g., "Xerox two copies"), unless you are writing about a specific brand (e.g., "Xerox's Color Cube™ 9200 Series").

■ Use short sentences and simple sentence constructions.

■ Avoid phrasal verbs like *call up, put up, drop down,* and the like; such phrases can easily be used as a single word (*call, put, drop*) and mean the same thing.

■ Make antecedents extremely clear when using pronouns.

■ Avoid clichés and slang.

■ Be careful with humor; a non-English-speaking person may not understand it.

■ Don't use contractions; they make translation more difficult.

■ Avoid cultural metaphors that are recognized in the United States but are meaningless to an international audience.

Examples: Big Apple, pigskin, brown-bagging

■ When using graphics in your document, avoid using human hands, animals, or religious symbols.

■ Use androgynous figures for humans.

■ Make sure you use *which* and *that* correctly.

■ Write out dates by spelling the month (September 23, 2012, not 09/23/2012).

■ If you must refer to gender, use the terms *man* and *woman* rather than *male* and *female*.

■ Do not use the word *domestic* to refer to the United States.

■ Avoid using symbols and special characters.

Examples: Use *pound,* not #; write *dollars,* not $; avoid the ditto mark (″); spell *inches,* not ″; spell *feet,* not ′; ask for *help,* don't type *?.*

■ When your document will be translated, keep in mind that the same content may expand by 15% or more in the new language.

COLLABORATIVE WRITING

Large projects often involve teams of writers all working together on the same document. During the planning phase of the project, the team leader should work together with the team to:

■ Define the audience and purpose of the document.

■ Create content outline.

■ Plan the research effort.

■ Create a standard system for taking notes and gathering content.

■ Plan graphics for use in the document.

■ Agree on style and document formatting standards.

■ Create a style guide for the document.

■ Develop a work schedule for the team members.

■ Assign team members to various sections of the document.

■ Assign team members to research activities.

■ Create a formal progress reporting process.

■ Schedule team meetings to discuss issues.

■ Set up a peer-review process where team members review each other's work.

PROMOTIONAL WRITING

Promotional writing is used for sales letters, brochures, and newsletters. This style of writing not only explains a product or service but compels the reader to take action. A well written promotional piece doesn't provide every detail; instead, it is a creative introduction that causes the reader to seek more information.

When writing a promotional piece:

■ Make the document readable by using neutral-colored paper and a simple font such as 12-point Times New Roman or Arial.

■ Don't pack too much information into the document.

■ Use an attractive page layout that leaves some white space.

■ Write compelling headlines, titles, or headings that convey important information to the reader.

■ Avoid too much hype and sensationalism that can't be supported.

■ Avoid making claims or comparisons that you can't support in the content of the piece.

■ Use descriptive language so that the readers can imagine what you are describing using all five senses.

■ List the benefits and reasons why a reader should respond to your call for action.

■ Address any serious obstacles or misconceptions that may be in the reader's mind.

■ Include a compelling call to action that gives the reader specific instructions on what to do.

■ Provide multiple forms of contact information so that readers can reach you using email, on the Web, by telephone, or through the mail.

The Business Writer's Alphabetical Reference

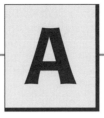

A, An

A and *an* are articles that proceed and identify nouns. *A* and *an* can also be used to mean one of something. The choice of *a* or *an* before a noun is based on the phonetic sound of the first letter in the word, not the written letter.

■ *A* is used before all words that begin with consonants.

Example: a kite, a man, a tomato, a large apple

Exception: *An* is used before words that begin with an unsounded *h*.

Example: an honor, an honest mistake

■ *An* is used before all words that begin with vowels.

Example: an apple, an egg, an Italian, an onion, an umbrella

Exception: When a word begins with *u* and sounds like *you,* then *a* is used as the article.

Example: a union, a used car

■ When a word begins with *o* and sounds like *won*, then *a* is used.

Example: A one-time offer

Abbreviations

Abbreviations are formed from the first letters of words or shortened versions of a word.

Example: Automated Teller Machine, ATM

Example: Professor, Prof.

Abbreviations are used as space savers. Abbreviations that can be pronounced are called **acronyms**.

Example: AIDS is an acronym; HIV is an abbreviation.

Do not use periods with acronyms.

Example: NATO, North Atlantic Treaty Organization

Titles Before and After Names

■ Use abbreviations for titles before names, and add a period after the abbreviation.

Example: Dr., Mr., Mrs., Rep.

Exception: *Miss* is not an abbreviation.

■ Use abbreviations for titles or degrees after names.

Example: Sr., Jr., M.D., Ph.D.

Exception: Some sources do not recommend using periods for degrees.

■ Don't use periods for abbreviations used both before and after a name at the same time.

Example: Dr. Gary Wilson Jr

■ Don't use a comma to separate *Jr.* or *Sr.* at the end of someone's name.

■ Don't abbreviate a title that is not attached to a name.

Correct: I went to the doctor yesterday.

Incorrect: I went to the dr. yesterday.

Names

■ Familiar institutions are often abbreviated.

Example: MIT, FBI, UN

■ Countries are often abbreviated.

Example: U.S.A.

U.S.A. can also be written as USA, but U.S. with periods is better. You can use U.S. as a modifier (U.S. foreign policy), but write it out (United States) when used as a noun.

Example: We want to visit the United States.

■ Company names are sometimes abbreviated.

Example: IBM, NBC, ITT

■ Famous people's names are sometimes abbreviated.

Example: MLK, JFK, FDR

■ Familiar objects are sometimes abbreviated.

Example: CD, TV, DVR, PC

Mathematical Units and Measurements

Mathematical units and measurements can be abbreviated in technical writing. Add a space between the number and the abbreviation.

Example: 20 ft, 30 lb

When used as a modifier, add a hyphen between the number and unit.

Example: a 20-ft ceiling

See *Abbreviations for Measurements* and *Abbreviations for Numbers*

Long Phrases

Long common phrases can be abbreviated and used without periods.

Example: miles per hour, mph; revolutions per minute, rpm

Words Used with Numbers

A.M. and *P.M.* can be written in upper or lower case with periods. *A.D.* and *B.C.* are written in upper case with periods. Here are some usage tips:

- *A.D.* appears before the date.

- *B.C.* appears after the date.

- *A.D.* and *B.C.* are sometimes replaced by *B.C.E.* (before the common era) and *C.E.* (common era).

Common Latin Terms

Common Latin terms are usually abbreviated.

Example: etc., et cetera, and so forth; i.e., id est, that is; e.g., exempli gratia, for example; et al., et alii, and others

Use a comma after *i.e.* or *e.g.* to set them apart as introductory modifiers. Do not italicize or underline the abbreviations of Latin terms. The use of periods to punctuate Latin abbreviations varies depending on the term. Table 2.1 lists Latin abbreviations and the proper period punctuation.

Table 2.1 Punctuation and English Meanings of Latin Abbreviations

Abbreviation	Latin	English Meaning
A.B.	*artium baccalaureus*	bachelor of arts
A.D.	*anno Domini*	in the year of the Lord
A.M.	*ante meridiem*	before midday
c., ca., or cca.	*circa*	around or about
cf.	*confer*	bring together
C.V.	*curriculum vitae*	course of life
cwt.	*centum weight*	hundredweight
D.D.	*divinitatis doctor*	teacher of divinity
DG, D.G., or DEI GRA	*dei gratia*	by the grace of God
D.Lit.	*doctor litterarum*	teacher of literature
D.M.	*doctor medicinae*	teacher of medicine
D.Phil.	*doctor philosophiae*	teacher of philosophy
D.V.	*deo volente*	God willing
ead.	*eadem*	the same man
e.g.	*exempli gratia*	for example
et al.	*et alia*	and others
etc.	*et cetera*	and other things
fl.	*floruit*	period when something flourishes
ibid.	*ibidem*	in the same place
id.	*idem*	the same man
i.a.	*inter alia*	among other things
i.e.	*id est*	that is
J.D.	*Juris Doctor*	teacher of the law
lb	*libra*	pound

(continues)

Table 2.1 *(continued)*

Abbreviation	Latin	English Meaning
M.A.	*magister artium*	master of arts
M.O.	*modus operandi*	method of operating
N.B.	*nota bene*	note well
nem. con.	*nemine contradicente*	with no one speaking against
op. cit.	*opera citato*	in the same article or book as mentioned before
p.a.	*per annum*	through a year
per cent.	*per centum*	for each one hundredth, used in English as *percent*
Ph.D.	*philosophiae doctor*	teacher of philosophy
P.M.	*post meridiem*	after midday
p.m.a.	*post mortem auctoris*	after the author's death
p.p. or per pro.	*per procurationem*	through the agency of
PRN	*pro re nata*	as needed for a dose of medication
pro tem.	*pro tempore*	for the time being
P.S.	*post scriptum*	after what has been written
Q.D.	*quaque die*	every day for a dose of medication
Q.E.D.	*quod erat demonstrandum*	which was demonstrated
q.v.	*quod videre*	which to see
Re	*in re*	in the matter of
REG	*regina*	queen
R.I.P	*requiescat in pace*	may he or she rest in peace
s.o.s.	*si opus sit*	if there is need
viz.	*videlicet*	namely, precisely
vs. or v.	*versus*	against

States and Territories

States and territories can be abbreviated in references and addresses, but do not abbreviate states and territories in normal writing. Abbreviations accepted by the U.S. Postal Service are listed on its Web site. Do not use periods with state abbreviations.

For addresses on envelopes, you do not need a comma to separate a city from a state abbreviation. If you spell out the state name, you do need a comma.

Example: Dallas TX or Dallas, Texas

For the District of Columbia, *DC* can be written with or without periods.

You can abbreviate *Saint* in place names.

Example: St. Louis

Things You Should Not Abbreviate

For formal business writing, do not abbreviate the following:

- Words like *through* (thru) or *night* (nite)

- Days of the week

- Months

- Words that begin a sentence

- People's names, such as Charles (Chas.) or James (Jas.)

- State names when not part of an address

- Military titles

Spacing and Periods for Abbreviations

Consider the following tips on the use of spacing and periods in abbreviations:

- Abbreviations of units of measure are written without periods.

Example: 30 ft, 20 lb

■ When abbreviating inches, you need a period to avoid confusion with the word *in*.

■ Use periods for lowercase abbreviations such as *e.g.* and *i.e.*

■ Common long phrase abbreviations do not use periods, such as *mph, mpg,* or *rpm*.

■ When an abbreviation with periods ends a sentence, the period for the abbreviation is used as the sentence period.

■ Academic degrees can be written with or without periods.

Example: MBA or M.B.A, BS or B.S.

■ People's initials should include a period and space.

Example: T. R. Smith

■ Don't let line breaks come in the middle of someone's initials.

Guidelines for Using Abbreviations in Your Writing

When introducing an abbreviation into your writing, spell out the term the first time it is used followed by the abbreviation in parentheses.

Example: cash on delivery (COD)

Use the abbreviation alone after the initial definition. Do not follow an abbreviation with a word that is included in the abbreviation.

Incorrect: ATM machine

Correct: ATM

To form the plural of an abbreviation or acronym, add a lower case *s*. Do not add an apostrophe. Do not make up abbreviations to save space in your business documents.

Abbreviations for Measurements

You can use abbreviations for common measurements when space is limited or when the measurements appear in a table. Table 2.2 lists the common abbreviations for measurements.

Table 2.2 Common Abbreviations for Measurements

Measurement	Abbreviation
Bits per second	bps
centimeters	cm
degrees	° or deg
dots per inch	dpi
feet	ft or '
gigabits per second	Gbps
gigabytes	GB
gigahertz	GHz
grams	g
Hertz	Hz
hours	hr
inches	in or "
kilobits per second	Kbps
kilobytes	KB
kilobytes per second	KBps
kilograms	kg
kilohertz	kHz
kilometers	km
lines	li
megabits per second	Mbps
megabytes	MB

(continues)

Table 2.2 *(continued)*

Measurement	Abbreviation
megabytes per second	MBps
megahertz	MHz
meters	m
miles	mi
millimeters	mm
milliseconds	msec or ms
picas	pi
points	pt
points per inch	ppi
seconds	sec or s
weeks	wk
years	yr

Abbreviations for Numbers

The abbreviation for number (no.) or the number sign (#) is normally not used.

Incorrect: Building No. 48

Correct: Building 48

Incorrect: Invoice #3219

Correct: Invoice 3219

Incorrect: Page no. 102

Correct: Page 102

In some situations, you may add the word *number* and not use the abbreviation.

Example: When we reviewed the list of charges against him, number five was discussed the most by the jury.

Above, Below

Do not use *above* or *below* to reference tables, visuals, or forms on the current page or on a previous or next page. When the page is laid out, these terms may cause confusion. Repeat the name when referencing a table, visual, or form.

Example: You will see a list in Table 3. Keyboard Shortcuts …

Absolute Form of an Adjective

An **absolute adjective** is an adjective that functions as a noun.

Example: the poor

Absolute Phrase

An **absolute phrase** is a group of words consisting of a noun or pronoun, a participle, and modifiers.

Example: President of the workers' <u>union three out of four years</u> [absolute phrase], his leadership experience really stood out.

Absolute phrases do not connect to or modify any other word in a sentence; instead, they modify the entire sentence. Absolute phrases are often treated as parenthetical elements set off from the rest of the sentence with a comma or a pair of commas.

Absolutely

The term *absolutely* should not be used in formal writing.

Incorrect: I am absolutely sure we'll win the contract.

Correct: I am very sure we'll win the contract.

Abstract Nouns

Abstract nouns describe qualities, feelings, states, concepts, and events that have no physical existence. Abstract nouns are used to describe things that cannot be detected by the five senses but that exist as ideas or feelings.

Example: hope, freedom, happiness, idea

Abstract nouns can be countable or uncountable. Abstract nouns that refer to events are usually countable.

Example: a concept

Accent Marks

Foreign language words adopted into the English language sometimes use the accent marks from their source language. Most word processing software automatically adds accent marks to the words that require them.

Example: fiancé, protégé, cliché

French and Italian source words often contain *grave* (left-leaning) accent marks (e.g., *è*). A *diaeresis* (··) over a letter signals the speaker that the letter begins a new syllable.

Example: noël and naïve

An *umlaut* (e.g., *ü*) looks similar to a diaeresis, but it modifies the sound of the vowel.

Some Spanish words use a tilde (*ñ*), which tells you that the *n* is pronounced like a *y*.

Example: piñata, niño

Accept, Except

Accept is a verb that means to agree to take something from someone.

Example: I always accept criticism from my mentor because I greatly respect her opinion.

Except is a preposition or conjunction that means not including.

Example: I work every day except Saturday.

Access, Excess

Think of *access* as part of the word *accessible* when determining its usage. *Access* means the ability to approach or enter, a way of approach, or the trait of being approachable.

Access can be a noun or verb.

■ Noun: The only access to the storage area is through the break room.

■ Verb: I can access my stock portfolio online.

Think of *excess* as part of the word *excessive* when determining usage. *Excess* means overabundance or overindulgence.

Excess can be a noun or an adjective.

■ Noun: He was happy to have an excess of red pens.

■ Adjective: We were charged an excess baggage fee of $25.

Acronyms

An **acronym** is a type of abbreviation that is formed by taking letters from a long phrase.

Example: radar, radio detection and ranging

Acronyms save time in speaking and writing, but they can be unclear and come across as jargon if used too much in business writing.

An **initialism** is an acronym whose letters do not make a word; the letters are pronounced individually.

Example: CBS, CIA, NFL

Action Verbs

Action verbs express achievement or something that a person, place, or thing does.

Example: eat, smile, think, run, jump, leap, cry

Action verbs are concise, persuasive, and easy for readers to understand. Use action verbs when writing résumés, cover letters, and sales copy.

Table 2.3 provides sample action verbs for use in your writing.

(text continues on page 52)

Table 2.3 Action Verbs

abandon	abduct	abolish	abscond	abuse
accelerate	accuse	achieve	acquire	act
adapt	add	address	adjust	administer
advance	advise	aim	allocate	analyze
answer	anticipate	apprehend	approach	appropriate
arbitrate	arrange	arrest	ascertain	assault
assemble	assess	attack	attain	audit
avert	bang	bar	beat	berate
bite	blast	block	blow	brighten
broke	buck	budget	built	bump
bury	bushwhack	calculate	catch	charge
chart	chase	check	choke	clap
clash	classify	climb	clip	clutch

coach	collapse	collar	collect	collide
command	commandeer	communicate	compile	complete
compose	compute	conduct	conserve	consolidate
construct	consult	control	coordinate	counsel
count	cram	crash	crawl	create
creep	cripple	crouch	cut	dance
dart	dash	deal	decide	deck
deduct	define	delegate	delineate	deliver
descend	describe	design	detect	determine
develop	devise	diagnose	dictate	dig
direct	discard	discover	display	dissect
distribute	ditch	dive	divert	do
dodge	dominate	dope	douse	draft
drag	drain	dramatize	drape	draw
dress	drill	drink	drip	drop
drown	drug	dry	duel	dunk
ease	edge	edit	eject	elevate
elope	elude	emerge	endure	engage
enjoin	ensnare	enter	equip	erupt
escape	establish	estimate	evacuate	evade
evaluate	evict	examine	exert	exhale
exit	expand	expedite	expel	experiment
explain	expose	extend	extirpate	extract
extricate	fade	fake	fall	falter
fan	fast	fear	feed	feel
fend	fight	file	fill	finance

(continues)

Table 2.3 *(continued)*

find	finger	fix	flag	flap
flash	flatten	flaunt	flay	flee
flick	flinch	fling	flip	flit
float	flog	flounder	flout	flush
fly	fondle	force	formulate	fornicate
found	fumble	furnish	gain	gallop
gather	generate	gesture	get	give
gnaw	gossip	gouge	grab	grapple
grasp	greet	grind	grip	gripe
grope	grow	growl	grunt	guide
gyrate	hack	hail	hammer	handle
hang	harass	haul	head	help
hesitate	hide	hijack	hit	hitch
hobble	hoist	hold	hover	hug
hurl	hurtle	hypothesize	identify	ignore
illustrate	imitate	implement	improve	improvise
inch	increase	indict	induce	inflict
influence	inform	inject	injure	insert
inspect	inspire	install	instigate	institute
interchange	interpret	interview	invade	invent
inventory	investigate	isolate	jab	jam
jar	jeer	jerk	jimmy	jingle
jolt	judge	jump	keel	kibitz
kick	kidnap	kill	kneel	knife
lash	launch	lead	lean	leap
learn	lecture	left	level	lick
limp	listen	log	lunge	lurch

maim	maintain	make	manage	mangle
manipulate	march	mark	massage	maul
measure	meddle	mediate	meet	mentor
mimic	mingle	mobilize	mock	model
molest	monitor	motivate	mourn	move
mumble	murder	muster	mutilate	nab
nag	nail	needle	negotiate	nick
nip	observe	obtain	occupy	offer
officiate	operate	order	organize	oversee
pack	paddle	page	pander	panic
parachute	parade	paralyze	park	parry
party	pass	pat	patrol	pause
paw	peel	peep	penetrate	perceive
perform	persuade	photograph	pick	picket
pile	pilot	pin	pinch	pirate
pitch	placate	plan	play	plod
plow	plunge	pocket	poke	polish
pore	pose	pounce	pout	pray
predict	preen	prepare	prescribe	present
preside	primp	print	process	prod
produce	program	project	promote	prompt
proofread	propel	protect	provide	provoke
pry	publicize	pull	pummel	pump
punch	purchase	pursue	push	question
quit	race	raid	raise	rally
ram	ransack	rape	rattle	ravage
rave	read	realize	receive	recline

(continues)

Table 2.3 *(continued)*

recommend	reconcile	reconnoiter	record	recoup
recruit	redeem	reduce	reel	refer
regain	rejoin	relate	relax	relent
render	repair	repel	report	represent
repulse	research	resign	resist	resolve
respond	restore	retaliate	retreat	retrieve
reveal	review	ride	rip	rise
risk	rob	rock	roll	rub
run	rush	sail	salute	sap
save	saw	scale	scamper	scan
scare	scatter	scavenge	schedule	scold
scoop	scoot	score	scour	scout
scrape	scrawl	scream	screw	scrub
scruff	scuffle	sculpt	scuttle	seal
search	seduce	seize	select	sell
sense	serve	set	sever	sew
shake	shanghai	shape	sharpen	shave
shear	shell	shield	shift	shiver
shock	shoot	shorten	shout	shove
shovel	show	shun	shut	sidestep
sigh	signal	sip	sit	size
skid	skim	skip	skirt	slacken
slam	slap	slash	slay	slide
slug	smack	smear	smell	smuggle
snap	snare	snarl	snatch	snicker
sniff	snitch	snoop	snub	snuff
snuggle	soak	sock	soil	solve

spear	spell	spike	spin	splatter
split	spot	spray	spread	spring
sprint	spurn	spy	squeak	stack
stagger	stamp	stand	start	startle
steal	steer	step	stick	stiffen
stifle	stomp	stop	strangle	strap
strike	strip	stroke	struck	stub
study	stuff	stumble	stun	subdue
submerge	submit	suck	summarize	summon
supervise	supply	support	surrender	survey
suspend	swagger	swallow	swap	sway
swear	swerve	swim	swing	swipe
switch	synthesize	systematize	tackle	take
tap	target	taste	taunt	teach
tear	tease	telephone	terrorize	test
thrash	thread	threaten	throw	tickle
tie	tilt	tip	toss	touch
tout	track	train	transcribe	transfer
translate	trap	tread	treat	trip
trot	trounce	try	tuck	tug
tumble	turn	tutor	twist	type
understand	undertake	undo	undress	unfold
unify	unite	untangle	unwind	update
usher	utilize	vacate	vanish	vanquish
vault	vent	violate	wade	walk
wander	ward	watch	wave	wedge
weed	weigh	whack	whip	whirl

(continues)

Table 2.3 *(continued)*

whistle	wield	wiggle	withdraw	work
wreck	wrench	wrestle	write	yank
yell	yelp	yield	zap	zoom

Active Voice

In sentences with an action verb (see *Action Verbs*), the subject performs the verb's action.

Example: John mailed the letter.

Because the subject (John) does the action (mails the letter), the sentence is said to be in the active voice.

When the subject is acted on by the verb, the sentence is said to be in the passive voice.

Example: The letter was mailed by John.

For your business writing, you should emphasize the who or what that performs the action; that is, you should write using the active voice. The active voice is concise, easy to read, and clear. Always use the active voice for policies, procedures, and instructions.

Example: You should review your emails before sending them.

Name the performer of the action to make it easier to identify the subject and avoid the passive voice.

Weak: It was discovered by the students that their new teacher had been in the Marines.

Better: The students discovered their teacher had been in the Marines.

A.D.

A.D. comes from the Latin phrase *anno Domini,* which means "in the year of the Lord." *A.D.* should be written in all caps with periods.

Adjectival Noun

An **adjectival noun** is an adjective that functions as a noun. Adjectival nouns are used to describe groups of people or things that share a common attribute.

Example: the poor, the rich, the young

Adjectival Opposites

Whenever you need to describe the opposite of an adjective, you can use an **antonym**. These opposite pairs of adjectives are called **adjectival opposites**. A thesaurus can help you find an appropriate antonym.

Example: The opposite of cold is hot.

Another way to form a negative adjective is with a prefix. Consider the following pairs:

- Fortunate, unfortunate
- Prudent, imprudent
- Considerate, inconsiderate
- Honorable, dishonorable
- Alcoholic, nonalcoholic
- Filed, misfiled

A third way to form an adjectival opposite is to combine the adjective with *less* or *least.*

Example: That is the least expensive building on the block.

Adjective Phrase

An **adjective phrase** is a group of words used as an adjective in a sentence.

> **Example:** The CEO is <u>fond of classic rock</u> [adjective phrase].

An adjective phrase can often include an adverb such as *very* or *extremely*.

> **Example:** The status report is very late.

> **Example:** My little brother is extremely afraid of the dark.

See *Adjectives*.

Adjectives

Adjectives are words that describe or modify a person, place, or thing.

> **Example:** tall, solid, cold, green

Articles such as *a, an,* and *the* are adjectives.

A group of words containing a subject and verb may act as an adjective. Such a group is called an **adjective clause**.

> **Example:** My best friend, <u>who is much older than I am</u> [adjective clause], is a doctor.

If the subject and verb are removed from an adjective clause, what's left is an **adjective phrase**.

> **Example:** He is the man ~~who is~~ <u>keeping me employed</u> [adjective phrase, once "who is" is removed].

Placement of Adjectives in a Sentence

Adjectives almost always appear immediately before the noun or noun phrase that they modify. Sometimes adjectives appear in a string; when they do, they must appear in a particular order according to category.

Adjectives appear in the following order:

1. Determiners—articles and other limiters

   Example: a, an, five, her, our, those, that, several, some

2. Observation—postdeterminers and limiter adjectives and adjectives subject to subjective measure

   Example: beautiful, expensive, gorgeous, dilapidated, delicious

3. Size and shape—adjectives subject to objective measure

   Example: big, little, enormous, long, short, square

4. Age—adjectives describing age

   Example: old, antique, new, young

5. Color—adjectives denoting color

   Example: red, white, black

6. Origin—adjectives denoting the source of the noun

   Example: American, French, Canadian

7. Material—adjectives describing what something is made of

   Example: silk, wooden, silver, metallic

8. Qualifier—final limiter that is often part of the noun

   Example: rocking chair, hunting cabin, passenger car, book cover

   Example: an expensive, square, antique, black, French, wooden chinaware closet

When indefinite pronouns—such as *something, someone,* and *anybody*—are modified by an adjective, the adjective comes after the pronoun.

Example: That is something useful to know.

Use of Multiple Adjectives

Multiple adjectives of the same class are called **coordinated adjectives** and require a comma between them in a sentence. Consider whether you could have inserted *and* or *but* between the adjectives. If so, then use a comma between them.

Example: inexpensive but comfortable car. [If the *but* were not in the sentence, you would punctuate it as "inexpensive, comfortable car."]

Degrees of Adjectives

Adjectives can express degrees of modification: positive, comparative, and superlative. Use the **positive** form when no comparisons are being made.

Positive form example: rich, lovely, beautiful

Use the **comparative** for comparing two things. Sometimes the word *than* accompanies the comparable adjective.

Comparable form example: richer, lovelier than, more beautiful

Use the **superlative** for comparing three or more things. Sometimes the word *the* precedes the superlative adjective.

Superlative form example: richest, the loveliest

The inflected suffixes *-er* and *-est* are used to form most comparative and superlative adjectives. Sometimes the suffixes *-ier* and *-iest* are added when a two-syllable adjective ends in *y.*

Example: friendlier, laziest

Be careful not to use the word *more* along with a comparative adjective formed with the *-er* suffix, or the word *most* along with a superlative adjective formed with the *-est* suffix.

Incorrect: more larger, most largest

Correct: larger, largest

Be careful not to form comparative or superlative adjectives that already describe a unique condition or extreme of comparison. *Perfect* and *pregnant* are good examples.

Incorrect: most perfect, more unique

Correct: perfect, unique

Irregular Form Adjectives

Some adjectives have irregular forms in the comparative and superlative degree, as seen in Table 2.4.

Table 2.4 Irregular Comparative and Superlative Degree Forms

Positive	Comparative	Superlative
good	better	best
bad	worse	worst
little	less	least
much, many, some	more	most
far	further	furthest

A-Adjectives

The so-called **a-adjectives** all begin with the letter *a*.

Example: ablaze, afloat, afraid, aghast, alert, alike, alive, alone, aloof, ashamed, asleep, averse, awake, aware

These adjectives are used after a linking verb.

> **Example:** The man was ashamed.

Sometimes you can use an a-adjective before the word it modifies.

> **Example:** the alert driver

A-adjectives are sometimes modified with *very much*.

> **Example:** The man was very much ashamed.

Adjuncts, Disjuncts, and Conjuncts

When adverbs are integrated into the flow of a sentence, the adverb is an **adjunct**.

> **Example:** Rebeccca, I don't <u>really</u> [adjunct adverb] care.

When an adverb does not fit into the sentence flow, it is said to be **disjunctive**.

Disjunctive adverbs are usually set off by a comma or a series of commas. A disjunctive adverb acts as if it is evaluating the rest of the sentence.

> **Example:** <u>Honestly</u> [disjunctive or conjunctive adverb], Rebecca,
> I don't really care.

Conjunctive adverbs serve as a connector within the flow of the text, signaling a transition.

> **Example:** If they start talking sports, <u>then</u> [conjunctive adverb]
> I'm leaving.

Adverbial conjunctions are words like *however* and *nevertheless*.

> **Example:** I love this town; <u>however</u>, I don't think I can afford to
> live here.

Adverbial Clause

A group of words containing a subject and a verb act as an adverb (modifying another verb in the sentence); this is called an **adverbial clause**.

Example: <u>When this conference is over</u> [adverbial clause], we're going home for dinner.

Adverbial Phrase

An **adverbial phrase** is a group of words that act as an adverb in a sentence.

Example: Our departmental budgets were due <u>in October last year</u> [adverbial phrase].

Adverbs

Adverbs modify verbs, adjectives, or another adverb. Adverbs often describe when, where, why, or under what circumstances something happened.

There are five main types of adverbs:

- Adverbs of manner

  Example: She spoke <u>slowly</u> and walked <u>quietly</u> [two adverbs of manner].

- Adverbs of place

  Example: She lives <u>there</u> [place] now.

- Adverbs of frequency

  Example: She drives to work <u>daily</u> [frequency].

■ Adverbs of time

> **Example:** She slept <u>late</u> [time].

■ Adverbs of purpose

> **Example:** She broke the window <u>intentionally</u> [purpose].

Adverbs usually end in *-ly;* however, many words not ending in *-ly* can serve as adverbs.

> **Example:** She drove <u>fast.</u> ... He bowled the <u>worst</u> of us.

Some words that end in *-ly* are not adverbs.

> **Example:** *Lovely, lonely, early, motherly,* and *friendly* are adjectives.

A small group of adverbs have two forms: those that end in *-ly* and those that don't. In some cases, the two forms have different meanings.

> **Example:** They departed <u>late</u>.

> **Example:** <u>Lately</u>, they can't seem to arrive on time.

In most cases, the form without the *-ly* should be reserved for casual conversation and not business writing.

> **Casual example:** He did her wrong.

> **Business writing example:** He treated her poorly.

Adverbs can modify adjectives, although adjectives can't modify adverbs.

> **Example:** The executive showed a <u>wonderfully</u> casual attitude.

Adverbs can have comparative and superlative forms.

Comparative example: You should walk <u>faster</u> if you want to get some exercise.

Superlative example: The candidate who types <u>fastest</u> gets the job.

Sometimes words like *more* and *most, less* and *least* are used to indicate the comparative or superlative forms.

Example: The house was the <u>most beautifully</u> decorated home on the tour.

Example: Her soup was <u>less tastily</u> seasoned than the others.

Another construction used to create adverbs is the use of *as-as*.

Example: He can't read <u>as</u> fast <u>as</u> his cubical mate.

Adverbs are often used as intensifiers to convey a greater or lesser meaning. Intensifiers have three functions:

■ Emphasize

Example: I <u>really</u> [intensifier] don't like him. He <u>simply</u> ignores me.

■ Amplify

Example: He <u>completely</u> wrecked his new car. … I <u>absolutely</u> love fresh fruit.

■ Tone down

Example: I <u>kind of</u> like this restaurant's food. … She <u>mildly</u> disapproved of his smoking.

Prepositional Phrases Acting as Adverbs

Prepositional phrases frequently function as an adverb.

Example: She works <u>on weekends</u> [prepositional phrase].

Infinitive Phrases Acting as Adverbs

An infinitive phrase can act as an adverb.

Example: The assistant ran <u>to catch the bus</u> [infinitive phrase].

Adverbs in a Numbered List

When you create a numbered list, do not use adverbs with an *-ly* ending (*secondly, thirdly,* etc.). Instead, use *first, second, third,* and so on.

Adverbs to Avoid

Adverbs like *very, extremely,* and *really* don't intensify anything. They are often too imprecise for business writing.

Positioning Adverbs in a Sentence

Adverbs have the unique ability to be placed in different places within a sentence. Adverbs of manner are unusually flexible about where they are located:

Example: <u>Solemnly</u> [adverb] the president returned the salute.

Example: The president <u>solemnly</u> returned the salute.

Example: The president returned the salute <u>solemnly.</u>

Adverbs of frequency should appear at specific points in a sentence:

■ Before the main verb

Example: He <u>never</u> gets up before noon.

■ Between the auxiliary verb and the main verb

Example: I have <u>rarely</u> called my sister without a good reason.

■ Before the verb *used to*

Example: I <u>always</u> used to talk to him on the phone.

Indefinite adverbs of time can appear either before the verb or between the auxiliary and the main verb:

Example: He <u>finally</u> showed up for the meeting.

Example: He has <u>recently</u> traveled to India.

The adverb *too* usually comes before adjectives and other adverbs.

Example: He ate <u>too</u> fast. ... He eats <u>too</u> quickly.

When *too* appears in a sentence after an adverb, it is a disjunct and is set apart with a comma.

Example: Linda works hard. She works quickly, <u>too</u>.

The adverb *too* and another adverb are sometimes followed by an infinitive verb.

Example: He talks <u>too slowly</u> to keep my attention.

The adverb *too* can also be followed by the prepositional phrase *for* plus the objective of the preposition plus an infinitive.

Example: This food is <u>too</u> spicy <u>for</u> Martha <u>to eat</u>.

Order of Adverbs

When a sentence contains more than one adverb, the adverbs should appear in a certain order. Shorter adverbial phrases should precede longer ones. The more specific phrase should go first.

Table 2.5 shows the correct order for adverbs.

Table 2.5 Correct Order of Adverbs

Noun/Verb	Manner	Place	Frequency	Time	Purpose
Horace jogs	enthusias- tically	in the park	every morning	before sunrise	to keep in shape.
Margaret drives	hurriedly	into town	every afternoon	before dinner	to do her shopping.

Inappropriate Adverb Order

Modifiers can sometimes attach themselves to the wrong word.

Example: They reported that M. B. Wilwau had won the lottery <u>on the evening news</u> [misplaced adverbial phrase].

Move the modifier immediately after the verb it is modifying (*reported*) or to the beginning of the sentence.

Example: They reported on the evening news that M. B. Wilwau had won the lottery.

Alternative example: On the evening news, they reported that M. B. Wilwau had won the lottery.

The adverbs *only* and *barely* are often misplaced modifiers.

Unclear: He <u>only</u> grew to be five feet tall.

Clearer: He grew to be <u>only</u> five feet tall.

Viewpoint Adverbs

A **viewpoint adverb** usually comes after a noun and is related to an adjective that precedes the noun.

Example: Investing all our money in technology stocks was probably not a good idea <u>financially</u>.

Focus Adverbs

A **focus adverb** is used to limit a specific aspect of the sentence.

Example: He got a promotion <u>just</u> for being there.

Negative Adverbs

Negative adverbs can create a negative meaning in a sentence without the use of words like *no, not, neither, nor,* or *never.*

Example: He <u>seldom</u> smiles.

Example: He <u>hardly</u> eats anything since he got sick.

Advice, Advise

Advice is a noun that means an opinion offered by someone suggesting how you should act or respond.

Example: I always talked to my uncle, whenever I wanted advice about business.

Advise is a verb that means to provide information or guidance.

Example: I advise my students to keep a dictionary handy whenever they are writing.

Affect, Effect

Affect is commonly used as a verb, meaning to influence. *Affect* can be used as a noun only as a psychological term, meaning feeling or emotion.

Effect is a verb meaning to bring about. It is also used as a noun, meaning a result or consequence, or a mental impression.

Incorrect: The light effects my vision.

Correct: The light affects my vision.

Incorrect: Can you affect a change in the operation?

Correct: Can you effect a change in the operation?

Affixes

An **affix** consists of one or more letters added to a word to change its meaning. There are two types of affixes:

■ Prefix—added to the beginning of a word

Example: im + possible = impossible

■ Suffix—added to the end of the word

■ Adding *-ly* to the end of some adjectives creates an adverb.

Example: wonderful + -ly = wonderfully

African-American

African-American is a term used to describe Americans of African descent. It is traditional to hyphenate African-American, but the hyphen is optional. Always use a hyphen if the term is being used as an adjective.

Example: He was an African American who idolized African-American business leaders.

Age

When giving the age of a person or a period of time, write out up to and including one hundred; use figures over one hundred:

Example: She is twelve years old.

Example: He has held the same position for twenty-six years.

Example: She is now 105 years of age.

Example: The company has been in this city for 102 years.

For compound adjectives denoting age, the words designating time may be used before *old,* but in that event the words *year* and *day* must appear in the singular:

Example: twelve-day-old baby elephant

Example: six-month-old pony

Example: 200-year-old building

Example: three-day-old kitten

Agents

The person or thing that performs the action described by a verb is called an **agent**. Agents are often used when writing in the passive voice along with the word *by.*

Example: The doctor's career was ruined by the lawsuit. [In this example, the *lawsuit* is the agent because it performed the act that ruined the doctor's career.]

Agreement

When the elements of a sentence have a grammatical relationship that affects the form of one or more of the words, **agreement** occurs.

Example: four boys [The word *four* requires the form of the word *boy* to become the plural *boys*.]

Agreement is also known as *concord*.

Aid, Aide

Both *aid* and *aide* mean helper or assistant. *Aide* comes from *aide-de-camp*, a military title. Use this form to describe people who serve as assistants.

Example: a congressional aide

Aid is often used for helpful objects.

Example: job aid, hearing aid, visual aid

Alike

See *Both, Alike*.

A Little

See *Little, A Little*.

Allegories

An **allegory** is a narrative that symbolically suggests something else. An allegory is an extended metaphor with two meanings. The underlying meaning of an allegory usually has moral or social significance.

Famous allegories are:

- *Aesop's Fables*

- *The Republic* by Plato

- *The Book of Revelation* from the Bible

- *The Masque of the Red Death* by Edgar Allan Poe

- *The Lord of the Flies* by William Golding

- *The Chronicles of Narnia* by C. S. Lewis

Alliteration

Alliteration is a narrative technique that uses words beginning with the same letter to sound poetic.

Example: "The moan of doves in immemorial elms, and the murmuring of innumerable bees."—Tennyson

---

All Right, Alright

All right means okay, acceptable, or unhurt. Always spell *all right* as two words, never one. *Alright* is an informal way to spell *all right* and should not be used in formal business writing.

Incorrect: It will be alright if you wish to go.

Correct: It will be all right if you wish to go.

Allusion, Illusion

An **allusion** is a reference to something. The words *allude* or *alluded* are more commonly used in writing. Allusions are often literary in nature.

Example: His allusion to water in his writing foreshadowed the great flood that would appear at the end of the book.

An *illusion* is a mirage, hallucination, or magic trick.

Example: The performance involved the illusion of sawing a woman in half.

Alone, Lonely

Alone can function as an adjective or adverb. *Alone* means to be without other people or to be on your own.

Example: Roger likes living alone.

Example: The child was left alone in the house.

Lonely is an adjective that means being unhappy because you are alone. Just being *alone* does not make a person lonely.

Example: Marcia felt lonely after her husband passed away.

A Lot, Alot, Allot

A lot, meaning a large amount or number, may be used to modify a noun. Using the word *many* or *numerous* instead of *a lot* is better form.

Example: We'll need a lot of hands to finish clearing the land.

Better: We'll need many hands to finish clearing the land.

A lot can also be used as an adverb to mean very much or very often.

Example: She looks a lot like her mother.

Alot is not a word.

Allot is a verb that means to give or share for a particular purpose.

Example: We were allotted one pillow and blanket per person.

Already, All Ready

Already denotes time and means before the present time or earlier than expected. *All ready* denotes preparation and means completely ready.

Example: She had already arrived.

Example: We are all ready to leave.

Altogether, All Together

Altogether is an adverb that means completely, in total, quite, or in all. *All together* is an adverb that means in one place or together as one group.

Example: She is altogether pleasant.

Example: His bills came to fifty-seven dollars altogether.

Example: The books were all together on one shelf.

Ambitransitive Verbs

An **ambitransitive verb** can be both transitive and intransitive without changing the verb form.

Example: I read the book. [*Read* is transitive and *the book* is the direct object.]

Example: I always read in the den. (*Read* is intransitive and there is no direct object after the verb.)

Other ambitransitive verbs are:

- Broke

Example: I broke the mirror. [transitive]

Example: The mirror broke. [intransitive]

■ Change

Example: I changed my pants. [transitive]

Example: The pants were changed. [intransitive]

■ Sunk

Example: I sunk the sailboat. [transitive]

Example: The sailboat sunk. [intransitive]

American English, British English

Certain words are spelled differently in **American English** than in **British English**. Table 2.6 is a list of words that have this peculiar treatment.

Table 2.6 Differences Between American and British Spellings

American	British
humor	humour
honor	honour
endeavor	endeavour
center	centre
fiber	fibre
theater	theatre
analyze	analyse
paralyze	paralyse

burned	burnt
dreamed	dreamt
spoiled	spoilt
canceled	cancelled
worshiping	worshipping
acknowledgment	acknowledgement
aging	ageing
usable	useable
anesthetic	anaesthetic
fetus	foetus
maneuver	manoeuvre
encyclopedia	encyclopaedia
catalog	catalogue
dialog	dialogue
check	cheque
draft	draught
plow	plough
program	programme

Among, Between

See *Between, Among*.

Ampersand

The **ampersand (&)** means "and." Do not use the ampersand in text, titles, or headings.

A.M., P.M.

A.M. means *ante meridiem,* which is Latin for "before midday." It stands for the time after midnight and before noon. *P.M.* means *post meridiem,* which is Latin for "after midday." It stands for the time after noon and before midnight.

When using *A.M.* or *P.M.*:

■ Don't write "12 A.M." or "12 P.M."; these forms cause confusion. Instead, write "12 noon" or "12 midnight."

■ You can use upper or lower case and periods: A.M. and P.M, or a.m. and p.m.

■ Do not add the word *o'clock* when writing times and including A.M. or P.M.

An

See *A, An.*

Anadiplosis

Anadiplosis is a narrative and speechwriting technique where a word or phrase at the end of a sentence or phrase is repeated at the beginning of the next sentence or phrase.

Example: Here, we expect commitment. Commitment is the key to being successful in this business.

Anaphora

Anaphora refers to the use of words or phrases such as pronouns that point backward to something earlier in a sentence.

Example: He wanted the newspaper and asked me to finish reading it [anaphoric, refers to the noun "newspaper"].

And Also

And also is a redundant phrase. Use either word separately, but not the two together.

And/Or

And/or is a legal term that means you can choose between two alternatives or choose both. Use *and/or* sparingly in your business writing because it is often seen as jargon. Check to make sure a simple *or* would do in your sentence. If choosing one of the alternatives eliminates the other, then it isn't an *and/or* situation.

Angry, Mad

See *Mad, Angry.*

Animate Nouns

Animate nouns refer to people, animals, and living things. **Inanimate nouns** refer to nonliving things.

Antagonyms

Antagonyms are words that can mean the opposite of themselves. Antagonyms are also known as **contranyms** or **autoantonyms**. The following are some examples of antagonyms:

■ Clip

> **Example:** <u>Clip</u> [attach] the receipts to your expense report.

> **Example:** <u>Clip</u> [cut from] the hedges.

■ Left

> **Example:** How much time is <u>left</u> [remaining]?

Example: They have already <u>left</u> [have gone].

■ Bound

Example: I'm <u>bound</u> [moving toward] for Los Angeles.

Example: The criminal was <u>bound</u> [unable to move] with handcuffs.

■ Buckle

Example: You had better <u>buckle</u> [hold together] your seatbelt.

Example: Her knees <u>buckled</u> [collapsed] under the weight.

■ Cut

Example: Those kids <u>cut</u> [got into] in line.

Example: Those kids <u>cut</u> [got out of] class.

■ Dust

Example: The maid is going to <u>dust</u> [remove dust] the living room.

Example: The police are going to <u>dust</u> [apply dust] for fingerprints.

■ Citation

Example: The city council gave me a <u>citation</u> [an award] for my volunteer efforts in the community.

Example: The police gave me a <u>citation</u> [a penalty] for speeding.

Antecedent

An **antecedent** is a word, phrase, or clause referred to by a pronoun. In a series of sentences, the antecedent is understood after being referenced once in a sentence or previous sentence, and therefore a pronoun is used to avoid repetition.

In the following example, the antecedent and pronoun are underlined.

> **Example:** The _Titanic_ was lost on its maiden voyage. It was said to be unsinkable.

Third-person pronouns (_he, she, it, they_) need an antecedent to be clear. First-person pronouns like _I_ and _you_ do not.

A pronoun must agree with its antecedent in three ways:

- Person—It must specify a particular person.

- Number—It must distinguish between singular and plural.

- Gender—It must distinguish between masculine and feminine.

Anti-

The prefix _anti-_ comes from Greek and means against. _Anti-_ is often added to words to create new words that mean the opposite of the original word.

> **Example:** anticrime, antisocial, antiglare

Antimetabole

Antimetabole is a technique where a word or phrase in one clause or phrase is repeated in the opposite order in the next clause or phrase.

> **Example:** "Ask not what your country can do for you; ask what you can do for your country."—John F. Kennedy

> **Example:** "The Sabbath was made for man, and not man for the Sabbath."—Jesus (Mark 2:27)

Example: "Now this is not the end. It is not even the beginning of the end, but it is, perhaps, the end of the beginning." —Winston Churchill

Antonyms

A word that means the opposite of another word is an **antonym**.

Example: Hot is the antonym of cold.

Antonyms can be made by adding the prefix *un-*.

Example: able, unable; happy, unhappy; suitable, unsuitable; likely, unlikely

Antonyms can be made by adding the prefix *non-*.

Example: sense, nonsense; conformist, nonconformist

Antonyms can be made by adding the prefix *in-*.

Example: sensitive, insensitive; discreet, indiscreet

Any, Either

Any refers to one of several. *Either* refers to one of two.

Correct: You may have any of the six books.

Correct: Either of those two cars will be acceptable.

Any, Some

Any and *some* are used to talk about indefinite quantities. Use *some* for positive statements and *any* for negative statements and questions.

Example: I asked the waiter to get me some water.

Example: Do you have any water?

Example: They don't have any.

Apart, A Part

Apart is an adverb that means separated by distance or time.

Example: I feel sad when we're apart.

A part is a noun that means a piece of something.

Example: I'd like to be a part of your team.

Apodosis

The main clause in a condition sentence is called an **apodosis**.

Example: If you ate there, you'd know what I mean. [The apodosis is "you'd know what I mean," and "if you ate there" is the if clause.]

Apostrophe

An **apostrophe** (') may denote that a word has been contracted intentionally.

Example: It's time to go.

Example: Haven't you finished the task?

An apostrophe can be used to show possession.

■   To show possession for a singular noun, add *'s*.

Example: the office's conference room

■   To show possession for a plural noun ending in *s*, add the apostrophe after the *s*.

Example: the employees' parking lot

■   To show possession for plural nouns not ending in *s*, add *'s*.

Example: men's room

The plural of compound nouns and joint possessive nouns is formed by adding *'s* to the second word only.

Example: Hitesh and Kalpana's house

If the items are separately owned, add *'s* to each of the compound nouns.

Example: Mary's and John's coats

For a proper name ending in *s*, use *'s*.

Example: Lewis's hat

Example: Miss Bliss's book

Note: Two proper names are traditionally observed as exceptions:

■   Moses' robe

■   Jesus' parable

For plural proper names ending in *s*, use only an apostrophe.

Example: The Joneses' boots were left in the hall.

No apostrophe is used with possessive pronouns.

Example: his, hers, its, yours, ours, theirs

The apostrophe is also used to express duration of time.

Example: a day's drive

Example: a year's worth of happiness

Appears, Displays

When writing about computer software, keep in mind that the word *displays* requires a direct object, while *appears* does not require a direct object.

Incorrect: The log-on screen displays.

Correct: The log-on screen appears.

Correct: The screen displays a warning message if you enter an incorrect password.

Appendix

An **appendix** is a separate section at the end of a document that provides supplementary information. An appendix provides additional reference material and details that were not necessary for all readers of the main document.

Example: statistics, detailed procedures, maps, diagrams

Documents can have more than one appendix, each containing a different type of information. Each appendix is labeled Appendix A, Appendix B, Appendix C, and so forth. When there is just one appendix in a document, title it Appendix.

If appendix items are referred to in the main document, arrange them in the same order as they are mentioned in the text.

Appendices should appear in the document's table of contents.

Apposition

An **apposition** is a writing technique that involves placing a noun or noun phrase next to another that explains it.

> **Example:** John Sullivan, <u>the mayor</u> [in apposition, explaining who John Sullivan is], will be visiting the high school on Wednesday.

Appositives

An **appositive** is a noun or phrase that renames or amplifies a word that immediately precedes it.

> **Example:** Gary, <u>my brother</u> [appositive], is a psychologist.

An **appositive phrase** renames or amplifies a word that immediately precedes it. Use commas to separate the nonessential appositive from the rest of the sentence.

> **Example:** My favorite professor, <u>a world famous author</u> [nonessential appositive], just won a prestigious literary award.

Be careful about the case of an appositive. Check the case by substituting the noun that the appositive modifies.

> **Incorrect:** My manager gave two of us, Ted and I, a bonus for our participation in the diversity task force.
>
> **Check:** My manager gave I a bonus.

> **Correct:** My manager gave two of us, Ted and me, a bonus for our participation in the diversity task force.
>
> **Check:** My manager gave me a bonus.

Articles

Articles, determiners, and **quantifiers** are little words that precede and modify nouns.

Example: the dog, a cat, those people, whatever purpose, either way, your choice

---

Sometimes these words tell you whether the subject is something specific or more general. Sometimes they tell you how much or how many.

The following is a list of determiner categories:

- Articles—*an, a, the*

- Determiners—articles and other limiters such as *a, an, five, her, our, those, that, several, some*

- Possessive nouns—*Kevin's*, the *worker's*, my *mother's*

- Possessive pronouns—*his, your, their, whose*

- Numbers—*one, two, three*, etc.

- Demonstrative pronouns—*this, that, these, those, such*

The three articles *a, an*, and *the* are a type of adjective. *The* is called the definite article because it tends to name something specific. *A* and *an* are called indefinite articles, because they refer to things in a less specific way. *The* is used with specific nouns and is required when the noun refers to something unique.

Example: The earth orbits the sun.

The is also used for abstract nouns.

Example: The City of Atlanta has encouraged the use of mass transit.

A is used before singular nouns that begin with consonants.

Example: a dog, a cat, a mountain

An is used before singular nouns that begin with vowels or vowel-like sounds.

Example: an apple, an eagle, an invitation.

As, Like

See *Like, As.*

Assure, Insure, Ensure

See *Ensure, Assure, Insure.*

Asterisks

Asterisks are used to call out a footnote on a page. The following are some uses for asterisks in your writing:

- Three spaced asterisks centered on a page may be used to signal a change in thought.

- One or more asterisks are sometimes used to strike out letters when writing profanity.

- Asterisks are sometimes used as bullets when creating a list.

- In computer science, an asterisk is used to represent a wildcard character.

- In telephony, an asterisk is included on the telephone keypad and is referred to as "star."

As to Whether

Avoid using the phrase *as to whether*. The word *whether* usually suffices.

As Well As

As well as is a synonym for *in addition to* and for the word *and*. Avoid using *as well as* in business documents. Instead use *in addition to* or *and*.

Correct: With the new printer, you can print beautiful color photographs in addition to normal black-and-white text documents.

Avoid: With the new printer, you can print beautiful color photographs as well as normal black-and-white text documents.

Autoantonyms

See *Antagonyms*.

Auxiliary Verbs

Auxiliary verbs are used to form verb phrases. There are four auxiliary verb groups:

- To be
- To have
- Model auxiliaries
- To do

The auxiliary verb *to be* is used in both the progressive tense and the passive voice.

Example of progressive tense: You are hitting.

Example of passive voice: You are hit.

The auxiliary verb *to have* is used in the perfect tense.

Example: I have finished my dinner.

Example: I had finished my dinner.

Example: I have been finished with my dinner.

Model auxiliaries determine whether a verb is a fact, desire, possibility, or command.

Example of fact: I can walk.

Example of command: I must walk.

Example of desire: I should walk.

Example of possibility: I may walk.

The auxiliary verb *to do* is used in questions, negatives, or emphatic statements.

Example of question: Does he smoke?

Example of negative: He smokes, doesn't he?

Example of emphasis: Despite the fact he's coughing, he does smoke.

Average, Mean, Median

Average is a mathematical term that is determined by adding two or more numbers together and dividing the sum by the number of items.

Example: The average of 2, 4, 6, 8, 10 is 6. [2 + 4 + 6 + 8 + 10 = 30, 30 ÷ 5 = 6]

Average is also known mathematically as the arithmetic mean. The middle number in a series of numbers is the *median*.

Example: The median of 2, 4, 6, 8, 10 is 6.

A While, Awhile

A while is a period of time. *Awhile* is an adverb that means for a time and should never be used as the object of a preposition (which can only be a noun or pronoun).

Incorrect: Please come to my home for awhile before you start your journey.

Correct: Please come to my home for a while before you start your journey.

Correct: Relax awhile before you begin the task.

Awful, Awfully

Awful can mean extremely disagreeable or exceedingly great.

Example: It was an <u>awful</u> experience. It was an <u>awful</u> lot of money.

Never use *awful* or *awfully* as a synonym for very.

Incorrect: She performed an awfully difficult task.

Correct: She performed a very difficult task.

Incorrect: Bill is awfully smart.

Correct: Bill is very smart.

Bad, Badly

Bad is an adjective and *badly* is an adverb. Use the adjective *bad* when referring to human feeling.

Example: I felt bad. [If you said, "I felt badly," you'd be saying that there was something wrong with your sense of touch.]

Badly is an adverb, but it is often mistakenly used as an adjective.

Incorrect: He wanted badly to go with them.

Correct: He wanted very much to go with them.

Incorrect: She felt badly after her operation.

Correct: She did not feel well after her operation.

Back-Channeling

In conversation, **back-channeling** is a natural response that shows you understand what a person is saying by using interjections such as *I see, yes, okay,* and *uh-huh*.

Backslash, Slash

The usual **slash** (/) is sometimes called a **forward slash**. Slashes are often used to indicate directories or folders in a computer filing system. Slashes are also used in Web addresses.

Example: http://www.videologies.com

A backslash (\) is often used in computer programming languages and to indicate the directory structure of a computer hard drive.

Back up, Backup

When used as a verb to describe the action of backing up, *back up* is two words.

> **Example:** It is important to back up your hard drive.

When used as an adjective or noun, *backup* is one word.

> **Example:** I searched my collection of backup CDs in order to restore my hard drive.

Base Form of a Verb

The base form of a verb is the same as the infinitive form without *to*.

> **Example:** wait, speak, come, see

Basically, Essentially, Totally

These words often add no additional meaning to a sentence and should be removed from your writing and speech.

B.C.

B.C. stands for *before Christ*. Some people use *B.C.E.*, which stands for *before the common era*.

B.C. is always written in all caps with periods.

Because, Since, As

Because is not to be used in place of *that*.

Incorrect: The reason he did not attend the company party is because he was in Chicago.

Correct: The reason he did not attend the company party is that he was in Chicago.

Better: He did not attend the company party because he was in Chicago.

Use *because* when referring to a reason for doing something. Use *since* when referring to a passage of time. Avoid using *as* referring to a reason for doing something. Use *because* instead.

Incorrect: As I forgot to get gas, my car stalled on the freeway.

Correct: Because I forgot to get gas, my car stalled on the freeway.

Correct: Since getting the new computer, I haven't had any problems with crashes.

Been, Gone

Been is the past participle of the word *be*. *Gone* is the past participle of the word *go*. *Been* is used to describe a past trip; a person has traveled somewhere and returned.

Example: Jennifer has been to India four times.

Gone is used to describe a trip from which a person has not returned.

Example: Jennifer has gone to India for the month of March.

Being That, Being As

Being that and *being as* are nonstandard substitutes for *because*.

Incorrect: Being that he was the only manager there on Saturday, everyone looked to him for answers when the network went down.

Correct: Because he was the only manager there on Saturday, everyone looked to him for answers when the network went down.

Below

See *Above, Below.*

Beside, Besides

Beside is a preposition that means close to or next to.

Example: The house is beside the river.

Example: He sat beside his girlfriend.

Besides can be a preposition that means in addition to or other than.

Example: What are you studying besides business administration?

Besides can be an adverb that means as well or furthermore.

Example: She was articulate and a strong leader. Besides, she was the owner's daughter.

Between, Among

Between is used to differentiate two, and only two, objects. *Among* is used to differentiate more than two.

Correct: The dog was sitting between John and me.

Correct: There were three good books among the many he gave me.

Bias, Biased

Bias is a noun used to describe a preference toward a particular ideology.

Example: His bias toward Hispanics prevented him from making friends with his new neighbors.

Biased is a verb used to describe an action or judgment influenced by prejudice.

Example: His vote on the jury was biased by his hatred for Hispanics.

Biased or Sexist Language

Avoid language that is stereotyped or biased in respect to gender, sexual orientation, ethnicity, or race. Stereotypical language assumes a stereotype about a particular group of people.

Incorrect: Although he was Jewish, he wasn't good with his finances.

Correct: He wasn't good with his finances.

Nonsexist writing is essential for most audiences.

Incorrect: He provides a great service to mankind.

Correct: He provides a great service to humanity.

Incorrect: Landing on the moon was one of man's greatest achievements.

Correct: Landing on the moon was one of humanity's greatest achievements.

Incorrect: The common man doesn't care anything about politics.

Correct: The average person doesn't care anything about politics.

Incorrect: We need to man the ticket booth.

Correct: We need to staff the ticket booth.

Avoid the use of *man* when describing various occupations.

Incorrect: businessman

Correct: businessperson

Incorrect: fireman

Correct: firefighter

Incorrect: mailman

Correct: mail carrier

Incorrect: stewardess

Correct: flight attendant

Incorrect: policeman

Correct: police officer

Incorrect: male nurse

Correct: nurse

Bibliography

A **bibliography** is a listing of books, magazines, Internet sources, and other reference materials used in writing a document. Bibliographies are located at the end of a document.

A bibliography is normally alphabetized by author's last name. If the author's name is unknown, alphabetize by title.

A bibliography is different from a series of footnotes. Footnotes are used to site references used in the text and are listed at the bottom of the page. See *Footnotes, Endnotes.*

For printed materials, a bibliography should contain the:

- Author's name.

- Title of the publication or title of the magazine article.

- Place of publication.

- Publishing company.

- Publication date.

- Volume number of a magazine.

- Page number(s).

Example of book: Wilson, Kevin. *The AMA Handbook of Business Writing,* New York: AMACOM Books, 2010: 50–51.

Example of journal article: Wilson, Kevin. "Alaskan B-24 Finds Home in Utah." *Aviation History,* October 2011.

For Internet sources, a bibliography should contain the:

- Author and editor names.

- Title of the page.

- Date of publication.

- Date you viewed the page.

- Web address.

Example: Wilson, Kevin. "Formatting a Bibliography." *Writing Toolkit.* http://www.videologies.com/amahandbook. 2010. Retrieved May 15, 2011.

Billion

A *billion* is equal to a thousand millions (1,000,000,000). You can write the number in words or numbers:

Example: five billion dollars, $5 billion

Biweekly, Bimonthly, Semiweekly, Semimonthly

To use these terms correctly, consider the following definitions:

- *Biweekly* means that something occurs every two weeks.

- *Semiweekly* means that something occurs twice in one week.

- *Bimonthly* means that something occurs every two months.

- *Semimonthly* means that something occurs twice in one month.

Blind

See *Visually Impaired, Blind.*

Blog, Weblog

Blog and *Weblog* are synonymous terms that describe Web-based journals. *Blog* can be both a noun and verb.

- *Blog* as a noun refers to the Web site where the content is published.

- *Blog* as a verb means to write articles for a blog.

Bold Fonts

Bold fonts are often used to identify key terms or phrases when writing technical documents or manuals. Consider the following tips for using bold fonts:

- Use bold fonts for emphasis to make certain words or phrases stand out.

- Use bold fonts for headlines and headings in your documents.

- In procedural documents, use bold fonts for warning or caution messages.

- Don't add bold to an entire paragraph of text.

- Use the bold font version of the typeface rather than the bold style function (the bold button) of your software. Use the bold style function only as a last resort if there is no bold typeface for the font you are using.

Bored, Boring

Bored is an adjective that describes when someone is uninterested, unhappy, or unoccupied.

Example: He was so bored that he started reading the phone book.

Boring is an adjective that means something is not interesting or exciting.

Example: The seminar was so boring that he fell asleep.

Both, Alike

Don't use the combination *both alike*.

Incorrect: The cars are both alike.

Correct: The two cars are alike. They are both the latest model.

Both, Each

Both is used to describe a condition that applies to two entities. *Each* is used to describe a single entity.

Incorrect: There is a picture on both sides of the mantel.

Correct: There is a picture on each side of the mantel.

Brackets

Brackets and **parentheses** are sometimes used interchangeably.

Changes to Quoted Material

If you are quoting someone, but make a change to the quote for clarity, you should put your change within brackets. Consider the following:

Original quote: "Everyone knew it was about to break any day now."

Revised quote: "Everyone knew it [the dam] was about to break any day now."

Digressions Within Parentheses

Sometimes you will find situations where you need an extra set of parentheses nested within a previous pair.

Example: The computer's memory (random access memory [RAM] and read only memory [ROM]) is where software is loaded.

Brake, Break

A *brake* as a noun means a device that slows a vehicle.

Example: I had to push hard on the brake to stop.

Break can be a noun or a verb.

■ *Break* as a verb means to damage something.

Example: He is going to break the chair.

■ *Break* as a noun means time off.

Example: I want to go outside on my break.

Brand Names

Capitalize the brand names of products. Some common brand names like Kleenex, Xerox, and Band-Aid are trademarked brand names and should be capitalized. You do not need to use the symbols ® or ™ when writing brand names.

If the product is part of the brand name, then it is also capitalized.

Example: Wonder Classic White Bread

If the product is not part of the brand name, then the product is not capitalized.

Example: Listerine mouthwash

Breath, Breathe

Breath is a noun that describes the air passing into and out of our lungs.

Example: The yoga teacher asked us to focus on our breath.

Breathe is a verb meaning to take a breath.

Example: Close your eyes, breathe deeply, and relax.

Bring, Take

Bring is used to denote movement toward someone or something. *Take* is used to denote movement away from someone or something.

Example: Bring me the book.

Example: Take the book to him.

British English

See *American English, British English.*

Bulleted List

Bulleted lists draw attention to important information. Consider these tips for the use of bulleted lists:

- Use a numbered list for a sequence of events or ranking items in a list.

- Use bullet symbols or checkmarks when the items in the list are not sequential or ranked.

- Make all the entries grammatically parallel.

- Do not mix clauses and sentences when creating bullet points.

- If the bullet points are not complete sentences, they do not need end punctuation.

- Indent subtext bullets that provide additional details about a main bullet point.

Bushel

Add an *s* when referring to more than one bushel.

Incorrect: Eight bushel of oats.

Correct: Eight bushels of oats.

Business, Right

Don't use *business* when you really mean *right*.

Incorrect: What business is it of theirs to question my action?

Correct: What right have they to question my action?

Buzzwords

Buzzwords are popular overused words that are common in business environments. Buzzwords are often pretentious and difficult to understand. Avoid them in your business writing.

Some buzzwords may be appropriate in the right context:

Incorrect: We need to architect a software solution.

Correct: John is the architect on the building project.

Common buzzwords to avoid are shown in Table 2.7.

Table 2.7 Common Buzzwords to Avoid

accountability	action items	architect	ballpark
benchmarking	best of breed	best practice	big picture
bleeding edge	bottom line	business case	buy-in
champion	cross-platform	customer-focused	deliverables
downsize	drill down	empowerment	enterprise-wide
fast track	front-end	game plan	globalize
goal-oriented	going forward	heads up	heavy lifting
herding cats	ideation	in the loop	in-market for
info superhighway	intellectual capital	key player	knowledge base
leading edge	lean and mean	level-set	leverage
long-term	low-risk/high-yield	matrix	methodology

mind-set	mission-critical	mission statement	monetize
multitasking	networking	on the same page	out-of-the-loop
out-of-the-box	outside the box	oxymoron	paradigm shift
partner	peel the onion	performance-based	play hardball
power shift	push the envelope	ramp up	reality check
re-engineer	resource-constrained	results-driven	right-size
risk management	ROI (return on investment)	rubber stamp	scalable
service organization	stand-alone	synergize	take that offline
talking points	task force	think outside the box	tip of the iceberg
total quality	touch base	touch points	train wreck
turnkey	24/7	user-centric	value-added
whiteboard	win-win	world-class	

By, Bye, Buy

By is a preposition and is commonly used in prepositional phrases.

Example: You should have learned that by now.

Bye is an abbreviated form of good-bye or a break in a sports team schedule.

Example: Because we had the best record, we got a bye for the first round of the tournament.

Buy can be both a noun and a verb. As a noun, *buy* means a very affordable purchase.

Example: The sweater was a great buy.

Buy as a verb means to make a purchase.

Example: I'm going to buy the sweater.

By, Until

By and *until* both indicate any time before, but not later than, a certain time. *Until* is used to tell how long a situation continued.

Example: He lived in Austin until May 2010.

Until is often used in negative sentences.

Example: Tickets will not go on sale until January 15.

By is used when something will happen before or at a specific time. It is often used to indicate a deadline.

Example: You have to finish the project by December 31.

Call Back, Callback

Call back is two words when used as a verb.

> **Example:** I need to call back two of the top candidates for the position.

Callback is one word when used as a noun or adjective.

> **Example:** After the audition, Chaital hoped for a callback.

Call Out, Callout

Call out is two words when used as a verb.

> **Example:** You should call out the processes in the diagram.

Callout is one word when used as a noun or adjective.

> **Example:** The illustration had a callout created as a text box.

Callouts

Callouts are text labels in an illustration that point out specific items that should be noticed by the reader. (See Figure 2.1.) Consider the following tips for using callouts:

- Callouts should have the first letter capitalized.

- Do not capitalize callouts that start with an ellipsis (…).

- If the callout is a complete sentence, end it with a period.

- Avoid a group of callouts for a single illustration where some are complete sentences and others are sentence fragments.

- Make all the callouts consistent grammatically for a single illustration.

Figure 2.1 Illustration with Callouts

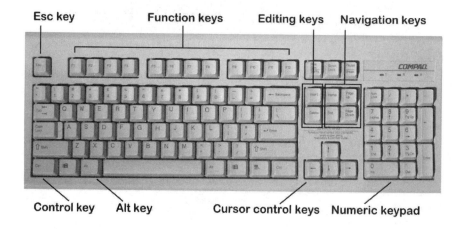

Came By

Came by is a colloquial phrase and should be avoided in business writing.

Incorrect: He came by to see me.

Correct: He came to see me.

Can, May

Use *can* to indicate capability.

Example: Can you read the bottom line on the eye chart?

Example: Yes, I can read it.

Use *may* to indicate possibility or when asking for permission.

Example: It may rain today.

Example: May I help you?

Cannot

Cannot is one word.

Incorrect: We can not make it to the performance.

Correct: We cannot make it to the performance.

Can't Seem

Seem is a verb that means look or appear. Using *can't* with *seem* is awkward.

Incorrect: I can't seem to make the journey in an hour.

Correct: It seems impossible for me to make the journey in one hour.

Canvas, Canvass

A *canvas* is a noun that means a heavy cloth that is, for example, stretched on a wood frame for painting or used to cover the floor of a boxing ring.

Example: The artist applied paint to the canvas.

Example: After the devastating punch, the unconscious boxer fell to the canvas.

Canvass is a verb meaning to survey.

Example: We went door-to-door to canvass voters.

Capital Letters

Capital letters are used at the beginning of a sentence or for a proper noun. Capital letters are also called **upper case**. See *Capitalization*.

Capital, Capitol

Capital can be a noun or an adjective. *Capital*:

- Can be the seat of government for a state or country.

- Can be an uppercase letter.

- Can be money or property owned by a business.

- Can be the top part of an architectural column.

- Can also mean "punishable by death."

    Example: Murder is a capital offense.

- Capital, as an adjective, means principal or chief.

    Example: It was the capital idea of the conference.

Capitol is the building where the U.S. Congress meets. It is capitalized when it refers to the U.S. Capitol. It is not capitalized when it refers to the main government building for a U.S. state.

Capitalization

Proper nouns that denote the names of specific persons or places are capitalized, though names that are common to a group are not. Consider the following *capitalization* guidelines:

Acts of Congress

- Civil Rights Act

- Taft-Hartley Act

- Child Labor Amendment

- Eighteenth Amendment

Associations

- Society of Professional Engineers

- American Business Association

- Young Women's Christian Association

- American Heart Association

Book Titles and Their Subdivisions

- *The American Way,* Chapter VI

- *Remembrance of Things Past,* Volume 11

- Bulletins and Periodical Titles

- *Wall Street Journal*

Railroad Cars and Automobile Models

- Car 54, Train 93

- Plymouth

- Cadillac

Churches and Church Dignitaries

- Fifth Avenue Presbyterian Church

- the Archbishop of New York

- Bishop John Barnes

Cities

- Jefferson City, Missouri

- Los Angeles

Clubs

- Leon Book Club
- The Do-Gooders
- Union League Club
- *But:* many Republican clubs in the West

Legal Codes

- the Code of Building Maintenance
- *But:* the building code
- Code VI

Compass Points Designating a Specific Region

- the Northeast [section of the country]
- the Pacific Northwest
- *But:* just drive north
- the West
- *But:* west of town

Constitutions

- the Constitution of Texas
- the Constitution of the United States
- *But:* the constitution of any nation

Corporations

- American Brake Corporation
- Container Corporation of America
- *But:* The corporation was dissolved.

Courts

- the Criminal Court of Appeals
- *But:* a court of appeals
- the Supreme Court
- the Magistrate's Court
- *But:* a county court

Decorations

- Purple Heart
- Good Conduct Medal
- Croix de Guerre
- *But:* Soldiers are given decorations to signal their acts of heroism.

Degrees (Academic)

- B.A.
- D.D.
- M.D.
- Ph.D.

Districts

- First Congressional District
- *But:* a congressional district

Educational Courses

- English 101
- Spanish Grammar
- Mathematics Made Easy
- *But:* He is studying physics and chemistry.

Epithets

- First Lady of the State
- Alexander the Great

Fleets

- the Third Fleet
- *But:* The ship was part of the fleet.

Foundations

- Carnegie Foundation
- Isha Foundation
- *But:* He established a foundation.

Geographic Divisions

- Lone Star State
- Sooner State
- *But:* There are fifty states in our country.
- Northern Hemisphere
- South Pole
- Old World Near East

Government Divisions

- Federal Reserve Board
- the Boston Fire Department
- *But:* The department was headed by Mr. Brian Wilson.

Historical Terms

- Dark Ages
- Renaissance

- Christian Era

- World War II

- Battle of the Bulge

- Declaration of Independence

- Magna Carta

Holidays

- Thanksgiving Day

- Passover

- Easter Sunday

- New Year's Eve

Libraries

- Library of Congress

- Albany Public Library

- *But:* The library is a source of information.

Localities

- Western Europe

- East Africa

- Wheat Belt

- West Side

- Mississippi Delta

Military Services

- United States Navy

- Signal Corps

- Second Battalion

- Company B

- Squadron 28

Nobility and Royalty

- Queen of Belgium

- *But:* Many queens were honored here.

- Duke of Windsor

- *But:* She was proud to have met a duke.

Oceans and Continents

- Pacific Ocean

- *But:* He was glad to be crossing the ocean.

Parks, Peoples, and Tribes

- Greenleaf Park

- Lake Texoma State Park

- Yellowstone National Park

- *But:* The park was in a southern state.

- Jews

- Christians

- Malay

- Chickasaw

Personification

- He was recognized by the Chair and spoke briefly.

- He sang about Summer in all its glory.

- *But:* In summer the days are longer.

Planets and Other Heavenly Bodies

- Mars

- Venus

- Big Dipper

Exceptions: moon, sun, stars

Rivers

- Mississippi River

- Wabash River

- *But:* The Mississippi and Wabash rivers were flooding after the torrential rains.

Sports Stadiums, Teams, and Terms

- Dallas Cowboys

- Madison Square Garden

- Super Bowl

- Dodgers

Captions

A **caption** is a short text message that appears below an illustration in a document that names and describes the image. A caption is usually placed directly below the illustration. Good captions pull a reader into the document.

A good caption should:

- Identify the subject of the illustration.

- Be short.

- Establish the relevance to the document.

Cardinal and Ordinal Numbers

Numerical symbols like 1, 2, 3 or numbers written as words like one, two, three are **cardinal numbers**.

Ordinal numbers express an order.

Example: first, second, third …

Case

Case is a grammatical term that refers to how nouns and pronouns are used with other words in a sentence. There are three cases:

- Subjective

- Objective

- Possessive

The **subjective** case is also called the **nominative** case. Subjective case includes:

- When a noun or pronoun is the subject of a sentence

  Example: I [pronoun] plan to go to India.

  Example: Mike [proper noun] sings in a band.

- When a predicate noun is used (a noun following a form of the *be* verb)

  Example: He is a singer [a predicate noun].

The **objective** case is used when the noun or pronoun is used in a sentence as a direct object, an indirect object, or the object of a preposition.

Example: Carl drew the picture [direct object].

Example: Jeff gave <u>us</u> [indirect object] the final presentation.

Example: Our team climbed up the <u>stairs</u> [objective of a preposition] together.

The **possessive** case is used to show ownership by a noun or pronoun.

Example: Paul washed <u>Nina's</u> [noun] clothes.

Example: Where did you find <u>her</u> [pronoun] clothes?

Table 2.8 provides a list of pronoun cases.

Table 2.8 Pronoun Cases

Subjective	Objective	Possessive
I	me	my, mine
you	you	your, yours
he	him	his
she	her	her, hers
it	it	its
we	us	our, ours
they	them	their, theirs

Cataphora

Cataphora is a writing technique that uses words or phrases such as pronouns to point forward to something later in the text.

Example: Since he was afraid of <u>it</u> [points forward to the noun "ocean"], John found it very difficult to go near the ocean.

Causative Verbs

Causative verbs are used to describe an action that is necessary to cause another action.

Example: My manager made me do it.

Other examples: let, make, help, allow, have, require, motivate, get, convince, hire, assist, encourage, permit, employ, force

---

Causative verbs are usually followed by an object (noun or pronoun) and an infinitive (*to* plus a verb).

Example: He allows his staff to work from home every Friday.

Three causative verbs do not follow this pattern: *have, make, let*. These verbs are usually followed by an object and the base form of the verb.

Example: She made her clients read the entire contract.

Caution Notice

See *Notices*.

CD, DVD

CD stands for compact disc. *CD-ROM* stands for compact disc, read-only memory. *DVD* stands for digital video disc. Do not add *disc* after CD or DVD.

Incorrect: Please give me the CD disc.

Correct: Please give me the DVD.

Censor, Censure, Sensor, Censer

Censor means to suppress someone's speech or writings to prevent them from being shared.

Example: The producer had to censor the interview by bleeping inappropriate language from the broadcast.

Censure means to denounce an offender.

Example: The lawyer who tampered with evidence was censured by the bar association.

A *sensor* is a device that detects changes in the environment.

Example: A motion sensor turns the light on when someone goes by.

A *censer* is an incense burner in a church.

Example: The priest swings the censer three times.

Champaign, Champagne

Champaign is a city and county in Illinois. *Champagne* is a type of sparkling wine and a region in France.

Check, Control

To *check* means to make certain something is correct, safe, or suitable by examining it.

Example: You should always check your wiper blades whenever you change your car's oil.

To *control* means to limit, order, instruct, or rule something or someone's actions.

Example: You need to control your dog while walking in the park.

Chiasmus

A **chiasmus** is a figure of speech created when two clauses use a reversal of structures. A chiasmus is often used to make a larger point.

Example: "Fair is foul, and foul is fair."—William Shakespeare

---

Chicano, Latino, Hispanic

To use these terms correctly in your writing, consider the following definitions:

- *Chicano* means Mexican-American.

- *Latino* means having Latin American heritage.

- *Hispanic* means having heritage from a Spanish-speaking country.

Choose, Chose

Choose is the present tense.

Example: Which one are you going to choose?

Chose is the past tense.

Example: I chose the purple one.

Cite, Site, Sight

To *cite* is a verb meaning to reference another person's words or writing.

Example: You cite the poet in your report.

A *site* is a noun meaning a location.

Example: That is the site of the car wreck.

Example: This is my Web site.

Sight can be a noun or a verb. As a noun, *sight* means the perception of something with your eyes, a view, or a glimpse.

Example: The ocean is in sight.

Sight as a verb means to see or to take notice.

Example: He sighted the enemy in his binoculars.

Citing Publications

Sources are often used in the creation of a new business document. Cited sources appear within the text and in a reference list at the end of the document.

■ Within the text, insert the last name of the author, a comma, and the publication date in parentheses.

Example: (Stroman, 2011)

■ For multiple authors, cite both names joined with an ampersand (&), a comma, and the publication date in parentheses.

Example: (Stroman & Wauson, 2011)

- If the name of the author is part of the text, cite only the missing information in parenthesis.

  Example: as reported by Stroman (2011)

- For citing works produced by an association, corporation, or government agency, the name of the group serves as the author.

  Example: (American Society for Training and Development, 2011)

- For citing works with no author, use the title of the book as the author.

  Example: (*The Urantia Book,* 1955)

Cite your sources in a reference list or bibliography at the end of the document. See *Bibliography.*

Clauses

A **clause** is a group of words that contains a subject and a verb but is not a complete sentence. A clause is different from a phrase because a phrase does not include a subject and a verb.

Cleanup, Clean Up

Cleanup is a noun that refers to a project or task involving cleaning.

Example: The oil spill resulted in a multimillion-dollar cleanup.

Clean up is a verb phrase that describes an action.

Example: You need to clean up your room before dinner.

Cleft Sentences

Cleft sentences are used to convert an original clause into two clauses to change the emphasis in the sentence.

Original clause: Mike ate the apple.

Cleft sentence: It was Mike who ate the apple. [puts the emphasis on Mike]

Cleft sentence: It was the apple that Mike ate. [puts the emphasis on the apple]

Clichés

Clichés are overused expressions that have become trite and even annoying. Avoid the clichés shown in Table 2.9.

Table 2.9 Common Clichés

acid test	at loose ends	babe in the woods
better late than never	black as night	blind as a bat
bolt from the blue	brought back to reality	busy as a bee (or beaver)
cat's meow	cool as a cucumber	cool, calm, and collected
crack of dawn	crushing blow	cry over spilt milk
dead as a doornail	dog-eat-dog world	don't count your chickens
dyed in the wool	easier said than done	easy as pie
face the music	feathered friends	flash in the pan
flat as a pancake	gentle as a lamb	go at it tooth and nail
good time was had by all	greased lightning	happy as a lark
head over heels	heavy as lead	horns of a dilemma
hour of need	keep a stiff upper lip	ladder of success
last but not least	looking a gift horse in the mouth	meaningful dialogue
moving experience	needle in a haystack	open-and-shut case
point with pride	pretty as a picture	put it in a nutshell
quick as a flash (or wink)	rat race	ripe old age

(continues)

Table 2.9 *(continued)*

rules the roost	sad but true	sadder but wiser
set the world on fire	sick as a dog	sigh of relief
slow as molasses	smart as a whip	sneaking suspicion
spread like wildfire	straight as an arrow	straw that broke the camel's back
strong as an ox	take the bull by the horns	thin as a rail
through thick and thin	tried but happy	to coin a phrase
to make a long story short	trial and error	tried and true
under the weather	white as a sheet	wise as an owl
work like a dog	worth its weight in gold	

Click

See *Press, Type, Click, Strike, Hit, Select,* and *Mouse Terminology.*

Click and Drag

See *Mouse Terminology.*

Click On

See *Mouse Terminology.*

Closed Compounds

See *Compound Words.*

Coleman-Liau Index

The **Coleman-Liau Index** is a readability test that is used to determine the grade level a student in the United States would need to be in order to read and understand a document. The index counts the number of characters in words.

The index is calculated using the following formula:

$$A - B = Index$$

where A = the number of characters divided by the number of words $\times$ 5.89 and B = the number of sentences in a fragment of words $\times$ 0.3.

Collective Adjectives

A **collective adjective** is formed when the article *the* is combined with an adjective describing a class or group of people. The resulting phrase can act as a noun.

Example: the meek, the rich, the poor

The difference between a collective noun and a collective adjective is that the collective adjective is always plural and requires a plural verb.

Example: The poor are always hungry.

Collective Nouns

A **collective noun** refers to people, animals, or objects as a group.

Example: The <u>company</u> [collective noun] has decided to expand internationally.

Example: I'm going to call the police [collective noun].

Collocations

Collocations are groups of words that are regularly used together in a certain order.

Example: hot and cold

Collocations are also word combinations that are common English sayings.

Example: middle management, nuclear family, heavy smoker, incredibly beautiful, wide awake

Colloquial

Colloquial is a term used to describe informal language that should not be used in formal speech or writing.

Example: ya'll, gonna, ain't, pop (for soft drink)

Colon

A **colon** generally follows a sentence introducing a list or a long quotation.

Example: The following quotation is from the *Atlanta Daily* newspaper: "Regardless of what may be accomplished, the company will still be involved."

Example: During your first year, you will study such subjects as these: algebra, physics, chemistry, and psychology.

Exception: When the list is the object of a verb or a preposition, a colon is never used:

Example: During your first year, you will study algebra, physics, chemistry, and psychology.

Emphasis or Anticipation

■ Colons are also used to stress a word, phrase, or clause that follows it or when a sentence creates anticipation for what immediately follows:

Example: The newspaper published a startling statement: the city is completely out of gasoline.

Time

■ Colons are used to separate hours and minutes in expressions of time:

Example: 5:15 A.M. EST

Titles

■ The colon is used to separate a title from a subtitle:

Example: *Gone with the Wind: A Story of the Old South*

Combination

Don't confuse *combine*—normally a verb unless referring to farm equipment—with *combination*, which is a noun referring to a group of entities.

Incorrect: That combine will be a large one.

Correct: That combination will be a large one.

Comma

A **comma** tells a reader to pause. Commas are used to separate nouns in a series or adjectives in a series of the same rank modifying the same noun.

Example: The workers picked cherries, peaches, and plums.

Example: We swam in the cool, clear, flowing water.

Commas are often used before an *and* in a sentence with a series of nouns or adjectives.

Example: At the zoo we saw elephants, tigers, bears, and monkeys.

Some writers prefer to omit the comma before the *and* in such sentences, unless it is needed for clarity. The same rules apply to using *but* and *or* in sentences with a series of nouns or adjectives. The comma is optional.

Example: His face was weathered, dirty, tired but handsome.

A term consisting of years, months, and days is considered not a series but a single unit of time. No commas are used.

Example: Interest will be computed for 6 years 3 months and 2 days.

Compound and Complex Sentences

Two sentences are often connected with a comma and conjunction, such as *and* or *but*. A comma is used between the clauses of a compound sentence.

Example: John went to the theater, but he left before the play ended.

Do not confuse this with a compound predicate, which takes no comma.

Example: John went to the theater but left before the play ended.

An adverbial clause usually follows the independent clause, and no comma is used. But for emphasis, the order of the clauses is sometimes transposed. Then a comma is used.

Usual Order: James was met by a large delegation when he came home.

Transposed Order: When James came home, he was met by a large delegation.

Introductory Expressions

Introductory expressions, such as transitional words and phrases, mild exclamations, and other independent expressions, are set off by a comma when they occur alone at the beginning of a sentence.

Example: Yes, I will go.

Example: Well, perhaps she is right.

Example: To tell the truth, I think you should not say anything.

A few introductory expressions are more emphatic without punctuation, however, and need not be followed by a comma.

Example: Doubtless she just couldn't be here.

Example: At least you tried.

Example: Indeed you may bring your friends with you.

Other Transitional Words

A comma is used to set off the transitional words *however, therefore,* and *moreover* when used within the sentence or as the first or last word of the sentence.

Example: Jean may not arrive until noon, however.

Example: Her problem, therefore, must be solved at once.

Example: I will be there, moreover, as soon as I can.

Sometimes *though* is used to mean *however* and should be set off with commas.

Example: I will be there, though, if at all possible.

Prepositional Phrases

No comma is used for prepositional phrases within a sentence unless the phrase comes between the subject and the predicate of the clause.

Example: I am sure that because of your generosity we will be able to build the new dormitory.

Example: The product sample, in addition to a diagram, will be sent to you today.

Contrasting Phrases

Contrasting expressions within a sentence are set off by commas.

Example: The lion, not the tiger, growled.

Example: We walk slowly, never quickly, to the garage.

Example: This letter was meant for you, not for me.

Nonrestrictive Modifiers

Nonrestrictive modifiers are phrases or clauses that could be omitted without affecting the meaning of the main clause. Nonrestrictive modifiers should be set off from the rest of the sentence by a comma or by parenthetical commas.

Example: Carlton, my favorite friend, is visiting me.

Example: That car is, I believe, a new model.

Example: Mary Brown, who works next door, is in charge of the festivities.

Infinitive Phrases

An infinitive phrase used independently is set off by commas.

Example: The color is too dark, to list one fault.

If the phrase is used as a modifier, it is not punctuated.

Example: The piano is too large to fit in the room.

Designating Dialogue

A comma is used to separate a dialogue quotation from the main sentence.

Example: "Please come with me," the boy said.

Example: "What do you think," Mr. Bleeker asked, "the mayor will do next?"

Commas also separate the name of the person addressed in dialogue from the remainder of the sentence.

Example: "Will you come with me, Luke?"

Example: "But, Amanda, how do you know that the plane is late?"

A confirming question within a sentence is set off by commas.

Example: "He left, did he not, on the noon plane?"

Repeated Words

A comma is used for clarity and to avoid confusion when the same word is repeated.

Example: Whoever goes, goes without my consent.

Word Omission

When words are omitted in one part of a sentence because they were used in a previous part, a comma is used to show where the words were omitted.

Example: Sam's first car was a Cadillac, and mine, a Ford.

Transposed Adjective Order

An adjective normally precedes the noun it modifies. When an adjective follows a noun, the adjective is set off by commas. When an adjective precedes a noun but also precedes the article before the noun, a comma follows the adjective.

Example: The physician, dignified and competent, told them the bad news.

Example: Dignified and competent, the physician told them the bad news.

Numbers

A comma is used in writing large numbers, separating the thousands digits from the hundreds, the millions digits from the thousands, and so forth.

Example: 249,586

Example: 1,345,000

A comma is used to separate two or more unrelated numbers.

Example: On August 1, 1992, 437 people visited the museum.

Example: Out of eighty, twenty were discarded.

Do not forget the second comma when the date occurs in the middle of the sentence.

Example: She left for England on June 22, 2009, and returned a month later.

Addresses

Elements of an address are set off by commas.

Example: He lives at 410 Hawthorne Street, Chicago, Illinois, near the University of Chicago campus.

On an envelope address, there is no comma between the state and the zip code.

Titles

A comma is used to separate a name and a title.

Example: The letter was from Mrs. Masterson, our president, and contained a list of instructions.

Do not set off *Jr.* and *Sr.* from proper names with a comma. A Roman numeral is not set off by a comma.

Example: Philip W. Thompson Sr.

Example: Philip W. Thompson III

Degrees are also set off by a comma.

Example: Jennifer Galt, M.D.

Descriptive titles are not set off by a comma.

Example: Ivan the Terrible

Company Names

Company names consisting of a series of names omit the last comma in the series.

> **Example:** Pate, Tate and Waite

When *and Company* completes a series of names, the last comma is also omitted.

> **Example:** Pate, Tate, Waite and Company

Do not use a comma before or after *Inc., Ltd., Limited,* or *Incorporated* unless the official name of the organization uses a comma.

> **Example:** Johnson Brothers, Incorporated

> **Example:** International Metrics Inc.

> **Example:** Benson & Sons, Limited

Common Adjectives

Common adjectives are not written with a capital letter.

> **Example:** a digital watch

Proper adjectives are written with a capital letter.

> **Example:** a Swiss watch

Common Nouns

Common nouns name ordinary people, places, or things. Common nouns are not written with a capital letter unless they begin a sentence.

Example: ball, flower, keys, cat, road, class, neighbors

Company and Product Names

The first time a product is mentioned, precede the name of the product with the company name. For subsequent usage, the product name alone can be used.

Example: Microsoft Windows [first mention] … Windows [subsequent usage]

Example: Ford Mustang [first mention] … Mustang [subsequent usage]

When listing multiple products from the sample company, precede the company name only for the first product.

Example: Ford Mustang, Escape, Explorer, and Focus

Comparatives

When an adjective or adverb is used to compare two things, the **comparative** form is used. To create the comparative form, some adjectives add an -er to the end, and some use a modifier before the adjective.

Example: The university is larger than the junior college.

Example: Many people find saving more difficult than spending.

See *Superlative*.

Compared to, Compared with

Compared to and *compared with* can sometimes be used interchangeably. When stressing similarities between items being compared, use *compared to*.

Example: David compared American coffee to French coffee and thought both had rich flavors.

When examining both similarities and differences, use *compared with*.

Example: Wes compared Jennifer's cake recipe with Emily's recipe to determine which one was easiest to prepare.

Complement, Compliment

Complement is a verb that means to add something or to make something better or more attractive.

Example: That blue dress complements your eyes.

Compliment is a noun that means an approving remark.

Example: It was the nicest compliment I'd received in years.

Complements

A **complement** is any word (or phrase) that completes a subject, object, or verb.

A **subject complement** follows a linking verb and is used to rename or define the subject.

Example: A tarn is a <u>small glacial lake</u> [subject complement].

An **object complement** follows or modifies a direct object and can be a noun or adjective.

Example: The players named Logan <u>captain</u> [object complement] to keep him happy.

A **verb complement** is either a direct or indirect object of a verb.

Example: Mark gave <u>Terry</u> [indirect object] all his <u>old albums</u> [direct object].

Complex Prepositions

A group of words that function as a preposition are a **complex preposition**. Complex prepositions consist of two or three words that act as a single unit.

Example: according to, apart from, because of, regardless of, with reference to, on behalf of, in line with, in relation to

Compound Nouns

Groups of words can form **compound nouns**.

Example: new moon

With compound nouns, the first word describes the second word. The second word identifies the thing in question. Sometimes two words are joined to form a new word.

Example: haircut, toothpaste, underground

Sometimes several words are joined to form a compound noun.

Example: daughter-in-law

Compound nouns can be formed using the combinations of words shown in Table 2.10.

Table 2.10 Compound Noun Combinations

Noun plus noun	mouthwash
Adjective plus noun	weekly lotto
Verb plus noun	wading pool
Preposition plus noun	underworld
Noun plus verb	grasshopper
Noun plus preposition	love-in
Adjective plus verb	dry cleaning
Verb plus preposition	stand by

Compound Predicates

See *Predicates*.

Compound Sentences

A **compound sentence** consists of two or more independent clauses, with two thoughts in the sentence, and either can stand alone.

The clauses of a compound sentence are separated either by a semicolon or by a comma and a coordinating conjunction. The most common coordinating conjunction is *and*; it simply links the two ideas. Other coordinating conjunctions, such as *but, or, for, yet,* and *so*, establish a relationship between the two clauses.

Compounding Sentence Elements

You can combine various sentence elements to create compound sentences.

- Subjects—Two or more subjects doing parallel things can be combined as a compound subject.

  Example: Working together, Acme and Industrial Pipe developed a new type of steel.

- Objects—When the subjects are acting on two or more things in parallel, the objects can be combined.

Example: The company president believed that the partnership between the two companies might help them increase sales and that he could eventually force a merger.

■ Verbs and verbals—When the subjects are doing two things simultaneously, the elements can be combined by compounding verbs and verbals.

Example: He studied sentence structure and grammar and learned how to speak and write effectively.

■ Modifiers—When appropriate, modifiers and prepositional phrases can be compounded.

Example: The company recruited its programmers from universities across the country and various competing companies.

Compound Words

Compound words are two or more words that are used to mean a single concept.

Open Compounds

Some compound words, called **open compounds**, are written as two separate words with a space between them. Table 2.11 presents a list of commonly used open compounds.

Table 2.11 Common Open Compounds

ad hoc	bed wetter	bona fide
drop in	half brother	life cycle
more or less	side effects	stick up
T square	time frame	under way
V neck	vice versa	

Closed Compounds

Some compound words, called **closed compounds**, are combined into a single word. Table 2.12 contains is a list of commonly used closed compounds.

Table 2.12 Common Closed Compounds

backslide	carryover	clearheaded
coldcock	crossbreed	deadpan
handwrite	layoffs	lifeline
longtime	makeup	ongoing
sendoff	shortlist	sidecar
standstill	stickhandle	twofold
waterlogged		

Hyphenated Compounds

Some compound words are separated by a hyphen. These are called **hyphenated compounds**. Table 2.13 presents a list of commonly used hyphenated compounds.

Table 2.13 Common Hyphenated Compounds

all-encompassing	all-knowing	anti-inflammatory
back-check	bed-wetting	cold-shoulder
community-wide	co-worker	cross-fertilize
dead-on	de-emphasize	do-able
drop-kick	ex-employee	ex-husband
multi-item	non-native	nuclear-free
off-color	pre-engineered	president-elect
self-doubts	self-esteem	stand-in
time-out	water-resistant	

Comptroller, Controller

A *comptroller* is the chief accountant in a governmental agency.

Example: the Georgia Comptroller of Public Accounts

A *controller* is the chief accountant in a business.

Example: Our controller, Mike Barrows, will be attending the board of directors meeting.

Concord

When combinations of words have a grammatical relationship that affects the form of one or more of the words, they show **concord**. Concord refers to the agreement between the form of the subject and the form of the verb. It also applies to noun phrases and personal pronouns such as *he, she, it,* and *they.* The grammatical relationship requires agreement in person, number, and gender.

Example: I sing, she sings, we sing. [Adding the *s* to *she sings* is required for third person singular and a present tense verb.]

Concrete Nouns

Concrete nouns refer to things that actually exist as opposed to abstract nouns, which refer to things that do not have a tangible physical existence.

Example: car, bus, airplane, tree, skin

Concrete nouns can be either countable or uncountable.

Conditional Perfect

Conditional perfect is a term used to talk about imaginary situations in the past. Conditional perfect is formed with the phrase *would have* plus the past participle of the verb.

Example: If he had seen the doctor, he would have not gotten sick.

Conditionals

Conditionals are used when writing about possible or imaginary situations.

The **first conditional** is used for future actions that are dependent on another future action. First conditional is composed of *if* + present simple + *will*.

Example: If he <u>wakes up</u> early enough, we <u>will</u> take him to breakfast with us.

Second conditional is used for future actions that are dependent on another future action where there is little chance of success. Second conditional is composed of *if* + past simple + *would* + base form.

Example: If I <u>found</u> a pot of gold, I <u>would share</u> it with my friends.

Second conditional can also be used for imaginary present situations when conditions for the action are not possible.

Example: If you had <u>visited</u> your mother, she <u>wouldn't</u> be so angry with you.

Third conditional is used for past situations where the conditional action did not occur. Third conditional is composed of *if* + past perfect + *would have* + past participle.

Example: If we <u>had seen</u> them, we <u>would have invited</u> them to dinner.

Zero conditional is used when actions will be true when the conditions are met. Zero conditional is composed of *if* + present simple + present simple.

Example: If you <u>put</u> honey in your tea, it <u>tastes</u> sweet.

Mixed conditionals involve combinations of second and third conditionals.

Other conditionals consist of using one of two formations. One is *if + will + will*.

Example: <u>If</u> you <u>will</u> write the report, I <u>will</u> do the research.

The other is *would + if + would*.

Example: I <u>would</u> appreciate it <u>if</u> you <u>would</u> help me more.

Conjunctions

Conjunctions are words that connect parts of a sentence. The simplest conjunctions are called **coordinating conjunctions**.

Example: and, but, or, yet, for, nor, so

And

The coordinating conjunction *and* can be used:

■ To suggest that one idea is sequential to another.

Example: Steve sent in his application and waited for the response in the mail.

■ To suggest that an idea is the result of another.

Example: Linda heard the thunder and quickly took shelter inside the house.

■ To suggest that one idea is in contrast to another.

Example: Carla is an artist and her sister is a doctor.

■ Frequently the conjunction *but* is used for this purpose.

■ To suggest an element of surprise.

Example: Atlanta is a beautiful city and has symptoms of urban blight.

■ Frequently the conjunction *yet* is used for this purpose.

■ To suggest that one clause is dependent.

Example: Drink too much water before the trip, and you'll soon find yourself stopping at every rest area.

■ To make a comment on the first clause.

Example: Horace became addicted to gambling—and that's why he moved to Las Vegas.

But

The coordinating conjunction *but* can be used:

■ To suggest an unexpected contrast.

Example: Tom lost money in his investments, but he still maintained a comfortable lifestyle.

■ To express positively what the first part of the sentence implies negatively.

Example: Tom never invested foolishly, but listened carefully to the advice of investment newsletters.

■ To connect two ideas with the meaning "with the exception of."

Example: Everyone but Tom is making money in the stock market.

Or

The coordinating conjunction *or* can be used:

■ To suggest that only one possibility is realistic and excludes the other.

Example: You can sell your investment now, or you can lose all
your money.

■ To suggest alternatives.

Example: We can go out to eat and to a movie, or we can just stay
home and see what's on TV.

■ To suggest a refinement of the first clause.

Example: The University of Texas is the best school in the state,
or so it seems to all UT alumni.

■ To suggest a correction to the first part of the sentence.

Example: There's no way you can lose money in this investment,
or so Eric told himself.

■ To suggest a negative condition.

Example: You have two choices: pay taxes or die.

Punctuation for Coordinating Conjunctions

When a coordinating conjunction connects two independent clauses, it is
often accompanied by a comma.

Example: Bailey wants to play football for Texas, but he has had
trouble with his grades.

It is also correct to use a comma with *and* when used to attach the items in a list.

Example: John needs to study harder in math, history, physics, and
economics.

When a coordinating conjunction is used to connect all the elements in a
series, a comma is not used.

> **Example:** Math and history and physics are the subjects that give John the most trouble.

Commas are also used with *but* when a sentence expresses a contrast.

> **Example:** Thomas is a great manager, but not very smart.

Other Conjunctions

The conjunction *nor* is used occasionally by itself; however, it is most commonly used in a correlative pair with *neither.*

> **Example:** He is neither rich nor poor.

Nor can be used with negative expressions.

> **Example:** This is not how I normally dress, nor should you get the idea I have no taste in clothes.

The word *yet* sometimes functions as an adverb and has various meanings such as in addition, even, still, and eventually. It also functions as a coordinating conjunction with a meaning of nevertheless or but.

> **Example:** Rosemary is an expert in computer programming, yet her real passion is poetry.

The word *for* is often used as a preposition, but it sometimes acts as a coordinating conjunction. When *for* is used as a coordinating conjunction, it has a meaning of because or since.

> **Example:** For he's a jolly good fellow.

The conjunction *so* can be used to connect two independent clauses along with a comma. It has the meaning of as well as, therefore, or in addition.

Subordinating Conjunctions

A **subordinating conjunction** comes at the beginning of a dependent clause and establishes the relationship between the clause and the rest of the sentence. Table 2.14 shows a list of subordinating conjunctions.

Example: He spoke Spanish <u>as if</u> he had been born in Mexico.

Many subordinating conjunctions also serve as prepositions.

Table 2.14 Subordinating Conjunctions

after	if	though
although	if only	till
as	in order that	unless
as if	now that	until
as long as	once	when
as though	rather than	whenever
because	since	where
before	so that	whereas
even if	than	wherever
even though	that	while

Correlative Conjunctions

Correlative conjunctions combine with other words to form grammatically equal pairs. The following is a list of correlative conjunctions.

- Both, and
- Either, or
- Not only, but also
- Neither, nor
- Whether, or
- Not, but
- As, as

Conjunctive Adverbs

A **conjunctive adverb** connects independent clauses. Common conjunctive adverbs include: *however, moreover, therefore,* and *nevertheless.*

Conjunctive adverbs require the use of semicolons.

> **Example:** The repairs to the space station should be successful; however, I'm a bit concerned about the long spacewalk.

Conjunctive adverbs are often confused with coordinating conjunctions (*and, but, for, nor, or, yet,* and *while*). Coordinating conjunctions do not require semicolons. See *Coordinating Conjunctions.*

Conjuncts

A **conjunct** is used to relate something said in one sentence to another sentence.

> **Example:** <u>That being said</u> [information from the previous sentence], we made money on the deal.

A conjunct can be removed without making the sentence ungrammatical.

Connote, Denote

Denotation is the literal meaning of a word.

> **Example:** Bullheaded and determined both denote stubbornness.

Broader associations with a word are its *connotations.*

> **Example:** Being determined connotes an adherence to purpose.

Considered to Be

The phrase *considered to be* can often be eliminated from your sentences.

Consonants

The letters *B, C, D, F, G, H, J, K, L, M, N, P, Q, R, S, T, V, W, X,* and *Z* are consonants in the English language.

Continuous Verbs

Continuous verbs are used to describe action that is taking place in the past, present, or future.

One use for continuous verbs is to describe past actions that were in progress at some time in the past, but the actions were not yet finished.

> **Example:** At 10:30 this morning, Mark was talking to the board of directors.

Another use for continuous verbs is to describe two or more actions that were in progress in the past at the same time.

> **Example:** While I was meeting with the general manager, he was busy scanning email messages on his Blackberry.

A third use for continuous verbs is to describe something that was happening when something else happened.

> **Example:** I was deep in the middle of my sales pitch, when the fire alarm suddenly went off.

Contractions

A **contraction** is a shortened form of one or more words with an apostrophe taking the place of the missing letter or letters. Do not use contractions in formal business writing.

> **Example:** don't, I'm, you're, it's, we're, we'd

In spoken English, forms of the verb *to be* and other auxiliary verbs are often contracted.

Example: I am, I'm; you will, you'll, it is, it's

Contractions are often used with *not* to negate a verb.

Example: is not, isn't; are not, aren't; did not, didn't

Contractions are often used with *have*.

Example: I have, I've; would have, would've

Some single words are sometimes contracted.

Example: of, o'; of the clock, o'clock; madam, ma'am

Table 2.15 shows a list of common contractions.

Table 2.15 Common Contractions

	Be	Will	Would	Have	Had
I	I'm I am	I'll I will	I'd I would	I've I have	I'd I had
you	you're you are	you'll you will	you'd you would	you've you have	you'd you had
he	he's he is	he'll he will	he'd he would	he's he has	he'd he had
she	she's she is	she'll she will	she'd she would	she's she has	she'd she had
it	it's (or 'tis) it is	it'll it will	it'd it would	it's it has	it'd it had
we	we're we are	we'll we will	we'd we would	we've we have	we'd we had

they	they're they are	they'll they will	they'd they would	they've they have	they'd they had
that	that's that is	that'll that will	that'd that would	that's that has	that'd that had
who	who's who is	who'll who will	who'd who would	who's who has	who'd who has
what	what's what is what're what are	what'll what will	what'd what would	what's what has	what'd what had
where	where's where is	where'll where will	where'd where would	where's where has	where'd where had
when	when's when is	when'll when will	when'd when would	when's when has	when'd when had
why	why's why is	why'll why will	why'd why would	why's why has	why'd why had
how	how's how is	how'll how will	how'd how would	how's how has	how'd how had

Contranyms

Contranyms are words that can mean the opposite of themselves.

Example: *Overlook* can mean to look at closely or to miss completely.

See *Antagonyms.*

Control

See *Check, Control.*

Convince, Persuade

Convince and *persuade* are not synonyms.

- To *convince* is to influence someone to adopt a point of view by evidence or by an intellectual argument.

  Example: Mike convinced Janet that she was wrong about the incident at the conference.

- To *persuade* is to talk someone into something by appeals made to morals or emotion.

  Example: Mike persuaded Janet to sign up for Toastmasters.

Cooperate

Cooperate is a verb that means to work together. Therefore, *cooperate together* is redundant.

Incorrect: If they cooperate together, their purpose will be accomplished.

Correct: If they cooperate, their purpose will be accomplished.

Coordinated Adjectives

See *Adjectives*.

Coordinating Conjunctions

Coordinating conjunctions are used to join two clauses of equal importance. Words like *for, and, nor, but, or,* and *yet* are coordinating conjunctions.

Copula Verbs

Copula verbs are verbs that connect the subject to the complement. Copula verbs are also called **linking verbs**.

Example: That band <u>plays</u> [connects the subject to the adjective] great.

Common copula verbs are *be, look, feel, taste, smell, sound, seem, appear, get, become, grow, stay, keep, turn, prove, go, remain, resemble, run,* and *lie.*

Copyright

Copyright is a form of protection provided by U.S. law to the authors of books, films, plays, music, art, and other intellectual works. Protection under copyright law is available for both published and unpublished works.

Owners of a copyright have the exclusive right to reproduce, distribute, or display their intellectual property.

You must obtain permission before including copyrighted work in your own business documents or Web sites.

Copyrighted materials contain a notice of copyright and a copyright symbol (©).

Example: © Copyright 2009, M. B. Wilwau. All rights reserved.

Correlative Conjunction

See *Conjunctions.*

Could of, Might of

See *Might of, Should of, Would of, Could of.*

Council, Counsel, Consul

To use these words correctly in your writing, consider these definitions:

■ A *council* is a group of persons convened for advisory purposes.

■ *Counsel* is advice; the word sometimes means attorney.

■ A *consul* is an official appointed by a government to report on matters that the official observes while residing in a foreign land.

Count Nouns

Count nouns are nouns that have both a singular and plural form. The plural of a count noun is usually formed by adding *s*.

Credible, Credulous

Credible means believable or worthy of being believed. *Credulous* means inclined to believe too readily.

Correct: He related the incident in a credible manner.

Correct: She is too credulous for her own good.

Cross-Reference

A **cross-reference** is a link in a document to related or more detailed information. Cross-referencing can be accomplished by:

■ Adding the word *see* plus the term in italics.

Example: See *Operating Systems.*

■ Adding a hyperlink to Web-based documents.

■ Adding an index to the end of the document.

Cut-and-Paste

Cut-and-paste is a term commonly used to describe editing functions in software such as word processing.

When using the term *cut-and-paste* in business writing, use it only as an adjective, not as a noun phrase or verb phrase. Always include hyphens in *cut-and-paste*.

Incorrect: Go to the Edit menu and do a cut-and-paste.

Incorrect: In a word processor, you can cut and paste text.

Correct: In most word processors, you can perform a cut-and-paste operation.

Danger Notice

See *Notices*.

Dangling Modifiers

A **modifier** is a word or phrase that gives more detail about a subject. A **dangling modifier** modifies a word that is not clearly stated in a sentence.

> **Example:** Having struggled through the long commute, Dan parked his car in his usual spot.

The doer must be the subject of the main clause that follows. In the example, Dan is the logical doer; therefore this sentence does not have a dangling modifier.

> **Example:** Having struggled through the long commute, the car was parked in the usual spot.

"Having struggled" is a participle that expresses action, but the doer is not the parking spot. Because the doer of the action is not clearly stated, this participial phrase is a dangling modifier.

Characteristics of Dangling Modifiers

Dangling modifiers typically occur at the beginning of a sentence as an introductory clause or phrase. Dangling modifiers can also appear at the end of a sentence. Dangling modifiers often have a gerund (*-ing* word) or an infinitive (*to + be* word) near the beginning of the sentence.

> **Incorrect:** Not having made contingency plans, the project was a failure.

Revising Dangling Modifiers

Name the doer of the action in a sentence as the subject of the main clause.

Dangling modifier: Having arrived late for the meeting, a recap of the first 30 minutes was needed.

Revision: Having arrived late for the meeting, the project manager needed a recap of the first 30 minutes.

Revise the dangling phrase into a complete introductory clause by naming the doer in that clause.

Dangling modifier: Without knowing the reason, it was impossible to order larger displays.

Revision: Because my manager did not know the reason, it was impossible to order larger displays.

Combine the introductory phrase and main clause into one.

Dangling modifier: To improve his sales, the advertising budget was increased.

Revision: His sales improved by increasing the advertising budget.

Dangling Participles

Dangling participles modify the noun or pronoun to which they refer (the referent). Because position determines the referent, how you construct the sentence determines the meaning.

Incorrect: Walking down Main Street, the art museum is visible.

This implies the art museum is walking down Main Street.

Correct: Walking down Main Street, you can see the art museum.

Dash

The **dash** is used to introduce an added thought.

> **Example:** I shall go with you—you don't mind, do you?

The dash also breaks the continuity of a thought as a digression.

> **Example:** "The Scherzo Sonata" by Tolstoy is a sad story—but the writing is magnificent.

The dash is sometimes used before and after a parenthetical expression in place of commas.

> **Example:** Henry Higgins—bareheaded and without a coat—left the house and ran down the road.

The dash can also be a super comma. When a sentence already contains a series separated by commas, a dash is a good tool for setting off a clause that might otherwise look like it is part of the series.

> **Example:** The Mississippi River weaves through Tennessee, Arkansas, and Louisiana—a state famous for its French culture—before emptying into the Gulf of Mexico.

When typing, the dash is indicated by two hyphens (--). There are two types of dashes: the en dash (–) and the em dash (—). The en dash is a little longer than a hyphen and is used for ranges of time and other numbers in place of a hyphen when combining open compounds.

> **Example:** The years 2007–2009 were not good for investors.

The em dash is about the same width as the letter *m* and is used like a super comma to add emphasis or an abrupt change of thought.

> **Example:** The conference was attended by the leaders of France, Germany, and Spain—a country that recently elected its president— all of whom were enthusiastically welcomed during the opening night ceremony.

You can add the en dash and em dash using the Insert/Symbol function on a word processor such as Microsoft Word.

Data

Data is always plural. *Datum* is the singular form but is rarely used.

Incorrect: This data proves that our business is growing.

Correct: These data prove that our business is growing.

Dates

When writing a date, a comma is placed between the day and the year.

Example: September 16, 2012

There is no comma if the date is written in the European style.

Example: 16 September 2012

Dates can also be written using a slash or hyphen to separate the day, month, and year. When a slash or hyphen is used, numerals are used to represent the month.

Example: 9/16/2012 or 9-16-2012

Do not use slashes or hyphens when writing dates in formal business documents.

When including the day of the week, add a comma after the day.

Example: Monday, September 16, 2012

When just writing a month and year, do not add a comma between them.

Incorrect: September, 2012

Correct: September 2012

When abbreviating a decade, there are two options. Use no apostrophe between the number and the *s*.

Example: 1990s

Insert an apostrophe to show that something was left out.

Example: '80s

Use the cardinal number when writing the days of the month without a year.

Incorrect: His birthday is March 26th [ordinal].

Correct: His birthday is March 26 [cardinal].

When writing a century as a noun, do not use a hyphen.

Example: The twentieth century gave birth to the television.

When writing a century as an adjective, use a hyphen.

Example: It was the nineteenth-century medical practices that caused so many battlefield deaths.

Deaf or Hard of Hearing

Use the entire phrase *deaf or hard of hearing* when referring to people who are deaf. Use *deaf* when space is limited. Hyphenate *hard-of-hearing* when it precedes a noun that it modifies.

Example: A man doing sign language stood on the side of the stage for the deaf or hard-of-hearing audience members.

Deal

Deal should not be used informally to refer to a business agreement.

Incorrect: She made a deal to buy the house.

Correct: She made an agreement to buy the house.

Decimals

The **decimal system** is a number system based on 10 that allows us to write large or small numbers.

■ Numbers placed to the left of a decimal point are whole numbers.

■ Numbers placed to the right of a decimal point are fractions that are equal to less than one.

Figure 2.2 illustrates whole numbers and fractions.

Figure 2.2 Whole Numbers and Fractions

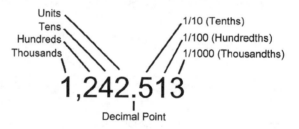

When writing decimals, you can write either the numerical form or the number in words.

Example: 0.3 or three-tenths

When writing a whole number and a fraction in words, add the word *and* to signal the location of the decimal.

Example: Two and three-tenths [written in numbers as 2.3]

When writing the numerical form of hundredths or thousandths, add zeros as place holders if there are no other numbers or if there is no whole number or decimal.

Example: 0.003 [written in words as three-thousandths]

A fraction can be written as a decimal.

Example: 0.5 [one-half]

Example: 0.25 [one-fourth]

Example: 0.333 [one-third]

Decimals can be written as a percentage. Move the decimal point two places to the right to translate a decimal into a percentage.

Example: 0.50 = 50 [fifty percent]

Example: 1.00 = 100 [one hundred percent]

Declarative Mood

Mood as a verb refers to the attitude of the speaker. The **declarative mood** is the normal form of a verb used to convey information or make statements of fact. The declarative mood is used to indicate that something has happened or will happen.

Declarative Sentence

A **declarative sentence** is used to state facts or an argument. Declarative sentences do not require an answer or reaction from the reader.

Example: Mike plays the guitar.

> **Example:** The weather is warm in Florida.

Declarative sentences are the most common type of sentence. Punctuate these sentences with a period.

Defining Relative Clause

A **defining relative clause** modifies a noun or noun phrase and provides essential information that is required for a sentence to make sense.

> **Example:** The bed and breakfast <u>that we stayed in</u> [defining relative clause] was really nice.

Defining relative clauses can begin with *who, whose,* and *that* for defining people and *which, whose,* and *that* for defining things.

Definite Article

Nouns are preceded by words like *the, a,* or *an.* These words are called **determiners**. The determiner *the* is a **definite article**. A definite article restricts the meaning of a noun to refer to something already known by the reader from earlier sentences.

> **Example:** A taxi pulled up next to Joe. He got into the taxi [the taxi that pulled up].

The is used before both singular and plural nouns.

> **Example:** the dog, the dogs; the notebook, the notebooks; the pear, the pears

Defuse, Diffuse

You can *defuse* a bomb or dangerous situation by removing the trigger or the fuse.

Example: Mike defused the situation by moving Mary to another project.

To *diffuse* is to spread something.

Example: Rotten smells from the refrigerator diffused through the office air conditioning system.

Degree Adverbs

Modifying adverbs like *very* and *extremely* are called **degree adverbs** because they specify the degree of another adjective or adverb. Other degree adverbs are *almost, barely, highly, quite, slightly, totally,* and *utterly.*

Degree Titles

When writing about college degrees, use lowercase spelling.

Example: The university near my house, Kennesaw State University, does not offer a doctor of philosophy degree.

College degrees can be shortened for less formal writing.

Example: I received my bachelor's from the University of Texas at Austin.

Capitalize the degree name when specifying a particular degree.

Example: I received a Bachelor of Science in Communications from the University of Texas at Austin.

Capitalize the abbreviations for degrees.

Example: B.A., M.A., Ph.D.

Deixis

Deixis refers to words or phrases that make sense only in the context of a particular sentence.

> **Example:** Jeff's presentation was scheduled to begin in ten minutes, and <u>he</u> [refers to Jeff] was feeling nervous about it [refers to the presentation].

Demonstrative Adjectives

Demonstrative adjectives are words like *this, that, these,* and *those* that tell whether a noun they modify is singular or plural and where the noun is located.

> **Example:** I've been using <u>this</u> hammer.

> **Example:** I climbed <u>that</u> mountain when I was twelve.

> **Example:** <u>These</u> are the shoes I like best.

> **Example:** I would like some of <u>those</u> flowers on my desk.

Demonstrative Pronouns

Demonstrative pronouns are words like *this, that, these, those,* and *such* that can be used as either pronouns or as determiners.

As pronouns, the demonstrative pronouns identify a noun.

> **Example:** *That* is marvelous! I will never forget *this.* Such is life.

As a determiner, the demonstrative adjectivally modifies a noun that follows. It is used to convey a sense of time and distance.

> **Example:** *These* [strawberries that are in front of me] look delicious.

> **Example:** *Those* [that are further away] look even better.

A sense of emotional distance can also be conveyed through the use of demonstrative pronouns. Pronouns used in this way receive special emphasis in a spoken sentence.

Example: You're going to eat *that*?

When used as subjects, demonstrative pronouns can be used to refer to objects as well as persons.

Example: *This* is my partner. *This* is my book.

Denominal Adjectives

Denominal adjectives are words that act like adjectives but are actually nouns. Denominals are derived from nouns.

Example: I visited a stone fort.

Example: We watched the physics experiment.

Denominals include references to nationality.

Example: An Asian nurse helped my father in the hospital.

Denote, Connote

See *Connote, Denote*.

Dependent Clauses

A **dependent clause** cannot stand by itself like an independent clause. A dependent clause must be combined with an independent clause to make a sentence.

Dependent clauses can perform a variety of functions in a sentence. They can be noun clauses, adverb clauses, or adjective clauses.

Noun clauses can do anything a noun can do in a sentence.

> **Example:** <u>What he knows about boxing</u> is not important to me.

Adverb clauses tell us about what is going on in the independent clause: where, when, or why.

> **Example:** <u>When the game is over,</u> we'll go get some burgers.

Adjective clauses function just like multiword adjectives to modify a noun.

> **Example:** My wife, <u>who is a video producer</u>, has just completed an award-winning documentary about music.

Descriptive Writing

Descriptive writing is used to help the reader visualize the topic and to experience what the writer experienced. Descriptive writing uses language of interest to the five senses. It includes concrete details to describe people, places, things, and actions. Figurative language such as simile, metaphor, hyperbole, symbolism, and personification are often used in descriptive writing.

Desert, Dessert

To correctly use these words in your writing, consider their definitions.

- A *desert* is dry barren landscape.

- A *dessert* is a sweet food served at the end of a meal.

Determiners

Articles, determiners, and **quantifiers** are little words that precede and modify nouns.

> **Example:** the dog, a cat, those people, whatever purpose, either way, your choice

Sometimes these words tell you whether the subject is something specific or more general. Sometimes they tell you how much or how many.

The following is a list of determiner categories:

- Articles—*an, a, the*

- Determiners—articles and other limiters such as *a, an, five, her, our, those, that, several, some*

- Possessive nouns—*Kevin's*, the *worker's*, my *mother's*

- Possessive pronouns—*his, your, their, whose*

- Numbers—*one, two, three*, and so on

- Demonstrative pronouns—*this, that, these, those, such*

Predeterminers occur prior to other determiners and include:

- Multipliers—*double, twice, two/three times*, etc.

- Fractional expressions—*one-half, one-third*, etc.

- The words *both, half,* and *all.*

- The intensifiers—*quite, rather,* and *such.*

Multipliers precede plural count and mass nouns and occur with single-count nouns describing an amount.

> **Example:** This classroom holds <u>three times</u> the students as my old room.

> **Example:** This time we added <u>twice</u> the amount of air in the tire.

Fractional expressions have a similar construction as multipliers and optionally include *of.*

> **Example:** <u>One-half of</u> the voters favored lower taxes.

Intensifiers occur primarily in casual speech and are more common in British English than in American English.

> **Example:** This food is <u>rather</u> bland, isn't it?

Example: The voters made <u>quite</u> a fuss over the debate.

Device, Devise

To correctly use these words in your writing, consider their definitions.

- *Device* is noun that means a piece of equipment designed for a special purpose or a special technique or strategy.

- *Devise* is a verb that means to think of a new idea.

Diacritic

A mark added to a letter that changes the pronunciation is a **diacritic**. Diacritics can appear above or below a letter. Diacritics are used for words that come from other languages.

Example: café, façade

Different from, Different than

Different from takes an object. *Different than* introduces a clause.

Incorrect: That coat is different than mine.

Correct: That coat is different from mine.

Correct: He was different than I remembered.

Diffuse, Defuse

See *Defuse, Diffuse*.

Dimensions

The symbols reserved for technical writing are a single prime (') for feet, a double prime (″) for inches, and a multiplication sign (×) for by.

Example: 9′ × 12′ (9 feet by 12 feet)

Example: 8″ × 10″ (8 inches by 10 inches)

In regular prose text, write out the word *by* for ×.

Ciphers (zeros) can be used to indicate exact measurement if they improve clarity.

Example: 9′0″ × 12′0″ × 20′6″

Figure 2.3 shows how to interpret a ciphered measurement.

Figure 2.3   Interpretation of a Ciphered Measurement

Nine feet three inches by twelve feet four inches

9'3" x 12'4"

Direct Objects

In a sentence, the word or words that designate the person or thing receiving the action of a transitive verb is called the **direct object**.

Example: My brother wrecked the *car* [direct object].

Disability

See *Handicap, Disability.*

Disc, Disk

A compact *disc* is spelled with a *c*. *Discs* often are used for magnetic media that is reproduced using a laser.

A computer hard *disk* drive is spelled with a *k*.

Discreet, Discrete

Discreet means showing discernment or good judgment in conduct or speech.

> **Example:** You have to be discreet when talking politics around my parents.

Discrete means a separate or distant entity.

> **Example:** The study separated people into two discrete groups.

Disease Names

Many diseases are named after their discoverer. The *disease* or *syndrome* part of the name is not capitalized.

The medical profession has recommended dropping the *'s* from many disease names.

> **Example:** Ménière syndrome, Bright disease, Asperger syndrome, Huntington disease, Lyme disease

Some disease names still retain the *'s*.

> **Example:** Lou Gehrig's disease, Legionnaire's disease, Alzheimer's disease

Disjuncts

A **disjunct** is used to express the writer's attitude toward something being described in a sentence.

Example: <u>Happily</u> [shows the writer's attitude], I agreed to his marriage proposal.

Display, Monitor, Screen

Use the term *display* when referring to the computer output device, such as a flat-panel *display*.

Monitor is an older technological term that is synonymous with *display*; however, it is no longer often used.

Use the term *screen* to refer to the graphics that can be seen on the *display* or to the actual surface where the graphics appear.

Display should not be used as an intransitive verb. Use *appear* instead.

Incorrect: After clicking the Print button, the Print dialog displays.

Correct: After clicking the Print button, the Print dialog appears.

Correct: The Print dialog displays a list of printers.

Disyllabic

A **disyllabic** word has two syllables.

Ditransitive Verbs

A **ditransitive verb** can take both a direct object and an indirect object.

Example: She gave <u>him</u> [indirect object] the <u>book</u> [direct object].

Ditto Marks

Ditto marks (″) mean the same as stated above or before, a repeat, or a dupli-cate. Ditto marks are often used in lists or tables, but they should not be used in formal business documents.

Do, Does, Did

Do is used as an auxiliary verb to express negatives and to ask questions.

Example: I don't drive.

Example: Do you drive?

Does is used for third-person singular subjects in the present tense.

Example: Does she drive?

Did is used for first person and third person in the past tense.

Example: Did you drive?

Do, does, and *did* can be used for short answers where the main verb has been omitted.

Example: [Do you drive?] I do.

Example: [Does she drive?] She does.

Example: [Did she drive?] She did.

For yes-or-no questions, the form of *do* is put in front of the subject, and the main verb comes after the subject.

Example: Did your mother drive?

Forms of *do* can be used to express similarities and differences along with *so* and *neither.*

Example: My mother drives and so does my father.

Example: My mother doesn't like to drive; neither do I.

Do allows you to avoid having to repeat a verb.

Example: My mother drives as well as my father does.

Do can be used emphatically.

- To add emphasis—She loves you. She really does!

- To add emphasis to an imperative—Do sit down.

- To add emphasis to a frequency adverb—He always does manage to get to work on time.

- To contradict a negative statement—But, I didn't say that.

- To ask a clarifying question—Then who did say it?

- To indicate a strong concession—Though he didn't get a ticket this time, he did get a warning.

Dollars and Cents

It is best to use figures when writing about money.

Example: 1 cent or 1¢

Example: 20 cents or 20¢

Example: 20,000 dollars or $20,000

Amounts of money are always written out when beginning a sentence.

Incorrect: 1 cent was contributed by each child.

Correct: One cent was contributed by each child.

A series of prices is written in figures only.

Example: These shoes are priced at $50, $60, and $85.

Dollar and Cent Signs

Use the dollar sign before the number, not the word *dollar* or *dollars* after the number.

Example: The office space rents for $1,700 per month.

If a large number combines figures and words, use the dollar sign before the figure.

Incorrect: The budget calls for 850 billion dollars.

Correct: The budget calls for $850 billion.

Repeat the dollar sign with successive numbers.

Example: The bonds could be purchased in denominations of $10,000, $12,000, $15,000, and $20,000.

Exception: Omit all but the first dollar sign when numbers are in tabulated form.

Example: The bonds could be purchased in denominations of the following amounts:

$10,000
12,000
15,000
20,000

The dollar sign is not used when the figure given is in cents alone. Use the cent sign (¢) after amounts less than one dollar, but never use the cent sign with a decimal point.

Incorrect: .25¢ [That would mean one-fourth of a cent.]

Correct: 25¢

Exception: The only time the dollar sign is used when the figure is in cents alone is in statistical work when the part of the dollar is carried out to more than two decimal places.

Example: $0.3564

Decimal Points

Decimal points are another way of writing fractions, especially large fractions. When a decimal occurs with no unit before it, use a cipher (zero) for quick interpretation.

Example: a 0.75-yard measurement, rainfall of 0.356 inch

Sometimes the fraction is part of a dollar. When the amount of dollars given is not followed by cents, omit the decimal point and the ciphers.

Example: $3, $1,200, $17.75

The decimal point and ciphers are not used with even amounts of money unless in tabulated form. If tabulated and if some amounts contain cents and some do not, the even amounts should contain ciphers.

Don't, Doesn't

Don't means do not; *doesn't* means does not.

Incorrect: He don't care to go with us.

Correct: He doesn't care to go with us.

Do's and Don'ts

Pay attention to the placement of apostrophes when writing the phrase *do's and don'ts*.

Incorrect: do's and don't's

Correct: do's and don'ts

Dot-Com

Dot-com refers to a Web-based business. Use dot-com as an adjective, not as a noun or verb. Hyphenate dot-com. When using it in titles or headings, do not capitalize the letter following the hyphen.

Incorrect: The programmers worked in the garage with hopes of one day starting their own dot-com.

Correct: Last year those dot-com stocks were really inexpensive.

Double Negatives

Double negatives occur when you use more than one negative word or phrase to express a single negative thought. Double negatives should not be used.

Incorrect: He doesn't never want to work here again.

Correct: He doesn't ever want to work here again.

Words like *hardly, barely,* and *scarcely* are negative in effect and can lead to double negatives.

Incorrect: She hardly never reads the newspaper.

Correct: She hardly reads the newspaper.

Use of the contraction *not (n't)* is negative in effect.

Incorrect: She doesn't offer no reasons for being late.

Correct: She doesn't offer any reasons for being late.

Double Possessives

A **double possessive** is two or more consecutive nouns in the possessive case. All nouns in the series carry apostrophes.

Example: I visited the tombs under St. Peter's Cathedral's main floor.

Double-Click

When writing software instructions, hyphenate *double-click* to describe mouse commands. Hyphenate *right-mouse click* to describe that type of mouse command.

Download, Upload

To *download* is to transfer files to a computer from a network, the Internet, or storage device.

To *upload* is to transfer files from your computer to a network, storage device, the Internet, or another computer.

Downtoners

Downtoners are adverbs that are used to tone down a verb. Common downtoner adverbs are *kind of, sort of, mildly, to some extent, almost,* and *all but.*

Example: The church was all but destroyed by the fire.

Example: She almost resigned after the demotion.

Example: We can improve morale to some extent.

Example: She mildly disapproved of his drinking.

Example: Mike sort of felt betrayed by his boss.

Example: I kind of like this job.

Drag-and-Drop

Drag-and-drop is a term used to describe a software editing process in which a mouse user moves text or objects from one place on the screen to another.

Use *drag-and-drop* in business and technical documents only as an adjective. Do not use *drag-and-drop* as a noun or verb.

Incorrect: To move the files to your flash drive, open the flash drive and drag-and-drop [used as a verb] the files you want into the folder.

Correct: It is easy to move the paragraph using a <u>drag-and-drop</u> [used as an adjective] procedure.

Correct: To moves the files to your flash drive, open the flash drive and use a <u>drag-and-drop</u> [used as an adjective] operation to move the files.

Due to the Fact That

This phrase should be avoided; use the word *because* instead.

DVD

See *CD, DVD*.

Dynamic Adjectives

Dynamic adjectives are used to describe attributes that are under the control of the person, place, or thing that possesses them.

Typical dynamic adjectives are *calm, careful, cruel, disruptive, foolish, friendly, good, impatient, mannerly, patient, rude, shy, suspicious, tidy, vacuous,* and *vain.*

Dynamic adjectives can be used in imperative sentences.

Example: Don't be foolish!

Example: Be patient.

Dynamic Verbs

Dynamic verbs are used to show continued or progressive action. Dynamic verbs are used to describe an action that occurs over time and that may or may not have a specific endpoint or may not yet have occurred.

Example: He's lying on the sofa.

Dynamic verbs are also known as action verbs. Dynamic verbs often are used in the continuous *be + ing* forms.

Example: The sun is melting the snowman.

Each Other, One Another

Use *each other* when referring to two people.

Example: Mike and Susan looked at each other.

Use *one another* when referring to more than two people.

Example: The four people in the car looked at one another.

Each, Their

Pronouns must agree in number and person with the words to which they refer.

Incorrect: Each drives their own car.

Correct: Each drives his own car.

Correct: <u>Each</u> [singular pronoun, the subject] of the women listed her needs.

Effect, Affect

See *Affect, Effect*.

Eggcorn

Words that sound similar but that have different meanings may be used by mistake. Such words are called **eggcorns**.

Incorrect: Wet your appetite.

Correct: Whet your appetite.

e.g., i.e.

The term *e.g.* is an abbreviation for the Latin phrase *exempli gratia*, which means "for example."

The term *i.e.* is an abbreviation for the Latin phrase *id est*, which means "that is."

It is often better to avoid confusion and use the English words—*for example* rather than e.g.

Either, Neither

Either and *neither* refer to a choice between two things. For a choice among more than two things, use *none* or *any*.

Incorrect: Neither of the four books suited him.

Correct: None of the four books suited him.

Incorrect: Either of the three books is the one I want.

Correct: Any of the three books will suit me.

Correct: Either of the two books will do.

Elicit, Illicit

Elicit is a verb that means to obtain, to draw forth, to bring out something hidden. *Illicit* is an adjective that describes something illegal.

Ellipses

Ellipses (...) are used to show the omission of words in quoted material, if the material is deleted within the sentence.

When the last part of a quoted sentence is omitted, it is followed by three spaced dots plus its punctuation. At the end of the quotation, only the punctuation is used.

Example: "Five hundred firemen ... attended the ball ...."

Example: Mr. Brown went on to say: "The shoe department functions smoothly ... many salespeople have won prizes for efficiency."

An ellipsis may also be used to indicate a thought expressed hesitantly:

Example: He said, "If ... if I do go with you, will you return early?"

Elliptical Clauses

Elliptical clauses are missing either a relative pronoun or something from the predicate in the second part of a comparison.

Example: The elderly women knew the tour guide could walk faster than they [could walk].

The missing parts of an elliptical clause (the other members of the tour) can be guessed from the context.

Email

Email can be spelled "email" or "e-mail" depending on your preference. The *e* stands for "electronic."

Other similar words often use a hyphen in their spelling:

Example: e-commerce, e-learning

Here are some tips for your business emails:

■   Do not use all caps in your email messages or subject lines.

- Use the active rather than passive voice in your messages.

- To quote from a previous email, use << (less than) and >> (greater than) on each side of the quote.

- Always type your response to a quote from a previous email below the quote or copy.

Embedded Questions

Embedded questions are questions within another statement. They function as a noun and follow the statement rather than the question order.

Example of question order: What day is it?

Example of statement order: I know what day it is.

An embedded question is not punctuated as a question because of its context within a sentence.

Example: I wonder who is hungry.

Em Dash

See *Dash*.

Emigrate, Immigrate

Emigrate means to leave your country for another.

Example: He was forced to emigrate from Mexico.

Immigrate means moving into a new country.

Example: They immigrated to California from South Korea.

Eminent, Imminent, Immanent

To correctly use these words in your writing, consider their definitions:

- *Eminent* is an adjective that means to be noteworthy, prominent, or famous.

- *Imminent* is an adjective that means something is about to take place.

- *Immanent* is an adjective that means to have existence only within the mind.

Emoticons

Emoticons are textual expressions created using punctuation marks and other keyboard symbols to express the mood or feelings of the writer.

Example: :-) is a smile.

Emoticons can be used in email messages but should not be used in any other business writing. Emoticons are often used in online chat rooms and to signal your reader that you are being sarcastic or making a statement with a tongue-in-cheek attitude. They can also be used to soften a message.

Use emoticons only when necessary, directly after the comments that require them. Do not use them in every message you write, and do not include them in your signature file.

Empathic Forms

Emphatic forms are created with the auxiliary verb *do* in the present or past tense along with the base form of the verb.

Example: They don't speak English anywhere in Europe.

Example: I don't believe you—they <u>do speak</u> [emphatic form that contradicts the first statement] English throughout Europe.

Emphatic forms are also known as **emphatic tenses** or **emphatic mood**.

Empathy, Sympathy

To correctly use these terms in your writing, consider their definitions:

- *Empathy* is a noun that means to understand what another person is feeling.

- *Sympathy* is a noun that means to share a common feeling of being sorry for someone.

En Dash

See *Dash*.

Endnotes

See *Footnotes, Endnotes*.

End Result

End result is a redundant term. Drop the *end* and use just *result*.

Endophora

Endophora is a literary technique where words or phrases, such as pronouns, point backward or forward to something else in the text.

Example: Because he [endophoric, refers to "Mike"] arrived early, Mike wanted to call his wife and ask her [refers to "wife"] to come to the airport early.

Engine, Motor

Engines are normally powered by combustion from sources such as oil, gasoline, coal, or natural gas.

Example: The engine in the car was very powerful.

Motors are usually electrically powered.

Example: The elevator motor had stopped working.

Enough, Not Enough

The adverbs *enough* and *not enough* usually take a postmodifier position.

Example: Is your food hot enough? This food is not hot enough.

Enough can also be an adjective. When it is used as an adjective, it comes before the noun and is often followed by an infinitive verb.

Example: The teacher didn't give us enough time to finish.

Enquire, Inquire

Both *enquire* and *inquire* mean to seek an answer, ask about, or to make an investigation. *Enquire* is the more common spelling in the United Kingdom.

Ensure, Assure, Insure

- *Ensure* is a verb that means to make certain.

- *Assure* is a verb that means to make someone confident about something or to make something safe.

- *Insure* means to issue an insurance policy.

Enthuse, Enthusiastic

Enthuse is used only as a colloquialism. For the formal language needed for business writing, use *to be enthusiastic*.

Incorrect: He was enthused about winning the award.

Correct: He was enthusiastic about winning the award.

Entitled

See *Titled, Entitled.*

Envelop, Envelope

- *Envelop* means to enclose or wrap something with a covering.

- *Envelope* is paper container for documents and mail.

Epanadiplosis

Epanadiplosis is a literary term when a word or phrase is repeated at the beginning and end of a phrase, clause, or sentence.

> **Example:** The king is dead, long live the king.

Epanalepsis

Epanalepsis is the repetition of a word or phrase in no particular order or position within a sentence, except that other words must appear between the repeated words or phrases. This technique is often used for emphasis and for rhythm.

> **Example:** "To each the boulders that have fallen to each."
> —Robert Frost, *Mending Wall*

> **Example:** "It will have blood, they say, it will have blood."
> —William Shakespeare, *Macbeth*

Epistemic Modality

Epistemic modality is a literary term that describes a sentence where the speaker's opinion is expressed using a modal verb (*can, could, will, would, shall, should, ought to, dare,* and *need*).

Example: It can be hot in Texas this time of year.

Epistrophe

Epistrophe is a stylistic technique where the writer ends different phrases, clauses, or sentences with the same word.

Example: "What lies behind us and what lies before us are tiny compared to what lies within us."—Ralph Waldo Emerson

Epizeuxis

Epizeuxis is a literary technique where words or phrases are repeated without other words in between.

Example: "And my poor fool is hanged! No, no, no life! Why should a dog, a horse, a rat have life, and thou no breath at all? Thou'lt come no more, never, never, never, never!"—William Shakespeare, *King Lear*

Equally as Important

You can say something is *equally important,* but not *equally as important.* Drop the *as.*

Equations

Equations are statements used to express relationships in mathematics or chemistry.

Mathematical equations use mathematical symbols and letters of the alphabet to define conditions of equality, to indicate true or false, or to identify something. Letters of the alphabet are used to represent variables.

Example: $X + Y = 5$

Mathematical equations may become complex with various smaller equations grouped in brackets and positioned above and below other equations, separated by a line that represents fractional division.

Example: $\dfrac{X + \frac{1}{Y}}{A + B} = C$

Chemical equations are used to represent chemical formulas describing the reaction that occurs when different substances are mixed. The addition of one chemical to another is denoted using a plus sign. What the chemical mixture creates is separated from the result using a right arrow, which is read as "yields."

Example: $H_2 + O \rightarrow H_2O$

This formula can be read as "H two plus O yields H two O." The "2" that follows the "H" means that twice as much H (hydrogen), when mixed with O (oxygen), yields H_2O (water).

Ergative Verbs

Ergative verbs are verbs that change the state of the subject in a sentence.

Example: The needle burst the balloon.

There are several categories of ergative verbs:

- Verbs that cause a change of state

Example: break, burst, form, heal, melt, tear, transform

- Verbs used in cooking

Example: bake, boil, cook, broil, fry

- Verbs that describe movement

    Example: move, mow, shake, sweep, turn, walk

- Verbs that involve vehicles

    Example: drive, fly, reverse, run, sail

Ergative verbs allow a writer to omit the identity of the agent that caused the change while identifying the affected party or subject.

Example: The windshield was broken.

Essentially

See *Basically, Essentially, Totally.*

et al.

The term **el al.** comes from the Latin phrase *et alia,* which means "and others." This abbreviation is used much the same way as etc. when you don't want to name a complete list of people or things.

Example: The playwriting class included lessons on characterization, plot, pacing, conflict, et al., but it was very basic and not really designed for serious writers.

Et al. is punctuated with a period after *al* to indicate that it is abbreviated.

etc.

This is an abbreviation for the Latin phrase *et cetera,* which means "and other things." Do not write "and etc." because the *and* is redundant.

It is better not to use this term in formal business writing. Instead, add a few more examples to close out a list.

Euphemisms

Euphemisms are words or phrases that substitute for language that is considered offensive, harsh, politically incorrect, or embarrassing.

Examples: passed away, died; peacekeeping forces, army; sanitation engineer, garbage collector

Everyday

Everyday is an adjective that can be confused for the adverbial phrase *every day.*

Example as an adjective: You don't wear your everyday clothes to a wedding.

Example as an adverb: I work out at the gym every day.

Everyone, Every One

Everyone is used when you are referring to all of the people or things in a group. The word can also mean everybody.

Example: Everyone enjoys a big holiday dinner.

Every one is used when referring to individual people or things in a group.

Example: Every one of the players received personal congratulations from the coach.

Every Time

Every time should always be written as two words.

Except, Unless

Except is a preposition used to introduce a prepositional phrase. *Unless* is an adverbial conjunction used to introduce a subordinate clause. *Except* and *unless* are not interchangeable.

Except may be used as a conjunction only when it's followed by the word *that;* however, that construction, although correct, is often awkward, and *unless* is preferable.

Incorrect: The horse cannot be entered in the race except that the judges allow it.

Correct: The horse cannot be entered in the race unless the judges allow it.

Excess, Access

See *Access, Excess.*

Exclamation Point

An **exclamation point** is used when making extravagant claims or to express deep feeling.

Example: Here is the finest car on the market!

Example: The announcement was unbelievable!

An exclamation point is used after a word or phrase charged with emotion.

Example: Quick! We don't want to be late.

An exclamation point is also used for double emphasis.

Example: I'm insulted by the innuendo!

Caution: For effective writing, show emotion through the choice of words and reserve exclamation points for only the strongest of feelings.

Exclamatory Sentence

An **exclamatory sentence** is used to express strong emotion or emphasis.

Example: I hate rainy days!

Exclamatory sentences often begin with *what* or *how*.

Example: What a wonderful surprise!

Example: How great you look!

Exclusive Adverbs

Exclusive adverbs focus attention on the words that follow and exclude all other possibilities.

Example: He ran the marathon just [excludes all other reasons for running the marathon] to prove he could do it.

Example: He joined Toastmasters solely [explains the only reason for joining] for the purpose of preparing for job interviews.

Other exclusive adverbs are *alone, exactly, merely,* and *simply.*

Existential *There*

The word *there* is often used as an adverb.

Example: She went there last week.

Example: You can't bring food in there.

There can also be used to start a sentence. When it does, it is referred to as the existential there.

Example: There is a bird in the tree.

Example: There was a flat tire on the truck.

The existential there is usually followed by a form of the verb *to be*.

Example: There were dogs loose in the neighborhood.

When the existential there is used in a question, it follows the verb.

Example: Is there a problem with your knee?

The two different uses of there can occur together in the same sentence.

Example: <u>There</u> [existential there] is a grocery store <u>there</u> [an adverb].

Exit

See *Quit, Exit.*

Exophoric

When referring to something that is not in the same text but that is understood by the reader or listener, the language is said to be **exophoric**.

Example: What is wrong with <u>that</u> [refers to something mentioned earlier in the text]?

Expect

Don't use *expect* to mean *think* or *suppose*.

Incorrect: I expect she was well received.

Correct: I suppose she was well received.

Correct: I expect you to be there at 8 a.m.

Expletive Constructions

Expletive constructions are sentences that begin with words like *there is, there are,* or *it is.*

Example: There are many poor children in the city who have expressed a desire to attend the free summer camp.

Expletive constructions include a pronoun that does not refer to a specific noun plus the verb *to be.* Expletive constructions are placed at the beginning of an independent clause.

Expletive constructions should be avoided because they deplete the energy of a sentence and are not needed to express the same idea.

Revision: Many poor children in the city have expressed a desire to attend the free summer camp.

Expository Writing

Expository writing is a type of composition that seeks to inform the reader. Expository writing tells what happened, explains how to do something, describes people and places, and provides facts. Examples of expository writing are:

- Cooking instructions.

- Driving directions.

- Instructions on how to perform a task.

There are five main types of expository writing:

- Sequence—used to list events in chronological order or provide step-by-step instructions

- Descriptive essay—to enable the reader to feel whatever is being described by including details about the five senses: sight, smell, touch, hearing, and taste

- Classification—allows an author to arrange ideas or objects into categories

- Comparison—allows the author to compare two or more choices and discuss similarities or differences

- Cause and effect—identifies why something occurred and the result of the occurrence

Extranet

See *Internet, Intranet, Extranet.*

Extraposition

Extraposition is a construction where the subject of a sentence is postponed until the end of the sentence. It is a stylistic technique that disrupts the normal declarative order.

Declarative order: Two security officers were inside the building.

Extraposition: Inside the building were two security officers.

Declarative order: Beautiful antiques were inside the lobby.

Extraposition: Inside the lobby were beautiful antiques.

When a sentence is introduced by *it*, the construction can also be extraposed.

Example: It's a good idea to get in line early.

Example: It's not surprising he got an internship.

In some sentences, extraposition is not just stylistic; it's required:

Extraposition: It seems that she'll be early again.

Declarative order: That she'll be early again it seems.

Factitive Verbs

Verbs like *make, choose, judge, elect, select,* and *name* are **factitive verbs**. These verbs can take two objects.

> **Example:** The people elected <u>Barack Obama</u> [object] <u>president of the United States</u> [second complement].

Faint

See *Feint, Faint.*

Fair, Fare

Fare, as a verb, means to go, to carry, or to pass through.

> **Example:** How did you fare on your trip to Scotland?

Fare, as a noun, can also mean an assortment of food or any material provided for consumption, the price charged for transportation, or a paying passenger on a taxi or bus.

Fair has a variety of meanings:

- Adjective—fresh, smooth, pure, clean

- Adjective—not dark

- Adjective—not stormy

- Adjective—impartial and honest

- Adjective—done according to the rules

> **Example:** That's fair.

■ Noun—a gathering of buyers and sellers for trade or for a competitive exhibition.

Example: The State Fair of Texas is held every year in October.

FANBOYS

Coordinating conjunctions can be remembered using the acronym **FANBOYS:** for-and-nor-but-or-yet-so. A comma is often used when a coordinating conjunction connects two independent clauses.

Example: Eric wanted to play in the band, but he also wanted to pursue a career in engineering.

Farther, Further

Farther shows a specific, quantifiable distance.

Example: I walked farther than he did.

Further shows degree or extent.

Example: He will go further with your help than without it.

Faze, Phase

Faze is a verb that means to disturb. Faze is often used in sentences where something did not affect someone or something.

Example: The shouts from the audience did not faze the speaker.

Phase can be a noun or verb.

■ As a noun, it refers to a particular cycle or appearance.

Example: The astronomer eagerly awaited a new phase of the moon.

■ As a verb, it means to carry out a plan or introduce something in stages.

Example: The plan was to phase in the new software over a period of several months.

Feint, Faint

Feint can be either a noun or a verb.

■ When used as a noun, *feint* means to distract attention from the real center of attention. A *feint* often refers to a battlefield strategy that involves a diversionary attack to distract the enemy from the real intended point of attack.

■ When used as a verb, *feint* means to make a fake move during a battle or confrontation.

Faint can be used as an adjective, verb, or noun.

■ When used an adjective, *faint* means weakness or lacking vigor or distinctness.

Example: There was a faint red glow in the sky.

■ When used as verb, *faint* means to lose consciousness temporarily.

Example: Candace fainted in the middle of her wedding.

■ When used as a noun, *faint* refers to the medical condition of fainting.

Example: The patient went into a faint.

Female, Woman

When referring to human beings, use the word *woman* rather than *female*.

Incorrect: A female walked down the hall and entered her office.

Correct: A woman walked down the hall and entered her office.

When used as an adjective, it is often best to use *female* rather than *woman*.

Example: female firefighter, female astronaut

Fewer, Less

See *Less, Fewer*.

Few, A Few

There can be a big difference between *few* and *a few*. The following example implies that Linda has some biographies in her collection.

Example: Linda has a few biographies among the books in her library.

This example implies that Linda does *not* have many biographies in her collection.

Example: Linda has few biographies among the books in her library.

Figuratively

See *Literally, Figuratively*.

Figure of Speech

A **figure of speech** is a form of expression where a word or words are used to convey something different from their literal meaning.

Example: As we entered the restaurant, Evelyn said she was <u>starving</u> [not dying from hunger, just very hungry].

Other figures of speech are *break a leg, butterflies in your stomach, raining cats and dogs, got your back.*

There are a variety of classifications for figures of speech. Here are some examples:

- Alliteration
- Anaphora
- Antithesis
- Apostrophe
- Assonance
- Chiasmus
- Euphemism
- Hyperbole
- Irony
- Litotes

- Metaphor
- Metonymy
- Onomatopoeia
- Oxymoron
- Paradox
- Personification
- Pun
- Simile
- Synechdoche
- Understatement

Figures

Figures are drawings, pictures, or charts that appear as illustrations in a manuscript. Figures should complement the subject matter in the text.

Provide a brief introductory sentence to introduce a figure.

Example: The following pie chart shows the various classifications of users for the new software.

Include a short caption below the figure. Even if a figure repeats later in the same document, repeat the caption. Do not use end punctuation for the caption, unless it is a complete sentence. Figures should be numbered sequentially throughout the document, with the figure number included in the caption. Figure numbering can be 1, 2, 3 or include a chapter or section number, such as 1.1, 1.2, 1.3, and so on.

Example: Figure 1. Software user pie chart

Finite Verbs

Finite verbs are verbs that have a subject and can stand on their own as complete sentences. Finite verbs show tense and number.

Example: I [subject] <u>drive</u> [finite verb] a car.

Finite verbs can be contrasted with **nonfinite verbs**, which have no subject, tense, or number. Nonfinite verbs use the following forms:

- Infinitive: to go

- Gerund: going

- Participle: gone

First Conditional

A **first conditional** sentence consists of an if clause and a main clause. The first conditional is used to describe things that may happen.

When the if clause occurs first, a comma is required.

When the if clause is after the main clause, no comma is required.

Example: You will be sleepy the next day if you stay up all night.

Fix, Situation

Fix means to repair. Don't use it to mean a bad situation.

Incorrect: She is in a desperate fix.

Correct: She is desperate because of her present situation.

Flair, Flare

Flair is a noun that means a skill, talent, or natural ability. *Flair* can also mean a unique attractive quality or style.

Example: He has a flair for doing hair.

Flare can be a noun or a verb.

As a noun, *flare* is a fire, a bright light, or a burning safety warning device.

As a verb, *flare* means to become excited or angry or to shine with a sudden light.

Flesch-Kincaid Index

The **Flesch-Kincaid Index** is a measurement used to determine how easy or difficult a document is to read. The Index gives the years of education required to understand a document.

The following formula is used to calculate the Flesch-Kincaid Index:

$$0.39 \times \text{Average number of words in a sentence}$$
$$+\ 11.8 \times \text{Average number of syllables per word}$$
$$-\ 15.59$$

Flier, Flyer

A *flier* is a noun that means a person who flies. A *flyer* is a one- or two-sided advertising notice.

Focus Adverb

A **focus adverb** is used to limit the context of a sentence or to add additional context.

Example: He got a ticket <u>just</u> [focus adverb] for going five miles over the speed limit.

Example: He got a ticket <u>in addition to</u> [focus adverb] a long lecture from the police officer.

Fog Index

The **Fog Index** is a test to determine how easy or difficult a document is to read. The official name is the "Gunning Fog Index." The Fog Index uses the following formula:

Reading level (school grade) = (Average number of words in sentences
+ Percentage of words of three or more syllables)
× 0.4

The result of the formula is the Gunning Fog Index, which represents the number of years of education that a reader needs to have in order to understand the document.

Short sentences with small words score better than long sentences with complicated words. Business documents should have a Gunning Fog Index between 10 and 15. If the Index exceeds 18, the document should be rewritten.

Font, Typeface

A *typeface* refers to the design of printed letters on paper or in a computer display.

Example: Helvetica, Times New Roman, Arial

A typeface is composed of different *fonts*.

Example: The Times New Roman typeface has a family of fonts: Times New Roman, Times New Roman Italic, Times New Roman Bold.

Foot, Feet

Foot is singular; *feet* is plural.

Incorrect: The room is twelve foot long.

Correct: The room is twelve feet long.

Footnotes, Endnotes

Footnotes are comments placed at the bottom of a page of text to explain a concept, define a term, or provide a reference.

A superscript number (for example, [1])is added after the text in the document that the footnote references. The footnote is numbered with the same superscript number at the bottom of the page.

Example: This is an example of a footnote reference[1].

Example: [1]This is a sample footnote.

Endnotes are similar to footnotes, but they appear at the end of a chapter, a section, or the document.

Forego, Forgo

Forego means to go before. *Forgo* means to do without something.

Example: After finishing dinner and feeling a bit too full, he decided to forgo dessert.

Foreign Words and Phrases

Non-English words and phrases, such as *etc., et al., de facto,* or *ad hoc,* should be avoided in most business writing.

Avoid the use of Latin abbreviations when a normal English phrase can be used instead. See Table 2.16.

Table 2.16 Latin Abbreviations and Their English Counterparts

Use ...	Instead of ...
for example	e.g.
that is	i.e.
namely	viz.
therefore	ergo
and so forth	etc.
and others	et al.
pseudo	de facto
special or specialized	ad hoc

Forever, For Ever

Forever is normally written as one word in the United States.

For ever is normally written as two words in the United Kingdom.

For, Fore, Four

To correctly use these words in your writing, consider their definitions:

■ *For* is a preposition that is used to indicate the purpose, goal, or recipient of an activity.

■ *Fore* can be an adverb or adjective that means something in front of something else.

■ *Four* is the number.

Formatting

Formatting a business document varies depending on the type of document. The most common formatting items are:

- Art or Figures
- Captions
- Callouts
- Cross-references
- Headings
- Subheadings
- Line spacing and breaks

- Lists
- Margins and margin notes
- Page breaks
- Tables
- Notes and tips
- Footnotes or endnotes

All these formatting items are covered elsewhere in this book.

Formulas

Formulas are used in mathematics and science to express information symbolically.

Example: $E = mc^2$

Writing formulas in business documents with a word processor may involve inserting special symbols and changing to superscript or subscript fonts.

Some of the latest word processors include the ability to insert and format complex formulas by using the Equation function.

Example: $(x + a)^n = \sum_{k=a}^{n} \binom{n}{k} x^k a^{n-k}$

Forward, Forwards, Foreword

Forward and *forwards* can both be used; however, *forward* is more formal. This usage also applies to *toward* and *towards* and *backward* and *backwards*.

A *foreword* is an introductory section of a book.

Fractions

Fractions can be written in words or decimals depending on the context. Avoid using numbers separated by a slash mark, unless you are writing an equation.

Hyphenate fractions written as words.

> **Example:** one-half, two-thirds, five-sixteenths

When writing fractions as decimal points, insert a zero before the decimal point for fractions that are less than one.

> **Example:** 0.25 inch

The unit of measure should be singular for amounts less than one, except zero, which is plural.

> **Example:** 0.75 inch, 0 inches, 10 inches

Fragments

See *Sentence Fragments*.

Full Time, Full-time

When used as a measure of time that denotes a complete work week, *full time* is a noun and is written as two words without a hyphen.

> **Example:** My job requires that I work full time Monday through Friday.

When used as an adjective to mean being employed full time, a hyphen is used.

> **Example:** She is looking for a full-time job.

Further

See *Farther, Further.*

Fused Sentences

Fused sentences are often referred to as "run-on sentences." Fused sentences have two parts that both can stand on their own as two independent clauses.

When two independent clauses are connected only by a comma, this is known as a comma-splice and the result is a run-on or fused sentence.

> **Example:** The weather is hot, let's go swimming.

To avoid a comma-splice and run-on sentence:

■ Connect the two independent clauses with a coordinating conjunction, such as *and, or, but, for, so, yet,* or *nor.*

> **Example:** The weather is hot, so let's go swimming.

■ Add a period to each of the independent clauses.

> **Example:** The weather is hot. Let's go swimming.

■ Link the clauses using a semicolon.

> **Example:** The weather is hot; let's go swimming.

■ Rewrite the sentences into one independent clause.

> **Example:** The weather is hot enough for swimming.

■ Rewrite the sentences so that one of the independent clauses becomes a dependent clause.

> **Example:** Since the weather is hot, let's go swimming.

■ Use a semicolon and a conjunctive adverb (*thus, otherwise, moreover, also, anyway, besides, furthermore, incidentally*) to separate the two independent clauses. Add a comma after the conjunctive adverb.

Example: The weather is hot; furthermore, let's go swimming.

Future Perfect

To describe an event that has not happened but is expected to happen before another event, the **future perfect** tense is used.

The future perfect is composed of a subject + *shall* or *will have* + the past participle of the verb.

Example: I [subject] will have already delivered [will have + past participle] the presentation by the time your plane lands.

Future Perfect Progressive

The **future perfective progressive** structure is used when an unfinished action will reach a certain stage. The form of the future perfect progressive is *will have been*.

Example: By this time next year, I will have been married half my life.

Future Progressive

To indicate action that will be taking place in the future as a part of normal events, the **future progressive** tense is used. The future progressive tense is composed of *will be* + the *-ing* form of the verb.

Example: I will be leaving for Detroit in the morning.

Gage, Gauge

Gage is an alternative spelling for *gauge*.

A *gage* is a measuring instrument that is used to measure the amount or the position of something. Gages are found in cars, airplanes, and industrial plants, among other places.

Gage can be a verb that means to estimate quantities or time.

Example: What do you gage the depth of the river to be?

Gage can also be a noun that is used to measure things, such as the distance between railroad rails, the thickness of wire, and the size of a shotgun's barrel.

Gender

In many languages, such as Spanish, French, and Italian, there is a grammatical category for **gender**: masculine, feminine, or neuter.

The only times that gender is indicated in English is when certain nouns refer to a male or female animal or person.

Example: lion (male), lioness (female); waiter (male), waitress (female); actor (male), actress (female)

Genitive Marker

When nouns take an *'s* to indicate possession, this is called a **genitive marker**.

Don't confuse the genitive marker with the *'s* that is added to contracted verbs.

Example: Horace's [Horace is] going to the store.

Gerund

A **gerund** is a verb form ending in *-ing* that acts as a noun.

Example: <u>Walking</u> [gerund] in the street after dark can be dangerous.

Gerunds are usually accompanied by other words that make up a **gerund phrase**.

Example: <u>Walking in the street after dark</u> [gerund phrase] can be dangerous.

Because gerunds and gerund phrases are nouns, they can be used just like nouns:

■ As a subject

Example: <u>Being president</u> is a difficult job.

■ As an objective of a verb

Example: He didn't really like <u>being poor.</u>

■ As an objective of a preposition

Example: He read a book <u>about being careful.</u>

Gigabyte

A *gigabyte* equals 1,024 megabytes, or 1,073,741,824 bytes. The abbreviation for gigabyte is GB (not G or Gbyte).

The first time that you use *gigabyte* in a document, spell out the word and put the abbreviation in parentheses.

When used as a measurement of computing speed, leave a space between the number and the abbreviation.

Example: The computer has 2 GB of memory.

When the measurement is used as an adjective preceding a noun, use a hyphen.

Example: Are those 1-GB or 2-GB memory chips?

Gigahertz

Gigahertz is a measurement of computer speed. One gigahertz is equal to one billion cycles per second. Gigahertz is abbreviated as GHz.

The first time you use *gigahertz* in a technical document, spell out the word and put the abbreviation in parentheses. Leave a space between the number and the GHz.

Example: The computer has 2 GHz of processing speed.

If the number and abbreviation are used as an adjective preceding a noun, use a hyphen.

Example: Is that a 2-GHz processor in your laptop?

Glossary

A **glossary** is an alphabetical list of words or phrases and their definitions.

Example: RAM—Random access memory

A glossary is useful in reports and other long documents when readers may be unfamiliar with the terminology being used. A glossary usually appears at the end of the document.

A glossary is usually introduced by the same heading level used for other chapters or sections in the document.

The content of a glossary explains concepts that are unique to a particular business, industry, or technology.

Gone, Went

The past participle of *went* is *gone*.

Example: I went to the store.

Example: I should have gone to the store.

Good, Well

Good is an adjective and *well* is an adverb. When describing an action verb, the only choice is the adverb *well*.

Example: He speaks well.

When using a linking verb or a verb that has to do with the five human senses, use the adjective *good*.

Example: You smell good today.

Many writers use *well* after linking verbs related to health because *well* is related to wellness.

Example: How are you doing? I am well, thank you.

Got, Gotten

Don't use *got*, when you can use *have*, *has*, or *must*.

Incorrect: I got a new car.

Correct: I have a new car.

Correct: He has a new job.

Incorrect (colloquial): I've got to stop at his house.

Correct: I must stop at his house. ... I have to stop at his house.

Gotten is an obsolete term. Do not use it; replace it with *got*.

Grammatical Hierarchy

Grammatical hierarchy is a way of studying language by classifying it as sentences, clauses, phrases, and words. Consider the following example of a grammatical hierarchy:

- Sentences consist of one or more clauses. Sentences are at the top of the grammatical hierarchy because they are the largest unit.

- Clauses consist of one or more phrases.

- Phrases consist of one or more words. Words are at the lowest level of the grammatical hierarchy. (Morphology is the study of how words are constructed.)

Gray, Grey

Gray is the American spelling; *grey* is the spelling in the United Kingdom.

Guess

Don't use *guess* when you really mean *think*.

Incorrect: I guess you are right.

Correct: I think you are right.

Correct: In the word game, Marcus was the first to guess correctly.

Handicap, Disability

A *handicap* is a problem that can be remedied, whereas a *disability* is permanent problem.

■ People who have disabilities prefer the word *disability* to *handicap*.

■ The phrase "people with disabilities" is preferred over "disabled people."

Hard Disk, Hard Drive

A *hard disk* is the actual disk inside a hard drive where data are stored in a computer system. Refer to the storage device inside most personal computers as a "hard drive" or "hard disk drive." When using these terms, consider these tips:

■ *Hard disk* and *hard drive* are always written as two words.

■ Do not hyphenate *hard disk* or *hard drive*.

Headings and Subheadings

Headings are used to organize sections of content and make it easy for readers to locate information. Consider these tips when using headings and subheadings:

■ Headings should convey information about the content that follows. The text that follows the heading should stand on its own and not continue where the heading left off.

Incorrect:
Printing the Document [Heading]
This can be done from the File menu by clicking Print.

Correct:
Printing the Document [Heading]
To print a document, click the File menu, then click Print.

- Avoid headings that require two or more lines of text.

- Avoid using articles to begin a heading.

  Incorrect: The Print Dialog

  Correct: Print Dialog

- Use the gerund form of verbs rather than the infinitive form when using headings to describe tasks (the *-ing* form instead of *to*).

  Incorrect: To Format Your Text

  Correct: Formatting Your Text

- Avoid terms like *Using, Working with*

- Use noun phrases for headings that do not involve a particular task.

  Example: Exhaust System Components

- Headings should not be used as a lead-in to a lone list or figure.

- Use widow and orphan formatting controls on page layouts to prevent a heading from appearing at the bottom of one page with content following on the next page.

  - Include at least two lines of text with a heading that appears at the bottom of a page.

Headings can be formatted on different levels with different text styles for each level. Consider these tips for heading levels:

- Use the same typography for a given level.

- Different typefaces and font styles are okay for each level.

- Level-one headings are for general information.

  - If material that starts with a level-one heading contains subsections, the subsections should have level-two headings.

- Keep headings on the same level parallel in their wording.

  Example: Formatting Your Text, Adding Styles, Printing Your Document

- First-level headings should appear on a new page.
  - Use all caps for first-level headings.
  - First-level headings can be centered on the page or aligned left.
  - Separate text that follows a first-level heading by three blank lines.
- Second-level headings should use bold or underlined styles.
  - Second-level headings should be aligned left.
  - Leave one blank line before text that follows a second-level heading.
- Subsequent levels of headings can use bold, italic, or underlined styles.
  - Use standard paragraph spacing for the text that follows subsequent-level headings.

Helping Verbs

See *Linking Verbs*.

Hendiatris

Hendiatris is a figure of speech where three words are used to emphasize one idea.

Example: Wine, women, and song

Example: Eat, drink, and be merry.

Hendiatris is often used to create mottos for organizations.

Example: The motto at West Point is "Duty, Honor, Country."

Heteronyms

Words that are spelled the same but that have different meanings and are pronounced differently are **heteronyms**. Heteronyms are also known as **heterophones**. Table 2.17 lists common heteronyms.

(text continues on page 221)

Table 2.17 Common Heteronyms

Word	Part of Speech	Definition
Abuse	Noun	Bad treatment
	Verb	To treat badly
Advocate	Verb	To argue for someone
	Noun	A person who speaks on behalf of someone or something
Agape	Adjective	Wide open
	Noun	Asexual, spiritual love
Alternate	Adjective	Other
	Verb	To take turns
Appropriate	Adjective	Suitable
	Verb	To set apart for
Attribute	Noun	A characteristic
	Verb	To associate ownership
Bass	Noun	Low in pitch
	Noun	A fish
Blessed	Adjective	Having divine aid
	Verb	Past tense of bless
Bow	Noun	A stringed weapon
	Verb	To bend in respect
	Noun	Front of a ship

(continues)

Table 2.17 *(continued)*

Word	Part of Speech	Definition
Buffet	Noun	Self-service food
	Verb	To hit or strike
Close	Verb	To shut
	Adjective	Nearby
Compact	Verb	To compress
	Adjective	Small
Conduct	Noun	Acton
	Verb	To lead
Console	Verb	To provide comfort
	Noun	A control unit
Content	Noun	Information
	Adjective	Satisfied
Convict	Verb	To find guilty
	Noun	Someone who has been convicted
Desert	Noun	An arid region of the world
	Verb	To abandon
Does	Noun	Plural of doe (female deer)
	Verb	Form of do
Dove	Noun	A bird
	Verb	Past tense of dive
Entrance	Noun	Doorway
	Verb	To delight
House	Noun	Residential building
	Verb	To place in residence

Intimate	Verb	To suggest
	Adjective	Very close
Invalid	Adjective	Incorrect
	Noun	A person with a disability
Laminate	Verb	To assemble from thin sheets glued together
	Noun	Material formed by laminating
Lead	Verb	To guide
	Noun	A metal
Learned	Adjective	Having much learning
	Verb	Past tense of learn
Live	Verb	To be alive
	Adjective	Having life
Minute	Adjective	Small
	Noun	Unit of time
Moped	Noun	Small motorcycle
	Verb	Past tense of mope
Multiply	Verb	To increase
	Adjective	In multiple ways
Number	Noun	A numeral
	Adjective	More numb
Object	Noun	A thing
	Verb	To protest
Polish	Verb	To shine
	Adjective	Native of Poland

(continues)

Table 2.17 *(continued)*

Word	Part of Speech	Definition
Present	Verb	To reveal
	Noun	A gift
Primer	Noun	A book that covers basic content.
	Noun	An undercoat of paint
Produce	Verb	To make
	Noun	Fruits and vegetables
Project	Noun	An undertaking
	Verb	To cast an image
Read	Verb	Present tense
	Verb	Past tense
Rebel	Verb	To resist
	Noun	One who rebels
Record	Noun	Physical information
	Verb	To make a record
Refuse	Noun	Garbage
	Verb	To decline
Resign	Verb	To quit
	Verb	To sign again
Resume	Verb	To start again
	Noun	A written history of employment
Row	Verb	To paddle a boat
	Noun	An argument
Sake	Noun	Benefit
	Noun	Rice wine

Sewer	Noun	Drainage pipes
	Noun	One who sews
Shower	Noun	Rain
	Noun	One who shows
Sin	Noun	A moral error
	Noun	Abbreviation for sine
Sow	Verb	To plant seeds
	Noun	Female pig
Subject	Noun	Topic
	Verb	To cause to undergo
Tear	Noun	Liquid from crying
	Verb	To separate
Wicked	Adjective	Bad or evil
	Verb	Past tense of wick
Wind	Noun	Air movement
	Verb	To tighten a spring
Wound	Verb	Past tense of wind
	Noun	An injury

Highlighting

Highlighting is a technique for changing the font or font style for a word or phrase to add emphasis. Techniques include using italics, bold, all caps, underlines, and different sizes and colors. Using too much highlighting is distracting.

In business and technical documents, highlighting is typically used:

- To emphasize the word *not* in statements

- In headings

- For software commands, menus, fields, and buttons

- For keyboard or mouse buttons

- In special notices such as warnings, cautions, or dangers

- For buttons on computer hardware

- As labels in figures

- In titles for a table

- For column headings in a table

Hispanic, Latino, Chicano

See *Chicano, Latino, Hispanic*.

Hit

When writing about keyboard actions, use *type* or *press* instead of *hit*.

Homographs

Homographs are similar to **homophones** and **homonyms** in that they are words that are spelled the same but have different meanings.

Example: I'm going to read the book.

Example: I read that book last week.

Example: The wind blew through the trees.

Example: You have to wind the old clock.

Homonyms

Homonyms are words that are pronounced the same, spelled differently, and have different meanings. Table 2.18 contains a list of commonly confused homonyms.

Table 2.18 Commonly Confused Homonyms

altar	alter	
born	bourn	borne
breach	breech	
caret	carrot	
compliment	complement	
council	counsel	
cubicle	cubical	
discrete	discreet	
dual	duel	
foreword	forward	
led	lead	
loath	loathe	
mettle	metal	
peace	piece	
piqued	peaked	
principal	principle	
rein	reign	rain
ringer	wringer	
role	roll	
stationary	stationery	
tick	tic	
tow	toe	
vice	vise	
waved	waived	
yoke	yolk	

Homophones

Words that are spelled differently but sound the same are **homophones**.

Example: to, two, too; birth, berth

Hypallage

Hypallage is a literary technique that involves reversing the normal relation of two words.

Transferred epithet is a type of hypallage that involves applying an adjective to the wrong word in a sentence.

Example: "the winged sound of whirling" [instead of "the sound of whirling wings"]—Aristophanes, *Birds*

Hyperbaton

Hyperbaton is a figure of speech that occurs when two words that normally go together are separated for effect.

Example: "This is the sort of English up with which I will not put [instead of "put up with"]."—Winston Churchill

Example: "Object there was none. Passion there was none."
—Edgar Allan Poe, *The Tell-Tale Heart*

Hyperbole

Hyperbole is a figure of speech that occurs in exaggerated statements that should rarely be taken seriously. Hyperbole is used to create emphasis and to be humorous.

Hyperbole often involves an overstatement or understatement.

Example: I have a million things I should be doing right now.

Example: I'm so hungry, I could eat a horse.

Example: I nearly died laughing.

Hyperlinks

Hyperlinks are text or buttons that allow a user to click and access another document or a different place within the same document.

Hyperlinks are often found in Web sites and online documents. One of the most common hyperlinks is a Web address (URL).

Hyperlinks that link within the same document are sometimes called **bookmarks**. Text hyperlinks within a document are normally highlighted with either bold, underlining, or a different color.

Hyphens

Hyphens are used to join words, to show a connection between words, or to separate the syllables for a single word when splitting a word for a line break. Hyphens are used for various purposes.

Line Breaks

- Break closed compounds between the words.

Example: peace-/keeping

- Break hyphenated compound words after the hyphen.

Example: user-/friendly

- Break multisyllable words at the end of a line.
    - Don't break one-syllable words.
    - Don't break a word if just one letter is left on either line.

Substitute Words

If a word repeats with a different modifier in a sentence, the repetition can make the sentence sound long and difficult. One way to solve this problem is to use a hyphen.

Example: We both over- and underestimated the amount of driving time for the trip.

Example: The football team used a three-, four-, and five-man line.

Example: Most computers today have either a 32- or 64-bit processor.

Pronunciation

You can use hyphens when writing dialogue to achieve a particular pronunciation in the reader's mind.

Example: "S-s-s-s" said the snake.

Example: "Mr. S-s-smith," he stuttered, "May I p-p-please have some w-w-water?"

Compound Adjectives

Compound adjectives are groups of words or phrases used in a sentence to describe a noun.

Example: It was a once-in-a-lifetime opportunity.

Example: I wouldn't touch that line with a ten-foot pole.

Example: The computer's processor has a 512-single-byte bus.

Example: Eight-month-old kittens were given away.

Do not use hyphens when the first word of a compound adjective ends in *-ly*.

Incorrect: It was a highly-motivated student body.

Correct: It was a highly motivated student body.

Incorrect: It was a beautifully-made sweater.

Correct: It was a beautifully made sweater.

Hyphenated Compound Words

The following is a list of commonly used hyphenated compounds:

- all-encompassing
- anti-inflammatory
- cold-shoulder
- co-worker
- dead-on
- do-able
- ex-employee
- multi-item
- nuclear-free
- pre-engineered
- self-doubts
- stand-in
- water-resistant
- all-knowing
- back-check
- community-wide
- cross-fertilize
- de-emphasize
- drop-kick
- ex-husband
- non-native
- off-color
- president-elect
- self-esteem
- time-out

Hyphenated Numbers

Consider the following hyphenation tips when working with numbers:

- Written-out numbers of less than one hundred are hyphenated.

  Example: thirty-three

- Hundreds and thousands are not hyphenated.

  Example: six hundred thousand

- When modifying a noun, numbers are hyphenated, as are any compound adjectives.

  Example: five-thousand-foot mountain

  Example: three-foot rule

- Fractions of less than one are hyphenated.

  Example: one-third

  Example: three-quarters

- Mixed numbers are not hyphenated between the whole number and the fraction, both when written as words and figures.

  Example: one and one-half

  Example: 1 1/2

- Do not write one part of the fraction as a numeral and the other as a word.

  Incorrect: 1 fourth-inch bolt

  Correct: one-fourth-inch bolt

Hyponyms

Hyponyms are words that are in categories of other words.

Example: Red, scarlet, and crimson are all hyponyms of red.

Example: Red, green, and blue are all hyponyms of color.

Hypophora

Hypophora is a figure of speech where the writer or speaker asks a question and then answers it.

Example: "What is George Bush doing about our economic problems? He has raised taxes on people driving pickup trucks and lowered taxes on people riding in limousines."—Bill Clinton

Hypothetical Questions

A **hypothetical question** is a question that is based on assumptions instead of facts and that is intended to elicit an opinion. Hypothetical questions are often asked of politicians and during court trials.

Hysteron Proteron

Hysteron proteron is a literary technique that calls attention to an important idea by placing it first and then having a secondary idea direct attention back to the first.

Hysteron proteron involves an inversion of the normal sequence of events for effect or humor.

Example: Put on your shoes and socks, but not necessarily in that order.

Idiolect

Personal language, including the words people use and other characteristics of how they speak or write, is called their **idiolect**. Idiolect is similar to **dialect**; however, dialect relates to the way a group of people speak or write.

Idioms

An **idiom** is a phrase that is easily understood by the speakers of a particular language; however, the meaning is different from the normal meaning of the words.

Example: A bird in the hand is worth two in the bush.

Example: a chip on your shoulder

Example: a drop in the bucket

i.e., e.g.

See *e.g., i.e.*

If, When, Whether

If is often used in casual speaking. *If* is used when there is a condition.

Incorrect: If you don't know <u>if</u> [should be whether] the front door is locked, you better get up and check it.

Correct: If you don't change the oil in your car, your engine won't last long.

Whether should be used in formal writing.

■ When discussing two possible alternatives, *whether* should be used.

Example: It's important to find out whether your guests prefer red or white wine.

■ *Whether* is used when there is uncertainty about the possible outcome.

■ Do not use *whether or not* if there is uncertainty about the outcome.

■ Only use *whether or not* to mean *under any circumstances.*

When is used when the passage of time is involved in the condition.

Example: You can finish your homework when we finish discussing this matter.

Illicit, Elicit

See *Elicit, Illicit.*

Illusion, Allusion

See *Allusion, Illusion.*

Illustrations

See *Figures.*

I, Me, Myself

Speakers and writers are often confused on when to use *I, me,* and *myself,* especially in sentences involving other people.

■ Use the word *I* when speaking of yourself as the subject of a sentence.

Example: I live north of Atlanta.

■ Use the word *me* when someone else is doing something to or for you.

Example: John threw the football to me.

■ Use the word *myself* only when you are doing something to yourself.

Example: Rather than taking the train, I'm going to drive myself to work today.

When another person is added to a sentence and there is a choice between *I*, *me*, or *myself*, one good test is to remove the other person and see if the sentence makes sense.

Incorrect: Jennifer and me live north of Atlanta. [Remove "Jennifer": Me lives north of Atlanta.]

Correct: Jennifer and I live north of Atlanta.

Incorrect: John threw the football to Jennifer and I. [Remove "Jennifer": John threw the football to I.]

Correct: John threw the football to Jennifer and me.

Incorrect: Rather than taking the train, I'm going to drive Jennifer and me to work today. [Remove "Jennifer": I'm going to drive me to work today.]

Correct: Rather than taking the train, I'm going to drive Jennifer and myself to work today.

Immanent, Eminent

See *Eminent, Imminent, Immanent.*

Immigrate, Emigrate

See *Emigrate, Immigrate.*

Imperative Mood

Imperative mood is an attitude in writing or speaking that involves giving directives, orders, or strong suggestions.

Example: Get out of my office!

Example: Get those reports in my office by noon.

Imperative sentences do not have subjects. The pronoun *you* is understood to be the subject.

Questions are often tagged to the end of imperative sentences.

Example: Leave your shoes outside, will you?

Imply, Infer

To correctly use these words in your writing, consider these tips:

■ If you are giving someone else an idea, you can *imply.*

■ If you are receiving an idea from someone else, you can *infer.*

■ When deciding whether to use imply or infer, use *imply* when something is suggested without being clearly stated.

■ Use *infer* when trying to arrive at a decision based on facts.

Inanimate Nouns

Inanimate nouns are nouns that identify nonliving things. Inanimate nouns identify places, things, and ideas.

Example: Austin, Texas, car, house, ceremony, speech

Inaugurate

Don't use *inaugurate* in place of *started* or *began*.

Incorrect: The program inaugurated on August 1.

Correct: The program began on August 1.

Correct: The president of the United States was inaugurated on January 4.

Inchoative Verbs

Inchoative verbs describe states of change.

Example: The strawberries have ripened.

Example: She has aged a lot.

Indefinite Articles

The determiners *a* and *an* are **indefinite articles**. Indefinite articles are used before singular nouns that have a plural form.

Example: a tree, a boy, an apple

The indefinite article *a* is used before consonant sounds and *an* is used before vowel sounds.

Example: a woman, a display, an umbrella, an intellectual

Indefinite Pronouns

The **indefinite pronouns** *everybody, anybody, somebody, all, each, every, some, none,* and *one* do not substitute for specific nouns but act as nouns themselves.

One of the problems with the indefinite pronoun *everybody* is that it seems to be plural but takes a singular verb.

Example: Everybody is coming.

The indefinite pronoun *none* can be either singular or plural. It is usually always plural except when something else in the sentence forces it to be singular.

Example: None of the students are failing.

Example: None of the water is salty.

Some can be singular or plural depending on whether it refers to something countable or not countable.

Example: Some of the whipped cream is gone.

Example: Some of the footballs are not being used.

Some indefinite pronouns also double as determiners, such as *enough, few, fewer, less, little, many, much, several, more, most, all, both, every, each, any, either, neither, none,* and *some.*

Independent Clauses

An **independent clause** could stand by itself as a sentence. When an independent clause is included in a sentence, it is usually separated from the rest of the sentence by a comma.

Example: Charlie didn't mean to run away, but he did it because he was angry.

In this example, two independent clauses are separated by a comma and a coordinating conjunction *but*. If the word *but* was missing, this example would be a comma splice.

Being able to recognize when a clause is independent is essential to knowing when to use commas, thereby avoiding sentence fragments and run-on sentences.

Two independent clauses can be combined into a single thought. Clauses can be combined three different ways:

- With coordination—using coordinating conjunctions such as *and, but, or, nor, for, yet,* and sometimes *so.* By using a coordinating conjunction, you avoid monotony and what is often called "primer language," simple sentence constructions.

  Example: The book was long, but I couldn't put it down.

- With subordination—turning one of the independent clauses into a subordinate element using a subordinating conjunction or a relative pronoun. When the clause begins with a subordinating word, it transforms into a dependent clause.

  Example: Linda never liked to fly in airplanes, because she was afraid of heights.

- By using a semicolon—with or without the help of a conjunctive adverb. Semicolons should be used only when the two independent clauses are very closely related and nicely balanced in length and content.

  Example: Sheena is a very pretty girl; she looks like an angel.

Index

Indexes are often created for large business documents and included at the end of the manuscript. Indexes alphabetically list keywords with either the page numbers where they can be found or hyperlinks to the pages in online documents. Some word processing software, such as Microsoft Word, creates an index automatically; however, you must manually omit unneeded words from the index.

When creating an index, consider these tips:

■ All headings and subheadings in a document should be included in the index.

■ Also identify and include keywords. (Word processing software allows you to mark keywords throughout the document.)

■ Consolidate entries that are similar with common phrasing.

Example: Print Documents, Printing Documents, Using the Print Function all become *Printing.*

■ A detailed index may include synonym entries with a *See* reference to the actual keywords used in the document.

Example: Monitors—See *Displays*

■ Index entries that appear on many different pages should include sub-ordinated entries.

Example:
    hard drives:
        error checking, 218
        formatting, 166
        replacing, 172

■ The first word of each entry has an initial capital letter. Subsequent words should be lowercase. Add a comma between the index entry and the page number.

■ Index entries, as well as subordinated entries, should be alphabetized.

■ Numeric entries in an index should appear before the A-letter entries and should be ordered numerically with the smallest numbers first.

Figure 2.4 shows a sample index.

Figure 2.4 Sample Index

Index

Indicative Mood

The **indicative mood** is an attitude for writing or speaking and is used in sentences that make a statement, affirm or deny something, or ask a question.

Example: Larry writes in his notebook.

Example: Mary goes to bed.

Indicative mood deals with facts, as well as confirming or denying things.

Example: Is the city still working on a wastewater control plan?

Indirect Objects

An **indirect object** identifies to what or for whom the action of a verb is performed. A **direct object** receives the action in a sentence. There must be a direct object to have an indirect object.

Example: Mike gave <u>Sally</u> [indirect object] the report.

Example: The CEO told <u>us</u> [indirect object] about the layoffs.

Indirect Speech

Indirect speech is commonly used in journalism to report what someone said without including his or her exact words. Indirect speech is often called "reported speech" and includes third-person narration.

The tense of the verbs is usually changed, and the verb *said* is often used.

Example: She said she wanted to visit Europe. [Her exact words were, "I want to visit Europe."]

Inductive Antonomasia

When a specific name or brand name becomes the general term in the language, this phenomenon is called **inductive antonomasia**.

Example: aspirin, Kleenex, Xerox, Google, Band-Aid

Infinitives

An **infinitive** is formed with the root of a verb and the word *to*.

Example: To be, or not to be.

A **present infinitive** describes a present condition.

Example: I like to dream.

The **perfect infinitive** describes a time earlier than that described by the verb.

> **Example:** I would like to have slept until nine.

When combined with auxiliary verb forms, infinitives can also express concepts of time.

■ Simple forms

> **Example:** We had planned <u>to watch</u> the Super Bowl.

> **Example:** <u>Seeing</u> the Cowboys win is always a great thrill.

■ Perfect forms

> **Example:** The Cowboys hoped <u>to have won</u> the Super Bowl.

> **Example:** I was thrilled about their <u>having been</u> in the big game.

■ Passive forms

> **Example:** <u>To be chosen</u> as an NFL player must be the biggest thrill in any football player's life.

> **Example:** <u>Being chosen,</u> however, doesn't mean you get to play.

Infinitive Phrase

An **infinitive phrase** consists of an infinitive—the root verb preceded by *to*—along with modifiers or complements.

Infinitive phrases can act as adjectives, nouns, or adverbs.

■ As an adjective

> **Example:** His plan <u>to eliminate smoking</u> [adjective modifying "plan"] was widely popular.

■ As a noun

> **Example:** <u>To watch him eat</u> [noun subject] ribs is something you have to see.

■ As an adverb

> **Example:** Eric went to college <u>to study to be an engineer</u> [explains why he went].

Inflection

Inflection involves changing the form of a word by adding an affix. Usually this is done to change the number of items or to change the tense. Adding an *s* or an *ed* to a word is a common example of inflection.

> **Example:** cat, cats; talk, talked

Inherent and Noninherent Adjectives

Adjectives that relate a certain attribute or the quality of a noun are known as **inherent adjectives**.

Noninherent adjectives do not relate any particular attribute or quality about the noun they modify.

The same word can be used as either an inherent or noninherent adjective depending on the context of a sentence.

> **Example:** He looked out at the <u>distant</u> [inherent] hills.

> **Example:** He didn't know much about his <u>distant</u> [noninherent] relatives.

Initialisms, Acronyms

See *Acronyms*.

Innuendo

Innuendo is a figure of speech that involves a remark about someone or something that suggests something bad or inappropriate.

When the implied content is sexual in nature, it is called **sexual innuendo**.

In Order to

In expressions with *in order* + infinitive, the *in order* can be omitted without affecting the meaning of the sentence.

Example: We will go to the library in order to get a book.

Example: We will go to the library to get a book.

In order to means the same as *so that*.

Example: We will go the library so that Susan can get a book.

No commas are used to punctuate *so that*.

Inquire, Enquire

See *Enquire, Inquire*.

In-Sentence Lists

See *Lists*.

Inside of, Within

Don't use *inside of* where you could use *within*.

Incorrect: He will visit us inside of a week.

Correct: He will visit us within a week.

Insure, Ensure, Assure

See *Ensure, Assure, Insure.*

Intensive Pronouns

Intensive pronouns (*myself, yourself, herself, ourselves,* and *themselves*) consist of a personal pronoun plus the suffix *self* or *selves.* Intensive pronouns are used to emphasize a noun.

> **Example:** I myself didn't play baseball.

Interjections

Interjections are words or phrases used to communicate excitement, orders, or protests. Sometimes interjections can be used by themselves, but often they are contained in more complex sentence structures.

> **Example:** Oh, I didn't realize you were here.

> **Example:** No, you shouldn't have done that.

Most interjections are treated as parenthetical elements and are set apart from the rest of the sentence by commas or a set of commas. If the interjection is very forceful, it is followed with an exclamation point.

> **Example:** Wow, I can't believe it!

Internet, Intranet, Extranet

The **Internet**, also known as the World Wide Web, consists of a network of computers that are accessible using an Internet protocol (IP) address. *Internet* is capitalized.

An **intranet** is a network within an organization or company. *Intranet* is not capitalized unless it starts a sentence.

An **extranet** is a part of an organization's intranet that is available to authorized outsiders. *Extranet* is not capitalized unless it starts a sentence.

Interrogative Pronouns

Interrogative pronouns (*what, who, which*) are used to introduce questions.

Example: What is that?

Example: Who is coming?

Example: Which dog do you like best?

Which is used for specific reference rather than *what*.

Example: Which dogs do you like best? [refers to individual dogs]

Example: What dogs do you like best? [refers to general dog breeds]

Interrogative pronouns can also act as determiners. In this role, the pronouns are called **interrogative adjectives**.

Example: It doesn't matter which road you take.

Interrogative pronouns are used to introduce noun clauses.

Example: what I thought about it

Like relative pronouns, interrogative pronouns play a subject role in the clause they introduce.

Example: I already said what I thought.

Interrogative Sentences

An **interrogative sentence** is used when asking a question.

> **Example:** Is that your dog?

Questions that can be answered with yes or no are called **yes/no interrogatives**.

Alternative interrogatives are questions that offer the possibility of two or more responses.

> **Example:** Should I use the post office or email to contact you?

Questions that begin with a *wh-* word are called **wh interrogatives**.

> **Example:** Who made those cookies?

> **Example:** Where did you go?

Intranet

See *Internet, Intranet, Extranet.*

Intransitive Verbs

Intransitive verbs do not require objects. Intransitive verbs usually have just a subject plus the verb and an optional adverb.

> **Example:** She complains too much.

Introductory Modifier

See *Prepositional Phrase.*

Invite

Don't confuse *invite* (a verb) with *invitation* (a noun).

Incorrect: I have an invite to the party.

Correct: I have an invitation to the party.

Irony

Irony is a literary technique where the speaker or writer says one thing, but the meaning is something completely different. Irony is often humorous in nature. When a statement uses irony, it is said to be *ironic*. Irony can also imply tragedy or a twist of fate.

Example: "It is a fitting irony that under Richard Nixon, launder became a dirty word."—William Zinsser

---

Irregular Plurals

Irregular plurals are words that change form and spelling to specify more than one.

Example: child, children; woman, women; man, men; mouse, mice; person, people

---

Irregular Spelling

Common **irregular spellings** to watch closely are:

- acknowledgment
- awful
- judgment
- ninth
- truly
- wholly

Words ending in *-ceed, -cede,* and *-sede* may sound the same, but pay attention to their spelling. Here are examples:

- exceed
- intercede
- precede
- proceed

- recede
- secede
- succeed
- supersede

The only English word that ends in *-sede* is *supersede.* The only English words that end in *-ceed* are *exceed, proceed,* and *succeed.*

Watch for *-ant* and *-ent* endings:

- correspondent
- eminent

- relevant

Watch for *-ance* and *-ence* endings:

- occurrence

- perseverance

Watch for *-able* and *-ible* endings:

- accessible
- affordable
- comfortable

- compatible
- deductible

Don't omit the silent letters:

- abscess
- acquisition
- diaphragm

- hemorrhage
- silhouette

Don't be confused over double consonants:

- accommodate
- commitment

- necessary
- occurrence

Some words are not spelled the way they are pronounced:

- asterisk
- auxiliary
- boundary
- prerogative
- separate

Irregular Verbs

Most verbs form the simple past and past participle by adding -*ed* to the base verb.

> **Example:** He walked. He has walked.

Some **irregular verbs** do not follow this pattern. Common verbs such as *to be* and *to have* have irregular forms.

> **Example:** He is. They are. He has. They had.

Isocolon

Isocolon is a figure of speech that uses parallelism involving words or phrases that are the same length.

> **Example:** No ifs, ands, or buts.

> **Example:** "They have suffered severely, but they have fought well."
> —Winston Churchill

> **Example:** "I speak Spanish to God, Italian to women, French to men, and German to my horse."—Charles V

Italics

Italics are sometimes used for emphasis.

Example: Notice where you are, not where you *have been*.

Italics are used for the names of books, pamphlets, and periodicals:

Example: *Saturday Evening Post, Black Beauty, Washington Daily News*

The names of ships are italicized but not the abbreviations preceding them:

Example: *Sea Witch*, USS *Heinz*

Its, It's

Its (without an apostrophe) is a possessive pronoun.

Correct: The ship was flying its flag at half-mast.

It's (with an apostrophe) is a contraction meaning "it is."

Correct: It's [It is] getting dark.

Jargon

People who work together or who share a common career or interest often develop their own specialized words and expressions, which outsiders may not understand. This unique language is often called **jargon**.

Many times, jargon is created from abbreviations and acronyms. Jargon often serves as shorthand for more complex terminology.

Jargon should not be used in business communications if:

- The readers are not part of the group that uses the specialized language.

- A more familiar term can be used.

- Abbreviations or acronyms are not defined.

Job Titles

When writing about **job titles**, do not capitalize the job title unless referring to a specific person and his or her job title.

Example: president, vice president, general manager

Example: President Barack Obama, Vice President Joe Biden, General Manager Phil Jackson

Joint Possessives

A **joint possessive** is a structure that involves expressing ownership of objects that are owned by two or more people.

When the same object is owned by two people, add an apostrophe only after the last name.

Example: That's David and Cathy's house.

If referring to objects that each person owns individually, add an apostrophe after each name.

Example: Those are David's and Cathy's motorcycles.

When one of the people is referred to by a pronoun, add the apostrophe only after the person who is named.

Example: Those are David's and her children.

Jr., Sr.

Junior and *senior* are abbreviated as *Jr.* and *Sr.* Both abbreviations capitalize only the first letter and add a period after the *r.*

Do not use a comma to separate *Jr.* or *Sr.* from the last name.

Example: Bob Stephens Jr.

When writing about a couple, *Jr.* or *Sr.* goes after both names.

Example: Gloria and John Jefferson Jr.

When only using the last name, avoid using the *Jr.* or *Sr.*

Example: Mr. Stephens

Kenning

A **kenning** is a synonym made from several words that can be used in place of a single word. Kennings are often used in poetic language. Kennings are used to add color and emphasis to a passage.

Example: wave's steed, a ship

Keyboard Terminology

The following is a list of keyboard keys that may be used in computer-related documentation:

- ALT
- Break
- Clear
- Delete
- End
- ESC (escape)
- Home
- Left Arrow
- Page Down
- Pause
- Reset
- Scroll Lock
- Shift
- Tab
- Windows Logo Key

- Backspace
- Caps Lock
- CTRL (control)
- Down Arrow
- Enter
- F1 through F12
- Insert
- Num Lock (number lock)
- Page Up
- Print Screen
- Right Arrow
- Select
- Spacebar
- Up Arrow

When writing documentation that instructs a user to type a particular key, use lowercase bold to highlight the key.

Example: Type **y** in the field, then click OK.

The first time a key is mentioned, use *the* and *key* with the key name.

Example: Press the Enter key.

For subsequent mentions of the same key, omit *the* and *key*.

Example: Press Enter.

Keys that are typed simultaneously are called keyboard combinations. Keyboard combinations are indicated by adding a plus sign.

Example: CTRL + Shift

When writing about keyboard combinations, don't use the word *key*.

Incorrect: Press CTRL + ALT + Delete keys

Correct: Press CTRL + ALT + Delete

Certain keyboard key names need to be spelled out when writing commands, because the key names are difficult to see or may be confusing. Spell *plus sign, minus sign, hyphen, period,* and *comma* when any of these keys are pressed as part of a command.

Kilobyte

A *kilobyte* is 1,024 bytes. *Kilobyte* is abbreviated as *KB*.

When used as an adjective, add a hyphen between the number and the abbreviation.

Example: That's an 800-KB data record.

When used in measurement, add a space after the number and add *of* to create a prepositional phrase.

Example: The data required 800 KB of storage.

Kilohertz

Kilohertz is a measurement of frequency that is equal to 1,000 cycles per second. The abbreviation for kilohertz is *kHz*.

Unless used as an adjective, leave a space between the number and the abbreviation. Spell *kilohertz* the first time it is mentioned and include the abbreviation in parentheses.

Example: The chip's memory is rated at 500 kilohertz (kHz).

When used as an adjective preceding a noun, use a hyphen between the number and the abbreviation.

Example: That's a 500-kHz processor.

Kind, Kinds

Kind is singular; *kinds* is plural.

Incorrect: She asked for those kind of flowers.

Correct: She asked for those kinds of flowers.

Correct: She asked for that kind of flower.

Kind of, Sort of

Kind of and *sort of* are unclear. Be definite when speaking or writing.

Incorrect: He appeared to be kind of ill.

Correct: He appeared to be rather ill.

Incorrect: She was sort of ill at ease.

Correct: She was somewhat ill at ease.

Latino, Hispanic, Chicano

See *Chicano, Latino, Hispanic.*

Latin Terms

See *Abbreviations.*

Latitude, Longitude

Latitude lines run horizontally around the earth (and on maps). To correctly write latitude measurements, consider these facts:

- Each degree of latitude is approximately 69 miles apart.

- Latitude degrees are numbered from 0° to 90°.

- 0° latitude is the equator.

- Latitudes north of the equator include "north" ("N") in their description.

- Latitudes south of the equator include "south" ("S") in their description.

- 90° north is the North Pole, and 90° south is the South Pole.

Longitude lines run vertically around the earth and converge at the North and South Poles. Longitude lines are also known as **meridians**. To correctly write longitude measurements, consider these facts:

- Each degree of longitude is approximately 69 miles apart at their widest distance, which is as they cross the equator.

- The meridian at 0° longitude runs through Greenwich, England.

- Longitudes extend east and west from Greenwich, England, and include "east" ("E") or "west" ("W") in their description.

■ Longitude lines extend to 180° east and 180° west at the International Date Line in the Pacific Ocean.

Longitude and latitude are used together to locate points on the earth. Degrees of longitude and latitude are divided into minutes (′) and seconds (″). Seconds can be further divided into tenths, hundredths, and thousandths.

To describe a location using longitude and latitude, latitude is listed first and is separated from longitude by a comma.

Example: The location of the United States Capitol is 38° 53′23″N, 77° 00′27″W. This translates into 38 degrees, 53 minutes, 23 seconds north of the equator and 77 degrees, 0 minutes, and 27 seconds west of the meridian passing through Greenwich, England.

Lay, Lie

Many people confuse the two words because the word *lay* is both the present tense of *lay* (*lay, lay, laid*) and the past tense of *lie* (*lie, lay, lain*).

Lie means to remain in position or to rest. *Lie* is intransitive, meaning that no object ever accompanies it. When the subject is lying down, use *lie*.

Example: I'm pretty tired, so I'm going to lie down.

Lay means to place something somewhere. *Lay* is transitive, meaning that an object always accompanies it. The verb *lay* takes an object in a sentence, whereas the verb *lie* does not. When the subject acts on something else, use *lay*.

Correct: I'm going to lay the book on your desk.

Incorrect: He lays down after lunch every day.

Correct: He lies down after lunch every day.

Correct: Yesterday he lay on the couch for two hours.

Correct: Will you please lay the book on the table?

Correct: The pen lay on the desk all day.

What can be confusing is that the past tense of *lie* is *lay*. Table 2.19 lists the various forms of the verbs *lay* and *lie*.

Table 2.19 Forms of Lay and Lie and Sample Sentences

	Lay	
	First Person	**Third Person**
Present	I lay the book down.	He lays the book down.
Past	I laid the book down.	He laid the book down.
Perfect form	I have laid the book down.	He has laid the book down.
Participle form	I am laying it down.	He is laying it down.
	Lie	
	First Person	**Third Person**
Present	I lie on my cot.	He lies on his cot.
Past	I lay in my cot.	He lay in his cot.
Perfect form	I have lain in my cot.	He has lain in his cot.
Participle form	I am lying in my cot.	He is lying in his cot.

Lay Out, Layout

Lay out as two words is a verb that means to display something in an orderly way, to spend or invest money, or to explain or show.

Example: I'm going to lay out my clothes before I start packing them into my suitcase.

Example: I've had to lay out thousands for car repairs.

Example: She laid out all the alternatives available to the company.

Layout, as one word, is a noun that describes a design plan.

Example: She was impressed by the layout of the loft apartment.

Lead, Led

Lead can be both a noun and a verb.

- As a noun, *lead* is a heavy metal.

- As a verb, *lead* means to guide others, and the past tense is *led*.

Learn, Teach

Before you can *learn,* someone must *teach* you.

Incorrect: She learned me how to type.

Correct: She taught me how to type.

Correct: If I teach him correctly, he will learn quickly.

Leave, Let

See *Let, Leave.*

Led, Lead

See *Lead, Led.*

Lend, Loan

See *Loan, Lend.*

Lessen, Lesson

Lessen is a verb that means to make something smaller.

Example: When the rain stopped, the flooding lessened.

Lesson is a noun for something that is learned, studied, or taught.

Example: Falling off the ladder taught me a valuable lesson about safety.

Less, Fewer

When you are talking about countable things, you should use the word *fewer*.

When you are talking about measurable quantities that cannot be counted, you should use the word *less*.

Example: He has fewer assets, but less worry.

Less refers to a smaller amount, degree, or value.

Example: There is less traffic today than yesterday.

Fewer refers to a quantifiable number.

Example: Fewer cars are on the road today than yesterday.

Let, Leave

Let means to permit.

Example: Let her go with us.

Leave means to depart, to bequeath, to allow.

Example: Leave her alone.

Lets, Let's

Lets without an apostrophe means to allow something.

Example: We can go get ice cream if my brother lets us use his car.

Let's with an apostrophe is abbreviated to mean let us.

Example: Let's go get ice cream.

Lexical Density

The **Lexical Density Test** is a readability test that is designed to measure how easy or difficult a document is to read. The test uses the following formula:

$$\text{Lexical Density} = \frac{\text{Number of different words}}{\text{Total number of words}} \times 100$$

A document with a low Lexical Density rating is relatively easy to read. A rating of 60–70% is difficult to read. A rating of 40–50% is the target range for business documents.

Liable, Likely

Liable should be used when referring to legal responsibility.

Example: The landlord is liable for damages.

Likely refers to a high probability.

Example: That horse is likely to win the race.

Lie, Lay

See *Lay, Lie*.

Lighted, Lit

Lighted and *lit* can both be used as the past tense and past participle of the verb *to light*. Both *lighted* and *lit* can also be used as adjectives. *Lit* is more often used as a verb, whereas *lighted* is more often used as an adjective.

Correct: He lit a candle.

Correct: He held a lighted pipe in his hand.

Like, As

Like is a preposition always followed by a noun or pronoun in the objective case.

Correct: Though he was only a little boy, he marched like a major.

As is an adverbial conjunction used to introduce a subordinate clause.

Incorrect: It appears like he isn't coming.

Correct: It appears as <u>if he isn't coming</u> [the subordinate clause].

Line

Line should not be used in place of *business*.

Incorrect: He has a jewelry line.

Correct: He is in the jewelry business.

Linking Verbs

Linking verbs connect a subject and its complement (a noun or adjective that describes the subject). Linking verbs often include forms of the verb *to be*.

> **Example:** These employees <u>are</u> [linking verb] all hourly workers.

Sometimes linking verbs are related to the five senses.

> **Example:** look, sound, smell, feel, taste

> **Example:** Those offices look vacant.

Sometimes they are related to a state of being.

> **Example:** appear, seem, become, grow, turn, prove, remain

> **Example:** Increased sales seem likely.

Lists

Lists can be used to highlight specific information or to make it easier to reference information. When creating lists, consider the following tips:

- List items should have parallel phrasing.

- Use a lead-in sentence to introduce the list.

- Each list item should be grammatically correct if it continues from the lead-in to form a sentence.

- Do not use headings instead of a lead-in sentence.

In-Sentence Lists

In-sentence lists are built into the flow of the text.

> **Example:** There are three things on our agenda: (1) minutes from last month's meeting, (2) treasurer's report, and (3) new business.

> **Example:** Remember three things about firearms: (1) they can be used for sport; (2) they can be used destructively; and (3) they do not care how you use them.

Note the characteristics of the preceding in-sentence lists:

- Use a colon to introduce the items only if the lead-in is a complete sentence.

- Punctuate list items with commas for sentence fragments.

- Use semicolons to separate the list items that are complete sentences.

- Add an *and* before the last item.

- Use numbers or letters within parentheses for each item.

- Avoid using in-sentence lists when there are more than four or five items.

Vertical Lists

Vertical lists are indented and lined up one over the other. Consider the following tips when creating vertical lists:

- List items should be indented three to five spaces from the lead-in sentence.

- Sentence-style capitalization should be used on each list item.

- Optionally add a comma after each item.

- If you add commas, add a period after the last item.

- If complete sentences are used for each item, semicolons may be used after each item.

Numbered Lists

In **numbered lists**, each item has a number. Consider the following tips when creating numbered lists:

- Use numbered lists when a specific order is required for the items in the list.

- For nested sublists, use letters for each item.

Example:

    1.   Two items need to be addressed first:
        a.   When to hold the meeting
        b.   Where to hold the meeting

Bulleted Lists

Bulleted lists are vertical lists where bullets or other symbols are used to introduce each item.

Multicolumn Lists

Multicolumn lists consist of items appearing in two or more columns. Column headings are not necessarily used in multicolumn lists.

Literally, Figuratively

Often the word *literally* is used when *figuratively* should be used.

Incorrect: Literally, it's a jungle in that office.

Correct: Figuratively, it's a jungle in that office.

It is best to omit both *literally* and *figuratively* from your business documents.

Lit, Lighted

See *Lighted, Lit*.

Litotes

A **litotes** is a figure of speech where a writer or speaker uses a negative word to express the opposite of what he or she means. Litotes are an understatement of reality.

Example: She's not the sharpest student in the class.

Little, A Little

Little means the same as *few* or *not much*.

Example: Mike has little experience with the software.

A little means the same as *some*.

Example: Sara has a little experience working with the software when she was with her previous employer.

Loan, Lend

Loan should be used as a noun to refer to an agreement to borrow.

Example: He went to the bank to receive a loan.

To allow someone to borrow is *to lend*.

Incorrect: Loan me your pen.

Correct: Lend me your pen.

Log On, Log Off, Logon, Logoff

When *log on* or *log off* are two words, they are treated as verbs.

Use the term *log on* when referring to the action of users when entering their ID and password to access a network or a secure Web site.

Example: You have to log on to gain access to the database.

Use the term *log off* when referring to the action of users when ending a session on a network or secure Web site.

Example: Make sure you log off before closing your browser.

When *logon* or *logoff* are one word, they are treated as adjectives.

Example: The Web site features a secure logon.

Example: The site has an automatic logoff if there's no activity for ten minutes.

Lonely, Alone

See *Alone, Lonely.*

Longitude, Latitude

See *Latitude, Longitude.*

Loose, Lose

Loose is a verb that means to allow to run free and an adjective that means not tight. *Loose* is pronounced with an *s* sound.

Example: My neighbors <u>loosed</u> [verb] their dogs in the neighborhood.

Example: He wore a <u>loose</u> [adjective] kerchief around his neck.

Lose is a verb that means to separate from possession or to suffer a loss from the removal of something. *Lose* is pronounced with a *z* sound.

Example: She tends to lose patience with her elderly parents.

Lost, Lost Out

Don't use extra words—like *out*—that are not necessary for meaning.

Incorrect: He lost out.

Correct: He lost.

Lots

Don't use *lots* when referring to an amount of something. *Lots* and *lots of* are colloquialisms that should be avoided. Alternatives include *many* and *much*.

Incorrect: She receives lots of fan mail.

Correct: She receives a great deal of fan mail.

Incorrect: He spent lots of money on that car.

Correct: He spent much money on that car.

Incorrect: She has lots of friends.

Correct: She has many friends.

Mad, Angry

Use *angry* rather than *mad*. Remember, dogs go mad, people get angry.

Incorrect: Chaital was mad at Ravi.

Correct: Chaital was angry with Ravi.

Margin Notes

Margin notes are often used in documents to provide tips and warnings. Tips can provide hints, shortcuts, or background information.

Margin notes can include a bolded heading that describes the subject of the note. Margin notes can also provide cross-references to direct readers to additional information elsewhere in the document.

Margin notes should be limited to three or four lines of text. Break the lines of margin notes so that they are all approximately the same width.

Mass Nouns

Mass nouns describe things that have no boundaries, such as liquids, powders, and substances.

Example: water, milk, juice, salt, sugar, sand, metal, wood

Mass nouns are also known as **uncountable nouns** or **noncount nouns**.

Mass nouns cannot be modified by a numeral without specifying a unit of measure.

Example: I had one quart of milk this morning.

Mass nouns can be combined with an indefinite article (*a* or *an*).

Example: Mercury is a metal.

Mathematical Equations

See *Equations*.

Maybe, May Be

Maybe is an adverb that means *perhaps*.

Example: Maybe she forgot to call me when she arrived.

May be is a verb and an auxiliary that suggests a possibility of something occurring.

Example: He may be on the football team next year.

May, Can

May refers to permission. *Can* refers to ability.

Incorrect: Can I help you?

Correct: May I help you?

Correct: Can he drive a car?

May, Might

Use *may* when seeking or granting permission for something or when suggesting something is possible. Use *might* to suggest a small possibility for something.

Example: May I help you with something?

Example: It may snow.

Example: I might attend the party.

May and *might* are interchangeable when expressing the possibility of something happening. *Might* is more tentative than *may*.

Example: She may be my new neighbor.

Example: She might be my new neighbor.

Mean, Median, Average

See A*verage, Mean, Median.*

Megabyte

A *megabyte* is 1,048,576 bytes or 1,024 kilobytes.

Megabyte is abbreviated as *MB*. Leave a space between a numeral and the abbreviation.

Example: I'll need at least 3 MB of storage for the files.

When used as an adjective preceding a noun, use a hyphen between the numeral and the abbreviation.

Example: I attached a 3-MB file to the email message.

Megahertz

Megahertz is a measurement for frequency that is equal to one million cycles per second.

The abbreviation for megahertz is *MHz*. Leave a space between a numeral and the abbreviation.

Example: The graphics processor accesses memory at 70 MHz.

When used as an adjective preceding a noun, use a hyphen between the numeral and the abbreviation.

Example: The computer had a 500-MHz graphics processor.

Meiosis

Meiosis is a figure of speech that is used to understate something or to imply that it is less significant or smaller than it really is.

Example: Bringing the gun to school was just a harmless prank.

Me, Myself, I

See *I, Me, Myself*.

Metaphor

Metaphor is a figure of speech where the speaker or writer equates one word to another in some way. Metaphors do not use *like* or *as* in the comparison.

Example: Mike was an angel in the eyes of his mother.

Example: Leslie is such a stubborn mule.

Metaphors are often used in literature and poetry. A **mixed metaphor** occurs when the comparison of the two subjects is nonsensical.

Example: The linebacker was a tank, a thunderstorm crashing through the offensive line.

Metonymy

Metonymy is a figure of speech where something is called not by its own name, but by the name of something with which it is associated.

> **Example:** The <u>White House</u> [instead of the president] is trying hard to explain the new policies.

Mfr., Mfg.

The abbreviation for *manufacturer* is *mfr.* The abbreviation for *manufacturing* is *mfg.*

Might Could

Might could is a colloquialism that should be avoided. The combination is redundant.

Might can be used alone when there is a possibility of something occurring. *Could* can be used alone when someone is able to do something.

Might, May

See *May, Might.*

Might of, Should of, Would of, Could of

This construction is the result of poor pronunciation. The correct phrases are *might have, should have, would have,* and *could have.*

> **Incorrect:** If you could of arranged it, I would of gone.

> **Correct:** If you could have arranged it, I would have gone.

Minimal Pairs

Two words that are very similar when pronounced but have different meanings are called **minimal pairs.**

Example: thick, sick; teeth, tea; that, sat; wonder, thunder

Misplaced Modifiers

When a modifier such as *only, just, nearly,* or *barely* appears in the wrong place in a sentence, it is called a **misplaced modifier**.

Incorrect: He nearly kicked the football fifty yards.

Correct: He kicked the football nearly fifty yards.

The best rule is to place the modifier immediately before the word it modifies.

Mixed Conditionals

A **mixed conditional** is a conditional sentence that uses an if clause and whose clauses refer to different periods of time.

Example: If I had studied [past] in school, I would be [present] rich now.

Example: If she had gone [past] on the interview, we would be [present] working in the same office.

Example: If I were [present] smarter, I would have [past] invested in Apple Computer back in the early 1980s.

Example: If she didn't work [present] so many hours, she would have [future] more time with her family.

Example: If I am going [future] to get that promotion, I would not have [past] sent out so many résumés trying to find another job.

Example: If I were [future] working for that company when it goes public, I would be [present] very rich.

Mixed Metaphor

See *Metaphor.*

Mnemonics

Mnemonics are memory devices that help you remember something. Mnemonics are often used to remember how to spell certain words.

Example: *i* before *e* except after *c*

Example: Scream *e-e-e* when walking past the cemetery.

Example: I lost an *e* in an argument.

Example: A desert is sandy, while a dessert is super sweet.

Modifiers

Modifiers are words that limit certain aspects of a sentence.

Some modifiers—such as *only, just, nearly,* and *barely*—can easily end up in the wrong place in a sentence.

Incorrect: He only threw the ball ten feet.

Correct: He threw the ball only ten feet.

The best rule is to place the modifier immediately before the word it modifies. When a modifier improperly modifies something, it is called a **dangling modifier**. See *Dangling Modifiers.*

Incorrect: Cleaning the windows every six months, the building seemed to look better. [Buildings can't clean their own windows.]

Correct: Cleaning the windows every six months, the maintenance staff made the building look better.

Adverbs can be placed almost anywhere in a sentence, but their placement can sometimes obscure their meaning.

Unclear: The people who listen to public radio <u>often</u> [adverb] like classical music. [Does everyone who listens to public radio, even for a few minutes, like classical music?]

Clear: The people who often listen to public radio like classical music.

You can add variety to your sentences by the way you place modifiers. You can use:

- Initial modifiers.

- Midsentence modifiers.

- Terminal modifiers.

- Combining modifiers.

Initial Modifiers

Consider these ideas for using initial modifiers:

- Dependent clause

  Example: Although he was tired, Bob wrote the report.

- Infinitive phrase

  Example: To please his boss, Bob wrote the report.

- Adverb

  Example: Slowly and laboriously, Bob wrote the report.

- Participial phrase

  Example: Hoping to be promoted, Bob wrote the report.

Midsentence Modifiers

Consider these ideas for using midsentence modifiers:

■ Appositive

Example: Bob, an expert on regulations, wrote the report.

■ Participial phrase

Example: Bob, hoping to catch up on his work, stayed after hours.

Terminal Modifiers

Consider these ideas for using terminal modifiers:

■ Present participial phrase

Example: Bob worked on the report, hoping to please his boss.

■ Past participial phrase/adjectival phrase

Example: Bob worked on the report demanded by his boss.

Combining Modifiers

Consider the following idea for combining modifiers:

Example: Slowly and laboriously, Bob, an expert on regulations, worked on the report, hoping to please his boss.

Misplaced Modifiers

See *Misplaced Modifiers*.

Monitor

See *Display, Monitor, Screen*.

Monosyllabic

Monosyllabic words have only one syllable.

Example: her, his, its, just, not, both, since

Mood

Mood refers to the attitude of the writer. Mood helps discern between facts and the hypothetical. Hypothetical statements use *could, would,* or *might.*

Three attitudes can accompany a verb:

- **Indicative mood**—used to make a statement or ask a question

- **Imperative mood**—used to give directions, to give orders, or to make a strong suggestion (these verbs don't need a subject, which is understood to be "you")

Example: Get out of my office.

Example: Answer the phone.

- **Subjunctive mood**—used with dependent clauses to express a wish

Example: He wishes she were fired.

This mood may be used with *if* and a condition:

Example: We could have won the contract if we'd bid lower.

The sentence may begin with *that* to express a demand.

Example: That would be in your best interest to do.

More Than, Over

More than and *over* can be used interchangeably to indicate an excess.

> **Example:** The thief took more than ten thousand dollars in the robbery.

Note: Some writers disapprove of using *more than* before a number.

Over is normally used when referring to age, time, distance, or height.

> **Example:** We rode together for over 50 miles without saying a word.

Morpheme

The smallest unit of meaning in the English language is a **morpheme**. A word can have more than one morpheme.

> **Example:** *Unhappy* has two morphemes: the prefix *un-*, meaning not, and *happy*.

> **Example:** The word *steel* consists of only one morpheme.

Most of All, Almost

Most of all is a colloquial expression. Use *most of* or *almost* instead.

> **Incorrect:** We walked most of all the way.

> **Correct:** We walked most of the way.

> **Correct:** We walked almost all the way.

Motor, Engine

See *Engine, Motor.*

Mouse Terminology

When writing about the use of a computer mouse in procedures and instructions, follow these guidelines:

■ Use *pointer* or *mouse pointer* rather than *cursor.*

■ Do not use the plural of *mouse* (mice).

■ Use *mouse button* for the left mouse button.

■ Use *right mouse button* for accessing secondary menus.

■ Use *right-click* to mean clicking the right mouse button.

■ Hyphenate *double-click* and *right-click.*

■ Use *click,* not *click on.*

■ Use *drag* rather than *click and drag.*

■ Do not combine keyboard and mouse actions in the same sentence.

Multicolumn Lists

See *Lists.*

Myself, Me

See *I, Me, Myself.*

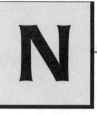

Names

See *Proper Nouns*.

Negative Adverbs

A **negative adverb** is used to create a negative meaning without using words like *no, not, neither, nor,* or *never.*

Negative adverbs include *barely, hardly, little, nowhere, rarely, scarcely,* and *seldom.*

Example: He seldom reads anymore.

Example: He hardly talks since the stroke.

Negative Formations

Just as not all plurals are made by adding *s* to a word, not all negatives are made by adding *un-* as a prefix.

There are many other ways to create negatives. Table 2.20 presents a list of common negative formation techniques.

Table 2.20 Common Negative Formation Techniques and Examples

	Meaning	Examples
a- or *an-* often used before words beginning with a vowel or *h*	lacking, without	amoral
		asexual
anti-	the opposite of	antibiotic
		antichrist
		antifreeze
		antimatter
counter-	the opposite of or contary to	counterclockwise
		counterculture
de-	the reverse of	decompose
		de-emphasize
		deforestation
		demagnetize
dis-	the reverse of	disarm
		discontented
		disrespectful
dys-	abnormal or impaired	dysfunctional
		dyspeptic
-free	without	caffeine-free
		crime-free
		sugar-free
-less	without	helpless
		motionless
		shoeless

(continues)

Table 2.20 (*continued*)

	Meaning	Examples
mal-	bad or incorrect	malformed
		malfunctioning
mis-	bad or incorrect	misfortune
		misinterpret
		misuse
non-	reverse of meaning	nonexistent
		nonfattening
		nonintoxicating
un-, in-, il-, im-, ir-	reverse of meaning	undressed
		undrinkable
		incapable
		illegitimate
		imbalance
		implausible
		irrefutable
		irrevocable

Negative Pronouns

Negative pronouns are used in negative noun phrases: *no one, nobody, neither, none,* and *nothing.*

Neither, Either

See *Either, Neither.*

Neologism

Neologism is a process where new words come into the English language from various sources, such as mass media, technology, other languages, and even slang.

Example: CD, PC, Internet, superhighway, shareware, going postal

Never

Never means never; it does not refer to a limited period of time.

Incorrect: We never saw your dog since yesterday.

Correct: We have not seen your dog since yesterday.

Correct: We never saw your dog. What breed was he?

Nominal Adjectives

Nominal adjectives act as both nouns and adjectives, and they are used to denote a class of people or things. They are preceded by a determiner (*the*) and can be modified by adjectives.

Example: the poor, the hungry, the sick, the blind

Nominal adjectives are also words that describe concepts.

Example: the opposite, the contrary, the good

Nominal adjectives reference certain nationalities.

Example: the French, the British, the Japanese

Comparative and superlative forms can be nominal adjectives.

Example: the greatest of these, the elder of the two

Nominative Absolutes

Nominative absolutes are a phrase consisting of a noun or pronoun, a participle, and any related modifiers. Nominative absolutes are also called **absolute phrases**.

Absolute phrases modify an entire sentence. They often appear as parenthetical elements that are set apart from the rest of the sentence by a pair of commas or by a dash or a pair of dashes.

Example: <u>The workday nearly finished</u> [nominative absolute], the programmers slowly began shutting down their PCs for the day.

Example: The authors signed autographs through the lunch hour, <u>their pens scribbling madly.</u>

Example: <u>Having been top performers for their entire careers,</u> the sales team was not surprised by the honors they received.

Noun phrases can also exist as absolute phrases.

Example: Then there was my college friend Mike—<u>the party animal</u> [noun phrase]—now a respected member of the legal profession.

Nominative Case

See *Case*.

Nominative Possessive

Nominative possessives are pronouns like *mine, yours, ours,* and *theirs.*

Example: Mine is a better dog than yours.

Noncount Nouns

See *Mass Nouns*.

Nondefining Relative Clause

A **nondefining relative clause** provides additional information about a noun or noun phrase. Nondefining relative clauses are separated from the rest of the sentence by commas.

> **Example:** My psychologist brother, <u>who lives in Nashville</u> [nondefining relative clause], is coming into town for the holidays.

Who and *whose* are used to refer to people.

Which and *whose* are used to refer to things.

That can't be used in a nondefining relative clause.

Nonfinite Verbs

Unlike finite verbs, **nonfinite verbs** have no tense, person, or singular and plural forms. Nonfinite verbs are called *verbals*.

There are three types of verbals:

- **Infinitives** are the *to* form of the verb.

> **Example:** to walk, to talk, to see, to jump

- **Participles** act as adjectives or as the main verbs in a verb phrase.

> **Example:** He put on a pair of <u>running</u> [participle acting as an adjective] shoes.

> **Example:** He knew he would <u>have to run</u> [verb phrase] to catch the bus. [verb phrase]

■ **Gerunds** are the *-ing* form of the verb and are used as nouns.

Example: <u>Walking</u> [gerund serving as a noun] is great for your health.

A clause needs a finite verb to serve as a predicate; therefore, nonfinite verbs can't serve as predicates.

Noninherent Adjectives

See *Inherent and Noninherent Adjectives.*

Nonrestrictive Clauses

Nonrestrictive clauses do not provide any essential information to a sentence and can be removed without changing the meaning of the sentence. They are often set apart from the rest of the sentence by a comma or pair of commas (if in the middle of the sentence).

Example: Doctor Early, <u>who lives in the same neighborhood as my friends Bill and Kathy</u> [nonrestrictive clause], is my mother's doctor.

Notices

Special **notices** highlight information that readers need to understand key points, avoid injuries or death, or prevent equipment damage when following procedures.

Five main types of notices are used in business writing:

1. Caution—to warn readers about damage to equipment, software, or problems with a particular outcome

2. Danger—to warn readers about possible fatal injuries to themselves or others

3. Note—to emphasize points, to serve as a reminder, or to point out minor problems

4. Warning—to warn readers about possible minor injuries

5. Tip—to help readers apply useful techniques or to point out benefits or capabilities

Consider the following tips when using notices:

- Place notices within the text where they are needed.

- Avoid all caps for special notices (except for *DANGER*).

Formatting for a special notice includes:

- Type the word (*Caution, Danger, Note,* or *Warning*), followed by a colon.

- Use bold font for the word *Caution, Danger, Note,* or *Warning*.

- Use your regular text font for the body of the special notice.

- Skip one space after the colon and begin typing the special notice.

- Single-space the text within the special notice.

- Skip one line above and below the special notice.

- Align the special notice with the text to which it refers.

- Use a numbered list for multiple special notices.

For special notices involving danger, enhance the formatting to include:

- *DANGER* in all capital letters.

- Setting the text of the special notice message in boldface.

- Drawing a box around the danger message.

Noun Case

Noun case tells you the role of a noun in a sentence:

- Subject

  Example: <u>The basketball player</u> jumped very high.

- Object

  Example: She selected a <u>paintbrush</u>.

■ Possessive (usually requiring an apostrophe and the letter *s* or *es*)

Example: The <u>policeman's</u> uniform was blue.

Noun Clause

A **noun clause** is a group of words that act like a noun in a sentence. A noun clause contains a subject and a verb.

Example: <u>What she said about Alex</u> was misunderstood.

Noun Phrase

A noun with several modifiers can act as a single noun in the form of a **noun phrase**. A phrase is a group of related words that does not include a subject and verb. If a subject and verb are present, the combination is a **clause**. A noun phrase includes a noun and its modifiers.

Example: college football team, extremely long hair, international bond fund, the tall dark man

The modifiers included in the noun phrase can be any of the following:

■ Adjectives

Example: <u>tall dark</u> man

■ Participial phrase

Example: the bushes <u>bordering the edge of the sidewalk</u>

■ Infinitive phrase

Example: the first woman <u>to fly around the world</u>

- Modifying clause

  Example: the mistakes <u>he had made the day before</u>

- Prepositional phrase

  Example: the trail next to the lake, <u>over by the dam</u>

Usually all the words in a noun phrase are together; however, occasionally they can be broken up into what is called a **discontinuous noun phrase**.

  Example: <u>Several burglaries</u> have been reported <u>involving people who were gone for the weekend.</u>

There is nothing wrong with a discontinuous noun phrase. It is sometimes useful for balancing a subject and predicate. Otherwise, the result can be a ten-word subject and a three-word verb.

A common problem to avoid is a long string of compound noun phrases. This often happens when the string also involves a group of compound nouns, such as *student body, book cover,* or *meeting place*. If you put together a long string of these phrases, the sentence can be very difficult to read.

  Example: The office supply store's computer section offered printer cartridges, inkjet printers, laser printers, desktop computers, laptop computers, hard drives, interface cards, and network routers.

An addressed person's name or substitute name is called a **vocative**. Vocatives sometimes take the form of a noun phrase. A vocative is treated as a parenthetical element and is set apart from the rest of the sentence by a pair of commas, if it appears in the flow of a sentence. You do not need to add commas every time someone's name is mentioned in a sentence. Commas are used only when the name refers to someone being addressed in the sentence.

  Example: Lieutenant, get those men moving.

There are four types of vocatives:

- Single names, with or without a title

■ The personal pronoun *you*

■ Appellatives of endearment, such as *darling, my dear, sweetheart,* and *sir*

■ Nominal clauses

Example: Whoever is singing, stop it now.

Noun Plurals

Normally, you can form the plural of a noun by adding *s*.

Example: Wilson, Wilsons

When the noun already ends in *s*, add *es*.

Example: file, files; desk, desks; lens, lenses

These rules apply to proper names as well as to common nouns.

Example: Jones, Joneses

Form the plural of a number by adding an *s* without an apostrophe.

Example: the 1990s

Avoid adding (*s*) to words so they can be interpreted as singular or plural.

Incorrect: Please keep your dog(s) on a leash.

Nouns

Nouns name a person, place, or thing. Nouns tell you who or what. There are several different types of nouns:

- **Proper nouns** name a specific person, place, or thing and are capitalized.

  Example: Jim, Alice, Canada

- **Nouns of address** are words used as someone's name.

  Example: Judge, Colonel, Mom

- **Common nouns** do not name a specific person, place, or thing.

  Example: candy, wool, tree

- **Countable nouns** are used for counting.

  Example: ten dollars, two dozen, fifty states

- **Mass nouns** refer to things that cannot be counted.

  Example: air, water

- **Collective nouns** are used to name groups of people or things.

  Example: class, fans, team

- **Abstract nouns** name intangible things.

  Example: hope, love, peace, war

- **Compound nouns** are composed of groups of words. See *Compound Nouns*.

- **Gerunds** are formed from a verb by adding *-ing*. See *Gerunds*.

Nouns of Address

See *Nouns*.

Number Abbreviations

See *Abbreviations for Numbers*.

Numbered List

A **numbered list** is an indented vertical list that is numbered. Numbered lists are useful for sequential steps in a procedure. Use these guidelines when creating a numbered list:

■ Introduce the list with a lead-in sentence.

■ Type the number followed by a period.

■ Use sentence-style capitalization.

■ Indent additional lines under the text rather than under the number.

■ Use regular line spacing for the list.

■ Indent the list items three to five spaces.

■ Punctuate the list items if they are complete sentences.

■ Avoid numbered lists with more than eight to ten items.

■ Break long lists into smaller ones if necessary.

■ Omit articles (*a, an, the*) from the beginning of list items.

Numbers or Words

Generally, numbers under 10 are spelled out, and numbers 10 and over are shown in figures. The only variation to this rule is when writing about a person's age. Then it is more accepted to write out ages. The more formal the text, the greater is the tendency to express the number in words.

Printed Text and Prose Text

In printed text, a number used for comparison with other numbers in the same section should be in numerical form.

Example: An excavation of 500 feet can be finished as rapidly as 200 feet if the right equipment is used.

At the Beginning of a Sentence

A number appearing at the beginning of a sentence, if it can be expressed in one or two words, should be spelled out.

Correct: Sixteen new cars were delivered.

Correct: Thirty or forty bushels were needed.

Incorrect: 2,746,892 copies were purchased.

Correct: They purchased 2,746,892 copies.

Legal Documents

In legal documents and in papers that transfer land title, numbers are written in both words and figures to prevent misunderstanding.

Example: West thirty (30) feet of Lot Nine (9) in Block Four (4)

Round Numbers

Approximate round numbers are spelled out.

Example: The station is about fifty blocks away.

Example: He found nearly two thousand dollars.

Sets of Numbers

To differentiate two sets of numbers occurring in the same sentence, use words for one and figures for the other.

Example: Three of the men drove 2,000 miles each; four drove 3,000 miles each; and only one drove the complete 5,000 miles.

If the sentence cannot be rewritten, use a comma or dash to separate the numbers.

Example: During the year 1992, 20 million people visited the park.

Example: We received 1,213—113 of which we couldn't use.

Large Numbers

If large numbers can be written in one or two words, do so.

Example: four hundred, five million, two billion

Use the short form for writing numbers over a thousand not pertaining to money.

Example: fourteen hundred [*not* one thousand four hundred]

Large, even amounts may combine figures and words.

Example: production of 37 million paper clips, a budget of $146 billion

If a number or the word *several* precedes *hundred, thousand, million, billion,* and so on, the singular form is used. After *many,* the plural form and *of* are used.

Example: six hundred pages, several million years, many hundreds of pages

Separating Digits

All numbers above 999 are written with commas to separate every group of three digits, counting from the units place.

Example: 1,001, 123,000, 1,436,936

Exceptions: Commas are omitted in long decimal fractions, page numbers, addresses, telephone numbers, room numbers, and form numbers.

Example: 0.10356, page 3487, 1467 Wilshire Boulevard, 201-555-9088, Room 2630, Form 2317-A

Commas are also omitted in four-digit year numbers, but they are added for years with five or more digits.

Example: The company began in 1992.

Example: The pottery shards were dated at about 14,000 B.C.

Example: This science fiction novel takes place in the year 27,345 A.D.

Patent numbers are written with commas.

Example: Patent No. 3,436,987

Serial and policy numbers are written without commas.

Example: Motor Number 245889954, Policy Number 894566

Object

The **object** is the part of a sentence that receives action.

Example: He threw the ball [direct object].

An **object complement** renames or describes a direct object.

Example: He named his monkey [direct object], Meep [object complement].

An **indirect object** identifies to what or to whom the action of a verb is directed.

Example: He sold me [indirect object] his car [direct object].

The word *me*—along with other pronouns such as *him, us,* and *them*—is not always an indirect object; it can also serve as a direct object.

Example: Save me!

Object Complement

See *Complements*.

Objective Case

See *Subjective Case*.

Off

Off is always used alone and not with *of*.

Incorrect: The ribbon was taken off of the package.

Correct: The ribbon was taken off the package.

Offline

See *Online, Offline*.

On Account of

Avoid this phrase and use *because* instead.

One

One can be a determiner, adjective, or pronoun.

■ Determiner—used before a proper noun to designate a particular person

Example: On September 1, did you make a phone call at 3:00 P.M. to one Horace Wauson?

■ Adjective—used to modify the number of a noun

Example: I'll have just one more piece of chicken.

■ Pronoun—used as numerical expression or to stand in for the speaker or a generic average person

Example: One of the students will volunteer.

Example: If one tries hard enough, one can be anything.

The possessive form of *one* is *one's*.

> **Example:** One must learn from one's mistakes.

In the United States, *one's* is often replaced by *his, her,* or *your.*

> **Example:** One must learn from his mistakes.

The reflexive form of *one* is *oneself.*

> **Example:** If one skips lunch, one will find oneself very hungry by dinner.

The plural of *one* is *ones.*

> **Example:** Which ones do you want?

One Another, Each Other

See *Each Other, One Another.*

Online, Offline

Online and *offline* are commonly written as one word, unless being used as an adverbial phrase.

> **Example:** Is the printer online or offline?

> **Example:** Mr. Smith used the computer at the library to go on line.

Only

Be careful of where you place this adverb; its position determines which word it modifies.

Incorrect: I could only get him to play one piece.

Correct: I could get him to play only one piece.

Onomatopoeia

Onomatopoeia is a term used to describe words that suggest the sound being described.

Example: bang, bash, clang, clap, crackle, fizz, growl, honk, knock, mumble, ouch, plop, rattle, screech, smack, sniff, splash, thud, tinkle, twang, tweet, whizz

Open

Open should be used without *up*.

Incorrect: We open up the doors promptly at noon.

Correct: We open the doors promptly at noon.

Open Compounds

See *Compound Words*.

Ordinal Numbers

Ordinal numbers describe the order or sequence of something.

Example: first, 2nd, third, fourth, 50th

Ordinal numbers can be written as words or abbreviations.

Example: 1st, first; 2nd, second; 3rd, third

Ordinal numbers usually appear before a noun.

Example: It was my parents' 60th wedding anniversary.

Over, More Than

See *More than, Over.*

Oxford Comma

When listing a series of items in a sentence, a comma is inserted between each item, and a final comma is inserted before the word *and* and the last item. The last comma is called a "serial comma" or **Oxford comma**. Oxford commas are optional but recommended.

Oxymoron

An **oxymoron** is a figure of speech that occurs when two terms that appear to contradict themselves are combined.

Example: minor crisis, alone together, living dead, original copies, pretty ugly, definite maybe, rolling stop
---

Page Breaks

Page breaks can be manually inserted into a document; however, they should not be added until all illustrations have been added and the document is ready for final delivery. When determining page breaks, consider the following tips:

- The goal is to keep related content together on the same page.

- New paragraphs that start at the bottom of a page should have at least two lines of text; otherwise they should be moved to the next page.

- A bulleted list that starts at the bottom of a page should have the lead-in sentence and at least two items in the list; otherwise it should be moved to the next page.

Avoid page breaks in the following situations:

- In the middle of a note, tip, caution, or warning message

- In the middle of a table

- In long tables (if they must spread over several pages, repeat the table title and heading when pages break from right to left)

- When separating content from any illustrations

Page Numbering

For all **page numbering**, use figures to show the numbers. Commas are not used in page numbers greater than 999.

Page Number Formats

On legal documents, a page number is centered at the bottom of each page; on other papers, it is usually shown at the top.

Manuscripts and briefs are numbered in the upper right corner; papers that are to be bound at the left are numbered in the lower right corner. In each case, all numbers should appear at exactly the same place on all pages in a document.

Title pages are not numbered. A first page of a work or of a chapter is not marked with a number, although the numbering of the following pages takes into consideration the number of the first page.

It is acceptable to use a hyphen before and after the page number (-3-) without a period.

Never use quotation marks around a page number, and never type the word *page* before the number.

Palindromes

Words or phrases that are spelled the same forward or backward are **palindromes**.

Example: madam, mom, level

Paragraphs

A **paragraph** is a group of related sentences that focus on a single topic. When writing paragraphs, consider the following tips:

- Keep the paragraph confined to one idea.

- Focus all sentences on the single idea or provide supporting evidence or details regarding it.

- If the single points in a paragraph get too long, break them up into separate paragraphs.

Elements of a Paragraph

A well-written paragraph includes the following elements:

- Unity—The entire paragraph should have a single focus. If it begins with one focus, it should not end with another.

- Coherence—The paragraph should be easily understandable to the reader.

- Logical bridges—Carry the same topic from sentence to sentence. Construct successive sentences in a parallel form.

- Topic sentence—One sentence in the paragraph should indicate the focus of the paragraph. (A topic sentence can be anywhere in the paragraph.)

- Verbal bridges—Create coherence using verbal bridges.
    - Key words can be repeated in several sentences in the paragraph.
    - Synonymous words can be repeated in different sentences.
    - Pronouns can refer to nouns used in previous sentences.
    - Transitional words can be used to link ideas from previous sentences.

Paragraph Development

When writing a paragraph, consider the following tips:

- Introduce the topic using the topic sentence.

- Beware of paragraphs that have only two or three sentences.

To develop a paragraph, do the following:

- Use examples and illustrations.

- Provide details, statistics, and evidence.

- Provide quotes and paraphrases from other people.

- Tell a story.

- Define terms used in the paragraph.

- Compare and contrast ideas.

- Evaluate causes.

- Examine the effects.

- Offer a chronological summary.

When to Start a New Paragraph

You should start a new paragraph in the following situations:

- When you begin a new idea

- To contrast, debate, or point out the differences between ideas

- When readers need a pause

- When ending an introduction or starting the conclusion

Paragraph Transitions

Sentences that outline what a document has covered and where the rest of the document is going are called **signposts** or **transitions**. Transitional sentences lead from one idea to the next. They are often used at the end of a paragraph to help one paragraph flow into the next.

Parallel Construction

Parallel construction is a stylistic technique for organizing expressions of similar content to improve readability. This technique involves the removal of repetitive words and combining similar sentences and ideas.

> **Nonparallel example:** John talked with Mike. John talked with Mary. John talked with Leon.
>
> **Parallel example:** John talked with Mike, Mary, and Leon.

Parallel construction also applies to things such as headings and bulleted lists. Headings should be a consistent part of speech or type of clause. List items should begin with the same part of speech or tense.

Paraphrasing

Paraphrasing is your own version of someone else's ideas and information. Paraphrasing allows you to use research and other resources without plagiarizing (as long as sources are cited in the document). Paraphrasing allows you to avoid quoting and gives you control over the writing style of your document.

To effectively paraphrase, do the following:

- Read and reread the original content until you fully understand it.

- Take notes.

- Set aside the original and write your paraphrased version.

- Compare your version to the original to make sure your version accurately expresses the idea or information.

- Use quotation marks to identify anything you have quoted verbatim from the original.

- Include the source in your notes to cite in your final document.

Parentheses

Parentheses are used to enclose matter that is introduced by way of explanation.

Example: If the lessor (the person owning the property) agrees, the lessee (the person renting the property) may have a dog on the premises.

Parentheses are used to enclose figures that enumerate items.

Example: The book contained chapters on (1) capitalization, (2) spelling rules, (3) troublesome verbs, and (4) punctuation.

Parentheses are also used to enclose citations of authority.

Example: The definition of action is "the process or state of being active" (*American College Dictionary*).

Parentheses are used to enclose figures repeated for clarity, as in legal documents:

Example: He was willed five thousand dollars ($5,000) by his uncle.

Example: You will be paid twenty (20) percent interest.

Parenthetical Elements

Nonessential information that is added to a sentence is called a **parenthetical element**. A parenthetical element is usually set apart from the main text by a comma or a pair of commas.

Example: The Lake Texoma bridge, <u>which connects Durant to Kingston</u> [parenthetical element], was originally designed by my grandfather.

Participle

A **participle** is a verb that acts like an adjective.

Example: The <u>running</u> dog chased the <u>speeding</u> [participles] car.

A **present participle** describes a present condition, while a past participle describes something that has already happened.

Example: Moses saw the <u>burning</u> [present participle] bush.

Example: The <u>burned</u> [past participle] tree fell down in the storm.

Participial Phrase

Present participles (verbals ending in -*ing*), past participles (verbals ending in -*ed*), or other irregular verbs can be combined with complements and modifiers to create a **participial phrase**. Participial phrases always act as adjectives. When they begin a sentence, they are set apart by a comma just like an introductory modifier. If they appear within the sentence, they are set apart with a pair of commas.

Example: <u>Working around the clock</u> [participial phrase], the workers repaired the airport runway in less than a week. The concrete, <u>having been damaged by the crash landing of the airliner,</u> needed to be replaced.

Parts of Speech

The eight parts of speech are:

- Nouns
- Verbs
- Adjectives
- Adverbs

- Pronouns
- Prepositions
- Conjunctions
- Interjections or determiners

Party

Party can be used to refer to a person in legal documents, but the word is too formal for common use. A party can also be a celebration.

Incorrect: The party I called was disturbed.

Correct: The person I called was disturbed.

Correct (in legal documents): The party of the second part hereby agrees …

Correct: He celebrated his birthday with a party.

Passed, Past

When referring to a period of time or distance, use *past*.

Example: We've always had good luck on these types of projects in the past.

When referring to movement, use *passed*.

Example: ABC just passed us to become number one in our market.

Passive Voice

Verbs can be either **active** or **passive** in voice. In the active voice, the subject is the do-er or be-er, and the verb describes an action. See *Active Voice*.

Example: The student <u>used</u> the computer.

In the passive voice, the subject is not a do-er or be-er. Instead, the subject is being acted on by something else.

Example: The computer <u>was used</u> by the student.

The passive voice has its uses. When it is more important to draw attention to the person or thing that was acted on, the passive voice can be used.

Example: Several quality control errors were made last month by <u>the third shift</u>.

The passive voice is also appropriate when the subject is not important.

Example: <u>The football tickets</u> can be picked up at the Will Call window.

The passive voice is sometimes required for technical writing, where the do-er or be-er can be anyone, and the process being described is more important.

Example of when the subject is not important: We developed a hard drive that can store several terabytes of data.

Example of emphasis on the process: A hard drive has been developed that can store several terabytes of data.

The passive voice is created by combining a form of the *to be* verb with the past participle of the main verb. Only transitive verbs (those that have objects) can be transformed into the passive voice. Some transitive verbs cannot be transformed into passive voice, such as *to have*.

Example in active voice: She has a new computer.

Example in passive voice: A new computer is had by her.

Other verbs that cannot be used with the passive voice are *resemble, look like, equal, agree with, mean, contain, hold, comprise, lack, suit, fit,* and *become*.

Past Perfect Progressive Tense

Past perfect progressive or **past perfect continuous** is used to describe events that were not finished when another event occurred. It is formed using *have been + -ing*.

Example: In November, I'll <u>have been living</u> [past perfect progressive] here for twenty-two years.

Past Perfect Tense

The **past perfect tense** is used to describe events that happened before another event or time period. Past perfect tense is formed using the verb *had* plus the past participle.

Example: After he was hired, we <u>had hoped</u> [past perfect] he would be a great leader.

An old term for past perfect tense is **pluperfect**.

Past Progressive Tense

Past progressive is used to describe events that were happening at some point in the past. Past progressive is used to indicate that something took place while something else was happening. It is formed using the past simple tense of *to be + -ing*.

Example: I <u>was eating</u> [past progressive] dinner, when the telemarketer called.

Past Simple Tense

Past simple tense is used to describe events that occurred in the past. Past simple tense is formed by adding *-ed* to the base form of regular verbs or *-d* if the verb already ends in *e*.

Example: I <u>liked</u> the play.

Example: I <u>walked</u> around the neighborhood this morning.

Irregular verbs change form to make past simple tense.

Example: I <u>ate</u> dinner after returning last evening.

People

People refers to a large group of individuals. When referring to people of a particular organization or place, it's better to use *people* before the name.

Incorrect: The General Motors people.

Correct: the people of General Motors, the people of Massachusetts

Per

Avoid using *per* and instead use *according to*.

Incorrect: The report was created per the manager's instructions.

Correct: The report was created according to the manager's instructions.

Percent

This is one word following an amount, never *per cent*.

Correct: Six percent interest was charged.

Percentage

Consider the following rules when using *percentage* or percentage signs in your writing:

- Use *percentage* when no amount is given.

  Example: What percentage of interest was charged?

- The numeral is retained whether or not a percentage sign is used.

  Example: 5% price reduction

  Example: loss of 10 percent

  Example: almost 30 percent of the population

- For percentages in succession, use the sign after each numeral.

  Example: 30% to 50%; 6%, 8%, and 10%

Perfect Aspect

The **perfect aspect** tense is used to describe completed events that are currently relevant or were relevant at a specific time. It is formed using the verb *to have* plus the past participle.

  Example: He has worked on my team for sixteen years.

Perfect Infinitive

See *Infinitives*.

Perfect Tense

Perfect tense is a category of tenses that includes:

- **Past perfect**—*had* + past participle.

- **Present perfect**—*have* + past participle.

- **Future perfect**—*will have* + past participle.

- **Conditional perfect**—*would have* + past participle.

Period

A **period** is used at the end of a declarative sentence to denote a full pause:

Example: I am going to town. You may go with me if you wish.

Use a period, not a question mark, when the sentence contains an indirect question.

Example: He could not understand why she was leaving.

Also use a period for a request phrased as a question.

Example: Will you please return the diskette when you are finished.

The period is used in decimals to separate a whole number from a decimal fraction.

Example: 5.6 percent, $19.50

A period is also used in abbreviations.

Example: Mrs., Ph.D., etc.

Person

Person involves the use of pronouns used as subjects of a sentence or clause. Categories of person include:

- First person singular—The subject is the writer or speaker.

- First person plural—The writer is part of a group that is the subject.

- Second person singular—The subject is the reader or listener.

- Second person plural—The audience is the subject.

- Third person singular—Someone else, a third person, is the subject.

- Third personal plural—The subject is a group that does not include the writer or the reader.

Personal Pronouns

Personal pronouns change form, or **case**, according to their use in a sentence. Consider the following guidelines:

- The pronoun *I* is used as the subject of a sentence.

  Example: I am tall.

- The pronoun *me* is used as an object in various ways.

  Example: He gave me a bonus.

- The pronoun *my* is used for the possessive form.

  Example: That's my password.

The same is true for other personal pronouns: the singular *you* and *he/she/it* and the plurals *we, you,* and *they.*

Table 2.21 shows the various cases for pronouns.

Table 2.21 Cases for Pronouns

	Subjective	Possessive	Objective
Singular first person	I	my, mine	me
Singular second person	you	your, yours	you
Singular third person	he, she, it	his, her, hers, its	him, her, it
Plural first person	we	our, ours	us
Plural second person	you	your, yours	you
Plural third person	they	their, theirs	them
Relative and interrogative pronouns	who, whoever, which, that, what	whose	whom, whomever which, that, what
Indefinite pronouns	everybody	everybody's	everybody

When a personal pronoun is connected by a conjunction to another noun or pronoun, it does not change case.

> **Example:** I am taking a course in PowerPoint. John and I are taking a course in PowerPoint. (Note in the second sentence that *John* is listed before *I*.)

The same is true when the object form is used.

> **Example:** The instructor gave the PowerPoint User Guide to me. The instructor gave the PowerPoint User Guide to John and me.

When a pronoun and a noun are combined, you must choose the case of the pronoun that would be appropriate if the noun were not there.

> **Example:** <u>We</u> teachers are demanding a raise.

With the second person, there's not as much confusion because the pronoun *you* is the same for both subject and object form.

Example: <u>You</u> teachers are demanding too much money.

Among the possessive pronoun forms are nominative possessives such as *mine, yours, ours,* and *theirs*.

Example: This new house is mine. Look at those houses. Theirs needs work. Ours is in good shape. Mine is newer than yours.

Personification

Giving human feelings and characteristics to nonliving things is a figure of speech called **personification**.

Example: My computer hates me.

Persuade, Convince

See *Convince, Persuade*.

Phase, Faze

See *Faze, Phase*.

Phatic Speech

Phatic speech involves words or phrases that are used in social settings to be polite rather than to be taken literally. Phatic speech is conversational informal speech.

Example: How are you doing? Fine, how are you? Thank you. You're welcome.

Phrasal Verbs

Phrasal verbs consist of a verb along with another word or phrase. The word that is joined with the verb is a **particle**.

Phrasal verbs often include a preposition and are used for casual and conversational phrases.

Example: The carpenters were <u>sitting around</u> eating lunch.

Example: He <u>looked up</u> his old customers in the database.

Phrasal verbs are often unclear. Avoid using them in business writing.

Phrases

Phrases are groups of words that do not include a subject and verb. A **clause** is a group of words that includes a subject and verb. The types of phrases are:

- **Noun phrases**—a noun and its modifiers

  Example: He ran briskly down <u>the zigzagging path.</u>

- **Prepositional phrase**—a preposition, a noun or pronoun, and sometimes an adjective

  Example: <u>On this side of the street,</u> there are no sidewalks.

- **Appositive phrase**—renaming a preceding word

  Example: My favorite football player, <u>a Heisman Trophy winner and number one draft pick,</u> played in three Super Bowl games.

- **Absolute phrase**—a noun or pronoun, a participle, and modifiers

  Example: <u>Their backpacks bulging with supplies,</u> the students waited at the bus stop on the first day of school.

- **Infinitive phrase**—an infinitive and any modifiers or complements

  Example: <u>His plan to write a little each day</u> resulted in a finished manuscript by the end of November.

- **Gerund phrase**—verbals that end in *-ing* that act like nouns along with modifiers or complements

  Example: Mike enjoyed playing the guitar <u>in the echoing hallway.</u>

- **Participial phrase**—verbals combined with complements and modifiers that act as adjectives

  Example: The house, <u>vacant since late last year,</u> is now slowly falling apart.

Phrases and Words to Omit

Table 2.22 presents a list of words that are usually not necessary in a sentence.

Table 2.22 Unnecessary Words

all things considered	as a matter of fact
as far as I'm concerned	at the present time
because of the fact that	by means of
by virtue of the fact	due to the fact
extremely	for all intents and purposes
for the most part	for the purpose of
have a tendency to	in a manner of speaking
in a very real sense	in my opinion
in the case of	in the event that
in the final analysis	in the nature of

(continues)

Table 2.22 *(continued)*

in the process of	it seems that
quite	really
severely	the point I am trying to make
type of	very
what I mean to say is	

Pidgin

Pidgin is a type of simple language that develops when people who do not speak the same language are required to communicate in order to live or work together.

Plagiarism

The use of written or spoken material including paragraphs, sentences, art-work, or research statistics without providing credit is called **plagiarism**.

Plagiarism can be avoided by paraphrasing and rewriting and by providing credit in the form of sources or acknowledgments.

Sources for quotes, facts, or research can be cited immediately after a bor-rowed statement or idea.

Example: See *Documenting Sources* in Section 1: The Writing Process

Pleonasm

Using more words than are really necessary or using redundant words or phrases is a stylistic problem called **pleonasm**. Pleonasm weakens a docu-ment and is distracting to readers.

Pluperfect

See *Past Perfect Tense*.

Plurals

The general rule is to form the plural of a noun by adding *s*.

Example: book, books; clock, clocks; pen, pens

A noun ending in *o* preceded by a vowel takes an *s* for the plural.

Example: curio, curios; folio, folios; radio, radios; ratio, ratios; studio, studios

Some nouns ending in *o*, preceded by a consonant, take *es* to form the plural, whereas others take *s*.

Example: banjo, banjos; buffalo, buffaloes; cargo, cargoes; Eskimo, Eskimos; hero, heroes; mosquito, mosquitoes; motto, mottoes; piano, pianos; potato, potatoes; soprano, sopranos; tomato, tomatoes

A singular noun ending in *ch, sh, s, x,* or *z* takes *es* for the plural.

Example: bush, bushes; chintz, chintzes; dress, dresses; inch, inches; wax, waxes

For a noun ending in *y* preceded by a consonant, the *y* changes to *i* and *es* is added for the plural.

Example: ability, abilities; auxiliary, auxiliaries; discrepancy, discrepancies; facility, facilities; industry, industries; lady, ladies; society, societies

A noun ending in *y* preceded by a vowel takes only an *s* for the plural.

Example: attorney, attorneys; galley, galleys; kidney, kidneys; monkey, monkeys; turkey, turkeys

Some plurals end in *en*.

Example: child, children; man, men; ox, oxen

For some nouns ending in *f* or *fe*, change the *f* or *fe* to *v* and add *es* for the plural.

> **Example:** calf, calves; knife, knives; leaf, leaves; life, lives; loaf, loaves; shelf, shelves

There are some exceptions.

> **Example:** bailiff, bailiffs; belief, beliefs; chief, chiefs; gulf, gulfs; roof, roofs

Some nouns require a vowel change for the plural.

> **Example:** foot, feet; goose, geese; mouse, mice; tooth, teeth

The plurals of numerals, signs, and letters are shown by adding an *s* (or *'s* to avoid confusion).

> **Example:** one B, four B's

For proper names ending in *s* or in an *s* sound, add *es* for the plural.

> **Example:** Brooks, the Brookses; Burns, the Burnses; Jones, the Joneses

A compound noun, when hyphenated or when consisting of two separate words, forms the plural form in the most important element.

> **Example:** attorney-general, attorneys-general; brigadier general, brigadier generals; brother-in-law, brothers-in-law; notary public, notaries public; passer-by, passersby

The plural of solid compounds (a compound noun written as one word) is formed at the end of the solid compound.

> **Example:** bookshelf, bookshelves; cupful, cupfuls; lumberman, lumbermen; stepchild, stepchildren; stepdaughter, stepdaughters

Some nouns have the same form for singular and plural.

Example: Chinese, corps, deer, salmon, sheep, vermin, wheat

Some nouns are always treated as singular.

Example: civics, mathematics, measles, milk, molasses, music, news, statistics

Some nouns are always treated as plural.

Example: pants, proceeds, remains, riches, scissors, thanks, trousers, tweezers

Plurals of Numbers

Form the plural of a numeral or other character by adding *s* or *es* to the word. If the number is a figure, use *s* or *es* depending on office policy.

Example: 5s and 6s or 5's and 6's or fives and sixes; the 1890s or the 1890's; MD88s OR MD88's

Plus

Avoid using *plus* as a conjunction. Instead use *and*.

Incorrect: We finished the market research on schedule, plus we discovered some new opportunities in the process.

Correct: We finished the market research on schedule, and we discovered some new opportunities in the process.

P.M.

See *A.M., P.M.*

Point in Time

Avoid this term in your writing and instead use *at this time, at this point*, or *now*.

Incorrect: At this point in time, everything seems to be working smoothly on the assembly line.

Correct: At this time, everything seems to be working smoothly on the assembly line.

Polyptoton

A **polyptoton** is a figure of speech that occurs when two words from the same root word are repeated. Polyptotons are used for stylistic emphasis.

Example: "Not as a call to <u>battle</u>, though <u>embattled</u> we are."
—John F. Kennedy

Polyseme

A word with at least two related meanings is a **polyseme**.

Example: milk [the noun *milk* and the verb *to milk*], bank [the noun *bank* and the verb *to bank*]

Polysyllabic

A word with three or more syllables is **polysyllabic**.

Example: January, wonderful, important

Possessive Adjectives

Possessive adjectives are words that are used before nouns to show ownership of the noun.

Example: his, her, its, my, our, their, yours

Example: That's his motorcycle.

Possessive Case

See *Case*.

Possessive Pronouns

Possessive pronouns are words that are used in place of a noun to show ownership.

Example: his, hers, its, mine, ours, theirs, yours

Example: Which one is your car? That one is mine.

Possessives

Consider the following guidelines when creating possessive forms:

■ Add *'s* to a singular noun to show possession. This rule applies also to nouns that end in *s*.

Example: Mike's car, a day's wage, Charles's plans

■ Add an apostrophe to the end of a pluralized family name to show possession.

Example: the Smiths' house

■ To show possession for inanimate objects, it may be best to rewrite.

Example: "The house's doors" might be rewritten as "the doors of the house."

■ For compound nouns, apostrophe placement determines which nouns show possession.

Example: Jeff's and Cathy's dogs are in the backyard. [Each person has at least one dog.]

Example: Jeff and Cathy's dogs are in the backyard. [Jeff and Cathy share ownership of the dogs.]

■ For a sentence where an appositive follows a possessive noun and renames or explains the noun, add the apostrophe to the appositive instead of the noun.

Example: We need to get Dr. Early, the family doctor's advice.

Posted, Informed

Don't use *posted* in place of *informed*.

Incorrect: You are well posted on the subject.

Correct: You are well informed about Australia.

Postmodifer

A modifier that appears in a sentence after the word it modifies is called a **postmodifier**.

Example: She was the girl <u>selected</u> [postmodifier] for the study.

Precede, Proceed

To go before someone or something else is to *precede*.

Example: The girls preceded the boys in the line of march.

To go forward is to *proceed*.

Example: We proceeded toward the treeline.

Predeterminers

Predeterminers are words that appear before other determiners in a sentence. There are three types of predeterminers:

- Multipliers—double, three times, twice

  Example: Now that I'm self-employed, I'm making <u>twice</u> [multiplier] the income.

- Fractional expressions—half, one-third, three-quarters

  Example: <u>Two-thirds</u> [multiplier] of the class were recent immigrants to the United States.

- Intensifiers—quite, rather, such

  Example: His college apartment was <u>quite</u> [multiplier] a dump.

Predicates

Predicates are used to complete a sentence. The subject names the person, place, or thing that is doing something. A simple predicate consists of a verb, verb string, or a compound verb.

Example: The flower <u>bloomed</u> [predicate]. The flowers <u>have been blooming.</u>

A **compound predicate** consists of two or more predicates connected.

> **Example:** The mountain biker <u>began to ride down the trail</u> and <u>eventually entered one of the most beautiful valleys in the area.</u>

A **complete predicate** consists of a transitive verb and all modifiers and other words that complete its meaning.

> **Example:** The slowly moving thunderstorm <u>flashed lightning across the dark foreboding sky.</u>

A **predicate adjective** follows a linking verb and describes the subject of the sentence.

> **Example:** The minerals in the water taste <u>bad.</u>

A **predicate nominative** follows a linking verb and describes what the subject is.

> **Example:** Linda Wauson is <u>president</u> of the firm.

Preface

A **preface** is an introduction to a book written by the author to:

- Acknowledge help and assistance provided.

- Explain how the project was started and the origin of the idea for the book.

A **prologue** is similar to a preface, except that it introduces the book and is written in the voice of the book's text, rather than the author's first-person voice.

Prefixes

Prefixes are letters that are added before a word that modify the meaning. Some prefixes show a change in quantity from the original word.

Example: semiannual, kilometer, millimeter, bimonthly

Some prefixes show negation or the opposite of the original meaning of the word.

Example: illegal, invalid, misjudge, counterclockwise

Some prefixes show a change in time.

Example: postwar, preschool

Some prefixes show a change in direction or position.

Example: circumnavigate, recede, infrastructure

Premodifier

A modifier that is placed before the word it modifies is called a **premodifier**.

Example: That's a big [premodifier] report.

Premodifiers help define and describe the words they modify. The most common premodifiers are adjectives; however, nouns can also serve in this function.

Example: He responded to an angry [adjective] caller.

Example: He was a right-wing [noun] radio talk show host.

Prepositional Phrase

A **prepositional phrase** consists of a preposition, a noun or pronoun that serves as the object of the preposition, and an adjective or two that modifies the object.

Prepositional phrases usually tell us when or where something is happening.

Example: in a half hour, at the community center

A prepositional phrase used at the beginning of a sentence is called an **intro-ductory modifier**. You can set apart an introductory modifier with a comma; however, the comma is optional unless the introductory modifier is long.

Prepositions

Prepositions are used to describe relationships between other words in a sentence. Prepositions like *in, on,* or *between* are good examples because they describe the spatial nature of things.

Prepositions are almost always combined with other words to become prepositional phrases. Prepositional phrases consist of a preposition and a determiner, along with an adjective or two, followed by a pronoun or noun that is called the "object of the preposition."

Prepositions can be divided into types:

- Prepositions of time

- Prepositions of place

- Prepositions of location

- Prepositions of movement

Prepositions of Time: At, On, In, For, *and* Since

At, on, and *in* often serve as prepositions of time. We use *at* to designate specific times.

Example: Meet me at five o'clock.

We use *on* to designate days and dates.

Example: I work all day on Saturdays.

We use *in* for nonspecific times.

> **Example:** He likes to read in the evening.

The preposition *for* is used to measure time.

> **Example:** He worked for twenty years.

The preposition *since* is used with a specific date or time.

> **Example:** I have known him since January 2003.

Prepositions of Place: At, On, In

At, on, and *in* can also serve as prepositions of place. We use *at* for specific addresses.

> **Example:** I live at 5203 Legendary Lane.

We use *on* to designate streets.

> **Example:** I live on Legendary Lane.

We use *in* for the names of towns, states, and countries.

> **Example:** I live in Acworth.

Prepositions of Location: At, On, In

At, on, and *in* can be used as prepositions of location. Their usage is specific to certain places.

> **Example:** at class, at home, at the library, at the office, at school, at work

> **Example:** on the bed, on the ceiling, on the floor, on the horse, on the plane, on the train

Example: in the bed, in the bedroom, in the car, in the class, in the library, in the room, in the school

Prepositions of Movement: To, Toward

The preposition *to* is used to express movement to a place.

Example: I am driving to work.

Toward and *towards* are also used to express movement. They are both the same word with a spelling variation. Avoid using *towards* in business writing, since its usage is out of date.

Example: We were working toward a common goal.

Combinations

Some prepositions are so commonly used with particular nouns, adjectives, and verbs that they have almost become one word.

The following is a list of noun-and-preposition combinations:

- approval of
- awareness of
- belief in
- concern for
- confusion about
- desire for
- fondness for
- grasp of
- hatred of

- hope for
- interest in
- love of
- need for
- participation in
- reason for
- respect for
- success in
- understanding of

The following is a list of adjective-and-preposition combinations:

- afraid of
- angry at
- aware of
- capable of
- careless about
- familiar with
- fond of
- happy about
- interested in

- jealous of
- made of
- married to
- proud of
- similar to
- sorry for
- sure of
- tired of
- worried about

A combination of a verb and a preposition is called a **phrasal verb**. The word that is joined with the verb is called a **particle**. The following is a list of verb-and-preposition combinations:

- apologize for
- ask about
- ask for
- belong to
- bring up
- care for
- find out
- give up
- grow up
- look for
- look forward to

- look up
- make up
- pay for
- prepare for
- study for
- talk about
- think about
- trust in
- work for
- worry about

Present Infinitive

See *Infinitives.*

Present Participle

The **present participle** is a form of the verb *to be* that indicates ongoing action.

Example: I am <u>eating</u> [present participle].

Example: I am <u>talking.</u>

A present participle can also serve as an adjective in a sentence to modify a noun.

Example: She is an <u>amazing</u> person.

Present Perfect Tense

The **present perfect tense** is used for unfinished past actions, for actions where no time is specified, or when a past action is important now. It is formed by using the verb *have* + past participle.

Example: I <u>have lived</u> [present perfect] here for twenty years.

Example: <u>Have</u> you <u>seen</u> that new movie?

Example: I'<u>ve overslept</u> and <u>missed</u> my meeting.

Present Progressive Tense

The **present progressive tense** is used to describe how long something occurred in the past or for activities that started in the past and are still happening now. It is formed using the verbs *have* + *been* + present participle.

Example: I <u>have been waiting</u> [present progressive] here for you.

Present Simple Tense

The **present simple tense** is used to state facts or for regular repeated actions.

Example: I <u>like</u> [present simple] chocolate.

Example: I <u>go</u> to the factory at six.

Press, Type, Click, Strike, Hit, Select

When writing instructions for computer and software usage, use the following guidelines to describe keyboard actions:

■ Press—when a keyboard key interaction is needed to perform a particular function

Example: Press Y to continue.

Do not use *depress, strike, hit,* or *type* for these types of keyboard interactions.

■ Use—for navigation purposes with an arrow key or when multiple keys are pressed at the same time to initiate a command

Example: Use the arrow keys to move up or down in the document.

■ Type—when a user enters information that appears on the screen

Example: Type your user ID.

■ Click—when using the mouse to make a selection

Example: Click the File menu.

■ Select—when marking or highlighting text in a document, when adding checks to checkboxes, or when picking an item from a list

Example: Select the desired text, then click Copy.

Example: From the list of values, select your choice.

Previous

Avoid using *previous* as in "our previous discussion." Instead use *earlier.*

Incorrect: In our previous discussion, you mentioned you might be interested in ordering a new delivery truck.

Correct: Earlier, you mentioned you might be interested in ordering a new delivery truck.

Principal, Principle

Principal can be the person—someone who runs a school or an important person such as the owner of a business—or it can be the amount borrowed in a loan.

Example: The principal actors had their own private trailers on the movie set.

Principle is a code of conduct usually involving law or a doctrine.

Example: The conversation was about the principle of subsidiarity.

Problem Pronouns

Pronouns in the nominative case—*I, we, he, she, they*—serve as subjects of verbs but never as objects of verbs or prepositions.

You can often tell that the case is wrong because the sentence sounds odd; however, when compound subjects or compound objects are used, it may be difficult to "hear" the correct case.

To test such an instance, drop the other subject or object and repeat the sentence with only the pronoun in question.

I: *Nominative Case, Never an Object*

Incorrect: This is just between you and I.

Correct: This is just between you and me.

Incorrect: He asked that the money be given to you and I.

Test: He asked that the money be given to I.

Correct: He asked that the money be given to you and me.

Test: He asked that the money be given to me.

She, He: *Nominative Case, Never an Object*

Incorrect: If you stay there, the ball will hit you and she.

Test: If you stay there, the ball will hit she.

Correct: If you stay there, the ball will hit you and her.

Test: If you stay there, the ball will hit her.

They: *Nominative Case, Never an Object*

Incorrect: I will give the money to you and they.

Test: I will give the money to they.

Correct: I will give the money to you and them.

Test: I will give the money to them.

Incorrect: You and them are welcome to come.

Test: Them are welcome to come.

Correct: You and they are welcome to come.

Test: They are welcome to come.

We: *Nominative Case, Never an Object*

Incorrect: Us boys are ready to play the game.

Test: Us are ready to play the game.

Correct: We boys are ready to play the game.

Test: We are ready to play the game.

Me, Us, Her, Him, Them: *Objective Case, Never a Subject*

■ Pronouns in the objective case—*me, us, her, him, them*—are always used as objects of either verbs or prepositions, never as subjects.

■ With a compound object, use the same way of testing, changing the number of the verb as needed.

Incorrect: Jim and me went to the movies.

Test: Me went to the movies.

Correct: Jim and I went to the movies.

Test: I went to the movies.

Better: Jim went to the movies with me.

Incorrect: Julie and us sat on the top bleacher.

Test: Us sat on the top bleacher.

Correct: Julie and we sat on the top bleacher.

Test: We sat on the top bleacher.

Better: Julie sat on the top bleacher with us.

Incorrect: Tommy and her [him, us, them] argued every day.

Test: Her [him, us, them] argued every day.

Correct: Tommy and she [he, we, they] argued every day.

Proceed, Precede

See *Precede, Proceed.*

Progressive Verbs

Progressive verbs, which indicate something that is being or happening, are formed by the present participle form (ending in *-ing*) and an auxiliary.

Example: She <u>is</u> [auxiliary] <u>crying</u> [present participle]. She <u>was crying.</u> She <u>will be crying.</u> She <u>has been crying.</u> She <u>had been crying.</u> She <u>will have been crying.</u>

The progressive form occurs only with **dynamic verbs** (verbs that show the ability to change). There are five types of dynamic verbs:

■ Activity verbs

Example: ask, play, work, write, say, listen, call, eat

■ Process verbs

Example: change, grow, mature, widen

■ Verbs of bodily sensation

Example: hurt, itch, ache, feel

■ Transitional events verbs

Example: arrive, die, land, leave, lose

- Momentary verbs

Example: hit, jump, throw, kick

Stative verbs describe a quality that is incapable of change. There are two classifications of stative verbs:

- Verbs of inert perception and cognition

Example: guess, hate, hear, please, satisfy

- Relational verbs

Example: equal, possess, own, include, cost, concern, contain

---

Pronouns

Usually **pronouns** refer to a noun, an individual or group, or a thing whose identity has been made clear previously.

The word a pronoun substitutes for is called its **antecedent**.

Example: Amanda accepted Nick's proposal. She [Amanda,
the antecedent for "she" and "her"] knew he [Nick, the antecedent]
was the right guy for her [Amanda].

Not all pronouns refer to an antecedent.

Example: Everyone [no antecedent] on this floor charges over
one hundred dollars an hour.

The types of pronouns are:

- Personal—*you, him, it, us, them.*

- Demonstrative—*this, that, these, those.*

- Indefinite—*all, any, anybody, anyone, everyone.*

- Relative—*whoever, whomever, whichever.*

- Reflexive—*myself, yourself, herself.*

- Intensive—*they themselves, I myself, the president himself.*

- Interrogative—*who, whom, which, what.*

- Reciprocal—*each other, one another.*

Pronouns and Antecedent Agreement

A pronoun usually refers to its antecedent and the two words must agree in number. If the antecedent is plural, the pronoun must be plural. If the antecedent is singular, the pronoun must be singular.

Certain pronouns like *anyone, anybody, everyone, everybody, someone, somebody,* and *nobody* are always singular.

Example: <u>Anyone</u> [antecedent] who says such a thing <u>is</u> [singular verb] just plain wrong.

The same is true for *either* and *neither.* Even though they seem to be referring to two things, they are singular.

Example: <u>Neither</u> Payal nor Charu <u>is</u> correct.

In other cases, the determination of singular or plural depends on what the pronoun refers to—a single person or a group.

Example: <u>The person</u> who broke my window <u>is</u> still unknown.

Example: <u>The people</u> who have been without power <u>are</u> now complaining.

One of the most frequently asked grammar questions is regarding the pronoun *who (who, whose, whom, whoever,* and *whomever).* A good way to understand the uses for *who* is to compare it with the pronouns *he* and *they.* Table 2.23 shows the comparisons between the pronoun *who* and the pronouns *he* and *they.*

Table 2.23 The Pronoun *Who*

	Subject Form	Possessive Form	Object Form
Singular	he who	his whose	him whom
Plural	they who	their whose	them whom

One good way to choose between the various forms of *who* is to think of the sentence in terms of the choice between *he* and *him*. If *him* feels right, choose *whom*. If *he* sounds better, pick *who*.

> **Example:** *Who* do you think is coming? [Do you think *he* is coming?]

> **Example:** *Whom* shall we invite to the movie? [Shall we invite *him* to the movie?]

> **Example:** Give the money to *whomever* you please. [Give the money to *him.*]

> **Example:** Give the money to *whoever* wants it most. [*He* wants it most.]

> **Example:** *Whoever* guesses my age will win the prize. [*He* guesses my age.]

Another related problem is confusing *whose* with *who's*. *Who's* looks like it is possessive; however, it is really a contraction of *who is*.

> **Example:** Who's going to take the assignment?

> **Example:** Whose glove is this?

Proper Adjectives

Proper adjectives come from proper nouns that act as adjectives to modify another noun. Proper adjectives begin with a capital letter.

Example: He was the first <u>Hispanic</u> [proper adjective] mayor in the history of the city.

Proper Nouns

Proper nouns are the name of a specific person, place, or thing. They are always capitalized.

Example: Atlanta, France, Linda

Protatis

Protatis is a term that describes an *if clause* in a conditional sentence.

Example: <u>If you buy a lottery ticket</u> [protatis], you might win a hundred million dollars.

Quantifiers

Quantifiers are words that precede and modify nouns and that are used to communicate how many or how much.

Selecting the correct quantifier depends on whether they are used with a count or noncount noun. The following quantifiers can be used with count nouns:

> **Example:** <u>many</u> [quantifier] people, a <u>few</u> people, <u>several</u> people, <u>a couple of</u> people, <u>none of the</u> people

The following quantifiers can be used with noncount nouns:

> **Example:** <u>not much</u> eating, <u>a little</u> eating, <u>a bit of</u> eating, a <u>good deal of</u> eating, <u>no</u> eating

Question Mark

A **question mark** closes a question.

> **Example:** What time is it?

A question mark is also used to express a doubt.

> **Example:** He is older (?) than she.

If the question is indirect, no question mark is used.

> **Example:** I wonder whether he will be here.

When a question is asked in the middle of a sentence, the question is set off by commas and the sentence ends with a question mark.

Example: They are arriving, aren't they, on the noon train?

When the question is enclosed in parentheses, the question mark is inside the parentheses, not at the end of the sentence.

Example: The magazine (did you see it?) describes the city in great detail.

If the question mark is part of a quotation, it is placed inside the closing quotation mark; if it is not a part of the quotation, it is placed outside the closing quotation mark.

Example: The statement ended, "And is that all?"

Example: What did she mean by "jobless years"?

If the last word in a question is an abbreviation and thus contains a period, the question mark is also used.

Example: Do you think he will arrive by 4 p.m.?

When a statement is made into a question, the question mark is used.

Example: He is arriving today?

Example: Really?

Question Types

A variety of **question types** are used in the English language.

- Academic—a question of interest but of no particular use or value

- Embedded—a question that is in a sentence but not a question in the context of the sentence

- Hypothetical—a question of interest but having no impact on the current situation

- Leading—a question that suggests a particular answer

- Question Tag—a statement with an auxiliary verb and pronoun added to confirm the statement

- Rhetorical—a question with an obvious answer that needs no response

- Yes/No—a question that can be answered with *yes* or *no*

Quitclaim

A **quitclaim** is a legal document that gives up title to property.

Note: Using *quick claim* is incorrect.

Quit, Exit

For computer-related procedures and manuals, avoid using *quit* to close a program.

- Use *exit* to describe ending a program.

- Use *close* to describe putting away a document or window.

Quotation Marks

Double **quotation marks** are used to set off any material quoted in a sentence or paragraph.

Example: The passage he read aloud was from the first chapter: "The discovery of this energy brings us to the problem of how to allow it to be used. The use of atomic power throws us back to the Greek legend of Prometheus and the age-old question of whether force should be exerted against law. The man of today must decide whether he will use this power for destruction or for peaceful purposes." When he had finished the reading, there was loud applause.

If the quoted material consists of several paragraphs, the opening quotation mark is used at the beginning of the quotation and at the beginning of each paragraph within the quotation.

A closing quotation mark, however, is used only at the conclusion of the quotation. It is not used at the end of each paragraph in the quotation, as many people mistakenly think.

Quotations Within Quotations

Single quotation marks indicate a quotation within the quotation.

Example: He said, "Did you hear John make the statement, 'I will not go with her,' or were you not present at the time he spoke?"

Quotations for Titles

In printed text, the titles of essays, articles, poems, stories, or chapters are set off in quotation marks; titles of plays, books, and periodical publications are italicized.

Example: The name of the article is "I Believe."

Example: The title of the book is *Project Bloom.*

Example: The article "A Brave Man's Journey" was first published in *Harper's Magazine.*

Quotation Marks and Punctuation

Place the close quotation mark outside the comma and the period.

Example: "Don't stop now," he said, "when you have so little left to finish."

Place the close quotation mark inside the colon and the semicolon.

Example: He called her a "little witch"; that was right after she broke his model plane.

Place the close quotation mark outside an exclamation point or a question mark when the quoted material itself is an exclamation or a question.

Example: "I passed my test!"

Example: Her response was, "Did he really say that?"

Place the close quotation mark inside an exclamation point or a question mark when the quoted material alone is not an exclamation or a question.

Example: I can't believe he actually used the word "idiot"!

Example: Didn't he claim to be "too tired"?

Raise, Rise

Raise is a transitive verb and always takes an object. *Rise* is an intransitive verb and never takes an object.

Correct: They raise <u>the question</u> [object] at every meeting.

Correct: I rise to make a motion.

Rational, Rationale

Rational is an adjective that means logical or reasonable. *Rationale* is a noun that means a belief or controlling principle.

Correct: Any rational person would agree.

Correct: My rationale is that centralizing control destroys individual initiative.

Real

Don't use *real* when you really mean *very*.

Incorrect: He is real assertive.

Correct: He is very assertive.

Reciprocal Pronouns

The **reciprocal pronouns**, *each other* and *one another*, are used to express mutuality.

> **Example:** My brother and I always give each other a hard time.

If more than two people are involved, use *one another*.

> **Example:** The team members gave one another high fives.

Reciprocal pronouns can also take the possessive form.

> **Example:** They borrowed each other's clothes.

Recur, Reoccur

Recur means to return to, to come back, or to occur again and again.

> **Example:** The problem recurred yesterday for the tenth time.

Recurrence means one of several repetitions.

> **Example:** If there's a recurrence of the fever, you must see the doctor.

Reoccur means a single repetition.

> **Example:** The creaking sound in the attic reoccurred an hour later.

Related words include *reoccurrence* and *recurrent*.

Redundancy

Although a well-rounded writing style includes compound and complex sentences, it is important to avoid **redundancy**, that is, saying the same thing twice. Table 2.24 presents a list of some of the most common redundant phrases.

Table 2.24 Common Redundant Phrases

12 midnight	12 noon
1 a.m. in the morning	circle around
close proximity	completely unanimous
continue on	cooperate together
each and every	enclosed herewith
end result	exactly the same
final completion	free gift
in spite of the fact that	in the field of
in the event of	new innovations
one and the same	particular interest
period of *x* days	personally, I think
personal opinion	refer back
repeat again	return again
revert back	shorter in length
small in size	summarize briefly
surrounded on all sides	the future to come
there is no doubt but	we are in receipt of

Reflexive Pronouns

Reflexive pronouns indicate that the subject in a sentence also receives the action of the verb. Reflexive pronouns are formed by adding *-self* or *-selves* to the pronoun.

> **Example:** People who cheat on their taxes are only hurting themselves [reflexive pronoun].

Whenever a reflexive pronoun is in a sentence, the sentence must contain a person to whom the pronoun can reflect.

Incorrect: Please give the food to <u>myself.</u> [The sentence contains no other subject such as "I."]

Example: I gave <u>myself</u> the credit.

Reflexive pronouns are the same as intensive pronouns (*myself, yourself, herself, himself, ourselves,* and *themselves*). There is a tendency to use reflexive and intensive pronouns (ending in *-self*) when they are not appropriate.

Incorrect: These books will be read by <u>myself.</u>

Correct: These books will be read by <u>me</u>.

The indefinite pronoun *one* has its own reflexive form.

Example: One must trust <u>oneself</u>.

Other indefinite pronouns use either *himself* or *themselves* as reflexives.

Regard, Regards

When making a reference to something, write *with regard to*. At the end of correspondence, write *regards*.

Regardless is often used as an adverb that means despite everything. The word *irregardless* is nonstandard and should not be used.

Regular Verbs

Regular verbs take an *-ed* to form the past simple and past participle tenses.

Example: talk, talked

Regular verbs that end in *e* take a *-d* to form these tenses.

Example: joke, joked

Relative Adverbs

Adjectival clauses can be introduced by **relative adverbs**: *where, when,* and *why.*

The relative word itself serves in an adverbial function, modifying the verb in the clause. The relative adverb *where* begins a clause that modifies a noun of place.

> **Example:** My family now lives in the town <u>where</u> [modifies "used to be"] my grandfather used to be sheriff. [The entire clause modifies the noun "town."]

A *when* clause modifies nouns of time.

> **Example:** My favorite day of the week is <u>Friday, when</u> the weekend is about to begin.

A *why* clause modifies the noun *reason.*

> **Example:** Do you know the <u>reason why</u> school is out today?

Sometimes the relative adverb is left out of these clauses and the writer substitutes *that* instead.

> **Example:** Do you know the <u>reason that</u> school is out today?

Relative Clauses

A **relative clause** modifies a noun or noun phrase in a sentence. Relative clauses are dependent clauses introduced by a relative pronoun (*that, which, whichever, who, whoever, whom, whomever, whose,* and *of which*).

> **Example:** John said that his knee, <u>which had bothered him ever since the accident,</u> [relative clause] needed surgery.

> **Example:** Cathy didn't get the promotion, <u>which really surprised everyone in the office.</u>

Relative Pronouns

The **relative pronouns** *who, whoever, which,* and *that* relate to groups of words, nouns, and other pronouns.

> **Example:** I don't know why she said that.

> **Example:** This is the house that had the fire.

The pronoun *who* connects the subject to the verb within a dependent clause.

> **Example:** That is the woman who used to be a teacher.

Choosing between *which* and *that* and between *who* and *whom* is difficult for many people. Generally, use *which* to introduce clauses that are parenthetical in nature; in other words, they can be removed from the sentence without changing the meaning of the sentence.

- A *who* clause is often set apart with a comma or a pair of commas.

- Use *that* to introduce clauses that are indispensable for the meaning of the sentence. *That* clauses are not set apart by commas.

- The pronoun *which* refers to things, *who* refers to people, and *that* usually refers to things but may also refer to people in a general way.

The expanded relative pronouns *whoever, whomever,* and *whatever* are known as **indefinite relative pronouns**. They do not define any thing or person in particular.

> **Example:** The company will hire <u>whomever</u> [indefinite relative pronoun] it pleases.

> **Example:** She seemed to say <u>whatever</u> came to mind.

> **Example:** <u>Whoever</u> took the money will be punished.

What can be an indefinite relative pronoun when used to introduce a dependent clause.

Example: He will give you <u>what</u> you need for the trip.

Reoccur

See *Recur, Reoccur.*

Reported Speech

Reported speech, also called **indirect speech**, is used to express what someone else said without using his or her exact words. The characteristics of reported speech are that:

- Exact quotes and quotation marks are not used.

- Pronouns are often changed.

- Verb tense is usually changed.

Exact quote: I'm going to declare bankruptcy.

Reported speech: He said he was going to declare bankruptcy.

Restrictive Clauses

A **restrictive clause** restricts the meaning of the preceding subject.

Nonrestrictive clauses also tell you something about the preceding subject, but they do not limit the possible meaning.

Restrictive clauses normally begin with *that*. Nonrestrictive clauses normally begin with *which*.

Example: The assistant bound the reports <u>that</u> were less than 30 days old [restrictive clause; the assistant bound only the reports that were less than 30 days old].

Example: The assistant bound the reports, <u>which</u> were less than 30 days old [nonrestrictive; the assistant bound reports and all of them were less than 30 days old].

Resultative Adjective

A **resultative adjective** is placed after the noun it modifies and changes the meaning of the verb and its action on the noun.

Example: He wiped the desk <u>clean</u>.

Example: He painted the office <u>green</u>.

Resumptive Modifier

A **resumptive modifier** takes a word from a sentence that appears to be ending and adds additional information.

Example: You'll find working with Videologies to be both enlightening and rewarding—<u>enlightening due to the many innovations we'll introduce to your company, rewarding because of the enhancements to productivity your company will experience</u> [resumptive modifier].

Rhetorical Question

A **rhetorical question** is asked to make a point and when an answer is not expected. The answer for a rhetorical question is usually obvious.

Example: Who is responsible for running the company—the customers, the employees, or the managers?

Rhyme

Rhyme is a literary technique used in poetry where words at the ends of lines sound similar.

Right, Business

See *Business, Right*.

Right-click

See *Mouse Terminology*.

Rise, Raise

See *Raise, Rise*.

Roman Numerals

Roman numerals are often used in outlines and some dates. Table 2.25 contains the most commonly used Roman numerals. Table 2.26 contains common Roman dates.

Table 2.25 Most Common Roman Numerals

Arabic	Roman	Arabic	Roman
1	I	30	XXX
2	II	40	XL
3	III	50	L
4	IV	60	LX
5	V	70	LXX
6	VI	80	LXXX
7	VII	90	XC

(continues)

Table 2.25 *(continued)*

Arabic	Roman	Arabic	Roman
8	VIII	100	C
9	IX	150	CL
10	X	200	CC
11	XI	300	CCC
12	XII	400	CD
13	XIII	500	D
14	XIV	600	DC
15	XV	700	DCC
16	XVI	800	DCCC
17	XVII	900	CM
18	XVIII	1,000	M
19	XIX	1,500	MD
20	XX	2,000	MM
		3,000	MMM

Table 2.26 Common Roman Numeral Dates

1900	MCM	1980	MCMLXXX
1910	MCMX	1990	MCMXC
1920	MCMXX	2000	MM
1930	MCMXXX	2010	MMX
1940	MCMXL	2020	MMXX
1950	MCML	2030	MMXXX
1960	MCMLX	2040	MMXL
1970	MCMLXX	2050	MML

Root, Rout, Route

Root can be:

- A noun that means the part of a plant that grows beneath the ground.

- A verb that means to develop roots or to dig in the earth.

- A verb that means to applaud or cheer for someone.

Rout can be:

- A noun that means a terrible defeat or retreat.

- A verb that means to defeat soundly.

Route can be:

- A noun that means an avenue of travel such as a road.

- A verb that means to select a particular pathway.

Run

When referring to a business or organization, don't use *run* in place of *manage*.

Incorrect: He runs the bakery.

Correct: He manages the bakery.

Run-On Sentences

See *Fused Sentences*.

Same

Don't use *same* to refer to the subject of a sentence.

Incorrect: Your letter arrived and I acknowledge the same with thanks.

Correct: Your letter arrived and I acknowledge it with thanks.

Sarcasm

Sarcasm is a figure of speech that describes a passage where the author means the opposite of what is actually said. Sarcasm is a form of irony. Sarcastic remarks are often rude or humorous.

Example: Maybe you should talk on the phone a little louder. I don't think everyone in the office could hear your conversation.

Satire

Satire is a literary technique where an author makes fun of someone or something in order to create a negative opinion. Satire often uses humor to ridicule the subject.

An author often uses satire to express a strong opinion about someone or something in order to damage or ruin the subject of the satire.

Screen

See *Display, Monitor, Screen.*

Screen Terminology

The screen captures in Figures 2.5 to 2.9 illustrate various features of Microsoft Windows–based software for the purpose of identifying elements that may appear in software-related procedures and manuals.

(text continues on page 361)

Figure 2.5 Windows Desktop

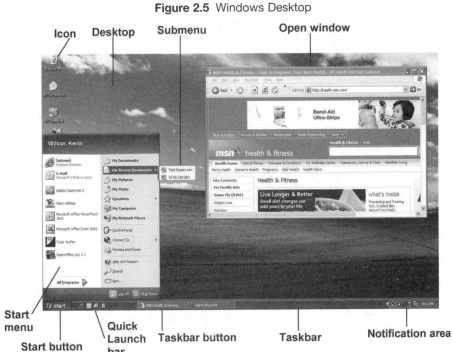

Figure 2.6 Open Window

Figure 2.7 Browser Window

Back to previous Web page

Reload Web page

Address bar

Search field

Search button

Web page

Figure 2.8 Web Page

Banner menu

Banner

Sign-in link

Navigation bar

Link

Figure 2.9 Program Window

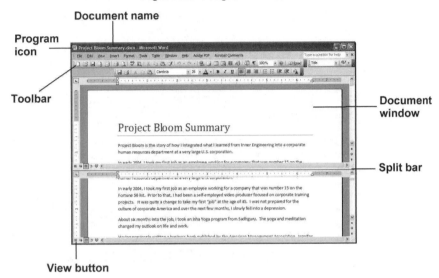

Second Conditional

The **second conditional** is used to express future actions that depend on the result of another future action. Usually, there is only a small chance both conditions will be satisfied.

The second conditional is formed with *if* + past simple tense + *would* + base form.

Example: If I found a buried treasure, I would buy my own island.

Select

See *Press, Type, Click, Strike, Hit, Select.*

Semicolon

A **semicolon** is used when the conjunction is omitted between parts of a compound sentence.

Example: I went with them; I should have stayed at home.

A semicolon precedes words such as *however, moreover,* or *otherwise* when they introduce the second of two connected full sentences.

Example: She is arriving at noon; however, she will not stay long.

If parts of a series contain inner punctuation such as a comma, the parts are separated by a semicolon.

Example: He came to see his mother, who was ill; his sister, who lived in the next town; and his old schoolmate.

Semiweekly, Semimonthly

See *Biweekly, Bimonthly, Semiweekly, Semimonthly.*

Sensor, Censor

See *Censor, Censure, Sensor, Censer.*

Sentence

A **sentence** has a subject and a verb (predicate) that can stand alone.

A sentence starts with a capital letter and ends with a period, question mark, or exclamation mark.

Sentence Fragments

A **sentence fragment** fails to be a sentence because it cannot stand by itself. It does not contain at least one independent clause.

A group of words may appear to be a sentence but turn out to be a sentence fragment instead for several reasons:

- The sentence fragment may contain a series of prepositional phrases without a proper subject-verb relationship.

Example: in Texas, sometime in early April, just before the
bluebonnets appear

- The sentence fragment may be a verbal phrase intended to modify
something that is missing.

Example: working deep into the night in an effort to get his
taxes completed

- The sentence fragment may have a subject-verb relationship, but it
has been subordinated to another idea or word so that it cannot stand
by itself.

Example: although he was taller than his older brother

Sentence Subject

The **subject** of a sentence is the person, place, or thing that is the main agent
in the sentence.

To find the subject of a sentence, first locate the verb. Then answer the question, what or who is being "verbed"?

Example: The monkeys in the treetops <u>must be observed</u>.
[verb; So, what must be observed? The answer is the monkeys.]

A **simple subject** is a subject without any modifiers.

Example: The upcoming <u>event</u> [simple subject], stripped of all
the hype, is nothing but a fund-raiser.

Sometimes a simple subject can be more than one word or even an entire
clause.

Example: <u>What he had forgotten about the law</u> was amazing
considering how many years he spent in law school.

Usually, when the subject of a sentence is *you* and the sentence is a suggestion, order, or command, the *you* is left out.

Example: Get out of the way! [*You* is understood to be the subject.]

For sentence analysis, the person who initiates an action in a sentence is called the **agent**. When the active voice is used, the subject is the agent.

Example: The class [subject/agent] failed the test.

When the passive voice is used, the agent is not the subject. Some passive sentences don't contain an agent.

Example: The test was failed by the class [object of the preposition "by"].

Sentence Types

The types of sentence structures are:

■ Simple—one independent clause

Example: He went to the store.

■ Compound—more than one independent clause

Example: He went to the store, and he bought groceries.

■ Complex—one independent clause and at least one dependent clause

Example: He went to the store, where he bought groceries.

■ Compound complex—more than one independent clause and at least one dependent clause

Example: He went to the library, and then he went to the store, where he bought groceries.

- Periodic—beginning with modifying phrases and clauses and ending with an independent clause

  Example: Having gone to the store, he bought groceries.

- Cumulative—beginning with an independent clause and ending with a series of modifying constructions

  Example: He ran his morning errands, buying groceries, dropping off his prescription, and getting cash from the ATM.

Sentence Variety

A **sentence** is a group of words containing a subject and a predicate.

How you use the many types of sentences in your writing, the order in which you use them, and how you combine and punctuate them determine your writing style.

It is relatively easy to write short sentences. However, if you use only short sentences, your writing will appear to be a primer style and give your reader a poor impression of your level of professionalism. To write more complicated sentences, you have to create constructions of clauses and phrases. Consider these tips:

- Long sentences and run-on sentences are not the same thing.

- Combining too long a series of clauses may confuse the reader.

- Many writers are afraid they'll create run-on sentences and tend to lean toward the shorter variety.

By coordinating clauses and punctuation, you can allow the complexity of a sentence to develop after the verb, not before it. The key is to make the subject-verb connection and then allow the sentence to paint the picture surrounding that subject and verb.

One issue that is difficult for many business writers is the need to repeat key terms in long sentences. The repetition feels awkward. When properly handled, though, repeated phrases can create a rhythm that helps to emphasize the meaning of the sentence.

Another way to enhance sentence variety and complexity is to avoid clumsy "which clauses" and replace them with dependent clauses.

> **Example**: Atlanta continues to grow in every direction, which means that homes are rapidly replacing the fields and forests in outlying areas.
>
> **Better:** Atlanta continues to grow in every direction, as homes rapidly replace the fields and forests in outlying areas.

When used sparingly, you can create an interesting twist to a sentence by ending it with a set of prepositional phrases, each beginning with a present or past participle.

> **Example:** You'll find working with Videologies to be an excellent experience, one that will develop into a lasting relationship, into a partnership, winning future business for us all.

Remember to throw an occasional question, exclamation, or command into your writing.

- *Questions* can be useful at the beginning of a paragraph to summarize the content that follows.

- *Exclamations* can be used to express strong feelings.

- *Commands* provide direction and energy by telling your readers what to do.

Occasionally, try to begin sentences with something other than the normal subject-verb combo. Consider these tips:

- Start with a modifying clause or participial phrase.

- Begin with a coordinating conjunction (*and, but, nor, for, yet,* or *so*).

- Many people think that they should never begin a sentence with *but* and that it should be linked to the previous sentence to make a compound structure. But a sentence like this calls attention to itself and can be a useful device.

Setup, Set Up

Setup is written as one word when acting as a noun or adjective.

Example: To install the software, run Setup [noun].

Example: The setup [adjective] process should take you approximately ten minutes.

Set up is written as two words when acting as a verb.

Example: Have you unpacked and set up your office?

Sexist Language

See *Unbiased Language*.

Shall, Will

Use *shall* to express a simple expected action by the first person.

Use *will* with second and third persons.

To express determination or command, reverse the order; use *will* for the first person and *shall* for the second and third.

Example: We shall go tomorrow.

Example: He will go, too.

Example: You will be at the conference by the time we arrive.

Example: I will go tomorrow.

Example: He shall go with me even if I must force him.

Example: You shall never do that again.

Shape

Don't use *shape* to refer to the status of something.

Incorrect: The transaction was completed in good shape.

Correct: The transaction was completed to everyone's satisfaction.

Should, Must

Should is used when an action is recommended but optional.

Example: I should clean the kitchen.

Must is used when an action is required.

Example: Mom said we must clean the kitchen.

Should of

See *Might of, Should of, Would of, Could of.*

Should, Would

Use *should* with the first person and *would* with the second and third persons to express expected action.

Example: I should run diagnostics again to look for errors.

Example: They would expect to have dinner with us after the play.

Using *should* and *would* instead of *shall* and *will* implies a doubt that the action will take place.

Should and *would* may also be used with all persons, but in these cases the meaning of the verbs is different. *Should* may be used with all persons to show obligation. *Would* may be used with all persons to show intent or determination.

Correct: A child should love his parents.

Correct: If I had enough money, I would buy a car.

Shut Down, Shutdown

Shut down is two words when used as a verb.

Example: You should shut down your computer during thunderstorms.

Shutdown is one word when used as a noun or adjective.

Example: To turn off your computer, click Start and then Shutdown.

Sic

Sic is a Latin word that means "in such a manner." When quoting a passage that has misspelled words or poor grammar, include [*sic*], italicized and within brackets, to show that the mistakes are an accurate part of the quote.

Example: Sprayed on the side of the wall was the slogan, "Eat moore chiken [*sic*]."

Sign In, Sign Out, Sign On, Sign Up

Sign in is used when entering a user ID and password to access a secure Web site. When you exit a secure Web site, you *sign out*.

Sign on is used as a noun to describe security software.

> **Example:** The Web site features a secure single sign on.

Sign up is when you register to access a secure Web site.

Simile

A **simile** is a figure of speech that is used to describe something by comparing it to something else using words such as *like* or *as*.

> **Example:** He was as nutty as a fruitcake.

> **Example:** She laughs like a hyena.

Since, Because

See *Because, Since, As.*

Singular

Singular is a grammatical term for a noun, pronoun, or verb that is used to describe something when there is only one item.

> **Example:** an office, a car, a laptop, a telephone

Plural is the grammatical term used when there is more than one item.

Sit, Set

Sit is an intransitive verb.

> **Correct:** She sits near her husband at every meeting.

Set is a transitive verb.

Correct: He sets the plates on the table in an orderly manner.

Site, Sight, Cite

See *Cite, Site, Sight*.

Slang

Slang is informal, sometimes grammatically incorrect language that is used by groups to bind the group together.

Usage of slang often spreads outside the group and becomes mainstream informal language.

Example: That's a cool hat you're wearing.

Example: He definitely has his game face on.

Slash

The **slash** is often used as shorthand or when the choice between alternatives is nebulous.

Because the slash is often ambiguous, use it with caution. The slash is used:

■ With *and/or* combinations.

■ To indicate other relationships between words.

And/Or Combinations

The slash can be used to indicate:

■ Options that are available.

Example: The ingredients of the drink are ice, rum, lime/lemon, and cola.

- Equal possibilities.

Example: Dear Sir/Madam:

- That something has more than one function.

Example: The potter worked alone in the cold garage/studio.

Indicating Other Relationships

The slash can be used to:

- Separate elements that are being compared.

Example: The Redskins/Cowboys rivalry has a long history.

- Separate origins and destinations.

Example: The Dallas/Atlanta flight was canceled.

- Separate the numerals in a date.

Example: 12/31/2012

- Indicate a period that spans two or more calendar years.

Example: For the 2011/12 school year, the eighth graders will be taking technology education for the first time.

- Mean "per."

Example: 1000 km/hour

- Write fractions.

Example: 1/4 + 1/4 = 1/2

Small Caps

Small caps are uppercase letters that are the same height as the surrounding lowercase letters. Small caps are often used for acronyms and abbreviations.

Example: THESE ARE SMALL CAPS.

So

Avoid overuse of this adverbial conjunction. *Consequently, therefore,* and *inasmuch as* are good substitutes when you want to vary the style.

Avoid: It had snowed over a foot that day; so we drove the jeep into town.

Better: It had snowed over a foot that day; consequently we drove the jeep into town.

Software Menus and Commands

Figure 2.10 shows an example of software menu elements.

Figure 2.10 Software Menu Terminology

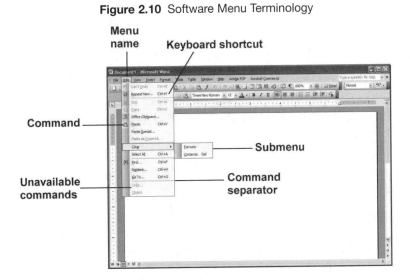

Solidus

Solidus is another name for **Slash**.

See *Slash*.

Some, Any

See *Any, Some*.

Sometime, Some Time

Sometime means occasional or at some point.

Some time means an amount of time.

> **Correct:** I will go sometime this morning.

> **Correct:** If I have some time this morning, I shall do the job for you.

Sort of, Kind of

See *Kind of, Sort of*.

Spaces After Periods

Only one space is needed at the end of a sentence after the period before starting another sentence. When people used typewriters, it was common to add two spaces after a period.

Split Infinitive

One of the most common writing mistakes is the **split infinitive**. An infinitive is said to be split when a word (usually an adverb) is placed between the *to* of the infinitive and the root verb.

Example: to boldly go where no man has gone before

The argument against split infinitives is based on the idea that an infinitive is a single unit and should not be divided. Because it is so easy to spot, many writers try to avoid a split. However, many style guides now say the rule against splitting infinitives can be ignored. To avoid the criticism, it is a good rule to avoid split infinitives in business writing.

Sr., Jr.

See *Jr., Sr.*

Stative Adjective

A **stative adjective** describes a condition or state that is not easily changed.

Example: large, blue, little

Stative Verb

See *Progressive Verbs.*

Subheadings

See *Headings and Subheadings.*

Subject

A noun, pronoun, or noun phrase that comes before the main verb in a sentence is called the **subject**.

Example: <u>She</u> [subject] went to the warehouse.

To find the subject in a sentence, ask the question, who or what did the action expressed by the verb?

Subject Complement

See *Complements*.

Subjective Case

The **subjective case**, also called **subjective pronouns**, consists of personal pronouns that can act as subjects in a sentence.

Example: I, you, he, she, it, we, they

The **objective case** consists of pronouns that act as objects in a sentence.

Example: me, you, him, her, it, us, you, them

Subjective Pronouns

See *Subjective Case*.

Subject-Verb Agreement

The basic rule of **subject-verb agreement** is that a singular subject needs a singular verb and that plural subjects require plural verbs.

Example: My brother is [singular subject and verb] a psychologist.

Example: My brothers are [plural subject and verb] psychologists.

Indefinite pronouns like *anyone, everyone, someone, no one*, and *nobody* are singular subjects and thus require singular verbs.

Example: Everyone is studying hard.

Some indefinite pronouns, such as *all* and *some,* can be singular or plural depending on whether what they are referring to is countable or not.

Example: Some of the candy <u>is</u> missing.

Example: Some of the dogs <u>are</u> barking.

One indefinite pronoun, *none,* can be either singular or plural, and it doesn't matter whether you use a singular or plural verb—that is, unless something in the sentence specifies its number.

Example: None of you <u>write</u> poetry.

Example: None of the cars <u>are</u> speeding.

Some indefinite pronouns like *everyone* and *everybody* sound as though they are talking about more than one person; however, they are both singular.

Example: Everyone is coming to the meeting.

The pronoun *each* is often followed by a prepositional phrase ending in a plural word.

Example: each of the monkeys

Each, however, is singular.

Example: Each of the monkeys is eating a banana.

Don't confuse the word *and* with the phrases *together with, as well as,* and *along with.* They do not mean the same and do not create compound subjects as *and* does.

Example: The boy, as well as his brother, is going to school.

Example: The boy and his brother are going to school.

The pronouns *neither* and *either* are singular even though they appear to be referring to two things.

Example: Neither of the two computers is obsolete.

Example: Either is a good choice for a student.

Sometimes *neither* and *either* take a plural verb when they are followed by a prepositional phrase that begins with *of*.

Example: Have either of you two kids seen my dog?

Example: Are either of you listening to me?

When the conjunctions *or* and *nor* are used, the subject closest to the verb determines whether the verb is singular or plural.

Example: Neither the bear nor the monkeys were outside when we visited the zoo.

It's also a good idea to put the plural subject closest to the verb because the sentence would be incorrect.

Example: Neither the monkeys nor the bear were outside when we visited the zoo.

The words *there* and *here* can never be subjects in a sentence. These words are used in what are called **expletive constructions** where the subject follows the verb and determines whether the verb is singular or plural.

Example: Here are <u>my two books</u> [subject].

Example: There better be <u>a good reason</u> [subject] you have them.

Verbs for third-person, singular subjects like *he, she,* and *it* have *s* endings.

Example: He loves to eat.

Sometimes modifiers slip between a subject and a verb, but they do not change the subject-verb agreement.

Example: The <u>workers</u> [subject], who always seem to be standing around taking a break, gathered in a circle like a football huddle, <u>are</u> [verb] being fired.

Sometimes nouns take peculiar forms that make it confusing to tell whether they are singular or plural. Words such as *glasses, gloves, pliers,* and *scissors* are thought of as plural unless they're preceded by the phrase *pair of,* in which case *pair* becomes the subject.

Example: My glasses are on the desk.

Example: The pair of glasses is on the desk.

Some words that end in *s* seem to be plural but are really singular and thus require singular verbs.

Example: The evening news is full of disasters.

Other words that end in *s* refer to a single thing but are actually plural and require a plural verb.

Example: His assets were totally wiped out by the bankruptcy.

Fractional expressions, such as *half of* and *a percentage of,* can be either singular or plural. The same is true when words like *some, all,* and *any* serve as subjects.

Example: One-half of the population is over sixty-five.

Example: One-quarter of the students were absent.

Example: Some of the houses are painted white.

Example: Some of the money is missing.

In a sentence that combines a positive and a negative subject and one is plural and the other singular, the verb should agree with the positive subject.

Example: The teacher not the students decides what to teach.

Subject-Verb Inversion

Normally, a sentence contains a subject and then a verb, in that order. This pattern is disturbed in only a few instances.

- In questions

  Example: Have you read that book?

- In expletive constructions

  Example: Here is your book.

- To put focus on a particular word

  Example: What's more important is his reluctance to find a job.

- When a sentence begins with an adverb, adverbial phrase, or clause

  Example: Rarely have so many been eaten in just one meal.

- After the word *so*
  Example: I believe him; so do the people.

Subjunctive

The **subjunctive** describes a verb mood and is used to express emotions, hope, opinions, commands, and wishes.

The subjunctive mood uses the simple form of the verb without *to*. The simple form of *to go* in the subjective mood is *go*.

Example: Is it necessary that we <u>be</u> [subjunctive] there?

Example: It's time that you <u>bought</u> some new shoes.

Example: I asked that the report <u>be</u> finished this morning.

The subjunctive mood is typically used in dependent clauses. It is also called the **conjunctive mood**.

Submittal, Submission

Submittal means the act of submitting, not the item being submitted.

Use *submission* when referring to anything that is being submitted.

Incorrect: Make sure you include a self-addressed stamped envelope with your submittal.

Correct: Make sure you include a self-addressed stamped envelope with your submission.

Correct: His submittal of the legal documents is now in question.

Subordinate Clause

A **subordinate clause** is subset within a larger clause. A **dependent clause** is a subordinate clause.

Example: I think <u>I'd like sushi</u> [subordinate clause].

The term **subordinate** describes the relationship between one clause and another in a single sentence. A sentence can have multiple subordinate clauses.

The largest clause in the sentence is called the **matrix clause** and is **superordinate** to any subordinate clauses nested within it.

Subordinating Conjunctions

Subordinating conjunctions are words that appear at the beginning of a subordinate or dependent clause. Subordinating conjunctions convert a clause into something that depends on the rest of the sentence for meaning.

Example: Because [subordinating conjunction] he loved driving fast, he often dreamed of becoming a professional race car driver.

Common subordinating conjunctions are shown in Table 2.27.

Table 2.27 Common Subordinating Conjunctions

after	although	as	as if
as long as	as though	because	before
even if	even though	if	if only
in order that	now that	once	rather than
since	so that	than	that
though	till	unless	until
when	whenever	where	whereas
wherever	while		

Suffix

Words whose roots end with -*ge* or -*ce* generally retain the *e* when a **suffix** is added.

Example: change, changeable

Example: damage, damageable

Example: disadvantage, disadvantageous

Example: outrage, outrageous

A final silent *e* is usually dropped before a suffix that begins with a vowel.

Example: argue, arguing

Example: change, changing

Example: conceive, conceivable

A final silent *e* is usually retained before a suffix that begins with a consonant.

Example: achieve, achievement

Example: definite, definitely

In words ending in *-c,* add *k* before a suffix beginning with *-e, -i,* or *-y,* so that the hard sound of the original *c* is retained.

Example: frolic, frolicked, frolicking

Example: mimic, mimicked, mimicking

Example: picnic, picnicked, picnicking

A word ending in *-ie* changes the *-ie* to *-y* when adding a suffix.

Example: die, dying

Example: lie, lying

Example: tie, tying

Example: vie, vying

Words that end in -*y* preceded by a vowel retain the *y* when adding the suffix.

Example: survey, surveying, surveyor

Words that end with -*y* preceded by a consonant change *y* to *i* when adding a suffix, except when the suffix is -*ing*.

Example: embody, embodying, embodied

Example: rely, relying, relied

Example: satisfy, satisfying, satisfied

A final consonant is usually doubled when it is preceded by a single vowel and takes a suffix.

Example: mop, mopping

A final consonant is doubled when it is followed by a suffix, and the last syllable is accented when the suffix is added.

Example: acquit, acquitted

The final consonant is not doubled when the accent is shifted to a preceding syllable when the suffix is added and when the final consonant is preceded by two vowels.

Example: refer, referring, reference

Example: fooled, fooling

Summative Modifier

A **summative modifier** renames or summarizes what has been going on earlier in the sentence and adds new information.

> **Example:** The email etiquette seminar promises to show employees how to write effective emails, emails that get results, and emails that result in a positive image for your business—<u>three benefits</u> [summative modifier] that can enhance the productivity of any business.

Superlative

A **superlative** is a type of adjective or adverb that depicts something that is of a higher quality than something else. There must be three or more items compared in order to use the superlative.

The superlative is formed by adding the definite article *the*, along with either a short adjective that adds the suffix *-est* or a longer adjective that adds *most*.

> **Example:** Mount Rainer <u>is the tallest</u> [superlative] volcano in North America.

> **Example:** He <u>is the most friendly</u> guy on the team.

Syllable

Syllables are individual sounds that make up a word. A syllable can be said without interruption.

Most syllables have at least one vowel and other consonants before or after the vowel.

> **Example:** *Syllable* has three syllables: syl-la-ble.

Symbols and Special Characters

Symbols and other **special characters** may be used in business documents for mathematical equations, formulas, measurements, and punctuation; they can also be employed as bullets and attention-getting characters in page layouts.

When instructing a reader to type a symbol or special character to complete a procedure, spell the name of the character and include the symbol enclosed in parentheses.

Example: In an email address, type the *at sign* (@) and a period (.) before the domain name.

Table 2.28 contains a list of symbols and special characters and their names.

Table 2.28 Symbols, Special Characters, and Their Names

Character	Name	Character	Name
´	acute accent	≥	greater than or equal to sign
&	ampersand	–	hyphen
< >	angle brackets	"	inch mark
'	apostrophe	<	less than sign
*	asterisk	≤	less than or equal to sign
@	at sign	–	minus sign
\	backslash	×	multiplication sign
{ }	braces	≠	not equal to sign
[ ]	brackets	#	number sign
^	caret or circumflex	¶	paragraph mark
¢	cent sign	( )	parenthesis
« »	chevrons	%	percent
©	copyright symbol	π	pi
†	dagger			pipe

º	degree	+	plus sign
÷	division sign	±	plus or minus sign
$	dollar sign	?	question mark
…	ellipsis	"	quotation mark
—	em dash	'	single quotation mark
–	en dash	®	registered trademark symbol
=	equal sign	§	section
!	exclamation point	/	slash
`	grave accent	~	tilde
>	greater than sign	™	trademark symbol
		_	underscore

Sympathy, Empathy

See *Empathy, Sympathy.*

Synecdoche

Synecdoche is a figure of speech where a phrase features one thing that is used to refer to a related thing.

Example: All <u>hands</u> [figure of speech for people or sailors] on deck!

Synonyms

A **synonym** is a word that has the same or a very similar meaning as that of another word. In most cases, a synonym of a word may be substituted for the original word.

Example: car, automobile; film, movie; woman, lady; happy, joyful; bad, terrible

Table of Contents

A **table of contents** appears at the beginning of a document after the title page and other front matter, such as a foreword or preface. Here are some things to remember about tables of contents:

- A table of contents includes titles or descriptions for first-level headings, which serve as chapter titles, along with second-level and sometimes third-level headings, which designate sections and individual topics. Page numbers are included for each level of heading. Second- and third-level headings are normally indented three to five spaces from the first-level headings.

- Leaders, which appear as a series of periods (. . .), can be used to align the page numbers along the right side of the page.

- The table of contents pages are often numbered with lowercase Roman numerals.

- In most business documents, it is recommended that a table of contents not exceed three pages.

- A table of contents can be created automatically using word processing software if consistent heading styles are used throughout the document.

Figure 2.11 is a sample table of contents page.

Figure 2.11 Table of Contents Page Example

CONTENTS

Tables

Tables are often used in business documents to organize information for reference purposes. Consider the following tips when creating tables:

- Tables contain rows and columns and column headings.

- Tables may have an optional title that is included within the frame of the table as the first merged row.

- Use title-style capitalization for the title.

- Tables need an introductory sentence that references the table.

- The introductory sentence for a table that immediately follows should end in a period rather than a semicolon.

- Column headings should be short, precise, and written in the active voice if they are sentences.

- Capitalize the first letter of the first word in each column heading.

- Text within the table should follow sentence capitalization and punctuation rules.

- Incomplete sentences do not need a period.

- Align the text within the columns consistently for all columns.

- Organize the content in the table from left to right.

- For definitions and descriptions, put the term in the leftmost column and the definition or description in associated columns to the right.

- Text entries within the table should have parallel structure. (For example, all entries begin with an article, a noun, an action first, and so forth.)

- Avoid blank column entries. Use *not applicable* or *none*.

- Tables with long entries should be limited to two or three columns.

- If a table must be divided over two or more pages, include the table title and column headings on each new page.

- Border rules between rows are optional but should be included if the row size is inconsistent due to the length of the content.

- Footnotes should be included at the end of the table.

Table 2.29 is a sample table, illustrating these tips.

Table 2.29 Table Example

Camera resolution	2 MP	3 MP	4 MP	5 MP	6 MP
Photo dimensions	1600 × 1200	2048 × 21536	2272 × 1704	2592 × 1944	2848 × 2136
File size	0.9 MB	1.2 MB	2 MB	2.5 MB	3.2 MB

Tag Question

A **tag question** is created by adding an auxiliary verb and pronoun to the end of a statement.

Example: He's happy, <u>isn't he</u> [tag question]?

Take, Bring

See *Bring, Take*.

Tautology

A **tautology** is a figure of speech that occurs when two near-synonyms are placed together for emphasis.

Example: free gift, unsolved mystery, new innovation, suddenly without warning, added bonus

Teach, Learn

See *Learn, Teach*.

Telephone Numbers

When including telephone numbers in your documents, consider these guidelines:

- For U.S. telephone numbers, use parentheses instead of hyphens to separate the area code from the rest of the number.

Example: (800) 555-1212

- For U.S. phone lists, do not include a 1 to indicate long distance.
- For international phone lists, include the country code.
- Use parentheses to separate the country code from the rest of the number.
- If a country code and city code are required, keep both the country code and the city code within their own set of parentheses.
- Put the country name or initials in parentheses at the end of the number.

Example: (22) (42) 0000 000 0000 (U.K.)

Temperature

When writing about temperatures, use figures for temperatures except zero.

Example: The high temperature today was 55.

Example: It looks like the temperature may get down to zero today.

To designate temperatures below zero, use the word *minus* or *below zero* rather than a minus sign.

Example: The temperature today was minus 20.

Example: The temperature today was 20 below zero.

Optionally, you can add the word *degrees* to designate a temperature.

Example: The temperature today was 55 degrees.

For tables and other scientific documentation, you may use the degree symbol.

Example: 55°

When you must designate whether the temperature is in Fahrenheit or Celsius, use either the word or the letter *F* or *C*, separated by one space from the number and with no periods.

Example: It was 55 degrees Fahrenheit.

Example: The temperature was 55° F today.

Example: It was 11 degrees Celsius.

Example: The temperature was 11° C today.

Tense

Tense is a way of expressing when an action of a verb occurs. There are present tenses, past tenses, and future tenses. The present tense is the base form of the verb. Regular verbs add *-ed* or *-d* to the end for the past tense. Irregular verbs may change forms to form the past tense.

The present tenses are:

■ Present simple—used to say what someone usually does

Example: I commute to work every day.

■ Present progressive or continuous—used to say what someone is doing now

Example: I am reading a book.

- Present perfect simple—used to show unfinished time

  Example: The meeting has not yet started.

- Present perfect progressive or continuous—used to say how long someone has been doing something

  Example: She has been in a meeting for the last hour.

The past tenses are:

- Simple past—used to show a completed action

  Example: I read the report.

- Past progressive or continuous—used to say when something was being done

  Example: I was reading email when he called.

- Past perfect simple—used to say when something was done by a certain time

  Example: You had studied Spanish before moving to Mexico.

- Past perfect progressive or continuous—used to say how long something was done for a specific time

  Example: They had been meeting for two hours before John arrived.

The future tenses include the following:

- Simple future—used to say what you will do in the future

  Example: You are going to read the report.

- Future progressive or continuous—used to say when something will be happening

Example: You will be in Mexico when the merger takes place.

■ Future perfect simple—used to say something will be complete by a specific time

Example: You will have read all of the reports by the time the meeting starts.

■ Future perfect progressive—used to say how long something will have been happening by a certain time in the future

Example: We will have been meeting for more than an hour when John plans to mention the contract terms.

Terabyte

A *terabyte* is equal to 1,024 gigabytes. Terabytes should not be abbreviated. Leave a space between a number and the word when used as a noun.

Example: My computer has over 3 terabytes of storage.

When used as an adjective, add a hyphen between the number and the word.

Example: I just purchased a 3-terabyte drive.

Than I, Than Me

When making a comparison between yourself and something or someone else, you will often end with a subject form or object form: "taller than I" or "taller than she" or the like.

When the comparison is made in the subjective case, normally we leave out the verb in the second clause: *am, are,* or *is.*

Example: He is taller than I [am].

Example: He is taller than she [is].

Be careful with comparisons in the objective case.

Example: I like him better than she. [You like him better than she likes him.]

Example: I like him better than her. [You are saying you like him better than you like her.]

To avoid confusion with the word *than*, add the verb or rewrite the sentence.

Example: I like him better than she does.

Example: I like him better than I like her.

Than, Then

Than is used when making comparisons or implied comparisons.

Example: Bongo would rather climb a tree than sit in his cage and eat.

Then is a conjunction, but it cannot be used as a coordinating conjunction.

Incorrect: Bongo ate an apple, then he climbed the tree.

Correct: Bongo ate an apple, and then he climbed the tree.

That, Which

In determining whether to use *that* or *which*, the choice of word depends on whether the clause that modifies the noun is a restrictive or nonrestrictive clause.

A **restrictive clause** means that the information is essential to the meaning of the sentence. Use *that* for restrictive clauses.

A **nonrestrictive clause** includes information that can be omitted without changing the meaning of the sentence. Use *which* for nonrestrictive clauses.

Incorrect: A high performance engine is an engine, which needs a high-octane fuel.

Correct: A high performance engine is an engine that needs a high-octane fuel.

When referring to people in a sentence with either a restrictive or nonrestrictive clause, use *who* instead of *that* or *which*.

There, Their, They're

Use *there* when referring to a place.

Example: Look over there at that horse.

Use *their* to indicate possession.

Example: My parents just celebrated their fiftieth wedding anniversary.

Use *they're* as a contraction of *they* and *are*. *They're* consists of a subject and a verb and is never used as a modifier.

Example: They're really nice to new employees here.

Third Conditional

The **third conditional** is used for imaginary past actions that could not have happened because conditions were not met.

Example: If I had studied harder, I probably would have gone to medical school.

Time

Consider the following guidelines when writing about time:

- When a figure and a word come together as an adjective to express time, connect the two with a hyphen.

  Example: a 24-hour day

  But: a day of 24 hours

  Example: two 2-year, 12-percent notes

  But: two notes for two years at 12 percent

- Hours, minutes, and seconds are separated by a colon.

  Example: 10:05:02 a.m.

- Never write "this a.m." to mean "this morning."

- With *a.m.* or *p.m.*, the word *o'clock* should not be used:

  Example: I will meet you at 4 p.m.

  Example: I will meet you at four o'clock this afternoon.

- Ciphers (zeros) after the number of the hour are unnecessary.

- For exact noon and midnight, it is correct to use the words *noon* or *midnight:*

  Example: I will meet you at noon.

  Example: The horn blew at midnight.

Dates

- The day is written in numerals, without *-th, -st -rd,* or *-nd,* unless the day is written before the name of the month.

Incorrect: May 1st, 2011

Correct: May 1, 2011

Correct: On the 2nd of June 2011

Incorrect: in the August 21st and September 3rd editions

Correct: in the August 21 and September 3 editions

- In legal documents, dates are spelled out.

Example: the twelfth day of May, A.D. Two Thousand and Eight

Time Zones

The names of time zones should be treated as proper nouns and capitalized.

Example: Eastern Time, Central Time, Mountain Time, Pacific Time

Avoid specifying standard time or daylight saving time when writing about time zones. Do not abbreviate time zones.

Titled, Entitled

Entitled should not be used as a synonym for *titled*. *Entitled* means that something is owed. Books are *titled*.

Incorrect: He was reading from a white paper entitled "Avoiding HR Litigation."

Correct: He was reading from a white paper titled "Avoiding HR Litigation."

Titles

Consider the following tips for formatting titles:

- Underlining and italics serve the same purpose. Never do both.

- For titles of standalone works, use underlining or italics. Works that are part of another work are enclosed in quotation marks.

Table 2.30 itemizes what gets quotation marks and what should be italicized or underlined.

Table 2.30 Use of Underlining, Italics, and Quotation Marks in Titles

Type and Formatting	Types of Titles
No quotation marks or underlining/italic	Your own works
Italics or underlined	Books
	Audio CDs
	Names of vehicles of transportation (ships, trains, airplanes, spacecraft)
	Long poems
	Television shows, plays, and movies
Quotation marks	Articles in a newspaper or magazine
	Chapter titles
	Poems
	Short stories
	Song titles

Formatting the Title of a Manuscript

The title page of a manuscript should be formatted as follows:

- The title should be positioned in the center of the page, between the top and bottom margins and left and right margins.

- Use a 12- to 14-point font, such as Times New Roman or Courier.

- Use the bold font.

- Capitalize the title properly.
  - Do not use all caps for titles.
  - Capitalize the first letter of each word, except for short words of less than four letters.
- Add quotation marks, underline, or italics if you use any other work as part of your title.

Tmesis

Tmesis is a literary device that involves splitting a word into two parts and adding another word in the middle with all three parts separated by hyphens.

Example: any-old-how, fan-blooming-tastic, un-bloody-believable

To, At

Do not use either *to* or *at* with *where.*

Incorrect: Where are you at?

Correct: Where are you?

Incorrect: Where did he go to?

Correct: Where did he go?

Tone

Tone is the writer's attitude toward the reader and the subject. Tone is a reflection of the writer and determined by the choice of words, the style, and level of care and detail.

To make sure a business document has the appropriate tone:

- Know the purpose of the document.
- Know the audience and what they need to understand.

- Be confident, courteous, and sincere as you craft your writing.

- Emphasize what's important and avoid getting lost in the details.

- Don't use discriminatory language.

- Stress the benefits.

- Write at the appropriate reading level for your audience.

Topic Sentence

A **topic sentence** is the main sentence in a paragraph that states the main idea of the paragraph. Although it is often the first sentence in a paragraph, if the purpose of the paragraph is to draw a conclusion, the topic sentence is usually the last sentence, stating the conclusion.

Totally

See *Basically, Essentially, Totally.*

Toward, Towards

Toward and *towards* are interchangeable.

- *Toward* is more common in the United States.

- *Towards* is more common in the United Kingdom.

Transitions

As you compound sentences and vary your sentence structures to add variety to your writing, consider using **transitions** between ideas. Transitions help guide a reader from one idea to the next.

You can add transitions between ideas by:

- Using transitional expressions.

- Repeating key words and phrases.

- Using pronoun reference.

- Using parallel forms.

Transitional Expressions

In addition to coordinating conjunctions—*and, but, for, nor, or, so*, and *yet*—you can use conjunctive adverbs and transitional expressions such as *however, moreover*, and *nevertheless* to transition your sentences from one thought to the next.

The key is to avoid using the same transitional elements because the repetition becomes boring.

Table 2.31 contains a list of some conjunctive adverbs that can add spice to your transitions.

Table 2.31 Conjunctive Adverbs

Type of Transition	Conjunctive Adverbs
Addition	again, also, and, and then, besides, equally important, finally, first, further, furthermore, in addition, in the first place, last, moreover, next, second, still, too
Comparison	also, in the same way, likewise, similarly
Concession	granted, naturally, of course
Contrast	although, and yet, at the same time, but at the same time, despite that, even so, even though, for all that, however, in contrast, in spite of, instead, nevertheless, on the contrary, on the other hand, otherwise, regardless, still, though, yet
Emphasis	certainly, indeed, in fact
Example	after all, as an illustration, even, for example, for instance, in conclusion, in short, it is true, namely, specifically, that is, to illustrate, thus

(continues)

Table 2.31 *(continued)*

Type of Transition	Conjunctive Adverbs
Summary	all in all, altogether, as has been said, finally, in brief, in conclusion, in other words, in particular, in short, in simpler terms, in summary, on the whole, that is, therefore, to put it differently, to summarize
Time sequence	after a while, afterward, again, also, and then, as long as, at last, at length, at that time, before, besides, earlier, eventually, finally, formerly, further, furthermore, in addition, in the first place, in the past, last, lately, meanwhile, moreover, next, now, presently, second, shortly, simultaneously, since, so far, soon, still, subsequently, then, thereafter, too, until, until now, when

Repeating Key Words

By repeating a key word or phrase, you can establish its importance in the mind of the reader.

Example: It is spending that got us into this mess. It is spending by consumers that will get us out.

Pronoun Reference

Pronouns can be used to refer the reader to something earlier in the text. A pronoun such as *this* causes the reader to summarize what has been said so far.

Example: There has been an increase in the number of earthquakes in California in the past ten years. This [pronoun summarizing previous sentence] is true because we have geological records that go back almost 150 years, and they [pronoun related to "geological records"] show a clear trend.

Parallelism

Parallel constructions are expressions with similar content and function. Their similarity enables the reader to more easily recognize the content and understand the message.

Articles (*the, a,* and *an*) must be used either only before the first term in a group or before every term in the group.

Example: At the World's Fair we saw all the latest model automobiles, including <u>the</u> new Hondas, Toyotas, and Nissans.

Example: We left on Sunday for vacation with <u>the</u> Wilsons, <u>the</u> Wausons, and <u>the</u> Bruecks.

Correlative expressions (*both, and; not, but; not only, but also; either, or; first, second*) should be followed by the same grammatical construction.

Example: It was not only the blowing wind, but also the freezing temperatures that made travel so treacherous.

Transitive Verb

A **transitive verb** requires both a subject and a direct object.

An **intransitive verb** does not take an object.

Example: He <u>lifted</u> [transitive] the box.

Example: She <u>died</u> [intransitive] last week.

Try and, Come and, Be Sure and

Don't use a word if it is not necessary to convey your meaning.

Incorrect: Try and be here at noon.

Correct: Try to be here at noon.

Incorrect: Come and see me tomorrow.

Correct: Come see me tomorrow.

Incorrect: Be sure and watch out as you cross the street.

Correct: Be sure to watch out as you cross the street.

Type, Enter

For technical documents involving computer-related procedures, use *type* when a user enters information to fill out a form or form field.

Example: Type your employee ID in the User Name field.

Use *enter* to instruct users what kind of data should be typed.

Example: Enter the file name and then click OK.

Typeface, Font

See *Font, Typeface*.

Unbiased Language

Most gender problems can be avoided without the use of *he/she, he or she, him or her,* or *him/her* constructions. Plural pronouns such as *they* can be very helpful in this regard.

An occasional *he* or *she* is okay, but after a while using the same pronoun becomes distracting.

When a singular pronoun is necessary, use either *he* or *she* consistently to avoid confusion.

Sexist Language

A variety of words and phrases make demeaning assumptions about gender-related roles. Substitutes should be reasonable and appropriate. Try not to look as though you are avoiding sexist language.

Table 2.32 contains a list of words to avoid and their alternatives.

Table 2.32 Biased Words and Their Alternatives

Instead of ...	Use ...
actress	actor
anchorman	anchor
businessman	businessperson
chairman	chairperson or chair
coed	student
forefathers	ancestors
foreman	supervisor
freshman	first-year student

(continues)

Table 2.32 *(continued)*

Instead of ...	Use ...
mailman	mail carrier
male nurse	nurse
man (meaning human being)	person, people
managers and their wives	managers and their spouses
mankind	humanity, people
poetess	poet
policeman	police officer
salesman	sales representative
stewardess	flight attendant
waiter or waitress	server

Uncountable Noun

Nouns with no plural form are called **uncountable nouns** or **mass nouns**.

Example: air, water, furniture, music, art, love, luggage, sugar, electricity, money, currency, information

Uncountable nouns are paired with a singular verb.

Example: This water is very refreshing.

Indefinite articles *a* and *an* are not used with uncountable nouns. *Some, any, a little,* and *much* are used with uncountable nouns.

Example: May I have a little water?

Underlining

Underlining is used the same way italics are used, to designate titles of publications, although italics are preferred.

Underlining is also used to designate hyperlinks in a document such as email addresses or Web addresses.

See *Titles* and *Italics*.

Understatement

An **understatement** is a figure of speech where a lesser expression is used than might be expected, usually for humorous or literary effect.

Example: The lean-to was hardly well-appointed.

Until, By

See *By, Until*.

Upload, Download

See *Download, Upload*.

Uppercase

Uppercase is an adjective meaning capital letters. **Upper case** (two words) is the related noun. Never use all uppercase letters for emphasis in emails.

For computer-related procedures, keyboard key names should be in upper case.

Example: Press the ENTER key.

Use upper case for acronyms.

Example: NASA, FIFO

See *Capitalization*.

URL

URL is an acronym for uniform resource locator. A URL is an address for a Web site on the Internet or an intranet.

When writing about URLs in technical documents, use the indefinite article *a* instead of *an*.

> **Example:** Each Web site has a URL.

A URL includes an Internet protocol name, a domain name, and other information such as file names, directories, and port names. Internet protocol begins with http:// and each of the elements after the Internet protocol is separated by a slash.

> **Example:** http://www.videologies.com

Most of the time, a URL can be typed in all lower case.

When including a Web address in a business document, it is not necessary to include the Internet protocol (http://).

> **Example:** www.videologies.com

When referring to an entire Web site, you can drop the *www* at the beginning of the address.

> **Example:** I do a lot of shopping on Amazon.com.

To include a URL as a hyperlink in a document, set the URL off on its own line of text.

U.S.

U.S. is an abbreviation for United States. It is appropriate to use U.S. as an abbreviation when it acts as an adjective.

> **Example:** They expect to be paid in U.S. dollars.

Do not use the *U.S.* abbreviation when it acts as a noun.

Example: They wanted to visit the United States.

Used to

Used to is a phrase that refers to something that happened often in the past but no longer occurs.

Example: I used to ride my bike every day.

Used to also refers to something that was true but is no longer.

Example: I used to live in Texas.

Use to without the *d* is incorrect for this purpose.

Utterance

An **utterance** is one complete unit of spoken language. It can be something as short as one word, such as *oh,* to a complete sentence from one speaker in a dialogue.

Vain, Vane, Vein

Vain means to be conceited.

Example: He's so vain he doesn't know when he's being insulted.

A *vane* is a blade that is moved by gas or liquid.

Example: a weather vane

A *vein* carries blood through the body or is a long slender deposit of a mineral.

Example: a vein of gold

Verbal Phrase

Verbals are words that seem to mean an action or a state of being but do not function as verbs. They are sometimes called **nonfinite verbs**. Verbals are frequently used with other words in what is called a **verbal phrase**.

Example: Frequenting the shady bars in that neighborhood [verbal phrase] is not a good idea.

Verb Complement

See *Complements*.

Verb Forms

Verbs have four basic inflections, or endings:

- Present tense—Something is happening now.

- Past tense—Something happened in the past.

  Example: I thought.

- Present participle—Something is happening now.

  Example: I am thinking.

- Past participle—Something happened in the past (the verb is combined with an auxiliary).

  Example: I have thought.

Verb Group

A **verb group** consists of an auxiliary or modal verb along with a verb.

Example: He wouldn't say [modal + verb] that.

Example: We haven't told [auxiliary + verb] her.

Verbiage

Verbiage is sometimes used to describe wording or text in a document; however, it is actually an insulting term that means overly wordy.

Verb Mood

Verbs can be used in three moods:

- **Indicative mood**—used for factual statements
  - Present indicative

    Example: He eats at school.

  - Past indicative

    Example: He ate at school.

  - Future indicative

    Example: He will eat at school.

- **Imperative mood**—used for requests or commands

  Example: Notice how nice the lake looks.

  Example: Email him tomorrow.

- **Subjunctive mood**—used to express doubts, wishes, or a request

  Example: He acts as if he doesn't know what he's doing.

  - Auxiliary verbs *could, would,* and *should* can express the subjunctive mood.

    Example: If Carl were to move to Dallas, he would be happy.

Verbose Expressions

Beware of words that do not mean exactly what you want to say and of phrases that are careless, vague, or wordy.

Table 2.33 contains a list of examples of such pitfalls.

Table 2.33 Verbose Expressions

Verbose Expressions	What You Really Mean
I beg to be advised	Please tell me
Thank you kindly	Thank you
I feel that you are able to appreciate	You can appreciate
Which you will remember is in connection with	Regarding
I am not at present in a position to	I am unable to
I would, therefore, ask that you kindly write	Please write
We would appreciate it if you would investigate the matter and inform us and report	Please check the matter
You have my permission to	You may
I am in receipt of the complaint from John Smith	John Smith complains
You have not, I believe, favored us with a reply	You have not replied
I acknowledge receipt of your letter	I received your letter

Verbs

Verbs describe an action or an idea of being in a sentence.

Example: I <u>am</u> [idea of being] an office worker.

Example: The manager <u>worked</u> [action] hard.

There are four ways to classify verbs:

■ **Transitive**—requiring an object

Example: Will you lay the report on my desk?

- **Intransitive**—not requiring an object

  Example: The project manager is sitting.

- **Finite**—standing alone as the main verb in a sentence

  Example: The layouts destroyed morale.

- **Nonfinite**—not standing alone

  Example: the devastated employees

Verb Tense

The form of a verb helps determine its tense, which tells you when something is happening.

- Happening now

  Example: They're serving dinner.

- Going to happen

  Example: It will be ready in the morning.

- Has already happened

  Example: The bus just left.

See *Verb Forms* and *Tense*.

Versus, vs.

The abbreviation for *versus* is *vs.* As an abbreviation *vs.* is always lowercase. Use the abbreviation in headings and titles; otherwise spell out *versus*.

Vertical Lists

See *Lists*.

Visually Impaired, Blind

A person with vision problems can be visually impaired; however, a person who can't see is blind.

Many people think using *visually impaired* is better than saying *blind*, but actually it is more polite to say *blind* when a person can't see.

Voice

Voice is a relationship between the action in a sentence and the participants.

When the subject of a sentence is the agent, we use the **active voice**.

When the subject of a sentence undergoes the action, we use the **passive voice**.

See *Active Voice* and *Passive Voice*.

Voice Mail

Voice mail is two words and should not be abbreviated as *v-mail* or *vmail*.

Vowels

All English words have at least one **vowel**. Vowels include *a, e, i, o, u*, and *y*. *Y* can act as a consonant when it begins a word.

Wait On

When *wait* refers to time, *on* is not needed.

Incorrect: Please do not wait on me if I am not at the station when you arrive.

Correct: Please do not wait for me if I am not at the station when you arrive.

When the word refers to the actions of a waiter or waitress, *wait on* is acceptable.

Correct: The headwaiter assigned the red-haired woman to wait on me.

Wander, Wonder

Wander means to walk around with no destination in mind.

Wonder, as a noun, means astonishment or curiosity. As a verb, it means to feel curiosity or doubt.

Web

Web is short for World Wide Web.

Spell out *World Wide Web* in your first usage and then use *Web* thereafter. When referring to the Internet, *Web* is always capitalized.

Example: Web page, Web browser, Web address, Web site

Although the abbreviation for World Wide Web is *www, Web* is the preferred abbreviation in business writing.

Weblog

See *Blog, Weblog*.

Web Pages, Web Site

A *Web page* is a individual page on a *Web site*, which is a collection of text and graphics at a particular IP address on the World Wide Web.

Capitalize *Web* in both Web page and Web site.

Weights and Measures

Consider the following guidelines when writing about weights and measurements:

- Abbreviations are used without capitalization.

   Example: 6 lb 3 oz, 6 pounds 3 ounces

   Example: 192 lb, 192 pounds

- In a compound adjective showing a weight or a measure, the numeral is hyphenated with a singular noun.

   Example: a speed of 600 miles an hour, a 600-mile-an-hour speed

   Example: a workweek of 40 hours, a 40-hour workweek

Well, Good

See *Good, Well*.

Went, Gone

See *Gone, Went*.

When, Whether

See *If, When, Whether.*

Where

Whether used as an adverb or a conjunction, *where* denotes position or place.

Where should never be used as a substitute for *that* when introducing a clause.

> **Incorrect:** Did you read in the paper where our mayor was honored at a banquet?
>
> **Correct:** Did you read in the paper that our mayor was honored at a banquet?

Whether or Not

When *whether* is used to introduce a statement involving multiple alternatives, do not use *not.*

> **Incorrect:** She didn't know whether or not to go first to the drugstore or to the cleaners.
>
> **Correct:** She didn't know whether to go first to the drugstore or to the cleaners.

Which

When used to introduce a clause, *which* must refer to a specific noun or pronoun and not to a whole situation.

> **Incorrect:** He did not arrive in time for the meeting, which caused the president embarrassment.
>
> **Correct:** His failure to arrive in time for the meeting caused the president embarrassment.

> **Correct:** His failure to arrive, which caused the president embarrassment, was the reason for his dismissal.

Who's, Whose

Who's is a contraction for *who is*.

Example: Who's working the night shift this week?

Whose is the possessive form of *who*.

Example: Whose work clothes are those on the floor?

Who, Which

Who is used to refer to people.

Which refers to objects.

Correct: She is the woman who smiled at him.

Correct: She is the kind of person whom everyone likes.

Correct: I read the book on bridges, which I found fascinating.

Who, Whom

When determining whether to use *who* or *whom* in a sentence, rephrase the sentence using *he* and *him*.

Example: Who/whom is responsible? He is responsible. Who is responsible?

Example: Give the box to who/whom? Give the box to him. Give the box to whom?

Will, Shall

See *Shall, Will*.

Within, Inside of

See *Inside of, Within.*

Woman, Female

See *Female, Woman.*

Wonder, Wander

See *Wander, Wonder.*

Word Classes

The major **word classes** include the following:

- Verbs
- Nouns
- Determiners
- Adjectives
- Adverbs
- Prepositions
- Conjunctions

Words or Figures

See *Numbers or Words.*

Wordy Expressions

See *Verbose Expressions.*

Would of

See *Might of, Should of, Would of, Could of.*

Would, Should

See *Should, Would.*

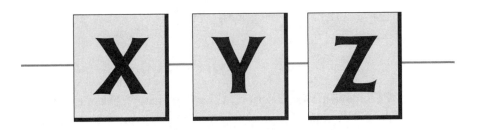

Xmas, Christmas

Xmas is an abbreviation for *Christmas* that should not be used in business writing.

Yes/No Questions

A **yes/no question** is one that can be answered with a yes or no response. These questions normally begin with an auxiliary or modal verb.

Example: Do you want to see it?

Example: Did you find it?

Example: Will they like it?

Zero Article

Zero article describes a situation where a noun is used without an article like *the*, *a*, or *an*.

Example: Money is power.

Example: We are studying French.

Zero Conditional

Zero conditional describes a situation that is always true when all the conditions are met. It is formed by adding *if* + present simple tense + present simple tense.

Example: If it rains, the roads get wet.

Zeugma

Zeugma is a figure of speech describing a word that is used to link two words or phrases; however, the word would normally be grammatically correct when used with only one of the words or phrases.

Example: She <u>lost</u> her purse and her temper.

Zip Code

Zip Code is always capitalized.

Sample Business Documents

ABSTRACTS

An **abstract** is a summary of a larger document, such as a report. Abstracts are also called **summaries** or **executive summaries**.

There are two types of abstracts:

- **Descriptive abstracts** are short summaries that appear on the front page of a formal report or journal article. (Figure 3.1.)
  - A descriptive abstract does not summarize the facts or conclusions of the report.
  - A descriptive abstract introduces the report and explains what the report covers.

Example: This report provides recommendations for the antivirus software currently available.

- **Informative abstracts** summarize the key facts and conclusions of the report. (Figure 3.2.)
  - Informative abstracts are usually one- or two-page documents.
  - Informative abstracts summarize each of the sections in the report.
  - Sentence structure is normally complex and packed with information.
  - An informative abstract is intended to allow readers to determine whether they want to read the report.
  - An informative abstract is not treated as an introduction.
  - Include any statistical details in an informative abstract.

Figure 3.1 Descriptive Abstract

Abstract

The U.S. Air Force Research Laboratory has been developing cost effective methods for gathering occupational and training requirements information. This information has most often been collected at an individual level of analysis focusing on the more behavioral aspects of work. Recent interest in both team and cognitive requirements for work has prompted renewed interest in team task analysis and accurately representing knowledge and cognitive components of work. The U.S. and Allied Military Services have pioneered the development of exemplar methods that serve as the foundation for recent advanced training. This paper highlights recent explorations and advanced training in team task analysis and cognitive task analysis methods. Implications for increasing the accuracy and efficiency of the requirements analysis process will also be discussed.

(Courtesy of the United States Air Force)

Figure 3.2 Informative Abstract

Summary

The U.S. Fish and Wildlife Service published special rules to establish nonessential experimental populations of gray wolves (*Canis lupus*) in Yellowstone National Park and central Idaho. The nonessential experimental population areas include all of Wyoming, most of Idaho, and much of central and southern Montana. A close reading of the special regulations indicates that, unintentionally, the language reads as though wolf control measures apply only outside of the experimental population area. This proposed revision is intended to amend language in the special regulations so that it clearly applies within the Yellowstone nonessential experimental population area and the central Idaho nonessential experimental population area. This proposed change will not affect any of the assumptions and earlier analysis made in the environmental impact statement or other portions of the special rules.

(Courtesy of the United States Environmental Protection Agency)

ACCEPTANCE LETTER

An **acceptance letter** is often written to formally acknowledge an employment offer, the receipt of a gift, or the appointment to a public office. An acceptance letter can also be written to formally accept someone else's resignation.

Consider these tips when writing an acceptance letter (Figure 3.3):

■ Begin the letter by thanking the person, business, or organization.

■ Identify what you are accepting and explain what it means to you.

■ Thank anyone who assisted you.

■ State the terms as you understand them.

■ If accepting an employment offer, summarize the start date, job title and description, compensation, benefits, and vacation days offered.

■ Use a positive tone.

■ Be gracious by showing your courtesy, tact, and charm in your writing style.

■ Restate your thanks and appreciation in the closing of the letter.

■ Use the spelling checker in your word processor to check for spelling errors.

■ Read the letter for clarity and to check for grammatical mistakes.

Acceptance letters are typically written to accept:

■ An invitation to a social event

■ A job offer

■ A request to serve in an honorary position

■ A resignation

■ An honor

■ An invitation to a business appointment

■ An invitation to speak

■ A gift

■ A proposal

Figure 3.3 Acceptance Letter

Evelyn Wauson
4212 West Church Street
Houston, Texas 77096
(713) 555-5555

October 20, 2011

Dear Mr. Harrison,

It was a pleasure speaking with you on the phone this afternoon.
I am very happy to accept the position of LMS supervisor with Harrison
Consultants. Thank you very much for the opportunity to join your team.
I am excited about the possibilities for this position, and I am eager to
work on the implementation of your new learning management system
and corporate online university.

As we discussed in our conversation, my starting yearly salary will
be $50,000. I understand that after being employed for 30 days, I will
receive health, dental, and life insurance benefits. After working for
Harrison Consultants for six months, I will receive one week's paid
vacation.

I am prepared to start work on December 1, 2011 as you requested.
If there is any paperwork I need to complete before I start work, or if
you need any additional information, please contact me.

I appreciate the help your associate Ken Knox provided by referring
me to you for this position.

Thank you.

Evelyn Wauson
Evelyn Wauson

ACKNOWLEDGMENT LETTER

An **acknowledgment letter** is a response that clarifies what is expected from you. An acknowledgment letter should be sent within two days of receiving the original letter, report, order, or request.

Consider these tips when writing an acknowledgment letter (Figure 3.4):

■ Include a short apology if the acknowledgement letter is delayed.

■ If you are responding to a complaint, be courteous and apologize for any inconvenience or problem.

■ Be sincere.

■ The letter should be addressed to a specific person if possible.

Acknowledgment letters are typically written to:

■ Accept a request to serve in an honorary position or a resignation.

■ Express appreciation for a suggestion.

■ Acknowledge a customer's order or donation or payment of an overdue balance.

■ Acknowledge the receipt of a report or letter, the receipt of a résumé, or the return of an item for refund, exchange, or credit.

■ Confirm an appointment or meeting, a business agreement, or an error, revision, or correction.

■ Celebrate an anniversary of employment.

Figure 3.4 Acknowledgment Letter

Isha Foundation
951 Isha Lane
McMinnville, TN 37110

August 20, 2011

Jeff Collins
3111 North Amber Lane
Nashville, TN 37213

Subj.: Tax Year 2011

Dear Mr. Collins,

Thank you for your recent donation of $500 for our outreach program,
Isha Care. Your gift will allow us to continue our efforts to provide free
medical care to the residents of rural Tennessee.

Your donation is fully tax-deductible, and this letter may serve as
a receipt for your tax records. This letter also verifies that you have
not received any tangible benefits in return for your donation.

Your generous gift assures a continued investment in the future of
Tennessee.

Thank you.

Dr. Jane Morgan
Dr. Jane Morgan
President, Isha Foundation Inc. USA

ADJUSTMENT LETTER

Adjustment letters are responses to written complaints. The purpose of such letters is to acknowledge the complaint. The letter is also a legal document that records what action will be taken.

Consider these tips when writing an adjustment letter (Figure 3.5):

- Reference the date of the original complaint letter.

- The letter should review the facts of the case and offer an apology for any inconvenience.

- When there is no truth to the complaint, courteously explain the reasons as clearly as possible.

- When the customer's request is denied, offer some compensation or advice.

- Take a positive approach to the letter to counter any negative feelings of the reader.

- The solution is more important than the reasons why something occurred.

- Cordially conclude the letter and express confidence that you and the reader can continue doing business.

Adjustment letters are typically written to apologize for:

- A defective or damaged product

- A missed deadline

- Making a mistake on a customer's account

- A shipping error

- Damaged property

- Poor quality or service

Figure 3.5 Adjustment Letter

Snack Makers, Inc.
1234 West Main Street
Los Angeles, CA 90036

April 20, 2012

Mr. Carl Luntz
Store Manager
Luntz Grocery
2411 Third Avenue
Atlanta, GA 30134

Dear Mr. Luntz:

I would like to apologize for the damaged shipment of Humus Chips.
At Snack Makers, we always try to package our product as securely
as possible, but it appears this time we failed.

We have shipped a replacement case of Humus Chips today at no charge.
You should receive them within two days. There's no need to return the
damaged product. You may dispose of the crushed chips anyway you
wish.

Being a new company with a new product, we want you to know that
we value your business and will do everything we can to make sure
this doesn't happen again.

In addition, I am crediting your account for $155 to reflect a 20% discount
off your original order.

I hope you will accept my apologies and will continue to do business with
Snack Makers.

Sincerely,

Morton Boyd

Morton Boyd
President
Snack Makers, Inc.

ANNOUNCEMENT LETTER

Announcement letters should be written in a straightforward and concise style so that readers can get information quickly.

Consider these tips when writing announcement letters (Figure 3.6):

- For positive announcements, make the letter inviting and to the point.

- Build morale, confidence, and goodwill.

- When announcing achievements, try to motivate others to achieve the same goals.

- Use the announcement to promote your business.

- Include enough information so that you don't have to answer questions about the announcement later.

- When announcing bad news, be considerate and respectful.

Announcement letters are typically written to announce:

- A new address

- A change in company name

- The business schedule

- A new hire or promotion

- An employee's special achievement

- A retirement

- A new product

- A new store opening

- A layoff

- A store closing

- A new policy

- A contest winner

- A price change

- Bad news to employees

- A training session

Figure 3.6 Announcement Letter

System Golf Supplies
4143 Green Avenue
Baltimore, MD 21205

May 22, 2012

Ms. Susan Jones
Manager
Jones Golfing
1322 North Pleasant Street
Baltimore, MD 21075

Dear Ms. Jones:

Due to increased costs for materials used in our manufacturing process, we must unfortunately increase the wholesale cost of our products. We have examined other ways to reduce our manufacturing costs; however, we have been unable to reduce costs enough without sacrificing quality. To maintain the superior quality of our products, we must raise our prices. I have enclosed a new price list that will go into effect on July 1, 2012. Any orders placed between now and July 1 will be honored at our previous prices.

We want to thank you for your business in the past, and we hope you understand the necessity for this increase.

Sincerely,

Carl Richardson

Carl Richardson
Sales Manager
System Golf Supplies

ANNUAL REPORT

An **annual report** is a document used to disclose corporation information to shareholders—a state-of-the-company report. All U.S. companies that issue publicly traded stock are required to file an annual report with the Securities and Exchange Commission (SEC). The document that is filed with the SEC is the Form 10-K.

Many nonprofit organizations, foundations, and charities produce annual reports to assess their performance. Nonprofit annual reports include the following sections (Figures 3.7–3.11):

- Letter from the chairman of the board

- A description of the charity, its causes, actions, and accomplishments for the year

- The financial statement:

  - A letter from the organization's CPA

  - Income statement

  - Balance sheet

- A list of directors and officers

If a company is privately owned but has more than 500 shareholders and over $10 million in assets, it is also required to file an annual report.

In addition to Form 10-K annual reports, the same mandated corporations must also file a quarterly Form 10-Q as a quarterly report.

The annual reports required by the SEC follow a strict format and include the following sections (Figures 3.7–3.11):

- Business overview

- Risk factors

- Unresolved staff comments

- Properties

- Legal proceedings

- Submission of matters to a vote by shareholders

- Market for the company's common equity

- Related stockholder matters

- Management's discussion and analysis of financial conditions and the results of operations

- Disclosures about market risk

- Financial statements and supplementary data

- Changes in accounting

- Controls and procedures

- Other information

- Directors, executive officers, and corporate governance

- Executive compensation

- Security ownership of stock by management and certain beneficial owners

- Relationships and related transaction and director independence

- Accounting fees and services

- Exhibits and financial statement schedules

(text continues on page 444)

Figure 3.7 Annual Report Cover Page

2008 Performance and Accountability Report

U.S. Securities and Exchange Commission

(Courtesy of the U.S. Securities and Exchange Commission)

Figure 3.8 Annual Report Table of Contents

CONTENTS

(Courtesy of the U.S. Securities and Exchange Commission)

Figure 3.9 Annual Report Letter from the Chairman

Message from the Chairman

Christopher Cox
Chairman

Dear Investor,

The mortgage meltdown and ensuing global credit crisis during the past year have confronted our markets with unprecedented challenges. The government's response to the financial turmoil has been equally unprecedented: the Federal Reserve and the Department of the Treasury have together committed over one trillion dollars in taxpayer funds to support insurance companies, banks, thrifts, investment banks, and mortgage giants Fannie Mae and Freddie Mac.

The Emergency Economic Stabilization Act (EESA), signed into law in October 2008, gives the Chairman of the SEC a formal oversight role with respect to the Troubled Asset Relief Plan administered by the Department of the Treasury. In addition, the Housing and Economic Recovery Act of 2008 gives the SEC Chairman similar oversight and advisory responsibilities with respect to the conservatorship of Fannie Mae and Freddie Mac supervised by the Federal Housing Finance Agency. These duties come in addition to the new responsibilities the SEC is already discharging as the statutory regulator of credit rating agencies, and the mandate that the EESA has given the agency to report by January 1, 2009, on the results of a congressionally-mandated study of fair value accounting.

Response to the Credit Crisis

The agency has taken a number of other actions in recent months to address significant issues that have arisen in the credit crisis. When the auction rate securities market froze early in 2008, the Enforcement Division immediately commenced investigations of potential securities law

violations by the largest sellers of these instruments. Preliminary settlements were reached in principle with six of the largest firms, which would return more than $50 billion to injured investors and make these settlements, when concluded, by far the largest in the agency's history. (While settlements in principle were reached during FY 2008, the amounts were not included in the enforcement statistics for this report because they were not finalized by the close of the fiscal year on September 30.)

As of the close of FY 2008, the Commission had over 50 pending subprime-related investigations involving lenders, investment banks, credit rating agencies, insurers, and broker-dealers. During the past year the SEC charged the managers of two Bear Stearns hedge funds in connection with last year's collapse of those funds. The Commission returned $356 million to investors harmed when Fannie Mae issued false and misleading financial statements. And the Division of Enforcement is currently in the midst of a nationwide investigation of potential fraud and manipulation of securities in some of the nation's largest financial institutions through abusive short selling and the intentional spreading of false information.

As part of this aggressive law enforcement investigation into potential manipulation during the subprime crisis, the Commission approved orders requiring hedge funds, broker-dealers and institutional investors to file statements under oath regarding trading and market activity in the securities of financial firms. The orders cover not only equities but also credit default swaps. To assist in analyzing this information, the SEC's Office of Information Technology is working with the Enforcement Division to create a common database of trading information, audit trail data, and credit default swaps clearing data. Our Office of Economic Analysis is also supporting this effort by helping to analyze the data across markets for possible manipulative patterns in both equity securities and derivatives.

During FY 2008, the Enforcement Division also brought the highest number of insider trading cases in the agency's history. In addition, the SEC brought a record-high number of enforcement actions against market manipulation in 2008, including a precedent-setting case against a Wall

2   2008 Performance and Accountability Report

(Courtesy of the U.S. Securities and Exchange Commission)

Figure 3.10 Annual Report Organizational Overview

Vision, Mission, Values, and Goals

Vision

The Securities and Exchange Commission (SEC) aims to be the standard against which federal agencies are measured. The SEC's vision is to strengthen the integrity and soundness of U.S. securities markets for the benefit of investors and other market participants, and to conduct its work in a manner that is as sophisticated, flexible, and dynamic as the securities markets it regulates.

Mission

The mission of the SEC is to protect investors; maintain fair, orderly, and efficient markets; and facilitate capital formation.

Values

In managing the evolving needs of a complex marketplace and in pursuing its mission, the SEC embraces the following values:

- Integrity
- Accountability
- Fairness
- Resourcefulness
- Teamwork
- Commitment to Excellence

Goals

- **Enforce compliance with federal securities laws**
  The Commission seeks to detect problems in the securities markets, prevent and deter violations of federal securities laws, and alert investors to possible wrongdoing. When violations occur, the SEC aims to take prompt action to halt the misconduct, sanction wrongdoers effectively, and, where possible, return funds to harmed investors.

- **Promote healthy capital markets through an effective and flexible regulatory environment**
  The savings and investments of every American are dependent upon healthy capital markets. The Commission seeks to sustain an effective and flexible regulatory environment that will facilitate innovation, competition, and capital formation to ensure that our economy can continue to grow and create jobs for our nation's future. Enhancing the productivity of America is a key goal that the SEC works to achieve by increasing investor confidence in the capital markets.

- **Foster informed investment decision making**
  An educated investing public ultimately provides the best defense against fraud and costly mistakes. The Commission works to promote informed investment decisions through two main approaches: reviewing disclosures of companies and mutual funds to ensure that clear, complete, and accurate information is available to investors; and implementing a variety of investor education initiatives.

- **Maximize the use of SEC resources**
  The investing public and the securities markets are best served by an efficient, well-managed, and proactive SEC. The Commission strives to improve its organizational effectiveness by making sound investments in human capital and new technologies, and by enhancing internal controls.

2008 Performance and Accountability Report

(Courtesy of the U.S. Securities and Exchange Commission)

Figure 3.11 Annual Report Overview of Organization's Performance

Financial and Performance Highlights

- In FY 2008, the SEC was authorized by Congress to spend $906 million, a 2.8 percent increase over the $881.6 million authorized in FY 2007. Funding was offset by fees collected by the SEC. Of the total authority, $843 million was new budgetary authority and the remaining $63 million was carried over from prior year unobligated balances, as illustrated in *Chart 1.2*.

- In FY 2008, the SEC reduced its year-end unobligated balance over previous levels through rigorous oversight and management of budgetary resources made possible by improvements in technology such as the agency's budget and performance tool.

- The SEC employed 3,511 FTE in FY 2008. This represents an increase of 46 FTE over FY 2007.

- In 2002, Congress set by law the aggregate amounts the SEC is to collect annually through fees. These target amounts generally exceed the level of funding appropriated to the SEC, and are used by Congress to offset SEC and other federal spending.

- In order to meet the offsetting collections target in FY 2008, the SEC lowered the rates of fees it collects on securities transactions on the exchanges and certain over-the-counter markets. Additional discussion of the fees collected by the SEC can be found in *Note 1.L. Accounts Receivable and Allowance for Uncollectible Accounts* on page 66, and *Note 1.S. Revenue and Other Financing Sources* on page 68.

- While the transaction fee rate was cut by more than half from this time last year, there was significantly more transactional volume compared to last year. Therefore, the total collections dropped only 36 percent. In accordance with law, the SEC collected fees in excess of its appropriations from Congress. However, the excess amount is declining, as illustrated in *Chart 1.3*.

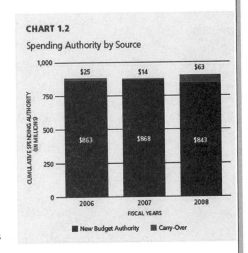

CHART 1.2

Spending Authority by Source

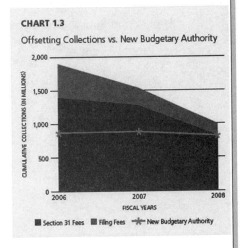

CHART 1.3

Offsetting Collections vs. New Budgetary Authority

2008 Performance and Accountability Report

(Courtesy of the U.S. Securities and Exchange Commission)

APPLICATION LETTER

In an **application letter** (Figure 3.12):

- In the first sentence, state what you are applying for.

- Explain the reasons you are applying and be specific.

  - Give the reasons why you are qualified including your experience, qualifications, accomplishments, and goals.

- Identify the response you would like to your letter.

- Identify the date you need a response.

- Reference any other materials included with the letter, such as a résumé, job application form, letters of recommendation, or work samples.

- Include your contact information and when you are available.

- Close the letter with a thank you.

Application letters are typically written to apply for:

- Employment

- Admission to a school

- Admission to a club

- A foreign work permit

- A grant

- A scholarship

- A travel visa

- A special program

- Credit

Figure 3.12 Application Letter

1322 Forest Lane
Dallas, TX 75214
August 11, 2012

Michele Phillips
APS Software
13211 Greenville Avenue
Dallas, TX 75212

Dear Ms. Phillips:

I am writing to apply for the position you advertised on Monster.com for a quality control manager. As you will see in my résumé, I have the experience to fill this position.

For the past ten years, I have been working in the information technology department at Hopewell Industries where I have been a software developer, project manager, and manager of QC Testing. My experience has ranged from coding, to managing teams of programmers, to creating test plans, running tests, and managing testers.

Recently, Hopewell Industries decided to outsource the IT function to IBM. While I am sad to leave the company, I am looking forward to a new assignment with fresh faces and new projects.

I have heard about APS Software in various trade journals and would be very interested in becoming part of your team. APS is well known for innovative quality products, and I am excited about the possibility of becoming a part of your success story.

I hope you'll give me an opportunity to discuss my qualifications and experience. I can be reached at (214) 555-5555 after 6 p.m.

Thank you very much for your consideration for this position.

Sincerely yours,

Alice Grassley

Alice Grassley

Encl.: résumé

BROCHURES

Brochures are often used by businesses to advertise products and services. There are several different types of brochures:

- Leave-behind brochures are left after a personal sales presentation.
  - These focus on a full description of the product and its benefits.
  - They echo the sales pitch given by the salesperson.
- Point-of-sale brochures are designed to catch your interest while waiting in line to check out in a store.
  - They are visually appealing with a catchy headline.
- Inquiry response brochures are sent to people who have asked for information about a product.
  - These brochures focus on a sales pitch that encourages the reader to take the next step and purchase the product or service.
- Direct mail brochures are sent to potential customers along with a sales letter.
- Sales support brochures are used by salespeople during their presentations.

In the planning phase of brochure creation, consider the following:

- Determine what you want the brochure to do: get orders, inform, get appointments.
- Determine the audience for the brochure and why they should be interested in your product or service.
- Develop an outline and divide the content you want to cover into sections.
- Consider the style of brochure you plan to create, and think about the content that is best for the cover, inside pages, and back cover.
  - Also consider content that is suitable for any sidebars.
- Determine whether photography or illustrations can be used.
  - If photography is used, also include captions for each photo that focus on benefits.
  - Photos should be at least 300 dpi resolution in order to print with the best possible print quality.

When writing copy for a brochure, keep the following in mind (see Figures 3.13–3.14):

- Write from the reader's point of view.
    - As the reader unfolds the brochure, present the information in the order that a reader would want to receive it.
    - On the cover or first page of the brochure, motivate readers to open the brochure and seek out additional information.
- For a brochure longer than eight or more pages, include a list of contents highlighted in bold and separated from the rest of the copy.
- Describe the product or service in terms of what it means to the potential customer.
    - Focus on the benefits rather than the features.
- Include helpful reference information that will make the reader want to keep the brochure on file.
- Write in an informal matter-of-fact style, as if you are having a one-on-one conversation with someone.
- Share your emotions and enthusiasm about the product or service.
- Don't waste time on all the details; instead, focus on the key selling points.
- Organize the content into easily identifiable sections.
- Ask for an order and provide simple instructions on how to order.
- Make a persuasive sales pitch.

In designing the brochure and doing the layout, consider the following:

- Study brochures from other companies and determine which designs are effective and which are not.
- Avoid packing in too much content.
    - Empty space is okay.
- Avoid using too many graphical boxes and lines to separate chunks of content.
    - They tend to make your design look cluttered.
- Use a consistent typeface throughout the brochure.

- You can change fonts within the same typeface family in various places for emphasis.

- Consider different fonts, font styles, sizes, and colors for key selling points and headings.

  - Use these techniques sparingly for greater emphasis.

  - Avoid all caps. Use bold style instead.

  - Avoid underlining. Use italics style instead.

  - Avoid putting text over images unless you make the image at least 80% transparent.

  - Avoid putting text columns on the first page or cover.

  - Use no more than 10 words on the cover.

  - Don't use more than two or three sentences per paragraph with a layout that is no more than nine or ten lines of type.

  - Add a space between paragraphs and do not indent the first word.

  - Use only one space after a period before starting the next sentence.

- If you have to start a sentence with a number, write it out.

Incorrect: 50% of the homeowners experienced hail damage.

Correct: Fifty percent of the homeowners experienced hail damage.

- Consider the use of multiple ink colors and colored paper.

- When creating a layout with photography, don't position the photos so that they are creased by a fold in the paper.

- Use desktop publishing software such as Microsoft Publisher, Adobe InDesign, or QuarkXPress.

  - Set the paper size before any design elements are created.

  - Confirm that the printer will be able to print on the intended size paper.

- Allow for print bleed in order to achieve edge-to-edge printing.

  - To create print bleed, expand your brochure design slightly beyond the edge of the paper with nonessential design elements to allow for trimming.

- Proofread your final design several times to avoid printing a brochure with a mistake or typo.

Figure 3.13 Brochure

Participants

Centers for Disease Control and Prevention
Central Intelligence Agency
Consumer Product Safety Commission
Department of Agriculture
Department of Army
Department of Commerce
Department of Education
Department of Energy
Department of Health and Human Services
Department of Housing and Urban Development
Department of Interior
Department of Justice
Department of Labor
Department of Navy
Department of State
Department of Transportation
Department of the Treasury
Department of Veterans Affairs
Environmental Protection Agency
Federal Bureau of Investigation
Federal Emergency Management Agency
Federal Trade Commission
Food and Drug Administration
General Services Administration
Government Printing Office
Internal Revenue Service
John F. Kennedy Center for the Performing Arts
Library of Congress
National Academy of Sciences
National Aeronautics and Space Administration
National Archives and Records Administration
National Endowment for the Arts
National Endowment for the Humanities
National Gallery of Art
National Institutes of Health
National Oceanic and Atmospheric Administration
National Park Service
National Science Foundation
National Security Agency
Nuclear Regulatory Commission
Office of Personnel Management
Peace Corps
Securities and Exchange Commission
Smithsonian Institution
Social Security Administration
U.S. Courts
U.S. Geological Survey
U.S. International Trade Commission
U.S. Holocaust Memorial Museum
U.S. Patent and Trademark Office
U.S. Supreme Court

www.ed.gov/free
Resources for Teachers, Parents, and Students

"One of the 16 best federal sites on the Web."
Government Executive

"A gold mine of information."
The Washington Post

"The absolute BEST Web site for using
technology in the classroom!"
Fifth-Grade Science Teacher

"Sometimes the government gets it right.
You made that happen."
Director of a Nonprofit Organization

Federal Resources for Educational Excellence
U.S. Department of Education
Office of the Under Secretary
Office of Intergovernmental
and Interagency Affairs
400 Maryland Ave., S.W.,
Washington, DC 20202-0498

free@ed.gov

Federal Resources for Educational Excellence

Federal Resources for Educational Excellence

Teachers, Parents, and Students—

FREE makes it easy to find learning resources
from more than 35 federal organizations.
Resources include teaching ideas, learning
activities, photos, maps, primary documents,
data, paintings, sound recordings, and more—
on thousands of topics. . .

The Constitution, photosynthesis, probability, American writers, women's suffrage, the
Renaissance, the Great Depression, Thomas
Jefferson, epidemiology, the human genome,
geology, cells, sun-earth connections, the
Civil War, African-American history, jazz,
aerospace careers, genealogy, immigration,
poetry, calculus, water in Africa, and more.

FREE is among the federal government's
most popular education Web sites because it
offers one-stop access to learning resources
developed by. . .

• Library of Congress
• NASA
• National Archives and Records Administration
• National Endowment for the Humanities
• National Gallery of Art
• National Park Service
• National Science Foundation
• Peace Corps
• Smithsonian Institution
• And other federal agencies and organizations.

Each week day, you'll find a new resource
featured on the FREE home page, such as. . .

• **School-Home Links**, part of the *Compact
  for Reading*, provides 400 activities for
  strengthening children's reading and writing
  skills in grades K-3.

• **Valley of the Shadow** looks at the Civil War
  through soldiers' letters, news articles, and
  other information from two communities
  separated by the Mason-Dixon line.

• **The Math Forum** highlights a Problem of
  the Week, Ask Dr. Math, Web units, and
  more.

• **Constitutional Community** presents lessons
  around images of the American Revolution,
  Civil War, and 33 other topics.

• **Find Out Why** explains why baseballs fly
  off bats, what makes playground slides
  slippery, and why hurricanes happen.

• **Art for the Nation** examines the works,
  techniques, and lives of more than a dozen
  famous artists.

FREE
www.ed.gov/free

(Courtesy of the U.S. Department of Education)

Figure 3.14 Brochure

"I was very satisfied with the process and I think all the managers would agree with that. The outcome was far better than anything that could have been obtained through administrative proceedings."
Mike Godfrey,
Senior Vice President and
General Counsel, FINA.

"I have been involved in four separate mediations conducted by the EEOC. I think the process is effective and efficient, particularly when an employee is still employed by the respondent."
Julia Carter,
Arizona Center for Disability Law.

"Our resolution rate in mediation between the EEOC and state and local agencies is 70 percent resolution at the table, and that typically is in the one-day mediation stage. You get it done and focus on resolution."
Deborah Lilly,
Director of Fair Employment for
Giant Food, Inc.

Publication EEOC-BK-26

For a list of EEOC publications, or to order publications visit our website at www.eeoc.gov or write, call or fax:
U.S. Equal Employment Opportunity Commission
Publications Distribution Center
P.O. Box 12549
Cincinnati, Ohio 45212-0549
1-800-669-3362 (voice)
1-800-800-3302 (TTY)
513-489-8692 (fax)

U.S. Equal Employment Opportunity Commission
Washington, D.C. 20507

MEDIATE!

Employment Discrimination Charges

Fair, Efficient *And* Everyone Wins

U.S. Equal Employment Opportunity Commission
Chairwoman Ida L. Castro

What is Mediation?

Mediation is a FAIR and EFFICIENT process to help you resolve your employment disputes and reach an agreement.

A neutral mediator assists you in reaching a voluntary, negotiated agreement.

How does it work at the EEOC?

The decision to mediate is completely voluntary for the charging party and the employer.

When a complaint is filed, the parties may be offered mediation.

If both the charging party and employer agree, mediation will be scheduled by an experienced mediator.

During mediation, both sides will be able to exchange information and express expectations for reaching resolution.

The parties work to reach common ground and resolve their differences. An agreement reached in mediation is as binding as any settlement reached through EEOC.

If an agreement is not reached, the case will be referred to EEOC's investigative process to be handled like any other case.

Information disclosed during mediation will not be revealed to anyone ... including other EEOC employees.

Choose Mediation to Resolve Employment Discrimination Disputes

Why labor through months of investigation or litigation?

Mediation ...

IS FAIR AND NEUTRAL

Parties have an equal say in the process and the parties decide the settlement terms. Not the mediator! There is no determination of guilt or innocence in the process.

SAVES TIME AND MONEY

Many mediated settlements are completed in one meeting and legal or other representation is permitted in all cases, but not required.

IS CONFIDENTIAL

All parties sign an agreement of confidentiality at the beginning of the process.

AVOIDS UNNECESSARY LITIGATION

Lengthy litigation CAN be avoided.

Mediation promotes a better work environment, reduces costs and works for the employer AND the employee!

How Can I Learn More?

For further information, visit our website at www.eeoc.gov or contact:

1-800-669-4000 (voice)
or
1-800-669-6820 (TTY)

This pamphlet is available in accessible formats for persons with disabilities.

Duplication of EEOC publications is permitted.

(Courtesy of the U.S. EEOC)

BUSINESS LETTER

The parts of a **business letter** are (Figure 3.15):

- Address or letterhead—usually a preprinted letterhead with the organization's name and address. (If letterhead is not used, include the address of the writer along with the date.)

- Dateline—two to six lines below the last line of the printed letterhead.
  - The date should be written out in this form: January 1, 2012 or 1 January 2012
  - The date can be centered if letterhead is used.
  - If letterhead is not used, the date is included with the address of the writer.

- Reference line—a numerical file number, invoice number, policy number, or order numbers on a new line below the date.

- Special mailing notations—special notations such as "Confidential" two lines below the date.

- Inside address—the addressee's title and full name, business title, business name, and full address.
  - Do not abbreviate the company's name unless it is registered that way.
  - Cities and states should not be abbreviated.
  - Do not use "care of" before a hotel name or company name.
  - Include the appropriate title: *Mr., Ms., Mrs., Miss,* or *Dr.*
  - Business titles are never abbreviated.

- Attention line—one line space and the phrase "Attention:_____" after the inside address, if the letter is not addressed to any specific person.
  - You can make the letter go to the attention of a department.
  - An attention line is never used in a letter to an individual but only in a letter having plural addresses.

- Salutation—"Dear [person's name]," "Ladies and Gentlemen," "Dear Sir or Madam," "Dear [company name]" one line after the attention line or the inside address.

- In business letters, the salutation is followed by a colon.
- In personal letters, the salutation is followed by a comma.

- Subject line—an overview of what the letter is about.
  - It can be used in place of a salutation.
  - A subject line can be centered in sales letters.
  - Do not include "Re" or "Subject" before the subject line.
  - Underline the subject line, unless it occupies two or more lines, in which case underline the last line, letting the underline extend the length of the longest line in the subject.

- Message—the body of your letter with paragraph breaks, optional indentions for paragraphs, bullet lists, and number lists.

- Complimentary close—two lines below the last line of the message.
  - The close is either left justified or five spaces to the right of center.
  - "Yours truly" or "Very truly yours" can be used when no personal connection exists between the writer and recipient.
  - "Sincerely" or "Sincerely yours" is appropriate when there is an established personal as well as business relationship.
  - "Respectfully yours" is appropriate on letters addressed to a person of acknowledged authority.
  - Avoid using closings such as "Yours for lower prices" or "I remain" or "Cordially yours."

- Signature block—justified with the complimentary close with options of typed name and title, signature, or just signature.
  - Never add a blank graphical line for the writer's signature.
  - A woman should include a courtesy title in her typed signatures to allow the recipient of the letter to reply appropriately.

Example: Miss Louise A. Scott, Ms. Tina Anderson-Tate, Mrs. Pat Brueck

---

- Identification initials—the initials of the typist aligned left two spaces below the signature block.
  - Writer's initials are typed in capitals; the typist's initials are in lower case.

■ A colon or slash is used to separate the initials.

■ Enclosure notation—located with the identification initials or in place of them with the notation "enc," "encl," "enclosures (3)," or "3 encs."

■ Copy notation—left-aligned two lines below identification initials with the notation "cc: [person's full name or initials]."

■ Postscript—two spaces below the last text on the page with a "P.S." and then a short sentence.

  ■ Use a postscript to dramatize something already included in the letter.

  ■ Never use a postscript to include something that was forgotten during the writing of the letter. Instead, rewrite the letter.

Figure 3.15 Parts of a Business Letter

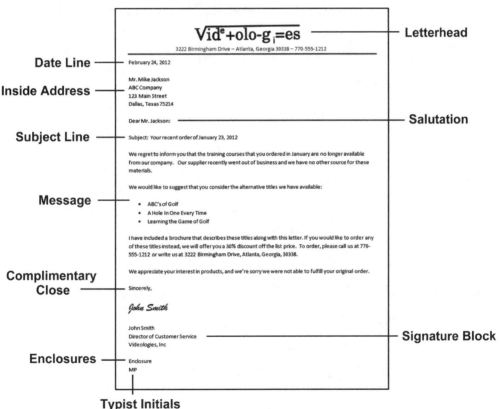

Business Letter Writing Style

Consider the following tips regarding business letter writing style:

- A good business letter advertises your capabilities and those of your company.

- A good business letter is neat and symmetrical, with no typographical, grammatical, or spelling errors.

- The language should be clear and simple.

- The first sentence should state the purpose of the letter.

- When responding to a letter, identify the subject and date of the previous letter in the first paragraph.

- Paragraphs should be short, and each paragraph should focus on a different topic.

- Use lists or italics where appropriate to make it easier for the reader to find important points.

- Focus on the reader's needs and interests.

- Avoid jargon.

- End with a call for action.

Example: Can we set up an appointment to discuss your needs on this project?

Business Letter Format

There are several different formats for business letters:

- Block letters (Figure 3.16)

- Modified block letters (Figure 3.17)

- Modified semiblock letters (Figure 3.18)

- Simplified letters (Figure 3.19)

(text continues on page 459)

Figure 3.16 Block Letter

5509 West 34th Street
Dallas, TX 75214
July 7, 2011

Michael J. Duffy
Intelligent Computer Systems
3121 Morris Lake Drive, Suite 211
Dallas, TX 75212

Dear Mr. Duffy,

I am writing to apply for the position you advertised in the Dallas Morning News for an e-learning developer. As you'll see in my résumé, I have the experience to fill this position.

For the past five years, I have been developing e-learning courses for three different companies: IBM, ATT, and Cox Enterprises. My experience has ranged from instructional design, technical writing, graphics production, multimedia production, and learning management system support.

Currently, I am working as a contractor for Cox Enterprises, where I am finishing a one-year assignment developing training for Oracle Financials. I have also recently developed documentation and training for PeopleSoft and for Hyperion Planning. I am currently the lead instructional designer on the Oracle Financials project that will conclude at the end of July.

Intelligent Computer Systems is famous for your innovative IT security systems and networking products. I would be proud to be part of the ICS team. I hope you will give me an opportunity to discuss my qualifications and experience. I can be reached at (214) 555-1212 after 6 p.m.

Thank you very much for your consideration for this position.

Sincerely yours,

Jeff Watkins
Jeff Watkins

Encl.: résumé

Figure 3.17 Modified Block Letter

5509 West 34th Street
Dallas, TX 75214
July 7, 2011

Michael J. Duffy
Intelligent Computer Systems
3121 Morris Lake Drive, Suite 211
Dallas, TX 75212

Dear Mr. Duffy,

I am writing to apply for the position you advertised in the Dallas Morning News for an e-learning developer. As you'll see in my résumé, I have the experience to fill this position.

For the past five years, I have been developing e-learning courses for three different companies: IBM, ATT, and Cox Enterprises. My experience has ranged from instructional design, technical writing, graphics production, multimedia production, and learning management system support.

Currently, I am working as a contractor for Cox Enterprises, where I am finishing a one-year assignment developing training for Oracle Financials. I have also recently developed documentation and training for PeopleSoft and for Hyperion Planning. I am currently the lead instructional designer on the Oracle Financials project that will conclude at the end of July.

Intelligent Computer Systems is famous for your innovative IT security systems and networking products. I would be proud to be part of the ICS team. I hope you will give me an opportunity to discuss my qualifications and experience. I can be reached at (214) 555-1212 after 6 p.m.

Thank you very much for your consideration for this position.

Sincerely yours,

Jeff Watkins
Jeff Watkins

Encl.: résumé

Figure 3.18 Modified Semiblock Letter

5509 West 34th Street
Dallas, TX 75214
July 7, 2011

Michael J. Duffy
Intelligent Computer Systems
3121 Morris Lake Drive, Suite 211
Dallas, TX 75212

Subj.: E-learning developer position

Dear Mr. Duffy,

I am writing to apply for the position you advertised in the Dallas Morning News for an e-learning developer. As you'll see in my résumé, I have the experience to fill this position.

For the past five years, I have been developing e-learning courses for three different companies: IBM, ATT, and Cox Enterprises. My experience has ranged from instructional design, technical writing, graphics production, multimedia production, and learning management system support.

Currently, I am working as a contractor for Cox Enterprises, where I am finishing a one-year assignment developing training for Oracle Financials. I have also recently developed documentation and training for PeopleSoft and for Hyperion Planning. I am currently the lead instructional designer on the Oracle Financials project that will conclude at the end of July.

Intelligent Computer Systems is famous for your innovative IT security systems and networking products. I would be proud to be part of the ICS team. I hope you will give me an opportunity to discuss my qualifications and experience. I can be reached at (214) 555-1212 after 6 p.m.

Thank you very much for your consideration for this position.

Sincerely yours,

Jeff Watkins
Jeff Watkins

Encl.: résumé

Figure 3.19 Simplified Letter

July 7, 2011
5509 West 34th Street
Dallas, TX 75214

Subj.: E-learning developer position

I am writing to apply for the position you advertised in the Dallas Morning
News for an e-learning developer. As you'll see in my résumé, I believe
I have the experience to fill this position.

For the past five years, I have been developing e-learning courses for
three different companies: IBM, ATT, and Cox Enterprises. My experience
has ranged from instructional design, technical writing, graphics
production, multimedia production, and learning management system
support.

Currently, I am working as a contractor for Cox Enterprises, where I am
finishing a one-year assignment developing training for Oracle Financials.
I have also recently developed documentation and training for PeopleSoft
and for Hyperion Planning. I am currently the lead instructional designer
on the Oracle Financials project that will conclude at the end of July.

Intelligent Computer Systems is famous for your innovative IT security
systems and networking products. I would be proud to be part of the ICS
team. I hope you will give me an opportunity to discuss my qualifications
and experience. I can be reached at (214) 555-1212 after 6 p.m.

Thank you very much for your consideration for this position.

Sincerely yours,

Jeff Watkins
Jeff Watkins

Encl.: résumé

BUSINESS PLAN

A **business plan** is a proposal for new business or a strategy for expanding an existing business. A business plan includes (Figure 3.20):

■ A detailed description of the product or service.

■ Technical background information that explains the technologies involved.

■ A discussion of the market for the new product or service, including how it compares to existing products and services currently available.

  ■ The sales of comparison products or services are listed along with projected sales of the new product or service.

  ■ The differences between the new product or service and existing similar products or services are detailed.

■ The day-to-day operations of the business, including information about how the product or service is produced.

■ Facilities and personnel that the business will require.

■ Project revenues, along with supporting material for how the revenues projections were calculated.

■ Funding requirements to get the business started.

■ Legal issues involving competitors or government agencies.

■ A feasibility section discussing the likelihood of success and the overall investment potential of the business.

■ Investment documentation that details the amounts required for shareholder purchase.

The overall elements of the business plan document include:

■ Cover sheet

■ Statement of purpose

■ Table of contents

■ Description of the business

- Marketing information

- Competition

- Operating procedures

- Personnel

- Business insurance requirements

- Capital equipment and supply list

- Revenue projections

- Investment requirements

- Copies of résumés of all principals.

(text continues on page 468)

Figure 3.20 Business Plan

STEWART LAKE STATE PARK BUSINESS PLAN

Submitted to:

Department of Natural Resources

Division of Parks and Recreation

Office of the Director

Prepared for the Director by:

Stewart Lake State Park Superintendent

and

Division of Parks and Recreation Budget Officer

Division of State Parks and Recreation

(Courtesy of the U.S. Department of Natural Resources)

(continues)

Figure 3.20 *(continued)*

EXECUTIVE SUMMARY/INTRODUCTION

The purpose of the business plan is to assist park management and staff at Stewart Lake State Park in making decisions regarding the management, operation, and development of park resources. This plan focuses on the financial impacts of management decisions. Information from this document will be used to inform State park management and State legislators of financial impacts at Stewart Lake State Park.

MISSION, VISION, VALUES, AND OBJECTIVES

The mission, vision, values, and objectives of Stewart Lake State Park are as follows:

Mission
Enhance the quality of life through outdoor recreation, leisure, and educational experiences.

Vision
Provide quality outdoor recreational experiences through camping, boating, fishing, biking, hiking, and off-highway vehicle (OHV) trails.

Values
Meeting customer needs; innovation; clean and well-maintained facilities; preservation of natural surroundings and resources; affordable, safe, and accessible recreational activities.

Objectives
1. Increase overnight camping revenue (number of visitors and nights stayed)
2. Increase day-use revenues and visitation
3. Increase fishing activities and revenues

PARK DESCRIPTION AND STRENGTHS, WEAKNESSES, OPPORTUNITIES, AND THREATS

Description

Stewart Lake State Park was established in 1972, 2 years after the Bureau of Reclamation built the reservoir as part of the Strawberry-Duchesne River Project. The reservoir is located off of Highway 40, next to the city of Duchesne (population 5,000), 1½ hours east of Salt Lake City and 6 hours from Denver, Colorado. Highway 40 is a main corridor from Denver to Salt Lake City. The reservoir has over 23 miles of sandy shoreline and rests at approximately 5700 feet above sea level. Many of its formations and geologic features are similar to Lake Powell, but with a shorter "warm season" limiting peak visitation to the summer months (late June to early September).

The park provides for a variety of experiences with six campgrounds and open "boat camping" on many of its shores.

Market Analysis

Stewart Lake State Park's primary customers are boaters form the Wasatch Front area and anglers throughout the State and neighboring States. Current demand is primarily for improved access and regress for boats and improved facilities (hookups, docks, camping, etc.).

Demographics

The makeup of the population that recreates at Stewart Lake State Park is identified in the following table.

Summary of Demographic Information

Demographic	Local	State	National	International
Population	1,932,967	2,550,063	296,410,404	6,451,392,455
Average age	28.4	28.5	36.4	26.9
Income	$74,078	$47,934	$46,242	N/A
Male	50.1%	50.1%	49%	50.4%
Female	49.9%	49.9%	51%	49.6%

(continues)

Figure 3.20 *(continued)*

Market Trends

General trends in outdoor recreation are as follows:

- Greater awareness of value of leisure—overall increased demand for leisure activities.

- Expectation of recreation facilities—more "comfort" oriented.

- Preference for individual or informal activities is increasing. People are looking for "experiences."

- Participation by older adults in active recreation and sport has increased.

- Average age of outdoor recreation participant is increasing (baby boomers).

- Number of minority participants is increasing (most notably the Hispanic community).

Market Needs/Demands

The following needs and demands have been identified by park staff based on visitor feedback, trend analysis, and community comments for Stewart Lake State Park.

1. More, larger campsites/hookups for recreational vehicles (RVs)

2. Larger or additional boat ramp

3. Additional fish-cleaning stations (improve existing)

4. Added roads and "turn-around" for boat launching

5. Expanded parking for boats and day users

6. Protected docks (breakwater wall/marina)

7. Improve/expand bathrooms and showers

8. Expand "sandy" beach area for day users

9. Fuel station for boats

10. Improved bathrooms/showers at Knight Hollow and Indian Bay

11. More "accessible" water; expand culinary water system

12. Connect OHV trails to system outside of park

13. Improve OHV trails inside park

14. Develop group site for Knight Hollow (OHV users)

15. Add paved and non-paved trails for hiking and biking; link to city of Duchesne

16. Emphasize partnership with local businesses for food, rentals, and supplies—no concessionaire

17. Develop comfort camping facilities (i.e., yurts, cabins)

Financial Analysis

The division staff evaluates potential projects, programs, events, etc., using return on investment (ROI) (the ratio of **money** gained or lost on an **investment** relative to the amount of money invested) and payback period as its methods to measure the acceptability of each project. For long-term capital projects, internal rate of return (IRR) (the annualized effective compounded return rate which can be earned on the invested capital, i.e., the **yield** on the investment) and/or net present value (NPV) measures the excess or shortfall of cash flows, in **present value** (PV) terms, once financing charges are met. By definition, net present value cash flow methods are used. As a standard of acceptability, project ROI must meet or exceed the current State Treasurer's money market fund. Capital project IRR uses a hurdle rate of 3 percent and payback period of 30 years, or the estimated life of the structure/facility, whichever is less. It should be noted, however, that certain projects may be accepted even if the minimum criteria are not met based on such factors as environmental justice, safety, resource protection, heritage preservation, or division objectives.

(continues)

Figure 3.20 *(continued)*

The following tables are a financial summary of the proposed plan.

Financial Summary of Proposed Plan

Investment summary strategy description	Net cash flow ($)	Initial Investment ($)	Pay-back[1]	ROI (%)	IRR (%)	NPV[2] ($)
Mountain View Alternative 2	$239,160	$4,666,000	20	5.13	3.04	$145,000
Indian Bay	26,310	579,000	22	4.54	2.13	(50,000)
Rabbit Gulch	25,300	434,000	17	5.83	4.07	75,000
Juniper Point	16,450	278,000	17	5.92	4.19	53,000
Knight Hollow	10,825	194,000	18	5.58	3.71	24,000
Strawberry River Above	(165)	38,000	-230	-0.43	-0.43	(41,000)
Strawberry River Below	125	43,000	344	0.29	-11.65	(40,000)
Special events	2,950	3,000	1	98.33	—	—
Marketing	—	6,000	0	0.00	0.00	(6,000)
TOTAL	$320,955	$6,241,000	19	—	—	$160,000

[1] Payback is in years.
[2] Based on a 30-year life (except for special events and marketing).

Summary of Annual Funding Sources

Revenue type	Current ($)	Proposed ($)	Net effect ($)
General funds	$103,095	$364,765	$261,670
10% of total incremental revenue	28,252	68,572	40,320
Federal funds	0	0	0
Grants	0	0	0
Restricted funds (law enforcement)	86,300	86,300	0
Other funding sources	250	250	0
TOTAL REVENUES	$217,897	$519,887	$301,990

Summary of Annual Expenses

Expense type	Current ($)	Proposed ($)	Net Effect ($)
Wages and benefits	$183,052	$336,872	$153,820
Operating suppies/maintence	4,970	88,890	83,920
Utilities	10,425	23,725	13,300
Other costs (contractor/professional services)	2,250	9,600	7,350
Overhead	17,200	60,800	43,600
TOTAL EXPENSES	$217,897	$519,987	$301,990

Success Monitoring

The performance measures in the following table will be used to monitor and measure the success of the implementation of the above-mentioned strategies.

Performance Measures

Goal	Action Item	Measure Description	Target Score or Range
Meet or exceed projected visitor use levels identified for camping, cabins, pavilions, boating, and day use	Promote new facilities as they are brought on line	Match or exceed projected revenues	Maintain or exceed projected use for 3 years
Organize and hold a fishing derby	Establish partnership with agencies, clubs, associations, and promoters	Schedule and follow through on a fishing derby	Hold an event each year for 3 years
Organize and hold a half triathlon	Establish partnership with agencies, clubs, associations, and promoters	Schedule and follow follow through on a triathlon	Hold an event each year for 3 years

COLLECTION LETTER

Collection letters are written to collect amounts owed on a past-due account. When writing a collection letter, consider the following tips (Figure 3.21):

- Gather all the facts about the customer's account.

- Be specific about the amount owed and the date the funds were due.

- Let the customer know what the penalty will be if he or she fails to pay by a specific deadline.

Example: If your payment is not received by November 1, 2012, your account will be sent to a collection agency.

- Offer assistance for customers having difficulty paying. Discuss new terms or a payment plan.

- If you must cancel a customer's credit, explain your reasons for doing so.

- Be courteous, but firm.

Collections letters are typically written to:

- Remind a customer that a payment is past due.

- Demand payment for a delinquent account.

- Inform a customer that legal action will be taken for failure to pay.

- Appeal to a customer to settle an account.

- Inform a customer of new business terms due to their failure to pay.

- Offer a customer a payment plan.

Figure 3.21 Collection Letter

AMC Corporation
1322 Westfield Lane
Los Angeles, CA 90025
September 21, 2011

Kenneth Barrymore
Eastern Distribution Company
41 West Mountain Highway
Denver, Colorado 80012

Dear Mr. Barrymore:

We currently have three outstanding invoices past the 30-day due date
for your account. These invoices are itemized below. All of these invoices
carry 30-day terms that were agreed upon in our distribution agreement,
and two of these invoices are over 90 days past due.

Invoice Number	Date	Amount
31431	05/22/2011	$2,134.99
31523	06/15/2011	$3,332.21
31731	08/01/2011	$2,451.31

We would appreciate your prompt payment by October 1, 2011;
otherwise, we will be forced to turn over your account to a collection
agency. In the meantime, any additional orders you make will have to
be on a cash-only basis until your account is paid in full.

Sincerely yours,

Albert Dayton
Albert Dayton
Accounts Receivable Manager
AMC Corporation

COMMENDATION LETTER

Commendation letters are often written to praise an employee's performance. Praise is a powerful motivator if it is genuine, specific, and timely. When writing a commendation letter, consider the following tips (Figure 3.22):

- Describe the work or accomplishment that deserves the commendation.
  - Use phrases such as "congratulations," "exceptional job," "very impressed," "must compliment you," "fine job," "outstanding success," "excellent quality," "professional manager," "your contribution," "positive impact."

- Describe the person's qualities that make him or her successful.
  - Use words such as *competence, expertise, diligence, commitment, enthusiastic, contribution, willingness, dedication, professional, extra time and effort, pride, invaluable, initiative, talent, leadership, ability.*

- Thank the person for his or her contribution to the organization.
  - Use phrases such as "job well done," "commend you," "vital to our success," "an asset to our company," "continued success," "further recognition," "thank you," "keep up the good work," "best wishes," "made the difference."

Commendation letters are typically written to:

- Praise an employee's performance.

- Compliment an employee from another organization.

- Praise a product or service.

- Compliment a guest speaker.

- Praise a salesperson from a supplier.

- Praise a chairperson or meeting planner.

- Compliment an instructor.

- Praise an employee's family for the employee's success.

Figure 3.22 Commendation Letter

Best Value Realty Company
4413 Lake Forest Drive
Woodstock GA 30189
October 22, 2012

Jack Moyer
1442 Pine Cliff Tarn
Woodstock, GA 30189

Dear Jack:

I wanted to congratulate you for achieving one million dollars in total sales this year.

In the history of Best Value Reality Company, we've only had two agents achieve this lofty goal. I would like to commend you for joining this elite group.

Your dedication in making cold calls, your helpful attitude when talking with homeowners, and your ability to help homeowners and buyers reach an agreement have all assisted you in achieving this outstanding success.

I want you to know that your efforts are vital to the success of Best Value Realty Company. You are indeed an asset to our company. Keep up the good work.

Sincerely yours,

Sherry Morgan

Sherry Morgan
President

COMPLAINT LETTER

Complaint letters are written to voice your opinion about something or to let a business know about an unsatisfactory situation. Remember, most errors are unintentional and most businesses want their customers to be satisfied.

When writing a complaint letter, consider the following tips (Figure 3.23):

- Write your complaint letter to a specific person at the organization, such as the manager, owner, or CEO.

- Write the letter with a positive tone without emotional language or obscenities.

- Keep the letter short, honest, and straightforward without omitting any relevant details.

- Send copies of any accompanying documentation and retain all the originals.

- Do not threaten or make generalizations about the organization.

- If other people you know were also affected by the problem, get multiple signatures on the complaint letter.

- Suggest a solution for the problem without destroying the relationship.

- Include your contact information including your name, address, phone number, and email address.

Complaint letters are typically written to:

- Complain about the quality of a product or service.

- Complain to governmental authorities.

- Complain to a landlord or neighbor.

- Complain about a billing problem.

- Complain about harassment at work.

- Complain to the news media.

- Complain about an order delay.

- Complain about an invoice.

- Reprimand an employee.

- Request a refund.

- Disagree with a coworker.

Figure 3.23 Complaint Letter

Leon Williams
14 Candler Avenue
Atlanta, GA 30311

August 8, 2011

Best Computers and Peripherals
32134 North 33rd Avenue
Tulsa, Oklahoma 74102

Gentlemen:

This letter is in reference to an Epson NX515 printer that I purchased online from your company on August 5, 2011. When the order arrived, the box contained an Epson NX415 printer.

While both printers are all-in-one printers, the NX515 has wireless networking capability, while the NX415 does not. There is also a price difference of $45.

I am enclosing a copy of my original online order for your reference.

I would like to return the Epson NX415 and exchange it for the Epson NX515 that I originally ordered. I would like for Best Computers and Peripherals to either send me a prepaid return authorization shipping label or reimburse me for the return shipping cost.

Earlier today, I checked your Web site which said the Epson NX515 is out-of-stock. The Web site did not say this last week when I placed my order. If you are unable to ship an Epson NX515, then I will keep the NX415, but I would like you to credit my credit card for the price difference of $45.

Sincerely yours,

Leon Williams

Leon Williams
(918) 555-6666
Lwilliams123@videologies.com

COVER LETTERS

Cover letters are often sent along with a résumé to emphasize what you can contribute to the hiring organization. When writing a cover letter, consider the following tips (Figure 3.24):

- Customize the letter for each job.

- Don't use a generic cover letter for every job application.

- Highlight your skills in bold font that match the job description.

- Make sure the cover letter does not contain any typos or grammatical mistakes.

- List specific examples of things you've accomplished and how each corresponds to the job description.

- Market your strengths, achievements, work ethic, and personality traits that will benefit the organization.

- Ask for an opportunity to interview.

Cover letters are typically written to:

- Respond to an advertisement for employment.

- Respond to a request for your résumé.

- Network with contacts during a job search.

- Accompany a proposal, report, or application.

- Respond to a job offer.

Figure 3.24 Cover Letter

12345 Heartside Drive
Western Branch, GA 31234
December 2, 2011

Mr. Kevin Wilson
President
Videologies, Inc.
10 North Main Street
Atlanta, GA 30303

Dear Mr. Wilson,

I am very interested in applying for the job of office assistant listed in
the Atlanta Constitution on December 1.

As you can see from my enclosed résumé, I have worked for both a still
photographer and a small video production company. I enjoyed working
at both of these companies, and I feel this past experience qualifies me
for the position described in your advertisement.

I have a good understanding of the visual medium and the many details
you must handle in your work. I believe I can help take responsibility for
some of these details with little additional training.

I would appreciate the opportunity for a personal interview. You can reach
me at (770) 555-1234.

Thank you for your consideration.

Sincerely yours,

Evelyn Boyd
Evelyn Boyd

Encl.: résumé

DIRECTIVES

Directives are memos or emails that give instructions for a task, project, assignment, or new procedure. Directives address a particular problem and indicate a solution.

When writing directives, consider the following tips (Figure 3.25):

- State the reason for the directive, including a legislative compliance requirement, if any.

- Include specific instructions on what the reader is expected to do.

- State deadlines for the task or project.

- List any benefits that will be achieved from following the instructions detailed in the directive.

- Include the names and contact information for any resources who can answer questions or assist employees in implementing the directive.

- Thank the reader, and express confidence that the task or project can be completed.

Directives are typically written to:

- Establish new policies or procedures.

- Notify employees of a change in policy or procedure.

- Announce a special project.

- Issue instructions regarding a specific task or project.

- Delegate responsibility.

- Adjust territories or organizational structure.

Figure 3.25 Directive

ANNOUNCEMENT

To: All Employees

Effective January 1, 2012, new guidelines will go into effect for the use of contractors and consultants.

A written contract must be executed with all contractors and consultants and must include the following:

- A definition of the services to be performed;

- The fees to be charged to the company or the method of charging the company for the services; and

- The length of time the services will be provided.

These guidelines apply to any contractor or consultant currently performing services and to those that may be retained in the future. I have approved contracts that I can share and will be glad to customize them for specific circumstances you may have.

Please send me a copy of your signed contracts with contractors and consultants, so that I can maintain the agreements in a central location and track contract expiration and compliance.

Finally, these new guidelines establish the dollar limits for approval. For contracts for fewer than 90 days and less than $25,000, a director may approve the contract. For contracts for more than 90 days or more than $25,000, a vice president must approve the contract. Please ensure that the appropriate approval is obtained prior to engaging a contractor or consultant.

Thank you for your attention to these guidelines. If you have any questions, please let me know.

Edward Gibson
Vice President

EMAIL

Email is used in many businesses as a substitute for memos and brief telephone calls. Short messages are sent to request information, to share information, and to provide progress reports. When writing email messages, consider the following tips:

- When sending a message to a group of people, use the BCC field to keep everyone's email address private.

- Include a meaningful subject line.
  - Avoid starting a message with *Re*.
  - Capitalize your subject like a book title.

  Example: ISS Meeting on Tuesday

- Mark a message *urgent* or *high priority* only when it really is time sensitive.

- Include a personal greeting.

  Example: Hello Jim,

- Keep your message short and limited to one subject.
  - Send a separate email if you need to discuss a different subject.

- Avoid sending long documents as email messages.
  - Instead send attachments that have been compressed using a program like WinZip or Stuffit.
  - If sending an attachment, explain what the attachment is within the email message.

- The formatting of a message may change when viewed by the recipient.
  - Internal messages in HTML format may hold their formatting.
    - With internal HTML format messages, you can use bold, italics, underlining, multiple fonts, bullets, special symbols, tabs, and spacing to indent paragraphs.
  - External messages should avoid special formatting.

■ Email messages may include hyperlinks to World Wide Web addresses.

■ Use the entire address, including the Internet protocol.

Example: http://www.videologies.com

■ Use the active rather than passive voice in your messages.

Example of passive: Documents were drafted by the committee.

Example of active: The committee drafted documents.

■ Avoid sexist language.

Example: salesperson instead of salesman

■ If you make a request in your message, say "please."

■ Avoid all capital letters in your messages unless it is a warning like "DANGER."

■ When replying to an email, send a copy of the previous message or use a few lines as a quote.

■ For selective quoting, mark the previous message by using two << (less than) and two >> (greater than) symbols on each side of the quote.

■ Type your message below the quote or copy.

■ Like a business letter, include a formal signoff.

■ Include a signature (which can be stored as a signature file) with your messages.

■ Include your name, company, email address, phone number, and Web site.

■ Do not include pictures in your signature.

■ Always read and spell-check your messages before you send them.

The following are examples of when email is an inappropriate medium for communication:

- Thank-you notes

- Long memos

- Yes-or-no answers (use the phone instead)

- Job praise (offer it in person or in a letter)

- Telling your boss you are sick (on the phone instead)

- Requests for raises, promotions, or resignations (meet in person or write a letter)

- Jokes

- Flirting

- Gossip

ENDORSEMENT LETTER

An **endorsement letter** is used to endorse a candidate for an award, to endorse a political candidate, or to endorse a person for a particular position. When writing an endorsement letter, consider the following tips (Figure 3.26):

- Include your name and organization and your relationship with the person being endorsed.

- Describe what you are endorsing and why.
    - Explain why the person is entitled to your endorsement.
    - List how long you've known the person.
    - List the person's qualities.

- Explain what this person will do in the future, given his or her skills and qualities.

- Include your contact information if the reader needs additional information.

- Conclude by restating your endorsement.

Endorsement letters are typically written to:

- Advocate legislation.

- Endorse a candidate.

- Endorse a person for a job.

- Endorse a nominee for an award.

- Endorse a product or service.

- Confirm a decision made by someone else.

- Endorse a report.

- Confirm authorization given to someone to act on your behalf.

- Endorse a business.

Figure 3.26 Endorsement Letter

May 10, 2012

Laura Johnson
1322 Flowering Field Circle
Roswell, GA 30123

Office of Admissions
Candler School of Theology
Emory University
Atlanta, GA 30322

Dear Emory University,

I am writing in regards to Darlene Williams, who has applied for admission to the Candler School of Theology. I have been asked to provide a work or character reference.

First of all, I would like to strongly recommend your acceptance of Darlene. She is a very talented, smart, and spiritual being. Wherever this path leads, it will surely be a blessing for those who come into contact with her in the future.

(continues)

Figure 3.26 *(continued)*

I have known Darlene both personally and professionally for over 12 years. She has worked for my company on numerous occasions as a professional on-camera presenter. She is one of the best in her field.

Over the years, I have become friends with Darlene and have discussed her past and present religious beliefs. Darlene grew up in Asheville, North Carolina, on a small farm where her parents still live. Her parents are active in the church and taught Darlene to pray, have faith, and be kind to others. I see the result today as someone who "shines."

While Darlene considers herself a Christian, she is accepting of other ideas and beliefs. She knows there is more to life than just following the dance steps to salvation. This was demonstrated recently, when she was counseling a woman at her church regarding the death of a loved one. The woman was afraid her dead husband wasn't going to heaven because he might have violated some of the belief system rules for obtaining salvation. Darlene told this woman something that summarizes why Darlene shines. She said, "People sometimes tend to underestimate the size of God's love."

If we jump into the future and listen to Darlene a few years from now after graduating from the Candler School of Theology, I'm sure I'll hear something just as comforting. Darlene's unique experience as an on-camera presenter, public speaker, and trainer, combined with the insights and knowledge acquired from this educational experience, should result in someone who not only communicates, but also counsels, heals, and inspires.

I'm excited that Darlene has chosen this path and has chosen to further her knowledge and spiritual growth by applying to Emory University. It is something to celebrate, a chance to see destiny fulfilled.

Sincerely,

Laura Johnson

Laura Johnson

FORMS

Business forms are created for common fill-in-the-blank documents such as job applications, health benefit claims, and legal documentation.

For legal documents, write numbers in words and then repeat them immediately in numerals inside parentheses.

Example: ten thousand five hundred and seventy-five (10,575)

For dates in legal forms, the month is always spelled out.

The following words and phrases often used in legal documents (Figure 3.27) are customarily written in full capitals, usually followed by a comma, a colon, or no punctuation:

- THIS AGREEMENT, made this second day of . . .

- KNOW ALL MEN BY THESE PRESENT, that . . .

- IN WITNESS WHEREOF, I have this day . . .

- MEMORANDUM OF AGREEMENT made this twenty-fifth day of . . .

Case titles in legal documents are always underscored, followed by a comma, the volume and page numbers, and date.

Example: Johnson v. Smith, 201 Okla. 433, 32 Am. Rep. 168 (1901).

Notary public forms are used to acknowledge and witness document signatures (Figures 3.28–3.30).

Figure 3.27 Contract

THIS AGREEMENT, made this _____day of _____, 20____,
between _____ of _____ , First Party (hereinafter
called the Seller), and _____a corporation under the laws of the
State of _____, with principal place of business in _____,
_____(city and state), Second Party (hereinafter called the
Purchaser).

WITNESSETH:

WHEREAS the Seller has this day agreed to _____; and
WHEREAS the Purchaser is willing to _____; and
WHEREAS_____; NOW, THEREFORE, it is agreed that
_____. WITNESS the signatures of the parties hereto on the
date aforesaid.

(S)_____
Seller

(S)_____
Purchaser

By_____
President

[Corporate Seal]

Figure 3.28 Notary Form for an Individual

For an individual
State of _____
County of _____
On the _____ day of _____, 20___, before me came _____
known to me to be the individual described in and who executed the fore-
going instrument and acknowledged that he (or she) executed the same.

(S)_____
Notary Public

[Stamp and Seal]

Figure 3.29 Notary Form for a Corporation

For a corporation

State of _____

County of _____

On the ____ day of _____, 20___, before me personally appeared

_____to me known, who, being by me duly sworn, did depose

and say that he (or she) resides at _____; that he (or she) is

_____(title) of _____(Company), the corporation

described in and which executed the foregoing instrument; that he

(or she) knows the seal of said corporation; that the seal affixed to said

instrument is such corporate seal; that it was so affixed by order of the

(title) of said corporation; and that he (or she) signed his (or her) name

thereto by like order.

(S)_____

Notary Public

[Seal]

Figure 3.30 Notary Form for a Partnership

For a partnership

State of _____

County of _____

On the ____ day of _____, 20___, before me personally appeared

_____ to me known, and known to me to be a

member of _____ (name of partnership), and the

person described in and who executed the foregoing instrument in

the firm name of _____, and he (or she) duly

acknowledged to me that he (or she) executed the same as and for

the act and deed of said firm of _____ (repeat name

of partnership).

(S)_____

Notary Public

[Seal]

FUND-RAISING LETTER

Fund-raising letters are written by nonprofit organizations, schools, civic organizations, and clubs to raise money from donors. When writing a fund-raising letter, consider the following tips (Figure 3.31):

- Use a personal and conversational tone.

- Introduce yourself and the organization, and thank readers for their support and interest in the organization.

- Describe the cause and credentials of the organization.
  - Explain the critical need, what the organization has accomplished in the past, and how the requested funds would be used.

- Ask for a specific donation amount and explain how that donation will help the organization.
  - Explain how donations of this amount have helped the organization in the past.
  - Specifically mention any previous donations from the person.

- Optionally, offer an incentive for a donation such as a tangible gift or a perceived value.

  Example: Imagine the impact your donation of $100 will have on the lives of ten children in rural India.

- Optionally, include a separate page or a brochure with detailed information about the program and fund-raising campaign.
  - Include photographs statistics, and the budget.

- Thank readers for their generosity.

- Conclude the letter by leaving a positive feeling about the needy cause.

- The letter should be personally signed by someone from the organization.

Fund-raising letters are typically to:

- Request a donation.

- Invite someone to attend a fund-raising event.

■ Thank someone for a donation.

■ Announce a new fund-raising campaign.

■ Inform members of the financial needs of the organization.

■ Introduce a new program offered by the charitable organization.

Figure 3.31 Fund-Raising Letter

September 12, 2012

Hopewell Middle School
131 Westfield Place
Kansas City, MO 67511

Alice Johnson
83 Cambridge Drive
Kansas City, MO 67511

Dear Mrs. Johnson:

As president of the Hopewell Middle School Parent Teachers Association, I want to thank you for your support last year. Involved parents like you are what help make Hopewell a great school and allow us to work as an effective PTA that supports the efforts of the teachers and staff.

For this new school year, Hopewell has been forced by the school district to reduce its operating budget by ten percent, which has resulted in layoffs of our art and music teachers. As a result, the PTA is now actively engaged in a campaign to raise funds to help the school hire at least one part-time art teacher and one part-time music teacher. Our goal is to raise $30,000 for the year through a variety of fund-raising efforts.

To start this effort, we are asking our PTA members to make a donation of $100 if at all possible. If you and other parents can contribute this amount, that will help us raise nearly one-third of our goal. That would allow the school to hire these part-time teachers. Additional fund-raising would be needed to cover their salaries through the end of the school year.

(continues)

Figure 3.31 *(continued)*

The value of including art and music education is extremely important in helping our children develop their cultural talents. As a community, we would be remiss to disregard this need and allow budget cuts to reduce the quality of the education our children receive.

I hope you'll join me and the rest of the PTA members in making this first step toward a successful 2012 at Hopewell Middle School.

Sincerely yours,

Carol Masters

Carol Masters
PTA President

GRANT PROPOSALS

A **grant proposal** should include the following elements (Figure 3.32):

- Cover letter
    - An introduction to the organization requesting the grant
    - A summary of the proposal
    - A summary of any previous communications with the funding organization
    - The amount of funding you are requesting
    - The population that will be served by the grant
    - The need the project will help solve
- Cover page
    - Grant proposal title
    - Submitted to: (funding organization's name)
    - Date
    - Your contact information including name, title, organization, address, phone, and email
- Proposal report

- The content and format, varying depending on the requirements of the funding organization

A basic grant proposal should include the following sections:

- Project abstract or summary—a concise summary of the project that is no longer than one page. Write this section of the proposal last.
    - Need for the project
    - Population served
    - Brief description of the project
    - Goals and objectives of the project
    - Applicant's history
    - How the program will be evaluated
- Statement of need
    - Description of the problem
    - Description of the population
    - Description of how the project will help solve the problem
- Goals and objectives
- Program description
    - Explanation of the program
    - Details on how the program will be implemented
    - Explanation of what will be accomplished
    - Timeline, the schedule for project implementation
- Evaluation—information on how the success of the project will be measured
- Organization and staff information
    - Description of the organization's experience
    - Staff qualifications
- Budget—a summary of the expenses for the project
- Appendix
    - Research support
    - Nonprofit tax status letter
    - Annual report

(text continues on page 496)

Figure 3.32 Grant Proposal

Date

Contact Person
Organization
Address
City, State, Zip

Dear _____,

Isha Foundation is a nonprofit 501(c)(3), international service organization that conducts various public welfare programs in parts of the world to advance physical and mental health. Isha Foundation is a volunteer organization funded with public and private assistance.

The Foundation's Action for Rural Rejuvenation (ARR) initiative is a comprehensive rural rehabilitation program that provides initial relief for urgent medical needs and ongoing services to restore inner well-being and rebuild communities in India. This project was launched in August 2003 with a mission to benefit 70 million rural people in 54,000 villages in Tamil Nadu, South India. It will be implemented in two phases over a period of 15 years. Thereafter, it is envisioned that local communities will sustain the project activities independently.

Currently, ARR operates nine Mobile Health Clinics (MHC) and provides services to 143,000 patients in 280 villages each year. Of these patients, 67,000 are elderly people, 87,000 are women, and 21,000 are children. Over 50% of the MHC patients suffer from chronic ailments such as ulcers, musculoskeletal disorders, hypertension, depression, and respiratory disorders including asthma. On average, each new MHC that is deployed can provide services for over 17,000 patients each year. Because rural children with conjunctivitis often scratch their eyes resulting in blindness, each MHC can provide timely medical services to over 2600 children each year. In addition to medical services for existing conditions, the staff on the MHCs offers preventive health care services in the form of yoga classes and provides sporting equipment to encourage physical activity.

ARR plans to launch 59 MHCs in the next three years, and 150 before the end of 2013. Isha Foundation is seeking funding to help us sustain and expand our ongoing ARR effort. Each MHC costs approximately $29,000 to purchase and equip. The yearly operating expenses for one MHC are approximately $17,000.

Isha Foundation is a nonreligious, nonpolitical, nonsectarian organization with over 250,000 active volunteers worldwide. Isha Foundation has over 150 centers in India and other parts of the world including the United States, Canada, Lebanon, Cyprus, France, and Germany. Based in Coimbatore, India, the foundation manages 87 centers in Tamil Nadu alone.

Over the past 14 years, Isha Foundation has successfully carried out several social outreach programs for rural people, as well as disadvantaged and often neglected segments of society, throughout Tamil Nadu, thereby gaining a reputable and trustworthy standing among the people throughout India.

Sincerely,
Your Name
Contact Information

(Courtesy of Isha Foundation)

ACTION FOR RURAL REJUVENATION

Submitted to: XYZ Foundation

October 10, 2011

Name
Isha Foundation
Address
Phone
Email

(continues)

Figure 3.32 *(continued)*

I. Summary

The Isha Foundation's Action for Rural Rejuvenation (ARR) initiative is a multi-pronged, multi-phased, holistic, outreach program whose primary objective is to improve the overall health and quality of life of the rural poor of India. ARR is a unique, well-defined philanthropic effort, which enhances existing development schemes by supporting indigenous models of health, prevention and community participatory governance, while offering primary health care services and allopathic treatment through its dedicated team of qualified and trained personnel.

At present, nearly 750,000 people in rural Tamil Nadu, India are served by Isha's ARR project. ARR features Mobile Health Clinics (MHC), which are able to traverse hard-to-reach regions and effectively operate in resource-poor environments.

In addition to medical services for existing conditions, the staff on the MHCs offers preventive health care services in the form of yoga classes and provides sporting equipment to encourage physical activity.

II. Statement of Need

Currently, ARR operates nine MHCs and provides services to 143,000 patients in 280 villages each year. Of these patients, 67,000 are elderly people, 87,000 are women, and 21,000 are children. Over 50% of the MHC patients suffer from chronic ailments such as ulcers, musculoskeletal disorders, hypertension, depression, and respiratory disorders including asthma.

On average, each new MHC that is deployed can provide services for over 17,000 patients each year. Because rural children with conjunctivitis often scratch their eyes resulting in blindness, each MHC can provide timely medical services to over 2600 children each year.

III. Goals and Objectives

This project was launched in August 2003, under the aegis of Isha Foundation. The project aims to benefit 70 million rural people in 54,000 villages in Tamil Nadu, South India. It will be implemented in two phases over a period of 15 years. Thereafter, it is envisaged that local communities will sustain the project activities independently.

The goals of Phase One include:

- Ensuring access to essential medical care by running mobile health clinics and distributing medicines free of cost

- Rejuvenating traditional well-being tools by introducing basic yogic practices

- Developing a sense of community involvement and joy by conducting games and inter-village tournaments

- Introducing the use of home remedies and herbs for cost effective and healthy living by providing free training and developing model herbal gardens

- Bringing awareness on preventive health, sanitation, and environmental conservation by conducting specially designed awareness programs

- Sustaining further development of the program by creating a local volunteer base

The goals of Phase Two of the project include building Rural Development Centers which will include a village library, computer center, yoga center, gymnasium, pharmacy, health clinic, and volleyball court. Phase Two will also include setting up contemporary crafts training and production units for economic development.

ARR plans to launch 59 MHCs in the next three years, and 150 before the end of 2013. Since Rural Development Centers (RDC) that are built in the second phase of the project will comprise a health clinic and pharmacy, the MHCs of the areas covered by these centers will be redirected to other regions. In villages where RDCs are not established or are remote, the MHC service will be sustained.

IV. Project Design and Implementation Plan

Central to the ARR project are the Mobile Health Clinics. These overcome two major barriers to appeasing existing illnesses: cost—by offering free examination and treatment; and access—by bringing the medical team to the rural people.

The MHCs are specially designed vehicles built on a conventional truck chassis incorporating all the built-in features of a clinic. They are outfitted with all common diagnostic equipment, a clinical laboratory, pharmacy, and an independent power and water supply. They are equipped so doctors can perform surgical treatments such as abscess draining, suturing, dressing, and childbirths. Immunizations for malaria and other diseases are provided. Whenever more complex care is needed, free medical examination and treatment or discounted fees and payment plans are negotiated at partnering local hospitals.

(continues)

Figure 3.32 *(continued)*

Each MHC includes a qualified allopathic physician, a trained nurse, two trained assistants and a pharmacist. The physicians are additionally trained in indigenous systems of healing. Prior to fieldwork, the MHC staff undergoes an intense training process including an orientation to working in resource-poor environments and guidance on how to effectively reach out and build rapport with the community in which they work.

In order to allow for maximal utilization of MHCs, standardized protocols have been implemented, including procedures for setup, data entry, and designations of roles and responsibilities of the staff. Apart from providing medical services, the MHC staff integrates with the local community. They share meals and reside in the homes of local villagers. Through these personal interactions, the MHC staff is better equipped to understand the needs and requirements of the local community. Furthermore, through these intimate interactions, they are able to ensure reciprocal dialogue with the community, mobilize support and by their example, inspire villagers to take responsibility for community health and well-being.

V. Timeline

Upon the funding of this grant request, a mobile health clinic can be purchased and equipped within three weeks. It can be on the road serving villages within one month.

Initially, a maximum of two villages are serviced daily by one MHC in order to assure adequate introductory and screening measures. Subsequently, a routine schedule is adopted during which each MHC typically services 4-5 villages daily, repeating these visits to each village on a fortnightly basis. Typically, one MHC serves 60-75 villages twice a month. Each clinic is in operation 24 days a month.

VI. Evaluation

The staff on each MHC maintains patient records, so the outcome of the project is easily measured in terms of number of patients served, the types of medical conditions treated, as well as demographic breakdown by age and sex.

For each MHC deployed, our target is to service 20,000 patients each year with a service area of approximately 60 rural villages.

VII. Organizational Capacity

Established in 1992, Isha Foundation is an international public service organization, founded by Jaggi Vasudev, dedicated to the enhancement of physical, mental and inner well-being of all people. Isha seeks to bring peace, inner balance and joy through the science of yoga and to relieve human suffering through a variety of initiatives on the individual, community and international level. Isha Foundation is a non-religious, non-political, non-sectarian organization with over 250,000 active volunteers worldwide.

Isha Foundation has over 150 centers in India and other parts of the world including the United States, Canada, Lebanon, Cyprus, France, and Germany. Based in Coimbatore, India, the foundation manages 87 centers in Tamil Nadu alone.

Isha is a predominantly volunteer-run organization. People who have been in some way touched and inspired by Isha Foundation comprise the volunteer base. Coming from all walks of life and all parts of the world, their quality of being dedicated, disciplined, and wanting to reach out is what is common across the organization.

Over the past 14 years, Isha Foundation has successfully carried out several social outreach programs for rural people, as well as disadvantaged and often neglected segments of society, throughout Tamil Nadu, thereby gaining a reputable and trustworthy standing among the people throughout India.

In addition to the selfless dedication of its volunteers, ARR is fueled and supported through its extensive partnerships with renowned national and international organizations, medical centers, and administrative centers, such as the Times Foundation, the Ramakrishna Hospitals, the Masonic Medical Center, the Kovai Medical Center Hospital, the KG Hospitals, the ELGI Group of Companies, and Shambhavi Trust, just to name a few. As part of their commitment to Action for Rural Rejuvenation, these organizations have pledged free and subsidized medical treatment to patients referred by the project, sponsored the design, construction or provision of the mobile health clinics and offered assistance of their own medical teams to go on rotation on the MHCs, among many other pledges.

(continues)

Figure 3.32 *(continued)*

VIII. Project Budget

We are seeking funding for:

One Mobile Health Clinic (MHC) Truck

Purchasing one additional MHC will allow Action for Rural Rejuvenation to serve up to 60 additional villages and as many 20,000 new patients the first year.

The cost for purchasing a MHC is $29,070.

While we can seek funding from other sources for the operating costs, the budget to operate the MCH for one year is an additional $17,442.

IX. Appendix

Attached are letters of support from our support organizations, such as the Times Foundation and the Kovia Medical Center Hospital, as well as our tax exempt status letter from the Internal Revenue Service.

INSTRUCTIONS

Instructions are step-by-step explanations of how to perform a particular procedure. Instructions are often written for product manuals, user guides, repair guides, and training manuals.

When writing instructions, consider the following guidelines (Figure 3.33):

- Instructions should be clear and written simply.

- The audience for the instructions should be clearly identified, and the instructions should be written to this audience's level of understanding.

- The instructions should have an introduction, listing:
  - Who should perform the procedure.
  - Any equipment, supplies, or documentation needed.
  - Special conditions or safety concerns, if any.
    - Warnings, cautions, and danger notices should alert readers of any possibility of hurting themselves or damaging equipment.

- Tasks involved in the procedure should be broken down into individual steps.

- Instruction steps should be numbered.

  - Substeps can be indented and alphabetized if they have to be performed in order.

  - If substeps can be performed in any order, bullets can be used.

- Supplementary information can provide commentary on what the process should look like at specific points in the instructions.

- Use the active voice for instructions.

Incorrect: The ENTER key should be pressed.

Correct: Press the ENTER key.

- Drawings, photographs, or screen captures are useful as roadmap illustrations.

- Major divisions of tasks can be grouped together under a heading.

Figure 3.33. Instructions

HOW TO ACCESS THE PRECLASS WEBINAR

Getting Started

Before attending the Technical Analysis class, you will need to sign in to the learning management system (LMS) and view a preclass webinar.

To access the LMS and view the webinar, you will need:

- The course password (tech123)

- Your employee identification number

- The Web address for the LMS: http://www.lms.com

You will need approximately one hour to view the webinar.

(continues)

Figure 3.33. *(continued)*

How to Find Your Employee ID

You will need your employee ID to sign in to the LMS. If you don't know your employee ID, follow these steps:

1. Open Internet Explorer and enter the following Web address: http://www.tech.com

2. Click the **Sign In** link in the top right corner.

3. On the Sign In page, change the Validation source to **Employee ID**.

4. New hyperlinks will be displayed. Click the link for **Forgot User ID**.

5. Answer the personal questions on the Verify Identity screen to get your employee ID.

Viewing the Preclass Webinar

Follow these steps to sign into the LMS and view the preclass Webinar:

1. Open Internet Explorer and enter the address for the LMS: http://www.lms.com

2. In the Quick Links section on the left side of the screen, click **Search Courses**.

3. On the Search Courses screen, select **Online Courses**; then click the **Go** button.

4. From the list of courses, select **TECH900**, and then click the **Select** button.

5. On the Sign On page, enter your employee ID and your last name as the password.

6. Click the **OK** button.

7. The preclass webinar will be displayed.

Warning: If you have a pop-up blocker running, the Webinar will not be displayed. To check, click the Internet Explorer **Tools** menu, then **Pop-Up Blocker**, and then check the setting. Make sure it is turned off.

INTRODUCTIONS

An **introduction** is usually the first section in a formal report. The introduction introduces the report to the reader.

The introduction explains what the report is about, why it was written, for whom it was written, and what it will cover. An introduction is usually no more than one or two pages (Figure 3.34).

Most introductions do the following:

■ Introduce the topic of the report.

■ Explain the purpose of the report.

■ Identify the target audience for the report.

■ Provide an overview of the content covered in the report.

■ Provide any history that may motivate readers to be interested.

Sections within the report may have their own introductions. A section introduction introduces a new topic, provides a content overview of the topic, and eases the transitions between sections.

Figure 3.34 Introduction

INTRODUCTION

America's Dynamic Workforce presents an overview of current conditions and notable trends affecting the American labor market and economic activity. Primary emphasis is on measures of labor market performance—employment, labor force participation, unemployment, and compensation. General measures of economic performance such as gross domestic product (GDP) and productivity growth are also described as they relate to labor market conditions and trends. Throughout this report the focus is on the data—what the numbers actually say about the American labor market—and on how individual data items fit together to present an overall portrait of the health and dynamism of the market.

There are six chapters:

Chapter 1 summarizes the current levels and trends of payroll jobs, total employment, job openings, turnover, unemployment, and GDP.

Chapter 2 provides a global context for understanding the U.S. labor market and compares the United States and other countries along common dimensions of labor market indicators.

Chapter 3 presents an overview of patterns, recent trends and projections regarding the distribution of employment across industries and occupations.

Chapter 4 examines the educational attainment of the labor force, including trends and comparisons of employment, earnings, and unemployment relative to educational attainment.

(continues)

Figure 3.34 *(continued)*

Chapter 5 examines the concept of labor force flexibility in terms of schedules, work arrangements, and other factors.

Chapter 6 highlights the dimensions of opportunity in the American workforce, including dynamic age, gender, race, and ethnicity perspectives.

The end notes provide important technical details, caveats, and references to additional information about the data items discussed in the main text.

Most of the tables and charts in America's Dynamic Workforce: 2006 reflect annual average data for calendar years ending in 2005 as the most recent full year available. In some cases, monthly data through the latest available month in 2006 (typically June) are also referenced.

In this report, the terms "population" and "labor force" refer to the civilian non-institutional population ages 16 and older and to the civilian labor force age 16 and over unless specified otherwise. Similarly, data on workers refer to employed persons age 16 and over unless otherwise noted. Monthly or quarterly labor market data are seasonally adjusted unless specified otherwise.

Much of the data in this report were compiled from the public access files of the Bureau of Labor Statistics' Web site at www.bls.gov.

(Courtesy of the U.S. Department of Labor)

INQUIRY LETTER

Inquiry letters are written to ask for information or to make a request. Don't send an inquiry letter for information you could easily obtain on the Internet or on the telephone. Allow two weeks after sending an inquiry letter and not getting a response before sending a follow-up letter.

When writing an inquiry letter, consider the following tips (Figure 3.35):

- Use a courteous tone because you are requesting the reader's time to fulfill your request.

- Begin the letter by stating who you are and how you found out about the reader's organization.

- State what you are requesting as clearly as possible.

- Explain the purpose of your request and how it will help you.

  - Mention your qualifications, if doing so is appropriate.

- The letter should be short but should adequately explain what you are requesting and what action you want the reader to take.

- Offer to pay for any copies or supplies that might be needed to fulfill your request.

  - Provide a self-addressed stamped envelope if you have requested documents.

- Include the date you need the information.

- When the person responds to your inquiry, send a thank-you note.

Inquiry letters are typically written to:

- Request technical assistance.

- Request a reprinted article or publication.

- Seek personal advice.

- Request information about a product or service.

- Request an official document.

- Request a reply to a survey.

- Request an application.

- Request an estimate or bid.

- Request information about a job seeker.

- Request information from a government agency.

- Request samples or information.

Figure 3.35 Inquiry Letter

May 15, 2012

654 West Lake Drive
Seattle, WA 98101

Technical Support
First Data Software
421 Research Drive, Suite 300
Research Triangle Park, NC 27709

Dear Technical Support Department:

I am writing to ask some questions about First Data's new upgrade for Kitchen Designer 4.0. I have been using Kitchen Designer 2.0 in my remodeling business for the past several years and it has helped me immensely.

I've read the latest sales literature about the software, but I was unable to find the answers to my questions. Since the new version has not yet been released, your online support pages also do not answer my questions.

To upgrade, I need to know whether the new software will operate properly with my current computer. Please let me know the answers to the following:

1. Does Kitchen Designer 4.0 still use a serial port security dongle?
2. Will the software support a geForce 800 video card using twin monitors?
3. Will designs created using Kitchen Designer 2.0 open in 4.0?

If your answer to all three questions is "yes," then I would definitely be interested in purchasing the upgrade.

You can respond to me by email at lsullivan@abcd.com or by calling me at (206) 555-1111. I appreciate your assistance.

Sincerely,

Louis Gullivan

Louis Sullivan

JOB DESCRIPTIONS

Job descriptions are often used when advertising an open position or when determining compensation.

A job description focuses on the job responsibilities, tasks, key qualifications, and basic skills needed to perform the job (Figure 3.36).

The categories that make up a typical job description include:

- Job title

- Department and to whom the person directly reports

- List of responsibilities

- List of other job titles and departments that the person will work with on a regular basis

- Terms of employment

- The necessary skills and experience required, including length of previous experience, educational requirements, and certifications

For existing positions, focus on the future needs and objectives of the business rather than on the current responsibilities of the position.

Be specific when describing tasks and responsibilities.

Any references to race, color, religion, age, sex, national origin, nationality, or physical or mental disability are illegal.

Figure 3.36 Job Description

Title of the position
Training Project Manager

Department
Human Resources

Reports to
Manager of Learning Technology

Overall responsibility
Provides project management and training development services for learning management system implementations and upgrades

Key areas of responsibility
- Provide project management services for e-learning course development.
- Provide training services for LMS administrators at subsidiaries.
- Develop training for LMS administrators and users.
- Provide support services for LMS users.
- Produce distance learning Webinars for Benefits and PeopleSoft instruction.
- Provide support to subsidiaries for e-learning implementations on the LMS.
- Manage the LMS administrator.
- Process training requests and assignments.

Consults with
- Human Resources Development department
- Training departments at subsidiaries

Term of employment
Full-time, on-sight, hours 8:00 A.M to 5:00 P.M.

Qualifications
- At least two years of project management experience for software implementations
- Experience working with learning management systems
- Experience conducting instructor-led training sessions
- Experience writing workbooks and job aids
- Experience supporting end users in a help desk function

JOB OFFER LETTER

Job offer letters are written by an employer to a job candidate to offer employment with the company.

Job offer letters should include facts about the following (Figure 3.37):

- Starting salary

- Job location

- Working hours

- Benefits

- Start date

- Job title

- Job responsibilities

The tone of the letter should be direct and encouraging. The offer may be contingent on providing proof of employment eligibility.

Figure 3.37 Job Offer Letter

January 20, 2012

Communication Enterprises
3211 West Peachtree Street
Dunwoody, GA 32311

Aileen Robertson
2422 Churchill Lane, Apt 233
Roswell, GA 30322

Dear Ms. Robertson:

It is my pleasure to present our offer of employment as training developer, reporting to me, Ken Wallace, Learning Technology Manager.

As training developer, you will be creating course manuals, PowerPoint presentations, and Help systems as a part of your normal job. In addition, you may also be asked to serve as an instructor from time to time.

Your annualized base salary will be $62,000, payable on a semimonthly basis. You will also be eligible for an annual incentive, which will range from 0% to 4% of base salary paid, with a target of 3% of base salary paid.

Communication Enterprises offers the following competitive benefits, all of which are subject to the terms of the company or benefit plan guidelines. All of these benefits are covered in detail in the enclosed documents. You will be eligible to participate in the company health plan upon hire and in the company pension plan upon hire or at age 21, whichever is later. Based on your projected hire date of February 1, 2012, you will be eligible to participate in the 401(k) plan on July 1, 2012. Additionally, you will have up to two weeks of paid vacation, nine company paid holidays, and two personal floating holidays.

Aileen, you bring a background of experience and capability that should greatly enhance our efforts in the training department. We look forward to the beginning of a long and mutually rewarding relationship.

Sincerely,

Ken Wallace

Ken Wallace
Learning Technology Manager

MEETING AGENDA

A **meeting agenda** is a road map for a meeting. The agenda provides the plan for the meeting and a sense of direction and purpose.

A meeting agenda should include (Figure 3.38):

- Meeting starting and ending times

- Meeting location

- Topic headings with topic details

- How much time each topic discussion is expected to last

- Which meeting participants will facilitate the topics

Figure 3.38 Meeting Agenda

Meeting Called By:	Session #:	Date:	Starting Time:
Mark Rivers		1/28/2011	9:30 a.m.
Location:	**Dress Code (optional):**		**Ending Time:**
Central Park Conference Room 11a			12:00 p.m.
Meeting Objective and Scope:			
JAD Session—The Big Picture.			
Time	**Topic**		**Leader**
9:30–9:35	Welcome and review agenda.		Mark Rivers
9:35–9:55	Basic data flow for enrollments.		Ritva Porter
9:55–10:15	Ongoing data requirements		Ritva Porter
10:15–10:35	Basic data flow for pay processing		Ritva Porter
10:35–10:45	Break		
10:45–11:10	Basic data flow for 401(k) billing.		Ritva Porter
11:10–11:30	Basic data flow for termination processing.		Ritva Porter
11:30–11:50	Basic data flow for loans.		Ritva Porter
11:50–12:00	Wrapup		Mark Rivers
Facilitator:	**Time Keeper:**		**Scribe**
Ritva Porter			Debra Miller
Attendees:			
Anne Fried, Mark Rivers, Donna Morgan, Tonya Smith, Debra Miller, Sally Roberts, Susan Mullins, Ebony Hollings, Tanya Sanchez, Mary McKnight, Daphne Johnson, Mike Harper, Kevin Wilson, Kendall Williams, Rita Zezula, Darlene Price			

MEETING MINUTES

Meeting minutes are a record of what took place during a meeting. They allow the meeting attendees to review the meeting later to look for outstanding issues and action items.

In some cases, such as stockholder and board of directors meetings, the minutes are required by law and are included in the corporate minute book.

Meeting minutes should include (Figure 3.39):

- The name of organization

- The name of body conducting the meeting

- The date, hour, and location of the meeting

- The list of those present and those absent

- A reading of previous minutes and their approval or amendment

- Unfinished business

- New business

- The date of the next meeting

- The time of adjournment

- The signature of the recorder

Corporate Minutes

All corporations must document the minutes of shareholder and board of directors meetings.

In many states, the absence of proper meeting minutes may be a liability for the corporation, especially when the shareholders are also on the board of directors or there are close relationships among board members.

All corporations in the United States are required to hold annual shareholder's meetings to elect directors. The bylaws of most corporations require the board of directors to have annual meetings.

At corporate meetings the following actions will normally be approved by the board of directors:

- Election of officers of the corporation

- New business policies and plans

- Creation of committees and assignments

- Issuing and selling stock

- Approval of the sale, transfer, lease, or exchange of any corporate property or assets

- Approval of mergers and reorganizations

- Adoption of a pension, profit-sharing, or other employee benefit plans and stock option plans

- Approval of corporate borrowing and loans

- Entry into joint ventures

- Designation of corporate bank accounts and authorized signatures

- Changing an officer's compensation

- Entry into major contractual agreements

Corporate Resolutions

Formal resolutions may be made in one of these forms:

- WHEREAS it is necessary to . . . ; and

- WHEREAS conditions are such that . . . ; and

- Therefore be it

- RESOLVED, That . . . ; and be it

- RESOLVED further, That . . .

Note that the word *whereas* is in caps with no comma following it; the first word after it is not capitalized unless it is a proper name.

The word *resolved* is also set in caps but is followed by a comma and a capital letter.

Figure 3.39 Meeting Minutes

Minutes of Meeting of
the Historical Society of the University of Texas
Hotel Driscoll, Austin, Texas
May 1, 2012

At the meeting of the Historical Society of the University of Texas at Austin, some 100 charter members being present, the Society was called to order at 1:05 p.m. by Mr. John R. Combs, chairperson, who requested Mr. Warren T. Scaggs to serve as temporary secretary.

Mr. Combs dispensed with the reading of the minutes of the last meeting because a copy had been previously distributed to all members.

A communication from the National Historical Society, read and accepted by the Society, dealt with the planting of redbud trees throughout America.

A communication from Miss Harriet Allen of New York City asked that the Society refrain from its normal pattern of conducting spring tours throughout the State of Texas. Several members, after the reading, expressed disagreement with the views given by Miss Allen.

There was no unfinished business.

New business was the election of officers for the remaining current year. The following nominations were announced by Mr. Warren T. Scaggs, chairperson of the Nominating Committee:

President	Mrs. Rutherford Tinsdale
Secretary	Mr. Joseph Mapes
Treasurer	Mrs. Theodore R. Tollivar
Members of the Council	Ms. Louise Allen
	Mrs. Philip W. Crossman
	Mr. John Stobaugh
	Mrs. John C. McCann

After an unanswered call for nominations from the floor, it was moved by Mrs. William R. Metcalfe that the secretary cast one ballot for officers nominated. The motion was seconded and carried, and the officers were declared elected.

The next meeting of the Historical Society of the University of Texas at Austin will be held on June 11 at the Hotel Driscoll in Austin, Texas, at 1:00 p.m.

After congratulations to the newly elected officers by the chairperson, the Society adjourned at 3:25 p.m.

Warren T. Scaggs
Temporary Secretary

MEMORANDUM

An office **memorandum** or memo is often used to communicate with the employees of a company (Figure 3.40).

Most memos are sent using email; however, some types of communication are not appropriate for email and should instead be printed on paper and distributed.

Example: Confidential information or information that should not be forwarded

Memos that are directed to individuals should be printed and signed. If copies are sent to other parties, a notation to that effect should be made at the lower left corner of the form.

If a memo is confidential, it should be printed and enclosed in an envelope.

Figure 3.40 Memo

TO: Mary Anne Scott, Shipping Department Manager

FROM: Bob Brueck, President

DATE: May 12, 2011

SUBJECT: Meeting to discuss various overseas carriers

A meeting has been scheduled for Tuesday, May 12, in my office to discuss with several carrier representatives suggested methods and costs to deliver our products to international markets. Your attendance is requested.

Distribution:
Tom Alberton
Martha Reeves

MISSION STATEMENTS

A **mission statement** explains an organization's purpose, function, and reason for existing. A mission statement motivates employees, customers, and stockholders.

A mission statement guides decision making throughout the organization. Mission statements are often included in annual reports, company brochures, and Web sites, and they may also be printed and framed.

When writing a mission statement, consider the following tips (Figure 3.41):

- Include a statement of purpose.

- Include a description of the organization's business or principal activities.

- Include acknowledgment of all stakeholders.

- Optionally include the organization's goals and how they can be measured.

- Optionally include the organization's values and establish a sense of identity.

When brainstorming and writing a mission statement, ask and answer the following questions:

- Why was the organization created?

- Who are the stakeholders?

- What services does the organization provide?

- What identity do you want to project for the organization's products or services?

- What do you want to communicate to the community?

- What does the future look like for the organization?

- What organizational values are needed to achieve?

Figure 3.41 Mission Statement

PROJECT BLOOM MISSION STATEMENT

To promote the recognition, appreciation, and development of the human resources team through direct involvement, exciting communications, and sharing of innovative ideas, which result in the fullest appreciation of the diversity of the team.

NEWSLETTERS

Corporate **newsletters** are written to publicize news about a company or department for reading by employees or customers. Newsletters can be distributed on paper, sent via email, or posted on a Web site (Figure 3.42).

Regardless of whether they are paper or electronic, corporate newsletters usually involve a front page, inside articles, and announcements on the back page.

- Front page news focuses on achievements, success stories, or changes that affect the audience.

Example: a new contract, completion of a project, opening of a new office, launch of a new product, hiring of a new executive

---

- Inside articles:

  - Usually include departmental news that lets readers know what various parts of the company are doing.

  - Focus on departmental achievements and information about specific projects.

  - Often introduce newly hired employees to the rest of the company.

  - Can also highlight personal achievements of individual employees.

- Company updates are often included to communicate information about policies and procedures, make announcements about new equipment, and tell about training opportunities.

- Employee news articles often highlight employment anniversaries with the company.

- Calendar items list company-wide events, such as parties, quarterly or annual meetings, and training events.

- Employee announcements may list job openings, transfers, promotions, and other similar events.

- Filler material is used when space is available, including art, cartoons, or humorous items.

Newsletter content depends on whether the audience consists of the entire company, a single department, and whether customers will see it. Some companies publish newsletters that are distributed exclusively to customers, usually via email.

Newsletters for a customer audience should include:

- Information about new products and services

- Helpful tips of interest to customers

- Calendar items of importance to customers

- Information about major promotions involving employees who work directly with customers

Newsletters are more visually appealing if they include photographs.

Newsletter Articles

Consider the following guidelines when writing a newsletter article (Figure 3.43):

- Develop a title for the article that will accurately convey the topic or theme.
- Use a title that arouses curiosity.
- Use photographs that illustrate the story.
- Optionally, write an opening story summary that can be set apart in bold and included at the beginning of the article or in a sidebar.
- The lead sentence should introduce the topic, engage the reader, and focus on the reader's point of view.
- The body of the article should include relevant background and history, explain the implications of the topic, provide specific examples, and make suggestions.
    - Use transitions to connect the main points of the article.
- The article's conclusion should repeat the most important point and emphasize why it is important to the readers.
- Use appropriate language for the audience.
    - Avoid using jargon and clichés.
    - Avoid complicated sentence constructions and wordiness.
    - Keep paragraphs short and focused.
    - Use quotes and testimonials when appropriate.

Figure 3.43 Newsletter Article

WHAT DO YOU HAVE TO LOSE?

Have you noticed something missing from the 11th floor? Like 91 pounds?

That's how much the participants of the "What Do You Have to Lose" challenge lost all together. We had three teams of five people, and the team that had the highest percentage of weight loss at the end of the challenge won. The challenge kicked off on July 10 and wrapped up on September 7. In addition to losing 91 pounds, some participants brought their blood pressure down to a healthier level, others started an exercise program, and some replaced their daily cokes and coffees with 64 ounces of water.

Congratulations to the winners, The Fabulous Five (Donna Gilbert, Ken Willingham, Sterling Mabry, Cathy Price, and Darlene Warren). Together they had a 21% weight loss. The winners each received a $110 Visa Gift Card.

Figure 3.42 Newsletter

GSA Office of Citizen Services and Communications

Intergovernmental Solutions Newsletter
Transparency and Open Government

Spring 2009

Transparency in Government

By Darlene Meskell
Director, Intergovernmental Solutions
GSA Office of Citizen Services and Communications

Newly elected President Barack Obama has taken bold steps to inaugurate an era of government openness and transparency. In one of his first official acts, the President issued a *Memorandum on Transparency and Open Government*, affirming his commitment to achieving an "unprecedented level of openness in government." Making known his belief that transparency is a fundamental responsibility of a democratic government, he called for the creation of an Open Government Directive that would require agencies to reveal their inner workings and make their data public.

A commitment to government accountability is at the heart of this message. By allowing citizens to "see through" its workings and investigate whether or not their leaders and organizations have met their expectations, the government brings the public into its inner circles and empowers citizens to contribute to decision-making. As citizens gain knowledge and understanding, their trust in government begins to grow.

Providing government data to citizens in a meaningful way will require a culture change, away from one where data are stored away for internal purposes to one that looks broadly at how data can be made accessible for re-use by the public. The federal website *Recovery.gov Reveals Details of the Stimulus Spending* on the $787 billion American Recovery and Reinvestment Act. It will put the data out in useable form so that people can slice, dice and mash it up to gain meaningful information about how government is working.

These data feeds create opportunities to look at government programs in new ways that could never have been imagined by the data collectors. The District of Columbia's *Apps for Democracy* Contest drew upon the public's imagination to make D.C. data more useful to constituents. Under the leadership of then-CTO Vivek Kundra, the District sponsored a contest seeking creative applications that use D.C. government data. The results were astonishing. The 47 entries submitted to *Apps for Democracy* within only 30 days "produced more savings for the D.C. government than any other initiative," according to Kundra, who has since been named federal CIO.

Continued on next page...

The Intergovernmental Solutions Newsletter is produced twice a year by the Intergovernmental Solutions Division, GSA Office of Citizens Services and Communications; Lisa Nelson, Editor. Send comments and suggestions to: lisa.nelson@gsa.gov.

(Courtesy of the U.S. General Services Administration)

NOTICES

Notices highlight information that readers must understand to avoid mistakes, injuries, or damage to equipment. Notices are often included in user and training manuals.

The most common types of notices are:

- Notes—to serve as reminders or to avoid problems or mistakes (Figure 3.44)

- Tips—to provide useful troubleshooting or time-saving information (Figure 3.45).

- Warnings—about things that can cause major problems or an injury (Figure 3.46)

- Cautions—about things that can result in damage to equipment or data loss (Figure 3.47)

- Danger—about the possibility of serious or fatal injuries (Figure 3.48)

Notices should not only provide warnings, they should also explain the consequences for failure to abide by the advice offered in the notice.

Notices are formatted differently from the rest of the text in a document. They are placed within the text when needed. Caution and danger notices are placed before the content to which they apply. Special icons are sometimes used to emphasize a notice.

Notes are usually set apart in their own paragraph with the word *Note* in bold followed by a colon.

- Skip a line above and below the note and single space the note.

- Additional lines in the note should align with the word *Note*.

Figure 3.44 Note

COBRA Overage

A COBRA overage process was put in place to keep the benefits plan in compliance with IRS guidelines. When COBRA overage processing runs on Sunday and Wednesday night, it evaluates all employees' benefits and their covered dependents.

When a dependent reaches his or her 23rd birthday (without the disabled indicator checked), the system **automatically** drops the dependent from any medical and/or dental coverage.

Note: Home Office changes the disabled indicator in the database once an dependent is approved per plan guidelines.

Tips should be formatted like notes with the word *Tip* in bold and followed by a colon.

Figure 3.45 Tip

With the exceptions of the employee's retirement or eligibility for long-term disability (LTD), domestic partners are not eligible for COBRA independently of the employee. Events where COBRA should not be offered to a domestic partner include termination of the domestic partner relationship and death of the employee. The domestic partner coverage is terminated due to the employee's retirement or eligibility for the LTD health care plan, at which time the domestic partner will be given the option to elect COBRA continuation for a period of 18 months.

Tip: If an employee terminates and has domestic partner coverage under domestic partner medical, dental, or vision, the COBRA forms generated do not include COBRA rates for the domestic partner. To ensure that the employee is offered COBRA for the domestic partner, write the domestic partner's name, Social Security Number and date of birth on the COBRA form in the "Eligible Participants" section.

Warning notices should be formatted with the word *Warning* written in italics with approximately a half-inch of tab space separating the word from the message.

- The text of the message should use the regular body font with no italics or bold.
- Skip one line before and after the warning.

Figure 3.46 Warning Notice

> The battery is one of the most important components on a vehicle today. It supplies not only the cranking amperage to start the engine, but also the initial voltage needed to run the onboard computer, ignition system, fuel injectors, lights, and all the vehicle accessories. Most of these systems require a minimum level of power to operate correctly. Having a good battery is absolutely essential for reliable vehicle starting and operation.
>
> *Warning:*   Be careful when handling batteries due to corrosive battery acid that may leak from the battery and damage your skin or eyes. Always wear gloves and eye protection.

Caution notices are formatted with the word *Caution* in bold and followed by a colon.

- Caution should appear on a line by itself.
- Skip one line before and after the caution notice.
- The text for the message is single-spaced and is aligned with the word *Caution*.

Figure 3.47 Caution Notice

> *Multimedia* is commonly defined as combining multiple forms of media such as audio, graphics, text, and video. Together, we will explore the multimedia control panel on your computer and find out how you can customize the features to enhance classroom presentations.
>
> **Caution:**
> Although we feel that it is important to show you how to control your settings, we recommend that you not make any changes to the system at this time. This is a multimedia course. It could be affected by any changes you make.

Danger notices should be formatted with the word *DANGER* in all caps, bold, and followed by a colon.

- Align the word *DANGER* with the normal text in the document.

- The rest of the text should be indented and aligned approximately 10 spaces from the left margin.

- Add a graphic box around the notice.

Figure 3.48 Danger Notice

It is a simple process to change wall switches around your home. You'll need a screwdriver, a replacement switch kit, a neon tester, and electrical tape.

> **DANGER:** Always shut off the power before beginning any electrical repair. Trip the breaker for the circuit that you will be working on. Use a neon tester on the outlet to be sure the power is off. If there is any doubt, trip the main breaker or remove the fuse and shut off power to entire house. Failure to follow these safety precautions may result in serious electrical shock, injury, or death.

PERMISSION LETTER

A **permission letter** is written to grant authority to someone for a specific purpose. Approval letters and authorization letters are similar.

When writing a permission letter, consider the following tips (Figures 3.49–3.50):

- Begin the letter by stating what permission is being granted and to whom it is being given.

- State the reasons for granting permission.

- Indicate the next steps the person is authorized to take.

- State any dates when the permission is effective, date of a specific event, and date the permission will expire.

- Include any other specific information regarding use of the permission.

- Include any special stipulations or guidelines that are required.
    - Outline any responsibilities.

Permission letters are typically written to:

- Approve a request.

- Approve a vacation or leave of absence.

- Approve the use of facilities.

- Give permission to be photographed as a model.

- Approve the use of a company vehicle.

- Authorize the use of copyrighted material.

- Grant permission to attend a conference or training session.

- Authorize medical treatment.

- Authorize work on a project.

- Delegate authority.

- Delegate a special project.

- Authorize research.

(text continues on page 524)

Figure 3.49 Permission Letter Granting Permission

PHOTO IMAGE GRANT OF RIGHTS AND RELEASE

In consideration of the opportunity to have my image published and other good and valuable consideration, the receipt and sufficiency of which is hereby acknowledged, the undersigned ("Releasor") hereby grants XYZ Corporation, its affiliates and their permittees (collectively, "Releasees") the following rights with respect to the use of the Releasor's image in the photographs taken on August 25, 2012 described as follows: XYZ Training Photos.

1. To alter and edit Releasor's image without limitation.

2. To use and publish Releasor's image and, in conjunction with it, Releasor's name and biographical information, in any medium, whether now or hereafter existing, including without limitation, any online service or Web site, and for any purpose, including, without limitation, promotional, advertising and marketing purposes.

With regard to these rights, Releasor releases and discharges Releasees and each of them from any and all claims and demands arising out of or in connection with the use of such photograph(s), the images therein (whether altered or unaltered) and Releasor's name and biographical information, including, without limitation, any claim for defamation, misappropriation, right of publicity, false light, invasion of privacy and copyright infringement.

The Photo Image Grant of Rights and Release constitutes an Agreement between Releasor and XYZ Corporation and contains the entire understanding between the parties. It cannot be modified except by written agreement signed by both parties and shall be governed and construed in accordance with the laws of the State of Georgia.

_____   _____

By: Signature   Date

_____

Name

_____

Address

_____

Figure 3.50 Permission Letter Requesting Permission

March 21, 2012

Communication Enterprises
3211 West Peachtree Street
Dunwoody, GA 32311

Dylan Wilson
Atlanta Community College
1311 West Northfield Drive
Decatur, GA 30133

Dear Mr. Wilson:

This letter confirms our recent telephone conversation regarding the use of a transcript of your Communications 101 course lecture on media responsibility in the June issue of our corporate newsletter.

I am responsible for editing the newsletter, and recently I heard you speak at a Technical Communications Association meeting on this subject. After speaking with you, I now know this talk is part of your regular course lectures at Atlanta Community College.

Our corporate newsletter is distributed to approximately 30,000 employees. It is an internal-only publication.

Please indicate your approval of this permission by signing this letter where indicated below and returning it to me as soon as possible. I have enclosed a self-addressed stamped envelope for that purpose.

Thank you very much for agreeing to let us publish your lecture.

Sincerely,

Al Gordon

Al Gordon
Communications Manager

Permission granted for the use requested above

_____   _____

Dylan Wilson   Date

POLICIES, RULES, OR GUIDELINES

Policies are rules or guidelines for a specific business process. They are formal corporate-wide instructions that must be followed by everyone within the organization. Violation of policies may result in disciplinary action. New policies must be approved by corporate management. (Figure 3.51.)

Rules are less formal than policies and define acceptable behavior within a particular department or division.

- Rules may not impact the entire organization.

- New rules must be approved by department or division heads.

- Violation of rules may result in disciplinary action.

Guidelines suggest ways of handling certain situations.

- Violating a guideline does not necessarily involve sanctions.

- A subject matter expert should approve guidelines.

Policies address a particular problem or issue and specific groups of employees.

- Policies must be formally shared with the group of employees who will be governed by the language.

- Employee handbooks are often published with company policies and distributed to all employees.

To write a policy, rule, or guideline, follow these steps:

- Create an outline of the topics that could be covered by the policy, rule, or guideline.

- State the purpose of the policy, rule, or guideline.

- State clearly what the policy, rule, or guideline allows and doesn't allow.

- Explain to whom the policy, rule, or guideline applies.

- Provide any background information that provides context on why the policy, rule, or guideline is needed.

- List any legislation that governs the policy, rule, or guideline.

- Describe any specific procedure that must be followed.
  - Use short paragraphs or numbered steps.
  - Group tasks together under subheadings.

- Explain what to do if violations occur.

- Explain any terminology that may be confusing to a general audience of employees.

- List any special circumstances when the policy, rule, or guideline does not apply.

- List any time restraints if applicable, including the effective date.

Figure 3.51 Policy

WHO IS ENTITLED TO BENEFITS UNDER COBRA

There are three elements to qualifying for COBRA benefits. COBRA establishes specific criteria for plans, qualified beneficiaries, and qualifying events:

Qualified Beneficiaries—A qualified beneficiary generally is an individual covered by a group health plan on the day before a qualifying event who is either an employee, the employee's spouse, or an employee's dependent child. In certain cases, a retired employee, the retired employee's spouse, and the retired employee's dependent children may be qualified beneficiaries. In addition, any child born to or placed for adoption with a covered employee during the period of COBRA coverage is considered a qualified beneficiary. Agents, independent contractors, and directors who participate in the group health plan may also be qualified beneficiaries.

Qualifying Events—Qualifying events are certain events that would cause an individual to lose health coverage. The type of qualifying event will determine who the qualified beneficiaries are and the amount of time that the plan must offer the health coverage to them under COBRA.

(continues)

Figure 3.51 *(continued)*

Qualifying Events for Employees:

■ Voluntary or involuntary termination of employment for reasons other than gross misconduct

■ Reduction in the number of hours of employment

Qualifying Events for Spouses:

■ Voluntary or involuntary termination of the covered employee's employment for any reason other than gross misconduct

■ Reduction in the hours worked by the covered employee

■ Covered employee's becoming entitled to Medicare

■ Divorce or legal separation of the covered employee

■ Death of the covered employee

Qualifying Events for Dependent Children:

■ Loss of dependent child status under the plan rules

■ Voluntary or involuntary termination of the covered employee's employment for any reason other than gross misconduct

■ Reduction in the hours worked by the covered employee

■ Covered employee's becoming entitled to Medicare

■ Divorce or legal separation of the covered employee

■ Death of the covered employee

POWERPOINT PRESENTATIONS

PowerPoint presentations are created to provide visual aids during oral presentations, sales presentations, and as stand-alone computer-based training. (Figures 3.52–3.55.) When creating PowerPoint presentations, consider the following tips:

■ Slide designs should focus the audience's attention on a particular aspect of each slide.

- Don't use too much text.
- Use contrasting colors, different text sizes, bold, or italics to set apart a particular element on the screen.
  - Highlight individual lines of text that are the focus of the slide.
- Bulleted text lines should be aligned to give the page an elegant look.
  - Keep all bullets on the same level grammatically parallel.
  - Indent text from the bullet symbols by a consistent space for all levels of bullets.
  - Avoid big paragraphs of text that fill the slide.
    - Use bullets, headings, and subheadings instead.
- Repeat visual elements and text throughout the presentation to focus on key points and to unify the presentation.
  - Repeat headings from slide to slide when appropriate.
  - Repeat text from slide to slide, while highlighting a different line on each slide.
- Group similar items on the slide to show a relationship.
  - Use subheadings with nested bullets for a list.
  - Use a graphic with associated text to show a visual connection to the text.
- Use sans serif fonts like Helvetica, Swiss, Arial, Avant Garde, and Modern.
  - Avoid mixing serif and sans serif fonts within the same presentation.
- Apply background shading for presentations that will be projected.
  - Use a white background for presentations that will be printed and distributed on paper.
  - If shading is used, use a gradient that gradually changes from light to dark or from one color to another to add visual depth to the presentation.
  - Apply a consistent color scheme to the entire presentation.
    - Do not use differently colored backgrounds for each slide in the presentation.

- Create styles for the entire presentation using Slide Master to:
    - Set the text placement as well as font size and color on all slides.
    - Keep the presentation consistent.
- Use Notes Master to insert speaker notes into the presentation.
    - When printed on paper, the slide appears at the top of the page and the notes appear at the bottom.
- Use Handout Master to add text and artwork to audience handouts.
- To save time when designing a presentation, use PowerPoint templates that are prebuilt and professionally designed.
    - Templates are available within the PowerPoint application.
    - Additional templates can be downloaded from the Internet.
- Use charts, photos, or illustrations that communicate visually.
    - Free clipart is available within PowerPoint.
    - Bar charts and pie charts can be created in PowerPoint.
        - Organizational charts can also be created within PowerPoint.
    - The Smart Art Graphics feature, available within the PowerPoint program, allows you to insert nice looking diagrams.
    - Digital cameras can be used to take photographs that can be imported into PowerPoint and placed on a slide.
    - AutoShapes allows you to create geometric shapes, arrows, and lines to help illustrate your slides.
- Videos, animation, and sound can be added to slides to create a multimedia presentation.

Planning a Presentation

Consider the following guidelines as you plan your presentation.

- Determine your goal and objectives.

Example: Do you want to persuade or inform?

- Keep the presentation simple and focused.

  - A clear message with more impact is more likely to achieve results than an unfocused one.

  - A complicated message is muddled and will leave the audience confused and frustrated.

  - Keep the number of topics covered to a minimum.

- Design the presentation like creating a story.

  - Organize the content with a beginning, middle, and end.

- Design for drama.

  - Pique your audience's interest toward the end of the presentation and deliver the central conclusion of your message when you have the full attention of everyone.

- Plan your media selection.

  - Will you use slides and a digital projector, printed handouts, or both?

- Think and plan ahead.

  - If you give the audience handouts before the show, they can follow along and write notes directly on the handouts.

  - Handouts also give the audience something to reference if they have trouble seeing the screen.

  - If you distribute handouts at the end of the presentation, you can avoid giving away any planned surprises.

- Consider the subject matter.

  - The tone of your presentation depends on the type of presentation: training seminar, presentation to managers or employees, or a sales presentation to customers.

- Consider the audience's:

  - Familiarity with the subject matter

  - Composition (will the audience be exclusively employees, or customers, or mixed?)

  - Size (large audiences dictate the need for more structure and formality; small audiences may be less formal, giving you more room for improvisation and one-on-one interaction)

- Consider the environment for the presentation.

    - How visible is the screen from each part of the room?

    - If visibility is in question, include handouts with printed versions of each slide.

    - If you are not familiar with the equipment, arrange time for setting up and rehearsing your presentation before delivering the real thing.

- Practice delivering your presentation.

    - Deliver your presentation to a coworker or friend and ask for a critique.

Figure 3.52 Slide with Bulleted Lists, a Graphical Background, and Photo

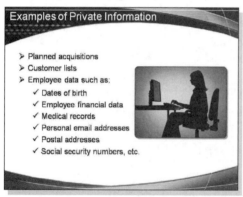

Figure 3.53 Slide with Title, Bulleted Subtitle, and Pie Chart

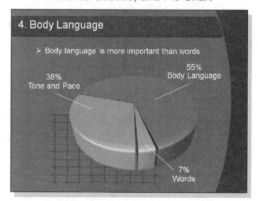

Figure 3.54 Slide with PowerPoint WordArt

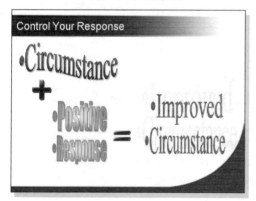

Figure 3.55 Slide with Graphics Rather Than Text

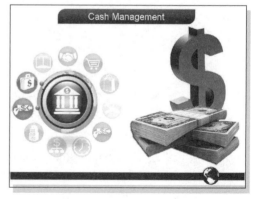

PRESS RELEASES

A **press release** is a written communication directed at the news media for the purpose of making an announcement. When writing a press release, consider the following guidelines (Figure 3.56):

- Lay out your document on an 8½ x 11-inch page.

- Provide wide margins and double-space the copy.

- Include a release date at the top of the page.

- Provide a contact name and address. Provide as much contact information as possible, including fax, email, and Web site addresses.

- Include the phrase "For Immediate Release" along with a contact name and phone number. If the release date is in the future, instead say, "For Release on [date]."

- Include a suggested headline.

- Start your first paragraph with the location in all caps, followed by the month and day.

- Summarize your story in the first paragraph, including who, what, why, where, when, and how.

- Make sure the first 10 words are effective; they are the most important.

- Elaborate on the details, including quotes from important sources.

- Make sure the information is newsworthy by suggesting other tie-ins. Pick an angle. Try to make your press release timely by tying it to current events or social issues.

- Avoid excessive use of adjectives and fancy language. Use only enough words to tell your story.

- Use the active, not passive, voice. Verbs in the active voice bring your press release to life.

- Avoid jargon specific to your organization that might not be recognized by other readers.

- Answer the question, why should anyone care?

- Use real-life examples, if possible, that include stories of the people involved.

- Raise other questions or suggest topics of interest, if you are trying to generate a feature story or radio or TV interview.

- Suggest in a covering pitch letter an interview with the principal person or organization involved, such as the company CEO or a book author.

- Type the word *more* at the end of each page.

- At the end of your release, type ### and center it.

Figure 3.56 Press Release

October 1, 2011

Contact Name
Address
City, State, Zip
Email
Web Address

For Immediate Release
Contact: Jason Brown—770-555-1234

BRONSON MEDIA SIGNS $8 MILLION CONTRACT WITH VIDEOLOGIES, INC. TO BE EXCLUSIVE PROVIDER OF CIRCULATION SYSTEMS, NETWORK, AND APPLICATIONS.

ATLANTA, Oct 1—Bronson Media, the largest American newspaper owner, signed an $8 million contract making Videologies, Inc. the exclusive provider of circulation systems, network and applications for print media holdings.

Videologies will now provide circulation software for all of Bronson Media's newspapers, including the *Los Angeles Herald, The Seattle Constitution,* and *the Atlanta Daily.* The contract was awarded to Videologies after an extensive product and company review. Bronson Media will take advantage of the entire line of Videologies circulation software. VID 4.2 is a program specially designed for print media to chart production and material costs to optimize productivity. VID Router allows newspapers to make routing decisions and design delivery routes based on scanned maps.

Mark Giddings, vice president of print media operations at Bronson Media, commented, "The contract with Videologies is a big step forward for Bronson's newspapers. It will allow us to standardize circulation and production systems, making cooperation between our print media holdings more efficient and effective."

###

PROCEDURES

Procedures are instructions that explain how to perform a particular task (Figure 3.57).

To write a procedure:

■ State the goal of the procedure.

> **Example:** This procedure tells you how to install a cable modem.

■ The heading for the procedure may also state the goal.

> **Example:** Installing a Cable Modem

■ If specific supplies or knowledge are needed for the procedure, provide a list before detailing the steps.

> **Example:** Before you start, you'll need the following: coaxial cable, pliers, and a screwdriver.

■ If a certain level of experience is necessary, provide a list for whom the procedures are intended.

> **Example:** Before attempting this procedure, you should have a basic understanding of an operating system.

- When is it necessary to use specific terminology to describe the procedure, use only what is absolutely necessary.
  - Don't overload the procedure with unnecessary jargon.
  - Explain any specialized technical terms that are used.
- Provide an estimate of how long it will take to complete the procedure.
- List the steps in the procedure using numbered lists.
- Break the steps in the overall procedure into smaller sections.
  - Limit the number of steps to 10 in each section.
  - Each section should have its own title.
- If a particular step has substeps, indent a secondary list using letters to designate them.
- Describe only one step at a time.
  - Each step should describe one task.
- Include illustrations where appropriate.
- If certain conditions apply or if performing a step will cause something to happen, present this information at the beginning of the step.

Example: To shut down the computer, click the **Start** button, then click **Turn Off the Computer**.

- When someone else is supposed to perform a particular step in the procedure, describe who is responsible and what he or she will do.

Example: The licensing department will accept your serial number, and will email you an activation code.

- At the end of the procedure, include a statement that tells users that the procedure is complete and what the result is likely to be.

Example: That completes the steps for installing the cable modem. The power and Internet lights should be solid green.

- Provide references to other useful information.

Figure 3.57 Procedures

WALKTHROUGH—PASTE SPECIAL > VALUES

In this walkthrough, you will use the Paste Special > Values function to convert the result of a formula to text.

1. Continue with the TTFFP—Daily Activity Exercise.xls file, which should already be open.

2. Select cell **I2**, the cell your concatenating formula is in.

3. Select **Edit > Copy**.

4. Select **Edit > Paste Special**.

5. Select the **Values** radio button.

6. Click **OK**.

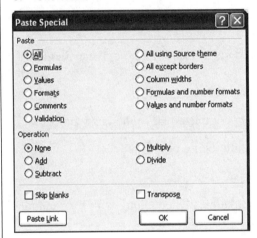

Note how your formula has been transformed into text.

---

7. Save your work by clicking **File > Save As**, and then changing the name of the file to **"Daily Activity Exercise A"** and then click the **Save** button.

8. Close the spreadsheet by clicking **File > Close**.

That completes this walkthrough.

PROGRESS REPORTS

Progress reports are written to inform a supervisor about the status of a project. These reports detail what was completed for the previous period, what percentage of the work has been completed, and what is planned for the next period. Any problems or issues are listed in the report.

Progress reports let management know about the overall health of a project and its team members. Progress reports also let everyone on the team know how the overall project is going.

These reports range from simple memos for small projects, to informal letters, to formal reports.

- Memos are often used for internal progress reports.

- Progress report letters are sent to outside clients.

- Formal progress reports are also sent to outside clients.

All progress reports include (Figure 3.58):

- What work has been completed since the last report

- What work is currently being performed

- What work is planned

- Individual tasks, sometimes listed, along with their completion percentages

- The progress of different stages of development and categories for different departments (may be listed for large projects)

Project reports prepared for outside customers may also include:

- The project purpose

- Objectives

- Scope or limitations

- Start date and completion date

- Current development phase

- Team members

(text continues on page 540)

Figure 3.58 Progress Report

ERP UPGRADE PROJECT STATUS REPORT

Name of Project: ERP Upgrade
Date: July 27, 2012
Project Manager: Mary Dawson
Sponsor: Allan Cummings

Project Objectives:
Upgrade the existing ERP application to position Acme Industries to maintain vendor support for the application and to consider undertaking projects, after the upgrade, which will implement new functionality offered in the ERP system.

Implementation Date: August 20, 2012
Current Phase: QA Testing/UAT Testing/Implementation Planning

Project Management Summary:
The upgrade project remains on track. 14 business days until we began our upgrade implementation!

ISSUE
Integrated QA test environment was planned for May 7 and is not completely ready.

Update—Stellent configuration issue was resolved and testing for Stellent will start next week.

QA Testing—The formal QA testing period is over; however, QA testing will continue for some items, including:

- HR/benefits—75% complete. Outstanding are items associated with HCFA, MSY, Retirees, and FSA.

- eApps—95% complete. Outstanding are items associated with integration testing that we delayed/not operating in our integrated test environment.

- Security—90% complete. Outstanding items are 4 reports that have been on hold pending resolution to reporting problems in QA. Testing planned for next week is in development.

System testing and UAT have been combined for HRM, HRM Data Prep, Hyperion, and Stellent. Status for these will be reported under user acceptance testing.

(continues)

Figure 3.58 *(continued)*

Third-party interface testing is in process. The team resolved outstanding issues with the integrated testing environment.

User Acceptance Testing—Continued formal UAT sessions. UAT testing is expected to be complete on August 3.

- HR/Benefits—50% complete—sessions scheduled through 8/3
- Payroll—85% complete—sessions scheduled through 7/27; interface testing will run into next week
- Authoria—80% complete—sessions scheduled through 7/30
- 401(k)—60% complete—sessions scheduled through 8/3
- Compensation—90% complete—sessions scheduled through 7/27
- HRM—90% complete—sessions scheduled through 8/3. Outstanding issue with home phone
- HRM Data Prep—50% complete—sessions scheduled through 8/3
- eApps—0% complete—session scheduled for 7/30
- Security—90% complete; retest sessions scheduled for early next week
- eRecruit—50% complete; sessions scheduled through 7/31
- Hyperion/EDW—70% complete; sessions scheduled through 7/30
- Stellent—0% complete; sessions scheduled though 8/3
- Pension—UAT is complete
- ESPP—UAT is complete
- Simple Steps—UAT is complete
- PDR—UAT is complete
- LMS—UAT is complete
- Total Comp—UAT is complete

Load Testing—Began load testing for eRecruit—expected completion is 7/31. Load testing for the eApps will follow with completion expected on 8/10.

Parallel Testing—Completed parallel #3 with excellent results. 34 of 36 sites have signed off as of 8 a.m. Friday.

Development: Development team is on track with issues and defects. Retrofitting for public and private queries continues. Continued refinement of implementation plan. Planned dress rehearsal—Test Move 7. Completed some pre-implementation tasks in PROD—copied software, set up data files, and added temporary space for backups.

eRecruit: Continued QA testing and UAT testing. Received signoff from subsidiaries. Additional sessions are scheduled for next week.

Training, documentation, and communication tasks are on schedule.

Deliverables completed last week:

Task	Complete Date	Comments
Milestone: Completed eRecruit system testing	7/23	No problems.
Milestone: PDR UAT complete	7/23	Report format issues were resolved.
Milestone: Simple Steps UAT complete	7/23	No problems.
Milestone: Total Compensation UAT complete	7/26	Data sync issue was resolved.

Deliverables scheduled for completion in next 2 weeks:

Task	Due Date	Comments
Milestone: eRecruit Query Development Complete	8/9	Mark Lester is out for medical leave.
Milestone: eRecruit Technical Process Flow Complete	8/13	
Milestone: Coordination of Division Portal links and URL changes for eRecruit complete	8/20	Outside focus group members are needed.

(continues)

Figure 3.58 *(continued)*

Resource Changes: None.

Future Meetings:

- Daily UAT testing sessions

- Daily Parallel testing sessions and morning meetings

- Full Team Status Meeting 7/31 ** Moved to Tuesday for this week only **

- Weekly Training, Documentation, and Communications Team Meeting 7/30

- Weekly Implementation Meeting 8/1

- Weekly IT Leads Team Meeting 8/1

- Weekly HR/Benefits Analyst Team Meeting 8/1

- Weekly QA Team Meeting 8/2

- Weekly Payroll Analyst Team Meeting 8/2

- Weekly Developers Team Meeting 8/2

PROPOSALS

Proposals usually consist of a bid and a description of a project, and they are sent to a customer. Many proposals are sent after a prospective customer makes a request for proposal (RFP).

There are several different types of proposals:

- Internal proposals written for someone within the same business

- External proposals written to another business or government agency

- Solicited proposals that are written and sent in response to and in accordance with the guidelines described in an RFP

- Unsolicited proposals that are sent to convince a potential customer to do business with you

Most proposals include the following sections (Figure 3.59):

- Cover letter—to be sent with a proposal

- Introduction—introducing the proposal, referring to previous contacts with the customer, and providing an overview of the contents of the proposal

- Background—information about the need for the project

- Benefits—describing how the proposed solution will solve the problems discussed in the background section

- Project description—describing what is involved in the project, including specifications for the end product

- Method—discussing how the project will be completed

- Schedule—detailing the project timeline

- Qualifications—discussing the organization's qualifications for completing the project

- Budget—listing the costs

- Conclusion—final words about why the submitter of the proposal should be awarded the project

When preparing a proposal, consider the following:

- Make sure you address everything asked for, if responding to an RFP.

- Identify all the tasks that are necessary to complete the project.

- Break out the budget into individual line items and include hourly rates if applicable.

(text continues on page 551)

Figure 3.59 Proposal for Video Production Services

LPS TRAINING
Video Production Proposal

Submitted to:

Andy Norvell

SAR Office Manager

BSP Energy Products Company

By:

Videologies

Acworth, Georga

(Courtesy of Videologies, Inc.)

(continues)

Figure 3.59 *(continued)*

INTRODUCTION

This proposal is for the production of an LPS training video for BSP Energy's SAR Department.

BSP Energy's request includes the following requirements:

- Limit video length to approximately 35 minutes
- Deliver the finished video by November 30, 2012
- Shoot at two sites in either New Jersey or Los Angeles basin area
- Create 10 minutes of material on drilling, monitor well installation, and sampling tasks
- Create 10 minutes of material on trenching, and SVE installation LPOs
- Create 6 minutes of material for supervisor feedback sessions
- Create 9 minutes of material featuring a host on camera for introductions and other commentary

After careful examination of these requirements, Videologies proposes the following:

- Research and scriptwriting with access to subject matter experts in the Atlanta area or via telephone or email
- Pre-production location visit by our producer
- Five days of production at two different locations in either New Jersey or Los Angeles
- One day of production in the Atlanta area for shooting an on-camera host
- Video still graphics to illustrate concepts
- Text and graphics
- Optional CD-ROM version
- Optional Streaming Video version for Web distribution

SPECIFICATIONS

The LPS Training video produced for BSP Energy will include the following specifications:

- 35-minute video script

- Producer services to coordinate all aspects of the production

- Video production using XDCAM HD format

- Video production crew including a director, camera operator, and lighting assistants as appropriate

- Use of a professional actor or actress for on-camera and voice-over narration

- One pre-production trip to either New Jersey or Los Angeles to scout locations and coordinate activities

- One five-day trip to either New Jersey or Los Angeles for shooting segments A, B, and C as outlined in the LPS Training Video Work Scope provided by Andy Nowell of BSP Energy

- Nonlinear post production to edit a master tape for duplication

- Video graphics for illustrating concepts

- Titles and transitional effects

- Background music

- Two approval copies

- One Blu-Ray DVD master for duplication

BSP Energy will provide the following logistical and review requirements:

- Script review and approval

- Locations

- All necessary props

- Personnel for demonstrations and activities described in the script

- Subject matter experts

- Company logos

(continues)

Figure 3.59 *(continued)*

TREATMENT

Based on our June 18, 2012 meeting, we propose a video treatment that utilizes an on-camera host to guide us through the video.

The host will be shot on location in the Atlanta area and will be used to introduce the content on camera and then narrate sequences shot on location.

Since the purpose of the video is to give viewers practice in observing LPO situations, we will divide the video into short two- to three-minute segments. Students will choose segments from a menu. Each segment will have a title screen describing its content. The on-camera host will introduce each segment and explain what viewers are about to see. Instructions will be given for viewers to practice their LPO observations as they watch scenes of various work practices. The narrator will describe the scene but will allow viewers to make and record their own observations. Following this sequence, we will replay the same sequence again, this time with the narrator pointing out all the possible observations. This will allow the viewers to check their answers.

Because students will watch these sequences twice, once with overview narration, and once again with the narrator describing the LPO observations, the finished video will be longer than 35 minutes. However, for purposes of budgeting, we are planning on no more than 35 minutes of original material. Repeating material in the same video will not increase the budget.

It is understood that only a sampling of possible LPO observations that may occur in an activity such as drilling will be featured in the video. We will work with BSP Energy's subject matter experts to construct scenes that feature as many work practice observations (both good and bad) as possible.

The training will be designed so that it can be self-paced. As part of our deliverables to BSP Energy, we will produce a short student guide (in Adobe Acrobat PDF format) that provides instructions for each video segment activity. We assume that BSP Energy will provide copies of LPO forms, so students can fill out the forms while watching the video.

The following LPO target areas will be featured in the video:

- Drilling, monitor well installation, and sampling tasks
- Trenching and SVE installation LPOs
- Supervisor feedback sessions

PRODUCTION

The production process will consist of the following stages:

- Content analysis and design
- Scriptwriting
- Video production
- Graphics production
- Post production
- Programming
- Study guide production
- Revisions
- Final mastering

Content Analysis and Design

Videologies will meet with subject matter experts and review previously produced materials, such as LPO forms and LPS handbooks. We will work together to plan our work practice scenarios to feature specific LPO opportunities for students. After completing content analysis, Videologies will create a design document that summarizes our plans for the video.

Scriptwriting

After a design is approved by BSP Energy, the scriptwriter will draft a script in a two-column format describing visuals and narration or suggested on-camera audio. This script will be submitted to BSP Energy for review. After this review, any revisions required will be made and a final script will be submitted for approval.

Video Production

After the script is approved, video production will begin. Video production will consist of the following:

- Five days of production on location at two sites in either New Jersey or Los Angeles
- One day of production in Atlanta to shoot the on-camera host
- Narration recording

(continues)

Figure 3.59 *(continued)*

Graphics Production

Video graphics will be created to illustrate concepts where appropriate. Title screens will also be created and added where appropriate.

Post Production

During post production, we will edit the raw footage, mix the audio, add music, insert graphics, and incorporate transitional effects where appropriate.

Study Guide Production

A short 10–20 page study guide will be created to facilitate the learning experience for self-paced training.

Final Mastering

After final approval of the video, a Blu-Ray DVD master will be delivered for duplication purposes.

OPTIONS

BSP Energy has requested that Videologies provide quotes on future upgrades of the video to CD-ROM and possible Web site delivery. In addition, we can provide VHS duplications upon request.

CD-ROM

The content created for the LPS Training video and study guide can be upgraded for delivery via CD-ROM. Depending on the design and content requirements, we can create a wide variety of CD-ROM–based programs ranging from a simple AVI video player to a more complex system incorporating additional audio instruction, graphics, simulations, and test questions.

The finished video segments can be converted to a Windows AVI video format at a screen size of 320 × 240 and played on a IBM PC compatible equipped with a CD-ROM drive, soundcard and speakers or headphones. We would recommend a minimum configuration of Pentium II 350 with an 8X CD-ROM drive.

As the least expensive option, we can create a CD that includes an autorun feature so installation is not necessary. Upon inserting the CD, the user will see a 640 × 480 menu screen that gives students access to a downloadable study guide, downloadable LPO forms, and menu choices for viewing the various video sequences (or lessons).

A more expensive alternative can include quiz and test questions, graphic and text screens, audio, and simulations for a more substantial learning experience. The course would require the use of a Web browser such as Internet Explorer to view content pages, access LPO forms, and view video and audio sequences. Test questions will provide feedback and remediation to ensure and document a student's comprehension.

Web Delivery

Videologies can provide streaming media versions of the finished video sequences in either Windows Media or Real Media formats compressed for playback at 300K speeds. Anything less than 300K compression produces quality that is too reduced for effective training. At least a 300K connection is required to view the files. This speed of connection is usually available with DSL, Cable Modem, or office LAN connections.

BSP Energy will need to provide a streaming media server (by purchasing a streaming media license from either Real Networks or Microsoft) in order to "stream" the videos. Without this server, the users must download each video sequence before playing it.

Videologies can provide services ranging from just supplying the media files to BSP Energy for posting on their own Web site, to creating a complete Web-based course similar to the CD-ROM version, complete with menus, graphics, and testing.

DELIVERABLES

This proposal calls for the following deliverables from Videologies:

- Design document
- Script
- One 10–20–page study guide in PDF format
- Two approval DVD copies
- One Blu-Ray DVD master

Optional deliverables include:

- CD-ROM version
- Windows Media or Real Media Web files
- DVD duplications

Figure 3.59 *(continued)*

LOGISTICS AND SCHEDULE

Videologies proposes the following schedule for the video:

Begin project	August 8, 2012
Content research	August 8–17, 2012
Content design delivered	August 21, 2012
Design approval from BSP Energy	August 28, 2012
Scriptwriting and revisions	August 28–September 18, 2012
Script approval from BSP Energy	September 25, 2012
Location shoot in either New Jersey or Los Angeles	October 1–5, 2012
Host shoot in Atlanta	October 8, 2012
Study guide production	October 8–26, 2012
Graphics production	October 8–26, 2012
Post production	November 5–19, 2012
Approval copy review	November 20, 2012
Revisions	November 26–28, 2012
Final master delivered	November 30, 2012

Any delay by BSP Energy in reviewing scripts, providing personnel, or locations, may delay delivery of the final video.

BUDGET

The services provided by Videologies will require the following development budget:

Production Category	Amount
Producer Services	$ 2,800
Design, Analysis, and Research	2,800
Scriptwriting	2,800
Production Equipment	4,200
Production Crew	16,000
Talent	1,500
Other Misc. Production Costs (crew meals, videotape)	1,350
Graphics	1,250
Post Production (editing, music, and master duplication)	8,270
Travel Costs (hotel, car, air, per diem)	5,880
10% Cost Contingency for overtime and Videologies overages	4,685
Total	$51,535

(continues)

Figure 3.59 *(continued)*

RATES AND MANPOWER

Rates are based on the following:

- Writing, producing, directing services, and production crew at $50 per hour or $500 per day per person.

- Video production equipment rentals at $700 per day, includes camera, tripod, lights, monitors, waveform, and grip equipment.

- Post production services at $125 per hour.

- Graphic services at $50 per hour.

- Computer programming services at $75 per hour.

- AVI and streaming media conversation at $40 per finished minute.

- Professional union actor at $1,500 per day.

Estimated manpower requirements include:

- Writer—14 days

- Producer—7 days

- Director—6 days plus 2 travel days

- Camera operator—6 days plus 2 travel days

- Lighting specialist—6 days plus 2 travel days

- Production assistant—6 days plus 2 travel days

- Editor—60 hours

- Graphic artist—25 hours

- Professional union actor—1 day

Estimated equipment rental days include:

- Camera package—6 days

- Nonlinear editor—60 hours

QUESTIONNAIRES AND SURVEYS

Questionnaires and surveys are used to gather data about customers and employees for use in decision making, marketing, and the development of new products and services. (Figure 3.60.)

Questionnaires can be distributed on paper or online. Online surveys are especially helpful because they can be emailed as links and the results can be automatically tabulated into a database or spreadsheet.

Using a questionnaire is a multistage process involving the design and development of the questions, determining the survey group, conducting the survey, and then interpreting the results.

Questionnaires are usually designed to gather qualitative or quantitative data.

- Qualitative surveys ask about opinions and ask respondents to rate the quality of a product or service.

- Quantitative surveys measure how many people do a particular thing, such as use a product or watch a particular television channel.

Questionnaires are often used instead of personal interviews because:

- They can be inexpensive to create and use.

- The privacy of the participants can be protected.

- When used with other data, such as sales trends, they can be useful as a confirmation tool.

Consider the following steps when creating a questionnaire:

- The first step in creating a questionnaire is to define the objectives.
  - The questions should focus on obtaining specific information.
    - To determine qualitative data about a product or service, you must break down the qualities into various aspects that can be isolated and measured.
  - The question order should have a logical flow.

- The second step in creating a questionnaire is to write the questions.
  - Write an introduction to the questionnaire that explains its purpose.

- Provide instructions on how to answer the questions.
  - Explain the rating scale if one is used.
- Include demographic questions to gather information about the respondents.
  - This information is helpful later when you are analyzing the results and comparing responses among different groups of people.
  - Common demographic questions, including age, sex, level of education, annual earnings, and so forth.
  - Demographic questions are normally asked at the beginning of the questionnaire.
- There are two general types of survey questions: multiple-choice or fill-in-the-blank.
  - Fill-in-the-blank questions are more time-consuming during the data analysis phase.
  - Multiple choice questions make it easier to tabulate the responses and calculate percentages.
  - Multiple-choice questions also make it easier to track opinions over time to see how the same questionnaire is answered by similar groups of people over a specific period.
- For multiple-choice questions involving a rating scale, it is best to have an even number of rating choices.
  - Having an odd number of choices leaves respondents with a middle neutral choice, which is often used by respondents who are bored.
  - Having an even number of choices eliminates the possibility of neutral answers.
- Multiple-choice questions should have clear, distinct answer choices.
  - "Very often," "Often," and "Sometimes" answer choices can be interpreted differently by different respondents.
  - "Every day," "2 to 5 times a week," and "Once a month" answer choices are easier to interpret.

- Avoid leading questions that imply a biased answer.

Example: A rating scale with choices like: "Incredible," "Superb," "Excellent," "Great," "Good"

Incorrect: Is this the best software you've ever used?

- Avoid adjectives and adverbs in your questions; they imply a biased answer.

- Avoid embarrassing questions that deal with personal or private matters.

- Avoid hypothetical questions; they are based on fantasy rather than fact.

- Avoid using *not* in your questions; this word can lead to double negatives and already implies a negatively biased answer.

After you've written the questions for the survey, proofread and test the survey on a small sampling of respondents.

- Review the questionnaire with the test audience and work together to resolve any problems.

- Revise the survey after the pilot test.

- Put a date on the questionnaire, so that you can keep track of versions.

Figure 3.60 Survey

United States Census 2010

This is the official form for all the people at this address.
It is quick and easy, and your answers are protected by law.

U.S. DEPARTMENT OF COMMERCE
Economics and Statistics Administration
U.S. CENSUS BUREAU

Use a blue or black pen.

Start here

The Census must count every person living in the United States on April 1, 2010.

Before you answer Question 1, count the people living in this house, apartment, or mobile home using our guidelines.

- Count all people, including babies, who live and sleep here most of the time.

The Census Bureau also conducts counts in institutions and other places, so:

- Do not count anyone living away either at college or in the Armed Forces.
- Do not count anyone in a nursing home, jail, prison, detention facility, etc., on April 1, 2010.
- Leave these people off your form, even if they will return to live here after they leave college, the nursing home, the military, jail, etc. Otherwise, they may be counted twice.

The Census must also include people without a permanent place to stay, so:

- If someone who has no permanent place to stay is staying here on April 1, 2010, count that person. Otherwise, he or she may be missed in the census.

1. **How many people were living or staying in this house, apartment, or mobile home on April 1, 2010?**
   Number of people = ☐

2. **Were there any additional people staying here April 1, 2010 that you did not include in Question 1?** *Mark [X] all that apply.*
   - ☐ Children, such as newborn babies or foster children
   - ☐ Relatives, such as adult children, cousins, or in-laws
   - ☐ Nonrelatives, such as roommates or live-in baby sitters
   - ☐ People staying here temporarily
   - ☐ No additional people

3. **Is this house, apartment, or mobile home —** *Mark [X] ONE box.*
   - ☐ Owned by you or someone in this household with a mortgage or loan? *Include home equity loans.*
   - ☐ Owned by you or someone in this household free and clear (without a mortgage or loan)?
   - ☐ Rented?
   - ☐ Occupied without payment of rent?

4. **What is your telephone number?** *We may call if we don't understand an answer.*
   Area Code + Number
   ☐ - ☐ - ☐

OMB No. 0607-0919-C: Approval Expires 12/31/2011.

Form **D-61** (1-15-2009)

5. **Please provide information for each person living here. Start with a person living here who owns or rents this house, apartment, or mobile home. If the owner or renter lives somewhere else, start with any adult living here. This will be Person 1.**
   What is Person 1's name? *Print name below.*
   Last Name ☐
   First Name ☐ MI ☐

6. **What is Person 1's sex?** *Mark [X] ONE box.*
   ☐ Male ☐ Female

7. **What is Person 1's age and what is Person 1's date of birth?**
   Please report babies as age 0 when the child is less than 1 year old.
   Print numbers in boxes.
   Age on April 1, 2010 ☐ Month ☐ Day ☐ Year of birth ☐

→ **NOTE: Please answer BOTH Question 8 about Hispanic origin and Question 9 about race. For this census, Hispanic origins are not races.**

8. **Is Person 1 of Hispanic, Latino, or Spanish origin?**
   - ☐ No, not of Hispanic, Latino, or Spanish origin
   - ☐ Yes, Mexican, Mexican Am., Chicano
   - ☐ Yes, Puerto Rican
   - ☐ Yes, Cuban
   - ☐ Yes, another Hispanic, Latino, or Spanish origin — *Print origin, for example, Argentinean, Colombian, Dominican, Nicaraguan, Salvadoran, Spaniard, and so on.*

9. **What is Person 1's race?** *Mark [X] one or more boxes.*
   - ☐ White
   - ☐ Black, African Am., or Negro
   - ☐ American Indian or Alaska Native — *Print name of enrolled or principal tribe.*
   - ☐ Asian Indian ☐ Japanese ☐ Native Hawaiian
   - ☐ Chinese ☐ Korean ☐ Guamanian or Chamorro
   - ☐ Filipino ☐ Vietnamese ☐ Samoan
   - ☐ Other Asian — *Print race, for example, Hmong, Laotian, Thai, Pakistani, Cambodian, and so on.* ☐ Other Pacific Islander — *Print race, for example, Fijian, Tongan, and so on.*
   - ☐ Some other race — *Print race.*

10. **Does Person 1 sometimes live or stay somewhere else?**
    ☐ No ☐ Yes — *Mark [X] all that apply.*
    - ☐ In college housing ☐ For child custody
    - ☐ In the military ☐ In jail or prison
    - ☐ At a seasonal or second residence ☐ In a nursing home
    - ☐ For another reason

→ **If more people were counted in Question 1, continue with Person 2.**

USCENSUSBUREAU

(Courtesy of the U.S. Department of Commerce)

REFERENCE LETTERS

A **reference letter** states the qualifications for a person seeking employment. It offers an endorsement of the person's job performance, skills, and character. A reference letter may be accepted in lieu of contacting references on the phone.

A reference letter should include (Figure 3.61):

■ How and for how long you know the person

■ Your qualifications for writing the reference letter

■ A list of the person's qualities and skills

■ Key points about the person that the reader should note

■ Examples that back up your opinions about the person

■ Your contact information

Reference letters are typically written to:

■ Recommend someone for a job.

■ Recommend someone who has applied to school.

■ Endorse a political candidate.

■ Provide a credit reference.

■ Recommend a service or product.

■ Recommend someone for club membership.

Figure 3.61 Reference Letter

John Davidson
Videologies, Inc.
1313 Old Alabama Highway
Atlanta, GA 30121

Hello,

This is a letter of recommendation for Peter Carson.

Peter has worked with me for the past year in the role of training technology manager at Videologies, Inc., a multimedia and training development business.

At Videologies, Peter worked on designing a training course for our Learning Management System. He designed and created a webinar presentation and a student exercise workbook.

Peter also worked on three multiday instructor-led courses on the subject of accounting practices. Peter did analysis, created the design, coordinated with the customer, and created workbooks and PowerPoint presentations.

I highly recommend Peter Carson for instructional design and course development projects.

Sincerely,

John Davidson

John Davidson
Vice President

REFUSAL LETTER

A **refusal letter** is written to deny a request, decline an invitation, or reply negatively to a suggestion. When writing a refusal letter, consider the following tips (Figure 3.62):

- Be as diplomatic as possible to avoid hurt feelings.

- Open the letter with a sincere statement that explains that you are refusing the request.

- Explain your reasons for the refusal, and include any evidence to back up your decision.

- Offer alternatives to the readers that might have a better chance of being accepted.

- Be courteous and wish the reader success elsewhere.

Refusal letters are typically written to:

- Decline an invitation or appointment.

- Decline a claim request from a customer.

- Turn down a request for a donation.

- Decline a job offer, promotion, or transfer.

- Reject an application for employment.

- Decline to join an organization.

- Terminate a business relationship.

- Decline a request to write a letter of recommendation.

- Turn down a suggestion.

- Decline a request for credit.

- Decline a gift.

- Decline orders or requests for information.

Figure 3.62 Refusal Letter

February 21, 2012

Buffalo Graphics
3133 Highway 9
Roswell, GA 32311

Dylan Wilson
Atlanta Community College
1311 West Northfield Drive
Decatur, GA 30133

Dear Mr. Wilson:

Thank you for invitation to be a guest lecturer in your communications class at Atlanta Community College. I'm sorry, but I'll have to decline the invitation.

I recently became the president of the Atlanta Communications Association, and these added responsibilities have already required more time than I have available. I would suggest that you contact Al Gordon, the ex-president of ACA. He may be available and with his experience, he should make an excellent guest lecturer.

I am honored to have been invited by you. You are well respected within the communications industry, and I wish you all the best with your class.

Sincerely,

Michael Woodson

Michael Woodson
President

REPORTS

There are four common **report** formats:

- Memorandum report

- Letter report

- Short report

- Formal report

Memorandum Report

The **memorandum report** is a routine and informal report that might be prepared on a weekly basis to report the status of projects to upper management. This type of report:

- Is objective and impersonal in tone.

- May contain brief introductory comments.

- Contains headings and subheadings, used for quick reference and to highlight certain aspects of the report.

- Is usually single-spaced and printed on plain paper. (However, in some businesses this report may be sent as an email or email attachment.)

Letter Report

The **letter report** is normally a one-page letter that is printed on company letterhead. If the reports contain second sheets, the continuation pages are also printed on letterhead. The letter report:

- Is typically sent outside the company to consultants, clients, or the board of directors.

- Should have headings and subheadings to organize its content.

Short Report

The **short report** has a title page, a preliminary summary with conclusions and recommendations, authorization information, a statement of the problem, findings, conclusions, and recommendations. The short report:

- May contain tables and graphs and can be either single- or double-spaced.

- Contains headings and subheadings to organize the content and to emphasize certain aspects.

- Has a title page with:

  - The report title (long titles are divided and centered)

  - The name, title, and address of the person or company to whom the report is being submitted

  - The preparer's name, title, and address

Formal Report

Included in the **formal report** are the:

- Cover
- Title page
- Flyleaf
- Title fly
- Letter of authorization
- Letter of transmittal
- Foreword and/or prefaces
- Acknowledgments
- Table of contents
- List of tables
- List of figures
- Synopsis
- Body
- Endnotes or footnotes
- Appendix
- Glossary
- Bibliography
- Index

When formatting your report, consider the following guidelines:

- The margin settings for a formal report are:

  - First page's top margin—2 inches.

  - Subsequent pages' top margin—1 inch.

  - Bottom margins on all pages—1 inch.

  - The left and right margins on all pages—1 inch.

- For bound reports, the left margin should be 1½ inches to allow extra room for the binding.

- The body of the report can be single- or double-spaced.

- Setoff quotations should be single-spaced, as are footnotes.

- Paragraph indentions should be five spaces.

- Long quotations should be indented five spaces from the left margin.

- Numbered and bullet lists should also be indented five spaces.

- Footnotes should match paragraph margins.

- Primary headings should be centered and bold, with additional space above and below.

- A 20- to 24-point sans serif font, such as Helvetica, should be used.

- Secondary headings should be aligned left justified, bold, with a 16- to 18-point sans serif font.

- Third-level headings should also be aligned left and bold, with 12- to 14-point sans serif font.

- There should be no page number on the title page, although a page number should be assigned for numbering purposes.
  - The front matter should use small Roman numerals (i, ii, iii, etc.) for numbering.
  - The body of the report should use Arabic numerals, starting with 1.
  - Page numbers should be either centered or in the right margin, either ½ to 1 inch from the top or ½ inch from the bottom.

Headings and subheadings should be parallel in structure.

Example of nonparallel structure:
1. Reading the Manual
2. The Instructions
3. How to Install the Software

Example of parallel structure:
1. Reading the Manual
2. Following the Instructions
3. Installing the Software

You should use a numbering system for headings. You can use numbers or a combination of numbers and letters.

Figure 3.63 shows two alternative heading numbering systems.

Figure 3.63 Heading Numbering Systems

System 1
1. Main Heading
    1.1 Subheading
    1.2 Subheading
        1.2.1 Third-level heading
        1.2.2 Third-level heading
System 2
I. Main Heading
    a. Subheading
    b. Subheading
        1. Third-level heading
        2. Third-level leading

The **cover** (Figure 3.64) should have the title and author's name, with the title printed in all capital letters.

The cover may be printed on card stock paper.

The **title page** should include:

- The title of the report in all capitals and subtitle if there is one

- The recipient's name, corporate title, department, company name, and address

- The preparer's name, corporate title, department, company name, and address

- The date the report is submitted

The **flyleaf** is a blank page that is inserted after the cover. It is also sometimes added to the end of the report just before the back cover.

The **title fly** is a single page with just the report title in all capitals, centered on the upper third of the page.

The **letter of authorization** should be printed on letterhead and explain who authorized the report and any specific details regarding the authorization.

The **letter of transmittal** (Figure 3.65) is a cover letter for the report. It explains the purpose of the report, the scope, limitations, reference materials, special comments, and acknowledgments.

The letter of transmittal may take the place of a **foreword** or **preface**.

The **acknowledgements** page should list individuals, companies, or institutions that assisted in creating the report.

The **table of contents** (Figure 3.66) should include headings, subheadings, and third-level headings with page numbers.

- You can use an outline style with a heading numbering system.

- If you are using a word processor, you can automatically generate a table of contents based on the heading styles.

If tables are used in the report, you should include a **list of tables** in the front matter. The list should include:

- Table numbers

- Page numbers

- The descriptions used as table titles in the body of the report

If illustrations are used in the report, you should include a **list of figures** (Figure 3.67) in the front matter. The list should include:

- Figure numbers

- Page numbers

- The captions used with the figures in the body of the report

The **body** of the report (Figure 3.68) should include:

- An introduction to the report.

- Introductions to the major sections—headings, subheadings, and third-level headings.

- A summary at the end of major sections.

■ Normal paragraph breaks, bullet lists, numbered lists, illustrations, and tables.

■ Footnotes or endnotes to present content that is not part of the main flow of the body.

■ Footnotes are short notes set at the bottom of the page.

■ Endnotes are placed at the end of the report.

Usually, footnotes or endnotes are numbered with a small, raised number ([1], [2], etc.) inserted at the end of the text, with the correspondingly numbered note at the bottom of the page or at the end of the report.

Footnotes and endnotes should include:

■ The author or author's names

■ The title of the source

■ The publisher

■ The date

■ A page reference

Example: [1]Kevin Wilson and Jennifer Wauson, *The AMA Handbook of Business Writing* (New York, AMACOM Books, 2010), page 201.

Sometimes a footnote is used for just the first reference to a source. Then, in subsequent references, just the author names and the page number are listed.

Example: Wilson and Wauson, 205.

Other parenthetical references are inserted in the text of the document inside parentheses.

If there are supplementary reference materials or sources of research—perhaps information that might be of interest to only some readers—you can include them at the end of the report in an **appendix**.

The **glossary** should include technical terms with definitions along with any abbreviations. In the body of the report, the abbreviations should be spelled out the first time they are used.

The **bibliography** lists:

■ All the sources of information used to compile the report

■ Research that was not cited as a footnote but used to create the report

The bibliography listings are ordered alphabetically by the authors' last names.

■ If there is no main author, then the book title is used.

■ The author's surname comes first.

■ Additional authors are listed first name, last name.

Example: Wilson, Kevin, and Jennifer Wauson. *The AMA Handbook of Business Writing* (New York, AMACOM Books, 2010).

An **index** is an option for many reports, and should be an alphabetical listing.

■ The first word of each entry has an initial capital letter, and the rest of the words are in lower case.

■ Subentries in the index are like subheadings and are indented one or two spaces.

■ Cross-references direct the reader to another location in the index.

(text continues on page 571)

Figure 3.64 Report Cover

ONLINE EMPLOYEE BENEFIT ELECTIONS

By:
Catherine Muncie
Muncie Consulting

Figure 3.65 Report Transmittal Letter

Muncie Consulting
1231 Peachtree Street
Atlanta, GA 30102

May 12, 2012

Mary Ann Cleveland
Vice President
Alstead Communications
3324 Interstate 75 Parkway
Atlanta, GA 30131

Dear Ms. Cleveland:

In accordance to our agreement for conducting research on alternatives
to paper-based benefit elections, I am pleased to submit this report
with my findings titled "Online Employee Benefit Elections."

The purpose of this report is provide information to the Alstead
Communications Executive Board for the purpose of determining whether
online employee self-service is a possibility for annual benefit elections.
The report describes the online process and compares it to the current
paper-based benefit election process. In addition, the report details
various policies and controls that would need to be implemented in order
to make online elections secure in order to protect sensitive personal
information.

I hope you will find this report to be informative.

Respectfully yours,

Catherine Muncie

Catherine Muncie
Muncie Consulting

Encl: Report on Online Employee Benefit Elections

Figure 3.66 Report Table of Contents

TABLE OF CONTENTS

ii

Figure 3.67 Report List of figures

LIST OF FIGURES

Figure 3.68 Report Body

Report on
ONLINE EMPLOYEE BENEFIT ELECTIONS

I. Introduction

During the annual benefits enrollment period, benefits-eligible employees may make changes to their benefits or enroll in flexible spending accounts for the upcoming plan year.

New benefit elections are effective January 1–December 31 of the following year. Once Open Enrollment has concluded, employees may change their benefits during the plan year only if they experience a qualified status change (marriage, divorce, birth/adoption of a child, or death of a dependent).

The human resources department must complete a number of tasks during August and September in order to ensure the online forms are correct. These tasks include the following:

- Determining wages for commissioned employees
- Verifying employment status
- Entering salary increases into the employee database
- Updating employee addresses

1

REQUEST LETTERS

A **request letter** is written to seek information, permission, or an explanation. This type of letter should (Figure 3.69):

■ Be courteous, tactful, brief, confident, and persuasive.

■ Be straightforward and include as much detail as possible about the request.

■ Not be overbearing or manipulative in trying to obtain the request.

　　■ Avoid apologizing for the request.

　　■ Make sure your request is reasonable.

■ Make the reader feel complimented to be asked for a favor.

■ Express your willingness to reciprocate.

■ Invite the person to contact you with any questions or concerns.

Request letters are typically written to:

■ Request a modification to an agreement.

■ Request a document or publication.

■ Seek a raise or promotion.

■ Request a response to a survey.

■ Ask for assistance.

■ Request a discount.

■ Ask for the correction of an error.

■ Ask for a favor.

■ Request a refund.

■ Extend an invitation.

■ Ask for more information.

■ Request an estimate or bid.

Figure 3.69 Request Letter

May 8, 2012

Roswell News Weekly
3233 Alpharetta Highway
Roswell, GA 32311

Captain Larry Muncie
United States Air Force
Dobbins Air Force Base
Atlanta, GA 30223

Dear Captain Muncie:

This is a request under the Freedom of Information Act (5 U.S.C § 552).
I request that the following documents be provided to me:

1.   Photographs of the B-29 airplane in the Dobbins Museum

2.   Mission information for the B-29 airplane on display

3.   Manufacturing information including when it was completed and
     what factory built the aircraft

To help you determine my status for the purpose of assessing fees,
you should know that I am a representative of the news media affiliated
with the *Roswell Weekly* newspaper, and this request is made as part
of news gathering, not for commercial use.

I am willing to pay the appropriate fees for this request up to a maximum
of $25. If you estimate that the fees will exceed this limit, please
contact me.

I have also included my telephone number and email address at which
I can be contacted if necessary to discuss any aspect of my request.

Sincerely,

Shelia Jefferson
Shelia Jefferson
Staff Reporter
(770) 555-1234
SJefferson@rosweekly.com

RESEARCH REPORT

Research reports summarize experimental findings and use additional reference sources to support the findings (Figure 3.70).

Research reports are commonly written in one of two ways:

- An argumentative research report makes a statement about a particular subject and then presents research to support the thesis.

- An analytical research report asks a question and then presents research describing various answers to the question.

A typical research report includes the following sections:

- Title page—a short 15-word-or-less description of the report

- Abstract—a short overview of the report that includes:
  - A statement of the problem
  - The study group
  - Dependent and independent variables
  - Research strategy
  - Major findings
  - Conclusions

- Introduction—a page that presents the investigated problem, explains the importance of the study, and supplies an overview of the research strategy

- Method—describing the sample, materials, and procedures used for the research (including all surveys, tests, questionnaires, interview forms, and laboratory equipment used in the research)

- Results—a summary of the findings from the research

- Discussion—an interpretation of the findings and the implications

- References—a list of sources used in the research

Figure 3.70 Analytical Research Report

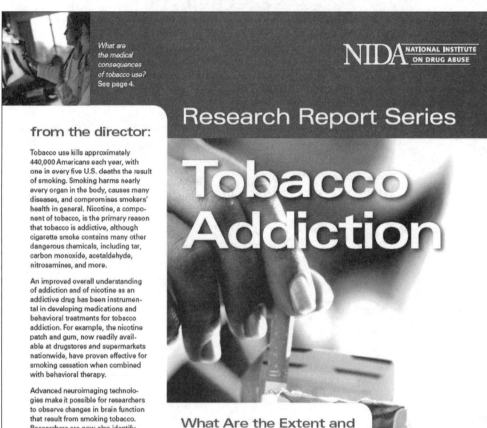

What are the medical consequences of tobacco use? See page 4.

NIDA NATIONAL INSTITUTE ON DRUG ABUSE

Research Report Series

Tobacco Addiction

from the director:

Tobacco use kills approximately 440,000 Americans each year, with one in every five U.S. deaths the result of smoking. Smoking harms nearly every organ in the body, causes many diseases, and compromises smokers' health in general. Nicotine, a component of tobacco, is the primary reason that tobacco is addictive, although cigarette smoke contains many other dangerous chemicals, including tar, carbon monoxide, acetaldehyde, nitrosamines, and more.

An improved overall understanding of addiction and of nicotine as an addictive drug has been instrumental in developing medications and behavioral treatments for tobacco addiction. For example, the nicotine patch and gum, now readily available at drugstores and supermarkets nationwide, have proven effective for smoking cessation when combined with behavioral therapy.

Advanced neuroimaging technologies make it possible for researchers to observe changes in brain function that result from smoking tobacco. Researchers are now also identifying genes that predispose people to tobacco addiction and predict their response to smoking cessation treatments. These findings—and many other recent research accomplishments—present unique opportunities to discover, develop, and disseminate new treatments for tobacco addiction, as well as scientifically based prevention programs to help curtail the public health burden that tobacco use represents.

We hope this *Research Report* will help readers understand the harmful effects of tobacco use and identify best practices for the prevention and treatment of tobacco addiction.

Nora D. Volkow, M.D.
Director
National Institute on Drug Abuse

What Are the Extent and Impact of Tobacco Use?

According to the 2007 National Survey on Drug Use and Health, an estimated 70.9 million Americans aged 12 or older reported current use of tobacco—60.1 million (24.2 percent of the population) were current cigarette smokers, 13.3 million (5.4 percent) smoked cigars, 8.1 million (3.2 percent) used smokeless tobacco, and 2 million (0.8 percent) smoked pipes, confirming that tobacco is one of the most widely abused substances in the United States. Although the numbers of people who smoke are still unacceptably high, according

continued inside

U.S. Department of Health and Human Services | National Institutes of Health

(Courtesy of the National Institutes of Health)

Research Report Series

Tobacco Addiction

to the Centers for Disease Control and Prevention there has been a decline of almost 50 percent since 1965.

NIDA's 2008 Monitoring the Future survey of 8th-, 10th-, and 12th-graders, which is used to track drug use patterns and attitudes, has also shown a striking decrease in smoking trends among the Nation's youth. The latest results indicate that about 7 percent of 8th-graders, 12 percent of 10th-graders, and 20 percent of 12th-graders had used cigarettes in the 30 days prior to the survey—the lowest levels in the history of the survey.

The declining prevalence of cigarette smoking among the general U.S. population, how-

ever, is not reflected in patients with mental illnesses. The rate of smoking in patients suffering from post-traumatic stress disorder, bipolar disorder, major depression, and other mental illness is two- to fourfold higher than in the general population; and among people with schizophrenia, smoking rates as high as 90 percent have been reported.

Tobacco use is the leading preventable cause of death in the United States. The impact of tobacco use in terms of morbidity and mortality to society is staggering. Economically, more than $96 billion of total U.S. health care costs each year are attributable directly to smoking.

However, this is well below the total cost to society because it does not include burn care from smoking-related fires, perinatal care for low-birthweight infants of mothers who smoke, and medical care costs associated with disease caused by secondhand smoke. In addition to health care costs, the costs of lost productivity due to smoking effects are estimated at $97 billion per year, bringing a conservative estimate of the economic burden of smoking to more than $193 billion per year.

How Does Tobacco Deliver Its Effects?

There are more than 4,000 chemicals found in the smoke of tobacco products. Of these, nicotine, first identified in the early 1800s, is the primary reinforcing component of tobacco.

Cigarette smoking is the most popular method of using tobacco; however, there has also been a recent increase in the use of smokeless tobacco products, such as snuff and chewing tobacco. These smokeless products also contain nicotine, as well as many toxic chemicals.

The cigarette is a very efficient and highly engineered drug delivery system. By inhaling tobacco smoke, the average smoker takes in 1–2 mg of nicotine per cigarette. When tobacco is smoked, nicotine rapidly reaches peak levels in the bloodstream and enters the brain. A typical smoker will take 10 puffs on a cigarette over a period of 5 minutes that

Trends in Prevalence of Cigarette Use for 8th-, 10th-, and 12th-Graders

Percentage of Students Using Cigarettes Over a 30-Day Period, 1992–2008

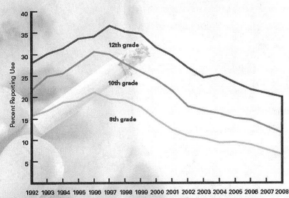

12th grade

10th grade

8th grade

1992 1993 1994 1995 1996 1997 1998 1999 2000 2001 2002 2003 2004 2005 2006 2007 2008

Source: University of Michigan, 2008 Monitoring the Future Survey.

RESIGNATION LETTER

A **resignation letter** becomes part of your personnel file and may be seen by future employers or if you reapply at the same organization. When writing a resignation letter, consider these tips (Figure 3.71):

- Highlight your accomplishments at the organization because your letter may be read by colleagues.

- Avoid emotion and maintain your dignity.

- Highlight your skills using action verbs.

- Emphasize the contributions you have made to the organization— be positive.

- Show enthusiasm and appreciation for what you have accomplished at the organization.

- The terms of your resignation should attempt to maintain a good relationship with your employer.

Resignation letters are typically written to:

- Resign from a job.

- Announce your retirement.

- Resign for health reasons.

- Resign to take another job.

- Resign for family reasons.

- Take early retirement

Figure 3.71 Resignation Letter

Dorothy Speers
7877 Bells Ferry Road
Acworth, GA 30188
(770) 555-1212
DorothySpeers@abcd.com

September 1, 2012

Sally Duffey
Industrial Lighting Supply
4300 Westfield Highway
Cummings, GA 30134

Dear Ms. Duffey:

This letter is to announce my resignation from Industrial Lighting Supply,
effective October 1, 2012.

I have enjoyed working for this company for the past five years, and it
was a difficult decision to leave. I have enjoyed working with you and
the rest of the sales department team. We accomplished a lot together.
I am especially proud of the sales order system that I helped implement
and for which I developed the training program.

I have accepted a position as general sales manager at Logan
Manufacturing in Douglasville, Georgia. This is a great career opportunity
for me, and it will reduce my morning commute substantially.

I wish you and everyone at Industrial Lighting Supply the very best.

Sincerely,

Dorothy Speers
Dorothy Speers

RÉSUMÉS

The purpose of a **résumé** to get the reader to give you an interview. A résumé should summarize and organize the information so that the reader understands that you are qualified for the job.

All résumés should include:

- Your name, address, and telephone number

- Educational background (schools attended, degrees, diplomas, special training)

- A listing of all previous employment:
  - The date, job title, and organization
  - A brief description of your job
  - *Not* salary

- Information about your current job:
  - Skills you have acquired
  - Your responsibilities

Optionally, a résumé can also contain:

- A job objective, which:
  - Should be tailored to each job for which you apply.
  - State the reason you are submitting your résumé for a particular job.

Example: To obtain a management position in human resources for a large communications firm that utilizes my leadership and organization skills

---

- Special skills, such as:
  - Software packages you've used
  - Languages you speak, read, and/or write

- Professional association memberships

- Honors and awards

Do not include references in your résumé. Instead, state that "References are available upon request." Have a list of references available with name, title, address, and phone number.

Use action verbs to describe your skills.

Example: Designed a new system to catch data entry errors.

Do not explain in your résumé why you are looking for a new job. Create several versions of your résumé, adapting the information to emphasize different skills required for different jobs. Emphasize your experience for various job possibilities.

There are two basic résumé formats:

- The history (or chronological) format focuses on where you have worked (Figure 3.72).

- The skills format lists skills you have acquired (Figure 3.73).

(text continues on page 582)

Figure 3.72 Chronological Format Résumé

Evelyn Flo Boyd
12345 Heartside Drive
Western Branch, GA 31234
404-555-1234

Experience

2009–Present   Lyon's Still Photography
                                                                    Acworth, Georgia

Office manager and assistant to business owner
Maintained files and records, accounts receivable, and customer database.
Assisted photographer with photo subjects, as well as sales of proofs
and prints. Handled scheduling of business activities, all correspondence,
and travel arrangements.

1997–2009   Third Coast Video, Inc.
                                                                    Austin, Texas

Office assistant
Scheduled clients and facilities for video production and postproduction
facility. Scheduled freelance crews and equipment rentals. Arranged
for shipping of equipment and travel for crews. Also handled invoicing
and correspondence.

Education
1993–1997: B.A. English
University of Texas
Austin, Texas

References furnished upon request.

Figure 3.73 Skills Format Résumé

Evelyn Flo Boyd
12345 Heartside Drive
Western Branch, GA 31234
404-555-1234

Experience

ADMINISTRATION—Maintained files and records, accounts receivable, and customer database. Handled scheduling of business activities, all correspondence, and travel arrangements.

SALES—Worked with customers to set appointments and to sell photography services.

VIDEO PRODUCTION—Coordinated scheduling of crews and facilities. Hired freelance crews and outline equipment rentals.

TECHNICAL SKILLS—Complete understanding of IBM-compatible software including Windows, Word for Windows, Excel, and WordPerfect. Also, some understanding of Apple Macintosh computers including Microsoft Word and Excel. Good typing skills, 50 wpm. Working knowledge of most office equipment, copiers, fax machines, and typewriters.

Work History
2009–Present
Office Manager and Assistant to Business Owner
Lyon's Still Photography
Acworth, Georgia

1997–2009
Office Assistant
Third Coast Video, Inc.
Austin, Texas

Education
1993-1997: B.A. English
University of Texas
Austin, Texas

References furnished upon request.

SALES LETTERS

Sales letters are written to catch the attention of readers in an attempt to sell them a product or service. When writing a sales letter, consider these tips (Figures 3.74 and 3.75):

A good sales letter focuses on what interests the readers:

- The benefits to the customer

- How the customer will use the product or service

If the letter is not personally addressed to the reader, start the letter with a headline that:

- Describes the key benefit to the reader.

- Uses power words such as *free, proven, imagine, how to, fast, cheap, save, enjoy,* and *introducing.*

- Gets the reader's attention, targets the audience, lists a benefit, and makes a promise.

Example: How to save 50% or more on office furniture

If the letter is personally addressed, the opening sentence becomes the headline.

Example: Dear Mr. Smith: How would you like to save 50% or more on office furniture for your business?

Keep the letter brief but interesting. Use short sentences, short paragraphs, bullet points, indented paragraphs, and subheadings to design the look of the letter and to make it visually attractive.

Start the letter by identifying the unique selling point of the product or service. Consider the following possibilities:

- Tell a story about the product or service and how it was used.

- Make an announcement of some important news about the product or service.

- Ask the reader a question that involves the unique selling point.

- Include a quotation from a testimonial.

- Include a celebrity endorsement.

- Provide surprising statistics to back up your claims.

Address the reader directly.

Incorrect: Many of you want . . .

Correct: You want . . .

Subheadings within the letter can be used to identify additional selling points.

Let the reader know how much the product or service costs.

The closing of the letter should include a call to action that asks for an order and explains how to order. The closing:

- May include a deadline.

- Always includes a thank-you.

Include a P.S. at the end of the letter to offer an incentive, sale, free trial, or gift. People often read a P.S.

Sales letters are typically written to:

- Announce a sale or a sales-related contest.

- Contact customers who have been inactive for a while.

- Send a thank-you note to an existing customer.

- Introduce a new catalog or product.

- Offer gifts and incentives to customers.

- Invite a customer to request a sample.

- Make an appointment for a sales presentation.

- Respond to customer inquiries.

- Solicit mail order purchases.

- Welcome a new customer.

- Strengthen a relationship with an existing customer.

(text continues on page 586)

Figure 3.74 Sales Letter

Business Furniture Liquidators
1245 North Main Street
Atlanta, Georgia 30322
December 1, 2012

Martha Sanchez
First Insurance
3211 Lake Tarn Terrace
Acworth, GA 30188

Dear Ms. Sanchez:

How would you like to save up to 75% on name-brand office furniture?
Business Furniture Liquidators specializes in preowned Herman Miller
and Steelcase desks and chairs. Why pay full price for new office furniture
when you can get quality refurbished furniture at up to 75% off?

Are you planning to expand your business or upgrade your existing
offices? Business Furniture Liquidators can help you design and furnish
offices, reception areas, and conference rooms. We have a network of
distributors throughout the southeast that allow us to offer you a wide
range of choices at a price you can afford. We'll personally deliver and
install your furniture to ensure your satisfaction.

Visit our Web site at www.bfl.com or call us at 1-800-555-1212 to request
a free quote. You'll find daily specials on our Web site and pictures of
our latest offerings.

Sincerely,

Warren Gladson

Warren Gladson
1-800-555-1212
Wgladson@blf.com
www.blf.com

P.S. For the month of December we are having a liquidation sale on all
Herman Miller office chairs. This is a great opportunity for you to upgrade
your office chairs to ergonomically friendly Herman Miller chairs at 80%
off the retail price. Call or email me today for an inventory list and a price
quote.

Figure 3.75 Sales Letter

Realty Investors
7788 Princeton Avenue
St. Louis, MO 63107

Do you have a house you would like to sell?

Dear Homeowner,

Do you own a home in St. Louis that you would like to sell? If so, we would like to meet with you to discuss some great opportunities.

Realty Investors specializes in helping investors find great opportunities in rental properties. We work with a large network of investors who are interested in purchasing rental properties. If you are interested in selling your property, now is a great time to talk to us and let us help you get the best price possible.

Last year, we helped our investors purchase over $20 million in properties in the St. Louis metro area and this year we will easily exceed that amount.

Here is a list of properties our investors are looking for:

- Single-family, 2- or 3-bedroom homes priced under $150,000
- Duplexes with 2 bedrooms and 1 bath on each side
- Mobile homes
- Two-story homes of any size

If you own a property like one of these, please give me a call and let me conduct a property evaluation. There's no obligation to sell, and the evaluation is completely free.

Selling your property with Realty Investors is an outstanding opportunity.

I look forward to hearing from you.

Sincerely,

Bill Stovall

Bill Stovall
(314) 555-1212

SEASONAL CORRESPONDENCE

Seasonal correspondence is a way of greeting customers and employees by writing holiday letters (Figure 3.76). Holiday letters to customers can include special offers and incentives with deadlines related to the holiday.

These letters to customers may also express appreciation for past business. When writing a holiday letter to customers, consider these tips:

- Greet the customer.
- Acknowledge the upcoming holiday.
- Describe the offer.
- Express appreciation for the customer's business.
- Close by offering warm wishes.

Holiday letters to employees can be used to express thanks for their hard work. When writing holiday letters to employees, consider these tips:

- Begin with a personal greeting.
- Acknowledge the upcoming holiday.
- Mention it in the letter if it includes a bonus or gift check.
- Announce any holiday parties, and include information about the date, time, location, and whether there is a need to RSVP.
- Include any messages about company accomplishments for the latest period and any goals for the future.
- Close by wishing the employee a happy holiday.

Holiday letters are most effective when they are personally addressed to the reader. Be sensitive to the fact that the individual may not celebrate the holiday.

Holiday letters are typically written to:

- Announce a holiday-related sale.
- Thank customers for their previous business.
- Announce a holiday-related open house.
- Announce a party.
- Offer season's greetings.
- Announce a holiday schedule.

Figure 3.76 Seasonal Correspondence

Acme Auto Supply
5353 Buffalo Speedway
Houston, TX 77097

December 7, 2012

Jeff Richardson
Jeff's Auto Repair
3221 Stella Link
Houston, TX 77098

Dear Mr. Richardson,

With the holiday season approaching, there is so much personal and business activity to take care of that it is sometimes easy to forget to thank our great customers who have helped make it a great year for us.

I want to personally thank you for your business and for being a loyal customer of Acme Auto Supply.

May this holiday season bring happiness to you and your family.

Very truly yours,

Sam Henderson

Sam Henderson
(713) 555-1212

SPECIFICATIONS

Specifications appear in various forms—the design of high-tech products, software development, engineering, and architecture (Figure 3.77). Specifications dictate the design of the project. They describe how the product should appear when completed. They can be included as part of a contract.

There are four major types of specifications:

- Requirement specifications (architecture and engineering) describe:
    - A product during the design phase
    - The functions the product will be capable of performing
    - The costs involved in making the product

- Functional specifications (manufacturing) describe:
    - The purpose, use, and operation of the product
    - How the components work together
    - The electronics that will be used
    - The power requirements
    - The production and maintenance costs

- Design specifications (software) describe:
    - The documents that contain information about the product
    - The product's functions, what it does, and how it does it
    - Any external components that interface with the product
    - The details of all the products' functions
    - The power requirements

- Test specifications (manufacturing and software) describe:
    - All the tests that will be run on the product during the development phase
    - All the tests that will be run on the production version of the product.

When writing specifications, keep the following language usage guidelines in mind:

- Keep sentences short and simple.

- Edit carefully to avoid mistakes that cause errors in the interpretation of the specifications and that result in manufacturing or development mistakes.

- Reference other documents and paragraphs rather than repeat content.

- Don't worry about repeating the same words and phrases.

- Use caution with ambiguous words like *any, include,* and *run.*

- Define acronyms the first time they are used.

- Avoid the use of words that may create logic errors in the specifications.

Example: all, always, never, every, none

- Do not use slash marks in specifications.

Incorrect: A/B

Correct: either A or B

- Use verbs in the future tense, using the emphatic form such as *shall.*
    - *Shall* expresses a requirement.
    - *Will, should,* and *may* do not express a requirement.
- Describe the person who will be using the product in the specifications.

Example: The operator will be a licensed engineer.

- Be specific when using noun modifiers that could be interpreted to apply to two or more nouns.

Incorrect: The cabin door will be connected to the doorway using metal pins and lock pins made of titanium.

Correct: The cabin door will be connected to the doorway using titanium pins and titanium lock pins.

- Use caution when writing essential and nonessential dependent clauses with words like *that* and *which*.

  - Essential clauses are required to specify a particular item and are often introduced by *that*.

  - Nonessential clauses are not required to specify anything and are often introduced using *which*.

  - Other introductory words that introduce essential and nonessential clauses are *after, as, as if, as though, as soon as, at which, because, before, by which, for which, if, in order that, since, so that, to which, unless, when, where, which, while, who, whom,* and *whose.*

- Avoid using multiple conjunctions in the same sentence.

  Incorrect: The cabin door will be sealed by gluing and clamping or riveting.

  Correct: The cabin door will be sealed either by gluing and clamping or by riveting.

- Use the third person.

  Incorrect: You will push the green on-screen **Start** button to begin the test.

  Correct: The operator will push the green on-screen **Start** button to begin the test.

- When including lists in specifications, make sure they are complete and parallel in structure.

  - The elements of the list should be the same part of speech.

Figure 3.77 Specifications

STUDENT COMPUTER SPECIFICATIONS

All students are required to have a desktop or laptop computer as well as a printer for use throughout the school year. Computers must also include a three-year on-site warranty for parts and labor, as well as telephone or Internet support.

Operating System

- Windows 7

Software Suite

- Microsoft Office Professional with Word, Excel, PowerPoint, and Outlook
- Internet Explorer browser
- Norton Antivirus

Computer Hardware

- Processor speed of at least 2 GHz
- Memory (RAM) of 2 GB or more
- Hard disk drive of at least 100 GB
- DVD burner CD-RW combo disc drive
- 19-inch flat panel display
- Inkjet printer and printer cable plus three additional sets of replacement ink cartridges
- 10/100Base-T Ethernet card or wireless Ethernet card
- USB Flash memory stick with at least 1 GB of capacity
- Multimedia sound capability
- Headphones

SPEECHES AND ORAL PRESENTATIONS

Writing a **speech** involves writing a script that can be memorized or read from a teleprompter, as well as speaker notes that the speaker can refer to during the presentation. (Figure 3.78.)

In *planning* a speech, keep the following in mind:

- Is the purpose of the speech to inform, instruct, or persuade?
    - An informational speech focuses on facts.
    - An instructional speech explains how to do something.
    - A persuasive speech attempts to convince the audience to think and act a certain way.
- Consider the audience for the speech and the location.
    - The audience and location will affect the tone of the speech.
    - Consider what the members of the audience have in common, such as age, interests, gender, and ethnicity.
    - Consider how much the audience already knows about the topic.
        - Will they already be familiar with the content, or will you be introducing new ideas?
        - What level of detail is appropriate for the audience?
        - What might offend the audience?
- Plan the presentation to avoid standing behind a podium.
    - Walk around but don't pace.
    - Plan on addressing different parts of the audience rather than one or two people in the front row.
- Determine whether accompanying visuals are appropriate. They may be appropriate depending on the audience and location.

In *writing* a speech, consider the following:

- Write a good introduction that gives a short overview and creates interest.
  - Create a hook that captures the audience's attention.
    - Offer shocking statistics.
    - Ask a thought-provoking question.
- Establish the reason you are speaking and why your topic is important.
  - Describe the topic from the audience's point of view.
- Divide your speech into sections, and give each section a verbal title.
- Use summaries and logical transitions to move from one section to the next.
  - Repeat crucial points to remind the audience.
  - Repeat crucial buzzwords to reinforce their meaning.
  - Use powerful transitions to reinforce or contrast ideas.
- Write the speech with short uncomplicated sentences.
  - Avoid using too many subordinate clauses.
  - Avoid the use of too many pronouns; it is hard for an audience to remember who and what *it, they,* and *this* mean.
- Use the strategies of ethos, pathos, and logos.
  - Ethos builds trust between the speaker and the audience.
  - Pathos appeals to the audience's emotions.
  - Logos provides facts, statistics, and logic.
- Conclude the speech by summarizing, stating your own conclusion, and then adding last thoughts as commentary.
  - Restate the main points of the speech, but don't repeat them the same way they were originally delivered.
  - End with a call to action that creates a connection with the audience.

(text continues on page 598)

Figure 3.78 Speech by John F. Kennedy

ASK NOT WHAT YOUR COUNTRY CAN DO FOR YOU
By John F. Kennedy

Vice President Johnson, Mr. Speaker, Mr. Chief Justice, President Eisenhower, Vice President Nixon, President Truman, reverend clergy, fellow citizens, we observe today not a victory of party, but a celebration of freedom—symbolizing an end, as well as a beginning—signifying renewal, as well as change. For I have sworn before you and Almighty God the same solemn oath our forebears prescribed nearly a century and three quarters ago.

The world is very different now. For man holds in his mortal hands the power to abolish all forms of human poverty and all forms of human life. And yet the same revolutionary beliefs for which our forebears fought are still at issue around the globe—the belief that the rights of man come not from the generosity of the state, but from the hand of God.

We dare not forget today that we are the heirs of that first revolution. Let the word go forth from this time and place, to friend and foe alike, that the torch has been passed to a new generation of Americans—born in this century, tempered by war, disciplined by a hard and bitter peace, proud of our ancient heritage—and unwilling to witness or permit the slow undoing of those human rights to which this Nation has always been committed, and to which we are committed today at home and around the world.

Let every nation know, whether it wishes us well or ill, that we shall pay any price, bear any burden, meet any hardship, support any friend, oppose any foe, in order to assure the survival and the success of liberty.

This much we pledge—and more.

To those old allies whose cultural and spiritual origins we share, we pledge the loyalty of faithful friends. United, there is little we cannot do in a host of cooperative ventures. Divided, there is little we can do— for we dare not meet a powerful challenge at odds and split asunder.

To those new States whom we welcome to the ranks of the free, we pledge our word that one form of colonial control shall not have passed away merely to be replaced by a far more iron tyranny. We shall not always expect to find them supporting our view. But we shall always hope to find them strongly supporting their own freedom—and to remember that, in the past, those who foolishly sought power by riding the back of the tiger ended up inside.

To those peoples in the huts and villages across the globe struggling to break the bonds of mass misery, we pledge our best efforts to help them help themselves, for whatever period is required—not because the Communists may be doing it, not because we seek their votes, but because it is right. If a free society cannot help the many who are poor, it cannot save the few who are rich.

To our sister republics south of our border, we offer a special pledge—to convert our good words into good deeds—in a new alliance for progress—to assist free men and free governments in casting off the chains of poverty. But this peaceful revolution of hope cannot become the prey of hostile powers. Let all our neighbors know that we shall join with them to oppose aggression or subversion anywhere in the Americas. And let every other power know that this Hemisphere intends to remain the master of its own house.

To that world assembly of sovereign states, the United Nations, our last best hope in an age where the instruments of war have far outpaced the instruments of peace, we renew our pledge of support—to prevent it from becoming merely a forum for invective—to strengthen its shield of the new and the weak—and to enlarge the area in which its writ may run.

Finally, to those nations who would make themselves our adversary, we offer not a pledge but a request: that both sides begin anew the quest for peace, before the dark powers of destruction unleashed by science engulf all humanity in planned or accidental self-destruction.

We dare not tempt them with weakness. For only when our arms are sufficient beyond doubt can we be certain beyond doubt that they will never be employed.

(continues)

Figure 3.78 *(continued)*

But neither can two great and powerful groups of nations take comfort from our present course—both sides overburdened by the cost of modern weapons, both rightly alarmed by the steady spread of the deadly atom, yet both racing to alter that uncertain balance of terror that stays the hand of mankind's final war.

So let us begin anew—remembering on both sides that civility is not a sign of weakness, and sincerity is always subject to proof. Let us never negotiate out of fear. But let us never fear to negotiate.

Let both sides explore what problems unite us instead of belaboring those problems which divide us.

Let both sides, for the first time, formulate serious and precise proposals for the inspection and control of arms—and bring the absolute power to destroy other nations under the absolute control of all nations.

Let both sides seek to invoke the wonders of science instead of its terrors. Together let us explore the stars, conquer the deserts, eradicate disease, tap the ocean depths, and encourage the arts and commerce.

Let both sides unite to heed in all corners of the earth the command of Isaiah—to "undo the heavy burdens—and to let the oppressed go free."

And if a beachhead of cooperation may push back the jungle of suspicion, let both sides join in creating a new endeavor, not a new balance of power, but a new world of law, where the strong are just and the weak secure and the peace preserved.

All this will not be finished in the first 100 days. Nor will it be finished in the first 1,000 days, nor in the life of this Administration, nor even perhaps in our lifetime on this planet. But let us begin.

In your hands, my fellow citizens, more than in mine, will rest the final success or failure of our course. Since this country was founded, each generation of Americans has been summoned to give testimony to its national loyalty. The graves of young Americans who answered the call to service surround the globe.

Now the trumpet summons us again—not as a call to bear arms, though arms we need; not as a call to battle, though embattled we are—but a call to bear the burden of a long twilight struggle, year in and year out, "rejoicing in hope, patient in tribulation"—a struggle against the common enemies of man: tyranny, poverty, disease, and war itself.

Can we forge against these enemies a grand and global alliance, North and South, East and West, that can assure a more fruitful life for all mankind? Will you join in that historic effort?

In the long history of the world, only a few generations have been granted the role of defending freedom in its hour of maximum danger. I do not shrink from this responsibility—I welcome it. I do not believe that any of us would exchange places with any other people or any other generation. The energy, the faith, the devotion which we bring to this endeavor will light our country and all who serve it—and the glow from that fire can truly light the world.

And so, my fellow Americans: ask not what your country can do for you—ask what you can do for your country.

My fellow citizens of the world: ask not what America will do for you, but what together we can do for the freedom of man.

Finally, whether you are citizens of America or citizens of the world, ask of us the same high standards of strength and sacrifice which we ask of you. With a good conscience our only sure reward, with history the final judge of our deeds, let us go forth to lead the land we love, asking His blessing and His help, but knowing that here on earth God's work must truly be our own.

SUMMARIES

Summary writing is a way of organizing and summarizing information that condenses large quantities of information into a shorter version that can be used for easy reference.

In technical writing, summary writing is employed to create abstracts, which provide a brief overview of a document.

To write summaries or abstracts, do the following (Figure 3.79):

- Read the longer document thoroughly, and make sure you completely understand the content.

- Review the longer document a second time, and strike out material that you feel isn't necessary and underline the most important points.

- Write a summary in your own words, following the organization of the original material.

- Mention the author, title, and publication date.

- Avoid unnecessary details and quotes.

- Don't give your own opinion.

- Any material used verbatim from the original should be properly documented.

- Compare your draft summary with the original for accuracy.

- The finished summary should be no longer than 20% of the original's length.

(text continues on page 602)

Figure 3.79 Summary

ENERGY AND ECONOMIC IMPACTS OF IMPLEMENTING BOTH A 25-PERCENT RPS AND A 25-PERCENT RFS BY 2025

1. Background and Scope of the Analysis

Background

This Service Report was prepared by the Energy Information Administration (EIA) in response to a request from Senator James Inhofe.[5] Senator Inhofe requested an analysis of a proposal (referred to as the 25 × 25 Policy Scenario in his letter request) to achieve a 25-percent renewable portfolio standard (RPS) and a 25-percent renewable fuel standard (RFS) by 2025. The combined RPS and RFS policy proposal is referred to as "the Policy" hereafter in the report. Copies of the request letter and a follow-up letter of clarification are provided in Appendix A.

Proposal Summary

The proposal analyzed in this study has two components: (1) an RPS, which requires that the percentage of electricity sales produced from renewable sources, excluding existing hydroelectric generation, must reach 25 percent by 2025; and (2) an RFS, which requires that the volumetric percentage of the transportation gasoline and diesel fuel market supplied from renewable resources, in the form of ethanol and biodiesel, must reach 25 percent by 2025 and then grow proportionately with growth in demand for transportation gasoline and diesel fuel. Each sector (electricity sales and gasoline plus diesel transport fuels) is required to meet its own target by 2025. Twenty-five percent of electricity sales would be from renewable generators and 25 percent of gasoline plus diesel fuel sales would be from either ethanol or biodiesel on a volumetric basis.

A key assumption in both the electricity and transportation sectors is that all tax or other policy incentives for domestic renewable fuels and ethanol import tariffs in current laws and regulations are allowed to sunset without extension.

The RPS target in the electricity sector is implemented using a credit trading system, where the qualifying renewables include:

(Courtesy of the U.S. Department of Energy)

(continues)

Figure 3.79 *(continued)*

- Biomass used in dedicated plants or co-fired with other fuels
- Geothermal
- Municipal solid waste (including landfill gas)
- Solar thermal
- Photovoltaic (PV)
- Wind (both onshore and offshore)
- Incremental new hydroelectricity above that existing in 2006

Further, existing qualifying generators, except existing hydroelectricity, receive credits under the proposed Policy. The renewable share is expressed as a share of electricity sales in kilowatt hours. The required share is set equal to the share of qualifying renewable generation sales in 2006 and increases to 25 percent in 2025. Thereafter, it is held at 25 percent. All retail electricity sellers are included. RPS credit trading is allowed only within the electricity sector, and there is no cap on the credit price.

The RFS target for the motor transportation sector is also implemented using tradable credits, where the qualifying renewable fuels include:

- Corn-based ethanol
- Cellulose-based ethanol
- Biodiesel production from all sources, including animal fats and oil-based beans/seeds

As with the RPS, existing qualifying sources receive credits. The renewable share is expressed as a share of all liquids sold in the motor transportation sector that displace either gasoline or diesel. The required share is set equal to the share of qualifying renewables sold in 2006 and increases to 25 percent in 2025. Thereafter, it is held at 25 percent. RFS credit trading is allowed only within the transportation sector, and there is no cap on the credit price. The existing import tariff on Brazilian ethanol imports (51 cents per gallon) is allowed to sunset in 2010. Finally, measures that facilitate compliance with the RFS, such as mandates to produce Flex Fuel Vehicles (FFVs) and the availability of E85 pumps at gasoline dispensing stations, are assumed as stipulated in Senate Bill 23 (S.23).

General Methodology

In this study, analyses of the energy sector impacts and energy-related economic impacts of the Policy proposal are based on the Annual Energy Outlook 2007 (AEO2007)[6] reference and high price cases, as amended to allow for the additional assumptions and modeling enhancements necessary to evaluate the proposal. As in the preparation of the Annual Energy Outlook and most EIA service reports, the National Energy Modeling System (NEMS) was used to evaluate the impacts of the Policy Case and alternative assumptions.

A number of changes were made in NEMS to address the Policy and to include enhancements relevant to the analysis. They included changes to the macroeconomic module to improve the representation of the impact on the entire economy of price increases for agricultural products, motor fuel, and electricity; changes in the Petroleum Market Module to ensure convergence of NEMS; and changes to the Renewable Fuels and Transportation Modules to incorporate the proposal's mandates. The changes made to the AEO2007 NEMS are summarized in Appendix B.

Sensitivity Cases

In addition to the four cases requested by Senator Inhofe (Reference, High Price, Policy, and High Price Policy), four additional cases are provided to illustrate the impacts of higher availability of ethanol imports and more optimistic assumptions for the cellulosic ethanol technology: Low-Cost Ethanol Imports, Low-Cost Ethanol Imports Policy, High Renewable Technology, and High Renewable Technology Policy. The cases analyzed for this request are shown in Table 1. High Renewable Technology and High Technology are used interchangeably throughout this text.

TERMINATION OF EMPLOYMENT LETTER

A **termination of employment letter** is an official announcement regarding a layoff or firing. A termination letter should come at the end of a termination process that involves personnel meetings.

Termination letters are usually written because of redundancy in positions, misconduct by an employee, or poor performance.

A termination of employment letter should (Figure 3.80):

- Be courteous and professional.

- Start by announcing the termination and the effective date.

- State the reasons for the termination.

- Clearly state any individual requirements, such as the return of a company car, credit card, computer, or cell phone.

- Clearly state any details regarding pay, holiday pay, benefits, pension, and other financial settlement.

- Describe the appeals process and schedule if an appeals process is required due to state law or union contract.

- Include a place for the employee to sign to confirm receipt of the letter.

Figure 3.80 Termination Letter

Credit Corp America
4300 Interstate Parkway
Dallas, TX 75301
September 6, 2012

Mary Sullivan
6426 Lakewood Blvd
Dallas, TX 75214

Dear Mrs. Sullivan:

As we discussed in our meeting on September 5, 2012, I regretfully must inform you that your employment with Credit Corp America will be terminated today, September 6, 2012.

As described in our meeting, the reason for termination of your employment is your failure to meet your sales quotas. You failed to meet your monthly quota three months ago and were given a warning at that time. You have continued to miss your quota for each of the past three months.

As part of the termination process, you must return your sales literature, customer lists, and company laptop.

You will receive two weeks' pay, which will be sent to your home within the next five days. You will also retain your 401(k) account. Your health insurance benefits will continue through the end of September. At that time, you have the option of continuing your coverage by purchasing it through the COBRA program.

To acknowledge your receipt of this letter, please sign and date below and return it to me.

We are sorry to see you leave and wish you the best for the future.

Yours,

Mary Ann Lemer
Mary Ann Lemer
Vice President of Sales

I acknowledge receipt of this letter.

_____   _____

Mary Sullivan   Date

TRAINING MANUAL

Training manuals are designed to instruct the reader on how to do something. There are two main types of training manuals:

- **Instructor-led manuals** may rely on lectures and demonstrations by the instructor (Figure 3.81).

- **Self-paced training manuals** must provide more instructions than an instructor-led manual (Figure 3.82).

A typical training manual includes:

- Cover (Figure 3.83)

- Table of contents (Figure 3.84)

- How-to-get-started information (Figure 3.85)

- Lesson modules

- Appendix items

- Glossary

- End-of-course quiz (Figure 3.86)

- Course evaluation form (Figure 3.87)

Training manuals are normally divided into lessons or topics. A typical lesson includes:

- Lesson overview and objectives (Figure 3.88–3.89)

- Explanation in the form of headings, subheadings, paragraphs of text, and lists

- Illustrations, diagrams, charts, screen captures, or photographs.

- Tables (Figure 3.90)

- Step-by-step instructions (Figure 3.91)

- Use of bold, italics, and all caps to highlight actions to be taken by the participant

- Exercises (Figure 3.92)

- Quizzes

- Summaries

Instructor-led manuals may include:

- Copies of PowerPoint slides used by the instructor as visual aids

- Speaker notes that summarize the instructor's lecture

- Speaker notes in the participant's version of the manual

Notes and warning messages may be formatted with icons and graphic boxes to focus the student's attention.

Training manuals may be integrated with other forms of instruction, such as:

- Hands-on exercises

- Team exercises

- Exercises involving online simulations

- Videos and audio recordings

- Computer-based training

- Webinars

- Job aids

(text continues on page 618)

Figure 3.81 Instructor-Led Training Manual

Topic 1:
Traditional Financial Statements

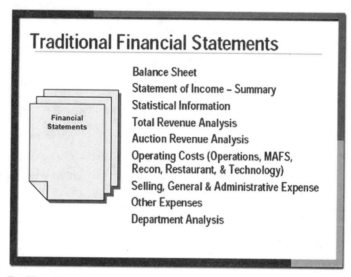

Traditional financial statements include information such as the current month, prior year, budget, year-to-date, and variance percentages. The traditional financial statements include:

- Balance Sheet
- Statement of Income – Summary
- Statistical Information
- Total Revenue Analysis
- Auction Revenue Analysis
- Operating Costs (Operations, MAFS, Recon, Restaurant, & Technology)
- Selling, General & Administrative Expense
- Other Expenses
- Department Analysis (One Statement of Income for each Department)

The Department Analysis provides the detail of revenues and expenses, gross profit, gross profit margin, IBD, and IBD Margin for each department and/or profit center, thus providing a basis to analyze operational performance by type of service.

Figure 3.82 Self-Study Training Manual

PERFORMANCE EVALUATION FORMS

For recording your written performance evaluation, Manheim has three Performance Expectations and Review forms:

- Employee form

- Managers, Supervisors, and Professional form

- Basic form

Goals

Page one of the form includes space for writing the goals for the year along with the tracking method. The first page should have been completed at the beginning of the review period. During the evaluation, you will determine if the goals were achieved. There are four possible ratings for each goal on the form: exceeded, met, did not meet, and not applicable.

Goals for the Review Period

Identify three goals to be accomplished during the review period by thinking of the key responsibilities for this job. At the end of the performance period, rate how well these goals were achieved.

	Goals for the Review Period Make goals SMART: Specific, Measurable, Attainable, Realistic, and Timely	Tracking Method How we know it was achieved	Exceeded	Met	Did Not	N/A
			Were the goals achieved?			
1	Maintain current Cust Sat Rating of 98%	Customer Survey	○	●	○	○
2	Increase dealer use of Recon Services over current level	Recon Sales Report	●	○	○	○
3	Increase dealer sales percentage by 5%	Dealer Sales Report	○	○	●	○

Figure 3.83 Training Manual Cover

PART 3:
Evaluate for Performance

Training Guide

Figure 3.84 Training Manual Table of Contents

Table of Contents

Figure 3.85 Training Manual Getting-Started Page

How to Take a Self Study Course

Welcome to Finance Training Self Study

This self study course allows you to learn independently and at your own pace. It contains many learning elements including a written presentation, associated activities, and online simulations and practices.

How to Take This Course

Study the written documentation and complete the associated activities, online simulations and online practice exercises.

Once you complete the course, you must register for the associated quiz on LMS and pass with an 80% or greater to receive credit for the self study.

Online Simulations:

Throughout the self study course, you will be able to watch demonstrations and then practice the same concepts in a simulated environment.

Self study online simulations allow you to view content in either See It! or Try It! mode.

Mode	Name	Description
	See It!	See It mode enables you to learn about the selected topic by displaying an animated demonstration of a task being completed.
	Try It!	Try It mode allows you to perform the selected task in a simulated environment

Steps to run simulations and practice exercises:

1. Access online simulations through the website and select the Online Simulations link.

2. Next, select the module you're studying.

3. This will launch the simulation player in a new window.

4. From this window, choose the topic you'd like to view in either See it! or Try it! mode.

Figure 3.86 Training Manual Quiz

Managing Performance Everyday

Quiz
Which Rating Error Are They Making?

1. Bob's latest project was great. He did miss on projects in the first half of the year, but he turned around nicely. I'm going to rate him exceeded expectations.
   a. Rating effort rather than performance
   b. Recent work focus (Recency Effect)
   c. Halo or horns effect

2. Stan made some people upset in the process, but he did get the job done. I'm going to rate him exceeded expectations.
   a. No news is good news
   b. Halo or horns effect
   c. Central tendency

3. Sara is one of my best friends, even though her performance is falling. I'm going to rate her meets expectations.
   a. Interpersonal relations bias
   b. Just like me or not like me
   c. Judging by association

4. There are no superstars in by book.
   a. Central tendency
   b. Judging by association
   c. Strictness

5. Janice and I used to work together at another company. We both understand what it takes to get ahead in this world.
   a. Leniency
   b. Just like me or not like me
   c. Central tendency

Figure 3.87 Training Manual Course Evaluation

Participant Feedback Survey

Please take a moment to complete the following survey. We are interested in learning about your experience with this course.

Instructor's Name

_____

Instructions

Please answer the questions below by circling the appropriate number on the right.

Scale

Strongly Disagree 1..2..3..4..5 Strongly Agree

1) I feel comfortable working with financial statements,	1..2..3..4..5
2) I feel comfortable finding information within the balance sheet.	1..2..3..4..5
3) I feel comfortable finding information within the statement of income.	1..2..3..4..5
4) I feel comfortable finding trends and other relationships within the financial statement data.	1..2..3..4..5
5) This course has taught me skills I need in my job,	1..2..3..4..5
6) The instructor effectively presented the course,	1..2..3..4..5
7) The instructor provided answers to my questions,	1..2..3..4..5

Figure 3.88 Training Manual Course Objectives

INTRODUCTION AND COURSE AGENDA

Welcome to the third module of Managing Performance Everyday. In this course, Evaluate for Performance, you will learn how to effectively evaluate performance and get prepared to confidently and respectfully discuss with your employees their performance and upcoming goals.

Performance Management Cycle

- **Set Goals** or expectations with your employees.

- **Feedback** is ongoing and lets employees know how they are doing and reinforces what the manager expects from the employee every day.

- **Track** how employees are doing against their goals.

- **Coach** the employee to make improvements.

- **Evaluate** the employee's performance on how they did against their goals and set new goals for next year.

	Part 3
Page 1	Facilitator Guide

Figure 3.89 Training Manual Lesson Contents and Objectives

Module 4: Accounting for Holds Roll-Forward Transactions

Module 4
Accounting for Holds Roll-Forward Transactions

This module focuses on the accounting procedures for Holds Roll-Forward transactions.

Module Objectives

This module explains:

- How to perform the accounting entries necessary to perform Holds Roll-Forward

Module Contents

This module contains the following topics:

Third Edition   4-1

Figure 3.90 Training Manual Table Reference

Oracle Forms Icons

	Icons	
Icon	**Name**	**Description**
	New	Creates a new record in the active form.
	Find	Displays the Find window to retrieve records.
	Show Navigator	Displays the Navigator window.
	Save	Saves any pending changes in the active form.
	Switch Responsibility	Allows you to select another Responsibility if you have more than one Responsibility.
	Print	Prints the current screen that the cursor is in. In some cases it may print a report associated with the current data.
	Close Form	Closes all windows of the current form.
	Cut	Cuts the current selection to the clipboard.
	Copy	Copies the current selection to the clipboard.
	Paste	Pastes from the clipboard into the current field.
	Clear Record	Erases the current record from the window.
	Delete	Deletes the current record from the database.
	Edit Field	Displays the Editor window for the current field.
	Zoom	Displays custom-defined Zoom (drilldown behavior).
	Attachments	Displays the Attachment window.
	Window Help	Displays help for the current window.

Figure 3.91 Training Manual Instructions

Changing Preference Settings

1. Log in to the Oracle application.

2. In the Oracle Applications Home Page, click **Preferences**.

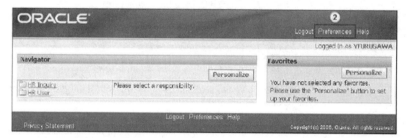

3. The **General Preferences** page is displayed.

4. *Date Format:* Change it to the desired format.

5. *Timezone:* Change it your time zone.

6. Click **Apply**.

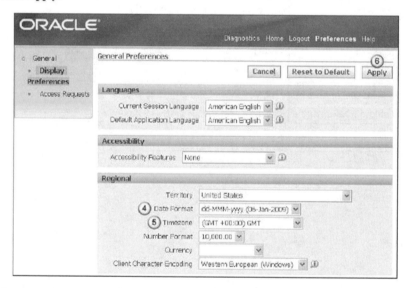

7. Verify that the message **Confirmation. Updated successfully.** appears at the top of the screen.

Oracle Human Resources

Page 21

Figure 3.92 Training Manual Group Activity

Financial Statement Review	Higher Up Increased	Lower Down Decreased
1 Are the YTD revenues for the location up or down when compared to prior year?	☐	☐
2 What revenue category has increased the most on a YTD basis when compared to prior year?	_____	
3 What revenue category has decreased the most on a YTD basis when compared to prior year?	_____	
4 Are the YTD Operating expenses up or down over last year?	☐	☐
5 Are the YTD SG&A expenses up or down over last year?	☐	☐
6 What category of Reconditioning revenue has had the greatest % change over prior year to date?	_____	
7 How many sale days did the location have in the most recent month?	_____	
8 What expense category (Operating or SG&A) has had the greatest percent change when compared to the prior year?	_____	
9 How many cars did the location register in most current month?	_____	
10 What was the average registration per sale in most current month?	_____	
11 How many cars did the location sell in most current month?	_____	
12 What was the location's sales ratio for most current month?	_____	
13 Was the location's sales ratio for current month higher or lower than the prior year?	☐	☐
14 Was the location's sales ratio for current month higher or lower than YTD for the prior year?	☐	☐

TRIP REPORT

A **trip report** is usually a simple memo that is sent to a supervisor after an employee returns from a business trip.

A trip report should include (Figure 3.93):

- The purpose of the trip

- A summary of what happened on the trip

- A discussion of any information learned on the trip that needs to be considered, such as customer needs or complaints

- Recommendations for any action that needs to be taken

Figure 3.93 Trip Report

MEMORANDUM

To: Jane Crosby, Sales Manager
From: Dirk Johnson
Date: July 11, 2012
Subject: Oklahoma sales trip

Purpose: This is an update of my sales trip last week
                     to Oklahoma City.

Summary: I called on four of our existing customers and three
                     new potential customers. The existing customers
                     (ABC, Dowd Electric, Pace Supplies, and Jumbo
                     Construction) all seemed pleased with our service.
                     The three new customers (Xecel, Jefferson Bingham,
                     and Winstead) are mainly interested in pricing.

Discussion: Jeff Brown at Xecel showed me our competitor's
                     price list. Our prices are about 10% more. Jeff
                     expressed interest in doing business with us if
                     our prices were comparable. I believe the same
                     would be true for Jefferson Bingham and Winstead.

> *Recommendation:*   I suggest we run some type of special sale or
> promotion for a specific period of time to get these
> guys to give us a try. Once they experience our
> level of service, if our prices increase later, they
> may not care.

USER GUIDE

User guides are documents about the operation of a product. The types of user guides are:

- Large user guides, for complex products

- Software user guides, published as books, online as Web pages (Figure 3.94), or both ways

- Small user guides, written for products ranging from toasters to automobiles

Some user guides may include tutorials for learning to use the product. Product tutorials are often published as separate documents (Figure 3.95). User guides often include troubleshooting procedures.

User guides often include:

- Heading organization with subheadings

- Numbered and bulleted lists

- Step-by-step instructions

- Graphics and illustrations.

- Tables

- Use of boldface, italics, all caps, and different fonts to highlight content.

- Special notices with notes, tips, warnings, cautions, and danger messages

User guides also include covers (Figure 3.96), title pages, list of trademarks, disclaimers, warranties, license agreements, appendix items, glossaries, and an index.

The product-related content included in a user guide is usually presented in one of the following ways:

- Step-by-step instructions guide users through operating the product (Figure 3.97). These guides often contain:

  - Illustrations as a road map

  - Numbered lists or list bullets as formatting

- Reference information provides content about all of the components, settings, controls, and options (Figure 3.98). Reference information is often presented in table form.

- Getting-started information provides users with a tutorial on how to start using the product immediately (Figure 3.99).

- Technical specifications provide reference information for maintenance and troubleshooting.

(text continues on page 626)

Figure 3.94 Online User Guide

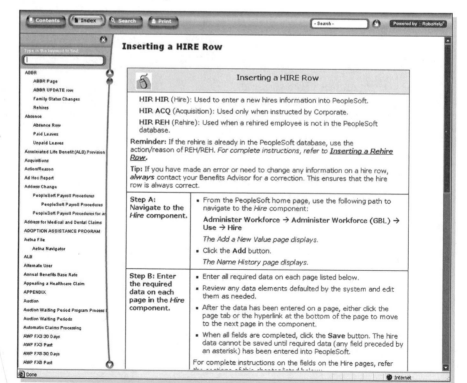

Figure 3.95 User Guide Tutorial

Walkthrough – Rounding

In this walkthrough, you would use the ROUND, ROUNDUP, and ROUNDDOWN functions.

Using the ROUND function

1.   Open the Round Exercise.xls file.

2.   In cell C2, enter the following formula: **=ROUNDUP(B2,0)**

3.   In cell C4, enter the formula: **=ROUND(B4,-1)**

4.   In cell C5, enter the formula: **=ROUNDDOWN(B5,0)**

	C5	▼	f_x	=ROUNDDOWN(B5,0)

	A	B	C
1			
2	Revenues	$ 3,423,117.80	$ 3,423,118.00
3			
4	Operating Expenses	$ (1,295,371.21)	$ (1,295,370.00)
5	SG&A Expenses	$ (862,595.52)	$ (862,595.00)
6			
7	IBD	$ 1,265,151.07	
8	IBD %	36.96%	
9			
10	Average # of Dealers registered	423.62	

Note how the value in cell C2 is rounded up to the nearest whole dollar, while the value in cell C4 is rounded to the nearest whole number (because of the -1) in the formula. The value in cell C5 is also rounded down because of the ROUNDDOWN function.

5.   Save your work by clicking **File > Save As**, and then changing the name of the file to "**Round Exercise A**" and then click the **Save** button.

6.   Close the spreadsheet by clicking **File > Close**.

Figure 3.96 User Guide Cover

Figure 3.97 User Guide Instructions

PeopleSoft Basics

Changing Your Password

Changing Your Password	
Step 1: Navigate to the *Change Password* **page.**	▪ From the PeopleSoft home page, click the <u>**Change My Password**</u> link in the Main Menu. *The Change Password page displays* **Note**: You can also change your password from the *General Profile Information* page. **Change Password** User ID: LBCTWO Description: LBC TWO *Current Password: *New Password: *Confirm Password: Change Password
Step 2: Change your password.	▪ Key your current password into the **Current Password** box. ▪ Key your new password into the **New Password** box. ▪ Key your new password again into the **Confirm Password** box. ▪ Click the **Change Password** button. Your password is immediately changed in PeopleSoft and the Password Saved page displays. **Password Saved** ✔ Your password has successfully been changed. OK ▪ Click the **OK** button.

Password Rules to Remember:

▪ Your User ID and Password cannot be the same.

▪ Passwords must be a minimum of 7 letters and/or numbers or special characters. At least 2 of the 7 characters must be numbers.

▪ The following characters can be used in your password:

! @ # $ % ^ & * ( ) _ - = + \ | [ ] { } ; : / ? . < >

▪ Passwords are case sensitive. PeopleSoft-generated passwords are all upper case. You can

Figure 3.98 User Guide Reference Information

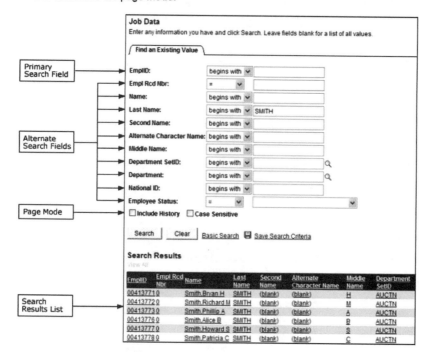

The Find an Existing Value Page

After navigating to a page or component, the *Find an Existing Value* page displays. This page allows you to input search criteria in order to access a specific employee's data. It is also used to determine the page mode.

Primary Search Field: The primary search field is the first field on the *Find an Existing Value* page. The *EmplID* field is the primary search field for most records in PeopleSoft 8.9.

Figure 3.99 User Guide Quick Start

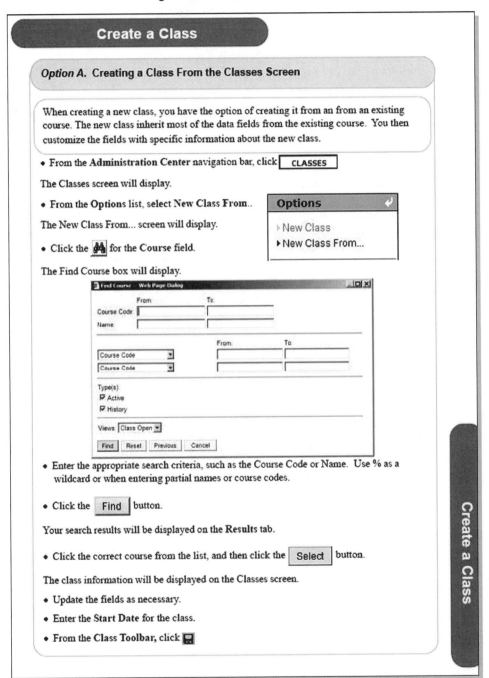

Create a Class

Option A. Creating a Class From the Classes Screen

When creating a new class, you have the option of creating it from an from an existing course. The new class inherit most of the data fields from the existing course. You then customize the fields with specific information about the new class.

- From the **Administration Center** navigation bar, click CLASSES

The Classes screen will display.

- From the **Options** list, select New Class From..

The New Class From... screen will display.

- Click the 🔍 for the Course field.

The Find Course box will display.

- Enter the appropriate search criteria, such as the Course Code or Name. Use % as a wildcard or when entering partial names or course codes.

- Click the Find button.

Your search results will be displayed on the **Results** tab.

- Click the correct course from the list, and then click the Select button.

The class information will be displayed on the Classes screen.

- Update the fields as necessary.
- Enter the **Start Date** for the class.
- From the **Class Toolbar**, click 💾

WARNING LETTER

Warning or **discipline letters** are written to make an employee aware of a problem and to define potential disciplinary action. A warning letter becomes part of an employee's personnel file and may be used later during the termination process.

When writing a warning letter, consider these tips (Figure 3.100):

- Start the letter by stating briefly what events led to the written warning. Include specific situations, dates, and times.

- Identify your expectations for the employee and what behavior the employee needs to change.

- Warn the employee that disciplinary action may have to be taken if the behavior is not corrected.

  - Provide details about what the disciplinary action may include.

  - State that failure to correct the situation may result in termination.

Warning letters are typically written to:

- Document a reprimand.

- Warn an employee for breach of policy.

- Warn an employee for poor performance.

- Reprimand an employee for poor attendance or lateness.

- Warn tenants in a rental property.

- Warn customers about a credit suspension.

Figure 3.100 Warning Letter

Credit Corp America
4300 Interstate Parkway
Dallas, TX 75301
June 2, 2012

Mary Sullivan
6426 Lakewood Blvd
Dallas, TX 75214

Dear Mrs. Sullivan:

As you will recall, the sales quota for our customer representatives
is $10,000 per month. I discussed with you at the end of April that it
was important for you to achieve this quota each and every month.
For the month of May, your sales totaled only $5,500.

Company policy states that any customer representative who fails to
achieve his/her sales quota for two consecutive months is subject to
termination. As a result of this situation, this letter will serve as a warning,
and a copy will be placed in your personnel file. To avoid termination,
you will need to achieve your quota for the month of June.

If you know of any problems that will prevent you from reaching these
goals, or if you wish to discuss this matter with me in more detail,
please arrange for a meeting.

Yours,

Mary Ann Lemer

Mary Ann Lemer
Vice President of Sales

WEB SITES

Writing for a **Web site** is different from writing for print.

- Writing for print is linear in nature, whereas writing for the Web is nonlinear.

- Web page content is usually chunked and packaged, so that a reader can quickly scan the page and decide whether to read more. (Readers spend very little time reading text on an individual Web page.)

- Web pages feature highlighted keywords, extensive use of subheadings, bulleted lists, and normally half the word length of a similar paper document.

When writing content for a Web site, consider these tips (Figure 3.101):

- Tone down promotional marketing hype and focus instead on reference and helpful information.

- Use an objective rather than a subjective tone.

- Use the active voice for Web content.

- Show numbers as numerals in all Web content.
  - Numerals are easier to scan and take up less room.

- Spell out large numbers, such as a million, billion, and trillion, because the words are shorter than the numerals.

When writing headlines for Web articles:

- Keep headlines short and format them in bold.

- Summarize the article so that users will know enough to determine whether they want to read it.

- Include the most important keywords first in the headline because readers often scan only the first few words of a headline.
  - Use keywords that match common user search criteria in search engines.

- Substitute commonly known words for technical jargon.

- Use generic names rather than brand names.

- Make the average headline five words.

When writing a Web article, consider the following:

- Use the inverted pyramid approach that is often used by journalists where you begin the article by telling the reader the conclusion, followed by important supporting information, and then end by providing background details.

- Use down-to-earth informal language to make the content easy to understand.

- Include hyperlinks to reference sources for added credibility.

- Use humor with caution because of the wide variety of user preferences.

- Use approximately 60% fewer words than you would if you were writing the same content for print.

- Chunk the content into sections and move nice-to-know content to other pages, and include hyperlinks to this content in the main article.

- Illustrations should always have a caption and complement the text rather than used just to make the page flashy.

- Segment the text to make it easier to scan the document.
  - Break up long paragraphs into smaller segments.
  - Include a heading that describes the subject of each segment, and capitalize the first letter of each word.
  - Include subheadings where appropriate, and capitalize only the first word.

- For lists of any kind, use bullet lists.

- Use the three aspects of rhetoric: ethos, pathos, and logos.
  - Ethos—Establish the credibility of the author by including references and hyperlinks to your sources.
  - Pathos—Make an appeal to the reader's emotions by writing from the reader's point of view.
  - Logos—Appeal to the reader's logic by providing statistical facts and convincing examples

Figure 3.101 Web Site

WHITE PAPERS

White papers are written to introduce an innovative product or technology to the industry, emphasize the unique qualities and advantages of a product or service, help influence customer buying decisions, and are the beginning steps in the creation of a product marketing strategy.

When preparing to write a white paper, read other white papers available on the Internet and look for successful models. Consider how the white paper will be published: paper-based or on a Web site.

When writing a white paper (Figure 3.102):

- Define the audience and understand their concerns.

- Be aware of the time investment required by the audience to read your white paper.
  - Make sure it is engaging and captures the audience's attention.

- Start with a one-paragraph executive summary with the key points the audience needs to know.

- State the problem faced by the customer that the product or service can solve.

- Describe the product and include the following details:
  - How the product was designed
  - What industry standards were used or considered
  - What type of testing was conducted on the product or service
  - What best practices were learned

- Keep a positive tone.

- Use the active voice.

- Avoid jargon and keep the presentation as nontechnical as possible.

- Include diagrams and illustrations.

- Explain how the product resolves the problem stated earlier.

- Tie the product to the problem, and include case study evidence of how the product solved the problem.

- Include testimonials and interview quotes, if available.

- Conclude by summarizing the benefits and discussing the return on investment for customers.

- Mention future product development and timelines for release.

Figure 3.102 White Paper

PUTTING CITIZENS FIRST:
Transforming Online Governement

A White Paper Written for the Presidential Transition Team by

The Federal Web Managers Council

Current and former members of the Federal Web Managers Council who contributed to this paper: Bev Godwin, General Services Administration/USA.gov (Executive Sponsor); Sheila Campbell, General Services Administration/USA.gov (co-chair); Rachel Flagg, Dept. of Housing and Urban Development (co-chair); Melissa Allen, Dept. of Interior; Andy Bailey, Dept. of Labor; Les Benito, Dept. of Defense; Joyce Bounds, Dept. of Veterans Affairs; Nicole Burton, General Services Administration/USA.gov; Bruce Carter, Social Security Administration (retired); Natalie Davidson, General Services Administration/USA.gov; Kate Donohue, Dept. of Treasury; Brian Dunbar, NASA; Tim Evans, Social Security Administration; Kellie Feeney, Dept. of Transportation; Sam Gallagher, Dept. of Housing and Urban Development; Colleen Hope, Dept. of State; Ron Jones, Dept. of Commerce/NOAA; Tina Kelley; Dept. of Justice; Gwynne Kostin, Dept. of Homeland Security; Jeffrey Levy, EPA; Beth Martin, Dept. of Health and Human Services; Leilani Martinez, GSA/GobiernoUSA.gov; Suzanne Nawrot, Dept. of Energy; Russell O'Neill, General Services Administration/USA.gov; Tom Parisi, Dept. of Treasury/IRS; Vic Powell, USDA; Rezaur Rahman, Advisory Council on Historic Preservation; Eric Ramoth, Dept. of Housing and Urban Development; Rand Ruggieri, Dept. of Commerce; Richard Stapleton, Dept. of Health and Human Services; Kim Taylor, USDA; Kirk Winters, Dept. of Education

We welcome your questions and comments. Please contact the Federal Web Managers Council co-chairs, Sheila Campbell (Sheila.campbell@gsa.gov) and Rachel Flagg (Rachel.flagg@hud.gov).

(Courtesy of the Whitehouse.gov)

Introduction

This White Paper recommends specific strategies for revolutionizing how the U.S. Government delivers online services to the American people. It was developed by the Federal Web Managers Council, comprised of Cabinet agency Web Directors.

The current state of government online communications

The importance of the Internet has grown exponentially over the last decade, but the government's ability to provide online services to the American people hasn't grown at the same pace. Building this capacity will present one of the biggest challenges—and most promising opportunities—for President-elect Obama. We need to build on the groundswell of citizen participation in the presidential campaign and make people's everyday interactions with their government easier and more transparent.

It won't be an easy task. There are approximately 24,000 U.S. Government websites now online (but no one knows the exact number). Many websites tout organizational achievements instead of effectively delivering basic information and services. Many web managers don't have access to social media tools because of legal, security, privacy, and internal policy concerns. Many agencies focus more on technology and website infrastructure than improving content and service delivery. Technology should not drive our business decisions, but rather help us serve the needs of the American people. Here's the result when communication takes a backseat to technology:

> "Often I can find the page on a government site that's supposed to contain the information I need, but I can't make heads or tails of it. I recently tried to Google a specific requirement for dependent care flex accounts. Although I got to the correct page, it didn't answer my question. The links took me to the typical, poorly written tax guidance. Where did I get the answer to my question? On Wikipedia."

We're working to address these problems. We've built a network of over 1,500 federal, state, and local web professionals across the country to share best practices; we created a large-scale training program for web managers; and we're working to support the use of social media while also addressing important privacy, security, and legal implications.

While our efforts have been very successful, a high-level mandate from the new Administration is needed to quickly and radically transform government websites.

A bold, new vision for the future

President-elect Obama should be able to promise the American people that when they need government information and services online, they will be able to:

(continues)

Figure 3.102 *(continued)*

- Easily find relevant, accurate, and up-to-date information;

- Understand information the first time they read it;

- Complete common tasks efficiently;

- Get the same answer whether they use the web, phone, email, live chat, read a brochure, or visit in-person;

- Provide feedback and ideas and hear what the government will do with them;

- Access critical information if they have a disability or aren't proficient in English.

The recommendations below are designed to help the new Administration increase the efficiency, transparency, accountability, and participation between government and the American people. Some of these changes can be implemented quickly and at minimal cost. Others will require significant changes in how agencies conduct business and may require shifts in how they fund web communications.

Establish Web Communications as a core government business function
One of the biggest problems we face in improving government websites is that many agencies still view their website as an IT project rather than as a core business function. Many government websites lack a dedicated budget. Only a minority of agencies have developed strong web policies and management controls. Some have hundreds of "legacy" websites with outdated or irrelevant content. With limited resources, many find it difficult to solicit regular customer input and take quick action to improve their sites. While there are many effective government websites, most web teams are struggling to manage the amount of online content the government produces every day.

- Agencies should be required to fund their "virtual" office space as part of their critical infrastructure, in the same way they fund their "bricks and mortar" office space.

- Agencies should be required to appoint an editor-in-chief for every website they maintain, as do the top commercial websites. This person should be given appropriate funding and authority to develop and enforce web policies and publishing standards, including ensuring that prime real estate on government websites is dedicated to helping people find the information they need.

- OPM should develop standard job descriptions and core training requirements so agencies can hire and retain highly qualified experts in web content and new media—not just IT specialists.

Help the public complete common government tasks efficiently

The U.S. economy loses millions of hours of "citizen productivity" every year when people can't efficiently accomplish basic government tasks online, such as filling out a form, applying for a loan, or checking eligibility for a government program. This adds to people's dissatisfaction with their government.

- Agencies should be required and funded to identify their core online customer tasks, and to develop service standards and performance benchmarks for completing those tasks. If the core customer tasks are not yet online, agencies should determine whether or not those tasks can be made available online, and if so, develop a plan for making them available online within one year.

- The Government should use social media, not just to create transparency, but also to help people accomplish their core tasks. For example, agencies could post instructional videos on YouTube to explain how to apply for a small business loan or learn about Medicare benefits. To do this, the government must ensure that federal employees who need access to social media tools have them, and that these new ways of delivering content are available to all, including people with disabilities.

- The new Administration should develop government-wide guidelines for disseminating content in universally accessible formats (data formats, news feeds, mobile, video, podcasts, etc.), and on non-government sites such as YouTube, Wikipedia, and SecondLife. To remain relevant, government needs to take our content to where people already are on the Web, rather than just expecting people will come to government websites. Having guidelines will ensure that we're part of the larger "online information ecosystem," without compromising the integrity of government information.

Clean up the clutter so people can find what they need online

President-elect Obama will inherit thousands of U.S. government websites. We have too much content to categorize, search, and manage effectively, and there is no comprehensive system for removing or archiving old or underused content. Some agencies have posted competing websites on similar topics, creating duplication of effort and causing confusion for the public. Much government web content is written in "governmentese" instead of plain language.

- The Government should set stricter standards for approving new, or renewing existing, government websites. All federally owned, managed, and/or directly funded websites must be hosted on .gov, .mil or fed.us domains. Where agency missions are related, a lead agency should be appointed to coordinate the online

(continues)

Figure 3.102 *(continued)*

"information lane," and all other agencies should defer to the lead agency for posting comprehensive government information on that topic. This will reduce duplication, save money, and help consumers find accurate information.

- Agencies should be required and funded to conduct regular content reviews, to ensure their online content is accurate, relevant, mission-related, and written in plain language. They should have a process for archiving content that is no longer in frequent use and no longer required on the website.

- Agencies should be funded and required to follow the latest best practices in web search. This will improve the quality and findability of online government information, and help agencies deliver the services most requested by their customers.

Engage the public in a dialogue to improve our customer service

Agencies often don't have resources to effectively manage customer input. For those that do, they must go through a clearance process before they can survey the public (requirements of the Paperwork Reduction Act, which was enacted before many agencies even had websites). Many web pages are developed without regular feedback or testing with customers. When people do provide feedback or ideas, they often never hear what the government will do with their suggestions.

- Agencies should be required and funded to regularly solicit public opinion and analyze customers' online preferences—just as Amazon, eBay, and other top commercial websites do. This can be done on an "opt-in" basis and without tracking personally identifiable information by using blogs, online surveys, a "Citizens Insight Panel" (such as that used by the Canadian government), or similar tools. Agencies should be required and funded to do user testing before undertaking major improvements to any current website, or launching a new website.

- Agencies should use their website to publish a summary of common customer comments and explain the actions they are taking in response to the feedback. Doing so will create better transparency and accountability.

Ensure the public gets the same answer whether they use the web, phone, email, print, or visit in-person

Agencies communicate with citizens via many different "delivery channels," including web, email, publications, live chats, blogs, podcasts, videos, wikis, virtual online worlds, and more. But it's difficult to ensure timeliness and consistency when various delivery channels are managed by different divisions within an agency.

■   Agencies should provide multiple ways for people to contact them and ensure that information is consistent across all channels. They should be funded to coordinate all types of content targeted to the general public (web, publications, call center, email, common questions, web chat, etc.). Agencies should be rewarded for delivering consistent information, both within agencies and across government.

Ensure underserved populations can access critical information online

Agencies are required to provide online information that's readily accessible by people with disabilities, as well as to people with limited English proficiency. However, few agencies have the funding, training or resources to meet these obligations.

■   The government should establish standards and guidelines for multilingual websites, and agencies should be funded and staffed with qualified bilingual web content professionals who can create and maintain them. This will help newcomers learn about the rights and responsibilities of living in the U.S.

■   Agencies should receive adequate resources to make their websites fully accessible to people with disabilities and meet requirements of the Rehabilitation Act. The new Administration should invest in government-wide solutions, such as captioning software to make videos and webcasts accessible to people with disabilities.

Conclusion

By harnessing the collaborative nature of the web, the new Administration has the potential to engage the public like never before. The web can foster better communication and allow people to participate in improving the operations of their government. By listening to our customers we can provide better services, focus on their most pressing needs, and spend their tax dollars efficiently. We're confident that President-elect Obama will appoint leaders who will invest in the web as a strategic asset and make these goals a reality. The millions of Americans who interact with their government online expect and deserve no less.